American Indian Stereotypes in the World of Children

A Reader and Bibliography
2nd edition

Arlene Hirschfelder
Paulette Fairbanks Molin
Yvonne Wakim

The Scarecrow Press, Inc.
Lanham, Maryland, and London
1999

SCARECROW PRESS, INC.

Published in the United States of America
by Scarecrow Press, Inc.
4720 Boston Way
Lanham, Maryland 20706
http://www.scarecrowpress.com

4 Pleydell Gardens, Folkestone
Kent CT20 2DN, England

British Library Cataloguing in Publication Information Available

Library of Congress Cataloging-in-Publication Data

Hirschfelder, Arlene B.
    American Indian stereotypes in the world of children : a reader and
bibliography — 2nd ed. / Arlene Hirschfelder, Paulette Fairbanks Molin,
Yvonne Wakim.
      p. cm.
Includes indexes.
ISBN 0-8108-3612-2 (cloth : alk. paper). — ISBN 0-8108-3613-0
(pbk. : alk. paper)
    1. Indians of North America—Public opinion. 2. Race awareness in
children. 3. Public opinion—United States. 4. Textbook bias—United
States. 5. Indians in popular culture—United States. I. Molin, Paulette
Fairbanks. II. Wakim, Yvonne. III. Title.
E98.P99H57   1999
970.004'97—dc21   98-49654
                                                     CIP

∞™ The paper used in this publication meets the minimum requirements of
American National Standard for Information Sciences—Permanence of
Paper for Printed Library Materials, ANSI/NISO Z39.48–1992
Manufactured in the United States of America.

This work is dedicated to the memory of Kathy Kerner,
whose The Thanksgiving Epidemic *is included in this book.*

For Kathy Kerner,
Who Knew They Taught Us All Wrong

Your spirit circled around us
as we gathered to honor you
with songs, stories, and memories,

of the days
you stood with a people,
whose struggles you adopted as your own.

You grew in the knowledge
that our struggles are intractable,
colonization-old and colonizer-fueled.

Still, you took them on,
and with rare courage and healing grace,
dared to speak the truth.

"They taught you wrong,"
you reminded us,
corrections must be made.

So, with your mindful intelligence
and compassionate heart,
you set out to right the wrongs of centuries.

Now, we remember you with great love, respect,
and thanksgiving,
as your strong, warrior spirit journeys home.

Paulette F. Molin
September 1998

Contents

Part 2: Bibliography

Foreword to the First Edition

Michael A. Dorris

I isn't for Indian. As the authors of the articles in this book know and demonstrate, it is often for Ignorance. In the Never-Never Land of glib stereotypes and caricature, the rich histories, cultures, and the contemporary complexities of the indigenous, diverse peoples of the Western Hemisphere are obscured, misrepresented, and rendered trivial. Native Americans appear not as human beings but as whooping, silly, one-dimensional cartoons. On occasion they are presented as marauding, blood-thirsty savages, bogeys from the nightmares of "pioneers" who invaded their lands and feared for the consequences. At other times they seem preconcupiscent angels, pure of heart, mindlessly ecological, brave and true. And worst of all, they are often merely cute, the special property of small children.

It's an easy way to dismiss an unproud history. A society that chooses to make a running joke of its victims embalms both its conscience and its obligations, relegating a tragic chronology of culture contact to ersatz mythology. It's hard to take seriously, to empathize with, a group of people portrayed as speaking ungrammatical language, as dressing in Halloween costumes, as acting "wild," as being undependable in their promises or gifts. Frozen in a kind of pejorative past tense, these make-believe Indians are not allowed to change or in any other way be like *real* people. They are denied the dignity and dynamism of their history, the validity of their myriad and major contributions to modern society, the distinctiveness of their multiple ethnicities.

It's a shame. To deprive our children (who grow up to become no less deprived adults) access to the wealth and sophistication of traditional Native American societies is indefensible. Among the several hundred separate cultures of North America alone, comprising as they did between twelve and twenty million people in 1491, there existed a pluralism of social experimentation and worldview unimagined by the melting pot theorists. Every known form of political system was practiced, from democracy to theocracy to communism to hereditary leadership. In the vast majority of these societies, power and decision-making rested with both women and men. Most Native peoples were village-based agriculturists, not "roaming hunters." A wide variety of sciences—astronomy, agronomy, medicine, mathematics, geology, meteorology and taxonomy, to name only a few—were highly developed and practiced. A wealth of spiritual and philosophical beliefs flourished. A tolerance for individual difference, either within one's own culture or in another society altogether, was the norm. Literature, music, dance, and art found widely divergent and brilliant expression. And yet this treasure trove of experience and intelligence, perfected over tens of thousands of years residence on this continent, is allowed to be eclipsed by dumb, racist drivel.

Real American history, abounding with confusion, misunderstanding, exploitation, good people and bad ones, cultural chauvinism and hard-won insight, contains lessons that vitally need to be learned, not forgotten or whitewashed. We, as a people, must not make the same mistakes again in other dealings with new societies that seem to be initially either strange or unfathomable to us.

Some readers may find individual instances of stereotyping cited in this book to be inoffensive, and individually they may be. Taken out of the general context, objection to a particular toy or school symbol or nursery rhyme might seem to be a case of over-sensitivity. "Where's your sense of humor?" they may ask. "Aren't all groups satirized or emblemized? Irish-Americans are proud of the Fighting Irish of Notre Dame! What's wrong with exhorting little boys to want to be brave and stoic? Can't you take a joke?"

No. It's no joke when a dominant group, with a sorry history of oppression towards its minorities, expropriates a shallow version of a subordinate, relatively powerless group and promulgates that imagery as valid. This realization may come slowly but it can come. Even the most hearty enthusiast can probably comprehend today the tastelessness of little black jockey statues in front of a house or the rolling-eyed parody of minstrel show revelry. Even the most oblivious observer cannot help but see the danger inherent in early Nazi caricatures of Jews or gypsies. Italian anti-defamation leagues are strong in their censure of media gangsters with Sicilian names. For most of us the Polish joke is at least suspect.

So why should standards of respect and restraint differ when it comes to Indians? Are Native people less worthy of serious consideration, less contemporary (the 1980 census revealed nearly one and one-half million Indians in the United States alone), less complicated? Is it any less demeaning or ridiculous to portray every Indian with feathers than it would be to present every Afro-American with a spear or every Hispanic with a sombrero?

This book is *about* context. It presents evidence from a variety of sources—toys, pageants, misrepresented "history," advertisements—that demonstrates the pervasiveness of the problem. The stereotype has even been exported: In duty free souvenir shops from Fiji to Freeport one can purchase stuffed animals wearing war bonnets or Hong Kong manufactured, dewy-eyed papoose dolls. Generations of German children have grown up reading "Westerns" about stalwart, crafty "redskins." Japanese baseball teams emulate their American counterparts and call themselves "Braves." The reality of American Indians, past and present, has been lost in the shuffle.

By legal definition, Indian tribes in the United States exist, in over two hundred treaty relationships with the federal government, as "domestic, dependent nations." They are self-governing, political entities, many of them rich in natural resources and all of them rich in human potential. For far too long they have been denied their legitimate place, their own voice, the public awareness of their diverse heritage. Let *I* be for someone else.

Introduction to the Second Edition

This first edition of this anthology was first compiled to "shock adults into realizing that the world of contemporary American infants and young children is saturated with inappropriate images of Indians." Unfortunately, almost twenty years later, too many toys, picture books, television programs, and sports team mascots bombard children with ignorant and insensitive images of Native people. Popular movies like *Pocahontas* and *The Indian in the Cupboard,* filled with offensive language and stereotypical characters, have turned the clock back on meaningful and realistic presentations of Indian peoples.

The second edition of this book has the same purpose. New material has been added to again shock parents, educators, and other caregivers into positive action. If Indian children are to build strong self-concepts, feelings of personal worth, and a sense of their place in United States history and the here-and-now, they are entitled to have culturally and historically accurate books, texts, movies, and other learning materials about their people. Constant encounters with specious images of Indians in school settings and popular culture result in Indian children losing self-esteem and pride in their identity. With constant rejection and denigration by society, Indian children soon learn to reject themselves. If non-Indian children are to learn to accept their Indian neighbors as friends and equals, they must have culturally and historically accurate accounts of Indians. Continuing encounters with racist imagery distorts the social and visual perceptions of European-American and other children and prevents them from developing appropriate attitudes—and behavior—about and toward Indians.

These racist images and even the complete omission of Indian peoples rob both Native and non-Native children of the opportunity to benefit from the richness and wisdom of Indian cultures, as well as the possibility of resolving many contemporary problems endemic in our society with solutions based on Indian life, thought, and philosophies.

The bibliography in this second edition has been tripled. Over the past decade, scholars in the United States and Canada have turned their minds to analyzing every conceivable form Indian imagery and stereotyping takes in both countries. It's nearly impossible to keep up with the scholarship, so the bibliography merely offers a sampling of the rich studies written during the twentieth century. A variety of new learning materials have been added so teachers and other educators can do battle with the worn-out images that belittle Indian cultures, traditions, and histories and replace them with accurate and respectful depictions.

Introduction to the First Edition

Adults who nurture, love, care for, educate, and work with children should heed the research findings regarding both the development of racial awareness and attitudes in very young children and their feelings about race differences. Psychologist Gordon Allport in his early work about prejudice generalizes that "The first six years of life are important for the development of all social attitudes, though it is a mistake to regard early childhood as alone responsible for them. A bigoted personality may be well under way by the age of six, but by no means fully fashioned."[1]

Mary Ellen Goodman, a cultural anthropologist who has done fundamental research in children's awareness and feelings about race differences, concludes that children begin to develop racial awareness at an extremely early age, perhaps as early as three or four years.[2] By upwards of age five, Goodman argues that incipient attitudes—and prejudice—are likely and by age seven true attitudes not unlikely.[3]

When infants are ready to focus their eyes on concrete objects, they are very likely to see angry-looking "I" for Indians brandishing weaponry on plastic or cloth block sets. By the time these infants are seven years old, they probably have seen hundreds of images of mean, silly, or noble Indians. It should come as no surprise that non-Indian children programmed on these stereotypes at early, formative developmental stages grow into adults who may unwittingly or knowingly discriminate against Indians. These children have been prevented from developing health attitudes about Indians. It also should come as no surprise that Indian children who constantly see their people stereotyped or treated in unfair ways grow into adults who begin to feel and act as if they were not as good as other people. These Native children are hindered in developing healthy self-images and racial identities; according to a group of scholars, they learn helplessness, the idea that they are incapable of making decisions for themselves.[4]

Children in America regularly see images of Indians that are inauthentic, unrealistic, and often offensive. Typical American children may dress in clothes decorated with headdresses, tipis, tomahawks, and faces of Indians and others may pin on pieces of jewelry shaped like one of these objects. Some youngsters pour "Life" cereal out of boxes that picture historic Indian cultures and offer free posters of Indians or dinosaurs. In school, children read social studies texts that portray Indians as obstacles to progress or incidental to the entire course of American history. Most routinely see silly or ferocious Indians in their story books and play with toys that demean important aspects of Indian cultures. After school, children watch Indians kill settlers, army regulars, or similar "good guys" on television or view the same scenarios on movie screens. They receive birthday cards that joke about Indian languages, dress, and customs, and presents wrapped in paper decorated with Indians. At Halloween or Thanksgiving, most nursery school children bring home a feathered headband they have proudly made themselves. Many youngsters across America cheer for sports teams that have names such as the "Redskins" and/or mascots that parade around at half-time in buckskin, beads, and feathers. Food packages, greeting cards, games, common household objects, songs, advertisements, and cartoons carry images of Indians that are either savage, noble, lazy, stupid, or subhuman.

This anthology has been put together to try and shock adults into realizing that the world of contemporary American infants and young children is saturated with inappropriate images of Indians. The carefully selected articles spell out the prevalent attitudes of children, explain the emergence of the Plains Indian stereotype, scrutinize in detail the images of Indians in children's story and textbooks, analyze toy Indian imagery, describe the misuse of Indian religion and customs in YMCA programs, and report on sports teams with Indian names and derogatory mascots. Essays discussing the images of Indians in the movies have been omitted because a number of them have been published in an anthology entitled *The Pretend Indians: Images of Native Americans in the Movies.*[5]

Following these readings, there is an annotated bibliography of articles and books about the images of Indians in the world of children and adults in America and other countries. The studies examine Indian imagery in art, literature, social science, children's story and textbooks, movies, television, European literature, and other fields. A shorter section of articles, books, curricula, and other materials suggests ways to correct the inauthentic, offensive, and unreal images of Indians. It is clear that much more work needs to be done in creating methods and materials that will counteract the harmful effects of so much negative and inappropriate Indian imagery.

Some of the articles in this anthology were written some years ago, but they are no less relevant today. For example, many of the findings regarding the social studies textbook treatment of Indians and Eskimos[6] are valid today. There have been *some* improvements, of course, in the history texts published in the 1970s, 1980 and 1981. A reader can find more accurate information about Indians prior to and subsequent to contact with Europeans. One textbook does an excellent job of presenting the viewpoints of contemporary Indians, an area sorely lacking in most texts; however, it contains meager information on the Iroquois and nothing about Eskimos.[7] Very few textbooks include enough information about Indians to suggest to young readers that there are hundreds of contemporary, dynamic Native societies in America.

A brief look at a few of the statements about Indians in a 1981 textbook entitled *History of a Free People* written by Henry W. Bragdon and Samuel P. McCutchen (New York: Macmillan Publishing Co., Inc.) illustrates the nature of information currently being published about Iroquois Indians. On page three, the Iroquois are called "northeast woodland" Indians, a map label deplored by scholars such as Jack D. Forbes because it is a non-Indian construct. The authors inform readers on page four that the Iroquois who lived in New York occupied a territory that they called a "longhouse" with its eastern "door" at Albany on the Hudson and its western "door" at Niagara Falls. There is no discussion of the Iroquois empire, which at its peak spread some 800 miles between the Appalachians and the Mississippi and which was strategically important land. In the few pages that discuss the traditional organization, beliefs, and actions of the Iroquois, the only observation quoted by the authors is one by a Jesuit priest likening the behavior of Iroquois warriors to foxes, lions, and birds. There is an illustration of Father Jogues, a Jesuit priest preaching to the Iroquois in one of their longhouses. The caption reads "Jogues was later tortured and put to death."[8] The authors write that Jesuit priests "Undaunted by starvation and torture"[9] made journeys far into the middle of the continent to convert Indians to Christianity. Thirty-two Indian scholars who investigated more than 300 books for a study about the treatment of Indians in textbooks[10] call such information the "semantics of racism." They argue that:

> Torture, human sacrifice, and delight in war are descriptions given of Iroquois customs by . . . textbook writers. Not to understand the differences in culture and standards of conduct, displays the lack of an objective, scholarly mind. Describing Roman history, for example, few if any historians and textbook writers give blow by blow accounts of the many atrocities committed by this society. It would appear that the contributions of the Iroquois would far outweigh any "strange" accounts of their religious customs (which are usually not understood and highly exaggerated).[11]

There is one paragraph about contemporary Iroquois keeping alive their traditions generation after generation, and there are several paragraphs at the end of the volume that deal with the new militancy of Indians. There are sixty-six maps that appear in the book, one of which depicts the location of Indian peoples before 1700—and which is left out of the table of contents. Not one map shows the boundaries of contemporary state and federal Indian reservations although there is room for a full-page map of Africa. It would be difficult for uninformed students to know that there are over 450 federally recognized tribes who live on or near 267 reservations, that there are over twenty state recognized Indian tribes, some of which are in New York State, that there are Indian groups without trust lands and certain tribes and groups that have been terminated by the federal government. As Michael A. Dorris remarks:

> The Indian, by and large, is a motif embedded in Americana, not perceived as a part of the American present. The confusion comes when we realize that Indian people, too often mistaken for The Indian, are still very much around.[12]

There are other social studies texts that contain statements and/or illustrations that distort Indian cultures and history. In *The American Adventure* published by Field Educational Publications, Inc. in 1970, there is a full page color illustration of a 1787 engraving of an Iroquois warrior in battle pose. The caption tells readers that "A scalp is draped over the end of his musket and a tomahawk hangs at his waist."[13] Iroquois men did not spend all their time dressed and ready for battle, equipped with weaponry and scalps, although some young readers might have difficulty believing otherwise. Probably the most important job of an Iroquois man was hunting. He was also a musician, dancer, physician, athlete, craftsman, politician, and religious leader. *The American Adventure* has nothing to say about present-day Indians and Eskimos.

After reading the essays about children's toys, books, and programs in this anthology, perhaps more adults will become convinced that it is essential to dispel the offensive, inauthentic, and unreal images of American Indians and replace them with accurate, authentic, and real depictions. After all, children's attitudes are at stake.

NOTES

1. Gordon W. Allport, *The Nature of Prejudice* (Cambridge, Mass.: Addison Wesley Publishing Co., 1954; Boston: Beacon edition), p. 297.

2. See Mary Ellen Goodman's study entitled *Race Awareness in Young Children*. Revised ed. (New York: Collier Books, 1964).

3. Ibid., p. 254.

4. "Stereotypes of Indians Decried at Conference on Native Americans." *New York Times*, November 28, 1976.

5. *The Pretend Indians* was edited by Gretchen M. Bataille and Charles L. P. Silet (Ames: Iowa State University Press, 1980).

6. See Chapter Five in this anthology.

7. Allan O. Kownslar and Donald B. Frizzle, *Discovering American History* (New York: Holt, Rinehart, and Winston, Inc., 1974).

8. Henry W. Bragdon and Samuel P. McCutchen, *History of a Free People* (New York: Macmillan Publishing Co., Inc., 1981), p. 18.

9. Ibid.

10. American Indian Historical Society, *Textbooks and the American Indian* (San Francisco: Indian Historian Press, Inc., 1970).

11. Ibid., p. 17.

12. Michael A. Dorris, "The Grass Still Grows, The Rivers Still Flow: Contemporary Native Americans," *Daedalus*, vol. 110, no. 2 (Spring 1981): 46.

13. Kenneth Bailey, Elizabeth Brooke, and John J. Farrell, *The American Adventure* (San Francisco: Field Educational Publications, Inc., 1970).

Chapter 1

Through the Eyes of a Child

Children's Impressions of American Indians: A Survey of Suburban Kindergarten and Fifth Grade Children: Conclusions*

League of Women Voters

The following conclusions are based on the results of a study conducted in 1974 with 238 kindergarteners and 239 fifth graders of the Mounds View School District, comprised of St. Paul suburbs. These students make up one-fifth of all the children in kindergarten and fifth grade. The children were asked twelve questions that brought out both their attitudes and information about Native Americans.

Most Children View Indian People as Far Removed from Their Own Way of Life. A careful analysis of all responses makes one conclusion very clear; most of the children surveyed view the American Indian as far removed from their way of life. When asked if they had ever seen an American Indian, only 16 kindergarteners (6%) and 31 fifth graders (13%) indicated they had seen one in person. This is interesting considering the number of Indian people living in the Twin City metropolitan area. Perhaps even more interesting are the comments of those who went on to state where they had seen an American Indian; almost everyone described places or situations outside his home, neighborhood, school, and circle of friends. For these children, the American Indian seems to exist "somewhere else"—the Black Hills, in North Dakota, at the fair, etc.

A number of other factors reinforce this conclusion: the many children who were unable to offer any description whatsoever of an American Indian, and the consistent recurrence of references to Indians of long ago in response to questions about Indian fathers, mothers, and children. When children were asked where Indian people live, they very clearly placed them "someplace else"— in dwellings very different from their own, such as tents and caves, in other states, in other time

---

*Reprinted by permission from "Children's Impressions of American Indians," League of Women Voters, New Brighton, Minnesota, 1975.

periods. For the most part, even those who placed Indians in another time period (by describing customs and practices of the past) also located them away from here. For example, little reference was made to the fishing, wild ricing, and maple sugaring so important to Indians in northern Minnesota. As a group, the children saw Indian people as far removed from themselves in location and in time.

Many Children Hold an Historic/Traditional Image of Indian People. Indians wearing traditional clothing and engaged in traditional activities were described by many children in kindergarten and fifth grade. Although few (no kindergarteners and 11 fifth graders) indicated they were speaking of the past, it is apparent that many of these students were describing the Indian in history. For example, children frequently mentioned skin clothing and feathers when describing Indians; they identified hunting as an Indian father's work and pictured mothers making clothes and food from the animals; they depicted children learning to hunt and shoot. This historical image was most evident in regard to an Indian father's work where 69% of the kindergarteners and 77% of the fifth graders who gave information mentioned traditional activities only. Furthermore, when asked specifically about today (question #11), 43% of the kindergarteners and 16% of the fifth graders who gave information mentioned the same traditional activities or stated Indians live the same as they always did. For these students, the historic/traditional image dominates.

Many Children, Particularly Kindergarteners, View Indian People as Warlike and Hostile. A distorted image of Indians as warlike has prevailed throughout much of American history. Indians defending their land against encroachment by European settlers have been termed "bloodthirsty savages" and their victories "massacres." Pictures showing Indians attacking so-called "innocent settlers" have been all too common.

In view of this, therefore, some comments reflecting this warlike image could have been anticipated. Yet we were surprised at the relatively large number of kindergarten children who described Indians as mean or killing or shooting people. This type of comment occurred in response to every question except number 7 (where do Indian people live?). Comments ranged from simply "Kill people" to "After them puts you in jail, that means they tie you up and shot you." The largest number occurred in relation to the father's activities, but even an Indian mother's activities were described as "kills people and goes to work." Even more startling were the eight kindergarteners who described Indian children shooting, catching, or killing people. Altogether almost one-fifth of the kindergarteners mentioned some type of hostile activity.

By contrast, only one fifth grader described this type of overt hostility. Other students implied a war-like image by speaking of Indian fathers going on war parties, children having game wars or Indians acting "wild-like." The total number of students who made these types of comments numbered 25, a decrease from the 43 kindergarteners, indicating a possible improvement in the image held by fifth graders.

Most of the Children Do Not Recognize the Great Diversity Among Indian People Which Existed in the Past and Continues Today. Gerald Vizenor, in his book *The Everlasting Sky: New Voices From the People Named the Chippewa*, speaks of an image of the Indian which is "homogenized" from more than 300 distinct tribal cultures, an image he feels the white dominant society prefers over the complexities of true Indian history. Many kindergarteners depicted this homogenized image by describing Indians wearing feathers, hunting, and living in teepees or tents in the woods. This simplistic overgeneralized view of Indian people has apparently been formed before kindergarteners enter school.

Because the majority of fifth graders did not specify whether they were speaking of one tribe or all Indians, they also seem to present a generalized view of Indians in the past. It is possible that they know from their studies in school that there were differences among tribes, but this was not expressed in their comments. For example, does the student who mentioned Indian mothers cleaning buffalo skins realize not all Indian tribes hunted buffalo?

Only a few fifth graders (16) indicated an understanding of tribal differences in the past. Some used tribal names in association with their information ("The Pueblo built homes, make clothing and clean food."). Others qualified their responses by saying "it depends" or "some." Only six students more explicitly indicated diversity among tribes by making comments such as "Some Indians were agriculturists, some hunters, depending on the part of the country."

When describing Indians today, children again generalized, not indicating whether they were referring to all Indian people or to some Indian people. For these children, Indians either live like we do ("They turned into Americans rather than keeping their own ways") or live the same as they did in the past ("They do the same things they did years ago"). Only a few fifth graders expressed some knowledge of diversity among Indian people today. Two exceptionally good answers reflect this broader, less generalized view. In describing where Indian people live, one fifth grader said "Depending on what kind of Indian they are, some live in pueblos, some in housing like ours"; another said an Indian father does "All kinds of different things, sometimes normal jobs, sometimes medicine men, I think that is what they are called. They can do anything they are qualified for. They could be a doctor if they had their degree."

There seems to be a definite need to emphasize the diversity among Indian people, both past and present. Information describing one tribe is easily generalized to all tribes and information about Indians of the past may be assumed to be true of all Indians today. Schools can help to counteract the homogenized view of the Indian by frequently identifying the specific Indian tribe being studied and reiterating that many Indian people do live differently today than they did in the past.

Fifth Grade Children Gave More Information Than Kindergarteners Did About Indian People. Fifth graders consistently gave more information and a wider range of answers to all the questions indicating they had more knowledge and were better able to express themselves. This is particularly evident in a number of areas.

When describing traditional/historical activities of women and children, more fifth graders responded and a few more activities were named such as grinding corn and craft activities. There were still quite a few children who simply said an Indian mother "cooks" or Indian children "play." Compared to the high number of responses in regards to an Indian father's activities, children show less knowledge about the historical activities of women and children.

More fifth graders than kindergarteners gave information about today. In contrast to the large number of students who seemed to be visualizing the Indian of the past a group of fifth graders (approximately 18%) answered most of the questions with information implying they were speaking about Indians today. Very few kindergarteners made this distinction. Almost one-fourth of the fifth graders are aware of reservations. However, some of these children have the misconception that Indians have to stay on a reservation. Others did not specify that Indian people also live in other places besides reservations.

Some fifth graders expressed a sensitivity to the problems of Indian people. A few were aware of prejudice today and 13% of the fifth graders made strong statements that Indians should have more rights or should be treated equally.

Even by Fifth Grade, Many Children Do Not Identify Positive or Negative Feelings Toward American Indians.   Two interesting observations from this study are (1) the largest group of children at both levels do not commit themselves to either positive or negative feelings toward Indian people, and (2) among those who do express feelings, fifth graders tend to be more positive than kindergartners.

It is possible, of course, that some of those who were noncommittal when asked how they felt about Indians were simply unwilling to admit their feelings or unable to describe them. For the remainder of this large group, however, the implications for education and the communications media are important; even after the fifth grade, children are forming attitudes toward the American Indian. Care should be taken to choose educational activities which present an accurate picture of Indian heritage and include the many contributions Indians have made and are making.

Among the children who do identify their feelings, fifth graders tend to be more positive than kindergarteners and will more frequently say they'd like to have an Indian for a friend. The reason for this shift is not clear. It may be the influence of schooling between kindergarten and grade five; or it may result from increased familiarity with Indian people through personal contacts and other experiences.

Those kindergarteners who make negative comments about Indian people base them on a different image than do fifth graders. Negative-feeling kindergarteners describe Indians as warlike, "I don't like them because they kill people." Negative feeling fifth graders, on the other hand, describe Indian people as lazy and unlawful, breaking into stores or breaking down houses.

Along with the conclusions from the data, we feel the following inference merits discussion.

Children's Images of Indian People Suggest the Influence of the Media. Kindergarten children were chosen for this study because their answers would reflect the image of the Indian people portrayed by influences outside of the schools. There are a variety of influences on children including the attitudes of parents and family as well as other group experiences. However, one which touches all children is the media, that is, television, movies, storybooks, toys and games. Considering the many references to Indians in the media, it is not surprising that many five-year-olds already have some impressions of the American Indian. That they do is clearly evidenced by the fact that all but 13 kindergarten children responded to at least one of the questions on this survey with a comment giving information.

What kind of an image did these kindergarten children portray? They are aware already of the traditionally dressed figure in feathers and skins living by hunting and dwelling in teepees. In fact, 182 children out of 238 (76%) answered at least one of the questions with some aspect of this image. In the case of 43 of these children, the Indian is a hostile enemy with which to contend, a fact that readily brings to mind the cowboys and Indians conflicts so common to movies and cartoons on television.

It is also interesting to note that a significantly larger number of kindergarten children gave answers about the traditional activities of Indian fathers (81) than about Indian mothers (20). It is apparent that the image of the Indian which children have is predominantly male. This, too, strongly suggests the influences of the media and games and toys in which the role of the Indian woman is seldom portrayed.

The primary image reflected by these children brings to mind the portrayal of Indian people in many story books. These books focus primarily on the past and portray a stereotyped image of Indian people. Mary Gloyne Byler,* a Cherokee, writes with concern about children's books:

> There are too many stories for very young children about little boys running around in feathers and headbands, wearing fringed buckskin clothing, moccasins and (especially) carrying little bows and arrows. The majority of these books deal with the unidentified past. The characters are from unidentified tribes and they are often not even afforded the courtesy of personal names. In fact the only thing identifiable is the stereotyped image of the befeathered Indian. . . . The device of repeatedly referring to people in this impersonal and anonymous way, and then reinforcing the anonymity with illustrations that are nondescript, creates the impression that one is not dealing with full-fledged human beings.

---

*Mary Gloyne Byler, *American Indian Authors for Young Readers*, New York: Association on American Indian Affairs, 1973, p. 5.

Fifth graders are also influenced by books as well as other forms of the media. It is interesting to note that, like the kindergarteners, a majority of the fifth graders responded to some of the questions with information about the Indian of the past even though all of the questions are worded in the present tense.

The media is reflected by a few fifth graders who mention "Wounded Knee."* Such present-day concerns of Indian people provide good openers for the very necessary emphasis on the Indian of today.

The task of the teacher is a challenging one. Not only does new information have to be given, but the misconceptions and stereotypes about Indian people which bombard the child from outside of the classroom need to be counteracted.

---

*The so-called "Indian occupation of Wounded Knee, South Dakota" had occurred one year earlier (1973) and the trial of two participants, Russell Means and Dennis Banks, had just ended in St. Paul when the survey was taken in the fall of 1974.

Chapter 2

The Only Good Indian Is a Plains Indian

The Emergence of the
Plains Indian as the Symbol
of the North American Indian*

John C. Ewers

One summer's day in 1941 I stood on the North Montana Fairground in Great Falls. From a stand in front of me a fast-talking patent medicine salesman was vigorously extolling the curative powers of his bottled wares. From time to time he pointed to the living advertisement standing beside him—a tall, erect, young White man whose paint-streaked face was framed by a beautiful, flowing-feather bonnet. The young man's body was clothed in a cloth shirt, leggings, and a breechclout dyed to resemble buckskin. His feet were clad in beaded moccasins. The audience, for the most part, was composed of Indians from Montana reservations wearing common White men's clothes—shirts and trousers. I was intrigued by the fact that this pale-faced symbol of an American Indian standing before us was wearing a close approximation of the same costume the Blackfeet, Crees, and Crows in the audience would put on when they staged an Indian show for the enjoyment of tourists.

How did this picturesque costume come to symbolize "Indianness" to the minds of Indians and Whites alike? How did the popular image of the Indian come to be formed in a Plains Indian mold? Why do people in Europe and America, when they think of Indians, tend to think of them as wearers of back-swept feather bonnets, as dwellers in conical tipis, and as mounted warriors and buffalo hunters? Surely our founding fathers had no such conception of the Indian in the days when the frontier of settlement extended only a short distance west of the Alleghenies, and the only Indians the remote frontiersmen knew were forest dwellers who lived in bark-covered houses, traveled in bark canoes or dugouts, hunted and fought on foot, and wore no flowing-feather bonnets. Nor was the pre-

*Reprinted by permission of the Smithsonian Institution Press from *Smithsonian Institution Annual Report 1964*, "The Emergence of the Plains Indian as the Symbol of the North American Indian," by John C. Ewers: pages 531–44. Washington, D.C.: Government Printing Office, 1965.

11

vailing popular image of the Indian an original creation of the motion pictures during the 20th century. How and when, then, did this image emerge?

Probing into history we find that the creation and clarification of this image was a prolonged process to which many factors contributed. Let us try to trace the development of this image from what appear to be its earliest beginnings. ⟩ 11-12

THE FIRST PICTURES OF PLAINS INDIANS (1804–40)

Obviously before non-Indians could begin to picture Indians in Plains Indian terms, they had to have fairly clear ideas of the appearance of the Indians of the Great Plains and of the those aspects of their culture that typified their way of life. European explorers and traders traversed considerable portions of the Plains in the 2½ centuries between Coronado's quest for the fabled city of Quivera on the grasslands of Kansas in 1541 and the purchase of Louisiana by the United States in 1803. Nevertheless, those Spaniards, French, and Englishmen produced no popular literature about and no known pictures of Plains Indians—either portraits or scenes of Indian life. At the time of the Louisiana Purchase these Indians remained virtually unknown to the peoples of Europe and the United States (although a number of earlier explorers' and traders' accounts have been published since that time).

The earliest known portraits of Plains Indians were made in the cities of the East during the first decade of the 19th century. They were likenesses of Indians whom President Jefferson urged Lewis and Clark to send to the seat of government in Washington. They were profiles executed by two very competent artists, who both employed versions of a mechanical device, known as a physiognotrace, to accurately delineate the outlines of their sitters' heads. The French refugee artist Charles Balthazar Fevret de Saint-Mémin made portraits of some of the 12 men and 2 boys of the Osages who comprised the first delegation of Indians from beyond the Mississippi. Thomas Jefferson welcomed these Indians to the Presidential mansion in the summer of 1804, and enthusiastically termed them "the most gigantic" and "the finest men we have ever seen" (Jackson, 1962, p. 199). Saint-Memin's most striking profile is that of the chief of the Little Osages.

Charles Willson Peale, prominent Philadelphia artist and museum proprietor, cut miniature silhouettes of 10 members of a second Indian delegation from the West. He sent a set of these profiles to President Jefferson on February 8, 1806 (Jackson, 1962, p. 299). One of these sitters was Pagesgata, a young Republican Pawnee from the Platte Valley.

After his return from the Pacific coast, Meriwether Lewis purchased several originals or copies of Saint-Mémin's Indian portraits. Undoubtedly he intended to reproduce them in an elaborately illustrated account of the Lewis and Clark explorations which he proposed, but never produced because of his untimely death in 1809. Peale also was to have furnished illustrations for this ill-fated work.

Doubtless they would have included accurate drawings of the Plains Indian costumes and other artifacts sent or brought back by Lewis and Clark, which Peale exhibited in his popular Philadelphia Museum.

More significant factors in the early diffusion of the Plains Indian image were the oil portraits of several members of an Indian delegation from the Lower Missouri and Platte Valley tribes who arrived in Washington late in the year 1821. Although Charles Bird King painted these Indians for Thomas McKenney, Superintendent of Indian Trade, he executed several replicas of the paintings that were diffused more widely—one set being sent to Denmark, another to London. The original portraits formed the nucleus of the National Indian Portrait Gallery, which became one of Washington's popular tourist attractions before it was almost completely destroyed in the Smithsonian Institution fire of 1865 (Ewers, 1954).

The most popular Indian in that 1821 delegation was Petalesharro, a young Pawnee warrior. He was hailed as a hero during his eastern tour because he had courageously rescued a Comanche girl captive just as her life was to be taken in the traditional human sacrifice to the morning star, an annual Pawnee ceremony. Petalesharro's portrait was painted by John Neagle in Philadelphia, as well as by King, and Samuel F. B. Morse placed him in front of the visitor's gallery in his well-known painting of "The Old House of Representatives," executed in 1822. All three paintings show this Indian hero wearing a flowing-feather bonnet. They are, to the best of my knowledge, the first of the millions of pictorial renderings of this picturesque Indian headgear produced by artist and photographers.

The popular novelist James Fenimore Cooper met Petalesharro during that Indian's eastern tour. This meeting was a source of inspiration to the author in writing *The Prairie*, the only one of the *Leatherstocking Tales* to have a Great Plains setting (Keiser, 1933, pp. 134–138). In the living Indians of the Plains, Cooper recognized the virtues he had imputed to his Woodland Indian heroes of an earlier period in *The Last of the Mohicans*. Writing of the Indians 2 years after that popular novel was published, he observed: "The majority of them, in or near the settlements, are an humbled and much degraded race. As you recede from the Mississippi, the finer traits of savage life become visible."

Cooper thought that Plains Indian chiefs possessed a "loftiness of spirit, of bearing and of savage heroism . . . that might embarrass the fertility of the richest inventor to equal," and he cited Petalesharro as a prime example (Cooper, 1828, vol. 2, pp. 287–288).

Some of the distinctive traits of the Plains Indians were pictured in illustrated books and magazines prior to 1840. The first published picture of the conical skin-covered tipis of the nomadic Plains tribes was a crude engraving after Titian Peale's field sketch on Major Long's expedition of 1819–1820, which appeared in Edwin James' account of those explorations (James, 1823). The first reproduction of a Plains Indian warrior on horseback probably was the lithograph of Peter Rindisbacher's drawing "Sioux Warrior Charging" that appeared in the October 1829 issue of *The American Turf Register and Sporting Magazine*. Young

Rindisbacher had ample opportunities to observe Plains Indian warriors and buffalo hunters during nearly 5 years' residence in Lord Selkirk's settlement on the Red River of the North, 1821–26. His lively portrayal of Indians on horseback chasing buffalo was offered as the colored lithographic frontispiece in the first volume of Thomas McKenney and James Hall's classic *History of the Indian Tribes of North America* (1836–44). However, of the 120 finely printed colored lithographs of Indians in that handsome work only a small proportion portray Plains Indians, and all of these were portraits of members of western delegations to Washington, the originals of which had been executed by Saint-Mémin, King, or the latter's pupil George Cooke.

In 1839 Samuel George Morton of Philadelphia, now known as the father of physical anthropology in America, published his major work, *Crania Americana.* Its frontispiece is a lithographic reproduction of John Neagle's portrait of the Omaha head chief Big Elk, a prominent member of the 1821 deputation from the Great Plains. Morton explained this selection: "Among the multitude of Indian portraits which have come under my notice, I know of no one that embraces more characteristic traits than this, as seen in the retreating forehead, the low brow, the dull and seemingly unobservant eye, the large aquiline nose, the high cheek bones, full mouth and chin and angular face" (Morton, 1839, p. 292).

The first illustrated schoolbook on American history was Rev. Charles A. Goodrich's *History of the United States.* First published in 1823, it went through 150 printings by 1847. However, Noah Webster's *History of the United States* was a popular competitor from its first appearance in 1832. The small and sometimes indistinct woodcuts in these books are not numerous. Nevertheless, some of them include Indians. A few scenes in Webster's history were adopted from John White's 16th-century drawings of Indian life in coastal North Carolina. But the scenes depicting early explorers' meetings with Indians, the making of Indian treaties, and the conduct of Indian wars seem to be based largely upon the imaginations of their anonymous creators. Plains Indians are conspicuously absent. They had yet to make an indelible mark upon American history in their determined resistance to the expansion of White settlement onto and across their grassy homeland.

THE INFLUENCE OF GEORGE CATLIN
AND KARL BODMER (1841–60)

No other mid-19th century factors had such a stimulating influence on both (1) the projection of the Plains Indian image and (2) the acceptance of this image as that of the American Indian par excellence as did the writings of the American artist George Catlin and the German scientist Maximilian Alexander Philipp, Prince of Wied-Neuwied; and the pictures of Catlin and the Swiss artist Karl Bodmer, who accompanied the prince on his exploration of the Upper Missouri in 1833–34.

Inspired by the sight of a delegation of western Indians passing through Phila-delphia on their way to Washington, and his own conviction that the picturesque Plains Indians were doomed to cultural extinction as the frontier expanded west-ward, Catlin determined to rescue these Indians from oblivion and to "become their historian" before it was too late. During the summers of 1832 and 1834 he traveled among the tribes of the Upper Missouri and the Southern Plains gathering infor-mation and preparing pictures for an Indian Gallery, which he exhibited to enthu-siastic audiences in the larger American cities. In 1840, he took the exhibition to England for a 4-year display in London; this was followed by a Paris exhibition that included a special showing for King Louis Philippe in the Louvre. In addition to his paintings this exhibition included costumed mannequins, a pitched Crow tipi, and enactments of Indian dances and ceremonies by Chippewa or Iowa Indians. No one had brought the Wild West to civilization as had Catlin, and his exhibition must have made a lasting impression upon all Americans and Europeans who saw it.

Nevertheless, Catlin's books must have had a still wider influence. His two-vol-ume *Manners, Customs and Condition of the North American Indians*, published in London in 1841, combined a vivid description of his travels and observations with 312 steel-engraved reproductions of his paintings. The work was enthusiastically reviewed in America and abroad, and was reprinted five times in as many years. Although Catlin included brief descriptions and illustrations, primarily portraits, of a number of the semi-civilized Woodland tribes, he concentrated primarily upon the wild tribes of the Great Plains. There could be no mistaking either from his text or from his pictures that the Plains Indians were his favorites. Repeatedly, if not con-sistently, Catlin sang their praises. He declared that the tribes of the Upper Missouri were the "finest specimens of Indians on the Continent . . . all entirely in the state of primitive rudeness and wildness, and consequently are picturesque and hand-some, almost beyond description." The Crows were as "handsome and well-formed set of men as can be seen in any part of the world"; the Assiniboins " a fine and noble looking race." There were no "finer looking men than the Sioux"; and Catlin used almost the same words to describe the Cheyennes. (Catlin, 1841, vol. 1, pp. 22–23, 49, 54, 210; vol. 2, p. 2) Catlin devoted several chapters of his book to Four Bears, the second chief of the Mandan, whom he called the "most extraordinary man, perhaps, who lives to this day, in the atmosphere of Nature's noblemen."

Prince Maximilian's *Reise in das Innere Nord-America in den Jahren 1832 bis 1834*, first published in Coblenz (1839–41), offered a more restrained, scientific description of the Indians of the Upper Missouri. Nevertheless, it was reprinted in Paris and London within 3 years, and the demand for it soon exceeded the sup-ply. Its great popularity was due largely to the excellent reproductions of Karl Bodmer's incomparable field sketches of Plains Indians that appeared in the ac-companying *Atlas*.

Together the works of Catlin and Maximilian-Bodmer, appearing almost si-multaneously, greatly stimulated popular interest in the Plains Indians in this country and abroad, and had a strong influence on the work of many other artists.

They influenced the pictorial representation of Indians during the mid-19th century in three important ways. First, the Catlin-Maximilian-Bodmer example encouraged other artists to go west and to draw and/or paint the Indians of the Plains in the field. Among the best known of these artists were the American John Mix Stanley, the German-American Charles Wimar, the Canadian Paul Kane, and the Swiss Rudolph Friederich Kurz.

Secondly, they encouraged some of the most able illustrators of the period, who had not visited the western Indian Country, to help meet the popular demand for pictures of Plains Indians by using the works of Catlin and Bodmer for reference. In 1843, 2 years after the first publication of Catlin's popular book, an enterprising Philadelphia publisher offered *Scenes in Indian Life: A Series of Original Designs Portraying Events in the Life of an Indian Chief. Drawn and Etched on Stone by Felix O. C. Darley.* This pictures episodes in the life history of a fictional Sioux chief. The artist was then an almost unknown "local boy," 20 years of age; but he possessed remarkable skill as a draftsman. Darley became the outstanding American book and magazine illustrator of the century. Even though most of his finely drawn illustrations are of non-Indian subjects, he repeatedly pictures buffalo hunts and other Plains Indians activities. He prepared the frontispiece and illustrated title page for the first edition of Francis Parkman's classic, *The California and Oregon Trail* (1849), and toward the end of his life designed a colored lithograph, "Return from the Hunt," which has the qualities of spurious realism that only a highly skilled artist who does not know his subject can impart to his work. The picture show a birchbark canoe in the foreground, a village of tipis in the middle ground, and a background of high mountains. Darley appears to have produced a handsome geographical and cultural monstrosity in which characteristics of the region from the Great Lakes to the Rocky Mountains are compressed into a single scene.

Darley was on firmer ground when he followed Catlin and Bodmer more closely. A few of his book illustrations are frankly acknowledged as "after Catlin."

Some of the most popular Currier and Ives prints of the 1850's and 1860's were western scenes, lithographed from very realistic drawings executed jointly by German-born Louis Maurer and English-born Arthur Fitzwilliam Tait, neither of whom had any first-hand knowledge of Plains Indians. Maurer acknowledged that they learned about Indians from the reproductions of Bodmer's and Catlin's works in the Astor Library in New York City (Peters, 1931, p. 21).

Finally Catlin and Bodmer powerfully influenced those lesser, poorly paid artists who anonymously illustrated a number of popular books on Indians as well as school histories; these began to appear within a very few years after the books of Catlin and Bodmer were published. One can trace the progressive degeneration of truthfulness in illustration in the copies of these once popular books preserved in the Rare Book Room of the Library of Congress.

A prolific writer of popular books of the 1840–60 period was Samuel Griswold Goodrich, who commonly used the pen name "Peter Parley," and who claimed in 1856 that he had written 170 books of which 7 million copies had been sold. Goodrich had discovered Catlin by 1844, when he published *History of the Indians of North and South America*; he quoted Catlin in the text and copied Catlin's "Four Bears" in one illustration. Two years later Goodrich's *The Manners, Customs, and Antiquities of the Indians of North America* derived all of its 35 illustrations of North American Indians from Catlin—28 of these being Plains Indian subjects. Finally, in Goodrich's *The American Child's Pictorial History of the United States*, first published in 1860, and adopted as a textbook for the public schools of Maryland 5 years later, the Indians of New England, Virginia, and Roanoke Island are pictured living in tipis and wearing flowing-feather bonnets of Plains Indian type, while 17th-century Indians of Virginia are shown wrapped in painted buffalo robes and performing a buffalo dance in front of their tipis.

Impressionable young readers of popular histories of the Indian wars published in the 1850's also saw the common traits of Plains Indian culture applied to the Woodland tribes. John Frost's *Indian Wars of the United States from the Earliest Period to the Present Time* pictures a buffalo hunt on horseback in the chapter on the French and Indian Wars, Catlin's Crow warrior on horseback in the one on the War of 1812, and the same artist's portrait of Eagle Ribs, a Blackfoot warrior, in the Creek war chapter.

Catlin's and Bodmer's representations of Plains Indians underwent even more miraculous changes in identity in William V. Moore's *Indian Wars of the United States from the Discovery to the Present Time*. In that book Catlin's "Four Bears" became "Pontiac," his Crow Indian on horseback "A Creek Warrior," and a ceremonial in a Mandan setting emerged as "Village of the Seminoles." Bodmer's well-identified portraits of Mandan, Hidatsa, and Sioux leaders became "Saturiouva," a 16th-century Florida chief, and two leaders in the Indian wars of colonial New England.

The first illustrated edition of Henry Wadsworth Longfellow's popular *Song of Hiawatha* was published in England in 1856. John Gilbert, its illustrator, did not copy Catlin slavishly but leaned heavily upon him in representing the poet's ancient Ojibwa of the southern shore of Lake Superior as typical Indians of the Upper Missouri. His portrait of "Paw-puk-keewis," for example, is but a slightly altered version of Catlin's Mandan hero, "Four Bears."

Nor were these Woodland Indians in Plains Indian clothing limited to the works of artists who had no firsthand knowledge of Indians. John Mix Stanley had known the Plains tribes well, yet when he attempted a portrait of "Young Uncas" (the 17th-century Mohegan) or "The Trial of Red Jacket" (the Seneca), he tended to clothe his Indians in the dress costume of the tribes of the western grasslands. And when Karl Bodmer collaborated with the French artist Jean François Millet to produce a series of realistic but imaginative scenes in the border warfare of the Ohio Valley during the Revolutionary War, the war-bonneted Plains Indian was clearly portrayed (Smith, 1910, p. 83).

INFLUENCE OF THE PLAINS INDIAN WARS (1860–90)

In 1860 a new medium appeared to exploit the American boy's fascination for the Indian's prowess as a warrior. Dime novels increased very rapidly in both numbers and sales. A favorite theme in this lurid literature was Indian fighting on the Western Plains in which many a wild Comanche, Kiowa, Blackfoot, or Sioux "bit the dust" before the hero ended his perilous adventures. Bales of these cheap "paperbacks" were sent to soldiers in camp or in the field during the Civil War, and reading them helped the boys in blue or gray to forget, for a time at least, their own hardships and sufferings (Johannsen, vol. 1, p. 39).

The horrors of Plains Indian warfare became very real as emigrants, prospectors, stage, and telegraph and railroad lines pushed across the Plains after the Civil War, and Sioux, Cheyenne, Arapaho, Kiowa, and Comanche resisted White invasion of their buffalo hunting grounds. Newspaper and magazine reporters were sent west to report the resultant Indian wars. Theodore R. Davis, artist-reporter for *Harper's Weekly*, was riding in a Butterfield Overland Coach when it was attacked by Cheyennes near the Smoky Hill Spring stage station on November 24, 1865. His vivid picture of this real-life experience, published in *Harper's Weekly*, April 21, 1866, was the prototype of one of the most enduring symbols of the Wild West—the Indian attack on the overland stage.

As the Indians of the Plains made their desperate last stand against the Army of the United States they again and again demonstrated their courage and skill as warriors. On the Little Bighorn, June 26, 1876, they wiped out Custer's immediate command in the most decisive defeat for American arms in our long history. Numerous artists, largely upon the basis of their imaginations, sought to picture that dramatic action. One pictorial reconstruction of a closing stage of this battle, Otto Becker's lithograph "Custer's Last Fight," after Cassilly Adams' painting, has become one of the best-known American pictures. Copyrighted by Anheuser-Busch in 1896, more than 150,000 copies of this large print have been distributed. It has provided a lively conversation piece for millions of customers in thousands of barrooms throughout the country (Taft, 1953, pp. 142–48).

Four years before his death, George Armstrong Custer published serially in the *Galaxy*, a respectable middle-class magazine, "My Life on the Plains," in which he expressed his admiration for "the fearless hunter, matchless horseman and warrior of the Plains." Many Army officers who had fought against these Indians expressed similar opinions in widely read books on their experiences, some of which were profusely illustrated with reproductions of drawings and photographs, including portraits of many of the leading chiefs and warriors among the hostiles—Red Cloud, Satanta, Gall, Sitting Bull, and others. The exploits of these leaders on the warpath became better known to late 19th-century readers than those of such earlier Indian heroes of the forest as King Philip, Pontiac, Tecumseh, Osceola, and Black Hawk.

THE WILD WEST SHOW AND ITS INFLUENCES (1883–)

On July 20, 1881, Sitting Bull, the last of the prominent Indian leaders in the Plains Indian wars to surrender his rifle, returned from his Canadian exile and gave himself up to the authorities of the United States. But within 2 years William F. Cody, pony express rider, scout, Indian fighter, and hero of hundreds of dime novels, whose hunting skill had earned him the name "Buffalo Bill," organized a reenactment of exciting episodes of the Old West that was so realistic no one who ever saw it could forget it. Buffalo Bill's Wild West Show opened in Omaha, Nebraska, on May 17, 1883. It ran for more than three decades, before millions of wide-eyed viewers in the cities and towns of the United States and Canada; in England; and on the continent of Europe. Sitting Bull himself traveled with the show in 1885. It always included a series of performances staged in the open by genuine Plains Indians—Pawnees, Sioux, Cheyennes, and/or Arapahoes—chasing a small herd of buffalo, war dancing, horse racing, attacking a settler's cabin and/or an emigrant train crossing the Plains. A highlight of every performance was the Indian attack on the Deadwood Mail Coach, whose passengers were rescued in the nick of time by "Buffalo Bill" himself and his hard-riding cowboys. This scene was commonly portrayed on the program covers and the posters advertising the show.

In 1887 this show was the hit of the American Exhibition at the celebration of Queen Victoria's Golden Jubilee in England, playing to packed audiences in a large arena that held 40,000 spectators. The *Illustrated London News* for April 16, 1887, tried to explain its fascination:

> This remarkable exhibition, the "Wild West," has created a furore in America, and the reason is easy to understand. It is not a circus, nor indeed is it acting at all, in a theatrical sense, but an exact reproduction of daily scenes in frontier life, as experienced and enacted by the very people who now form the "Wild West" company.

Except in Spain, where no outdoor drama could quite replace the bullfight, Buffalo Bill's Wild West Show met with almost equal success on the European continent. During its 7 months' stand at the Paris Exposition of 1889 it attracted many artists. The famous French animal painter Rosa Bonheur pictured the show Indians chasing buffalo. What is more, the Indians inspired Cyrus Dallin, a gifted American sculptor then studying in Paris, to create the first of a series of heroic statues of Plains Indians. "The Signal of Peace," completed in time to win a medal at the Paris Salon of 1890, now stands in Lincoln Park, Chicago. A second work, "The Medicine Man" (1899), is in Fairmount Park, Philadelphia. The famous sculptor Lorado Taft considered it Dallin's "greatest achievement" and "one of the most notable and significant products of American sculpture." Another, "The Appeal" (to the Great Spirit), winner of a gold medal at the Paris Salon of 1909, sits astride his horse in front of the Museum of Fine Art in Boston. And still a fourth, "The Scout," may be seen atop a hill in Kansas City. Taft termed Dallin's realistic equestrian Plains Indians "among the most interesting public monuments in the country" (Taft, 1925, pp. 476–8, 576).

The phenomenal success of Buffalo Bill's Wild West Show encouraged others to organize similar shows, which together with the small-scale Indian "medicine" shows toured the country and the Canadian Provinces in the early years of the present century, giving employment to many Indians who were not members of the Plains tribes. These shows played a definite role in diffusing such Plains Indian traits as the flowing-feather bonnet, the tipi, and the war dances of the Plains tribes to Indians who lived at very considerable distances from the Great Plains. A Cheyenne Indian who traveled with a medicine show is reputed to have introduced the "war bonnet" among the Indians of Cape Breton Island as early as the 1890's (Shaw, 1945, p. iv). Contacts with Plains Indian showmen at the Pan-American Exposition in Buffalo during 1901 encouraged New York State Seneca Indians to substitute the Plains type of feather bonnet for their traditional crown of upright feathers, and to learn to ride and dance like the Plains Indians so that they could obtain employment with the popular Indian shows of the period.[1] Carl Standing Deer, a professional sideshow and circus Indian, is credited with introducing the Plains Indian feather bonnet among his people, the Cherokee of North Carolina, in the fall of 1911.[2]

The acceptance of typical Plains Indian costume, of the tipi, and some other traits of Plains Indian culture as standard "show Indian" equipment by Indians of other culture areas is revealed through study of 20th-century pictures. My collection of photographic prints, post cards, and newspaper clippings dating from the turn of the century shows Penobscot Indians of Maine wearing typical Plains Indian garb (women as well as men), dancing in front of their tipis at an Indian celebration in Bangor; a Yuma Indian brass band in Arizona, every member of which wears a complete Plains Indian costume; dancing Zia Pueblo Indians of New Mexico wearing flowing-feather bonnets; Cayuse Indians of Oregon posing in typical Plains Indian garb in front of a tipi; and a young Indian standing in front of a tipi in the town of Cherokee, N.C., to attract picture-taking tourists and to lure them into an adjacent curio shop.

In 1958 I talked to a Mattaponi Indian in tidewater Virginia about the handsome Sioux-type feather bonnet he was wearing as he welcomed visitors to the little Indian museum on his reservation. He was proud of the fact that he had made it himself, even to beading the browband. With that simple and irrefutable

---

[1]Communication from Dr. William N. Fenton, director, New York State Museum, June 12, 1964.

[2]Communication from John Witthoft, anthropologist, Pennsylvania Historical and Museum Commission, August 2, 1964.

logic which so often appears in Indian comments on American culture, he explained: "Your women copy their hats from Paris because they like them. We Indians use the styles of other tribes because we like them too."

The trend toward standardization in Indian costume based upon Plains Indian models has also been reflected in the art of some of the able painters of the Taos, N. Mex., art colony, for whom a sensitive interpretation of "Indianness" was more important than tribal consistency in detail. Likewise, it appears in prominently placed paintings purporting to commemorate significant historic events of the colonial period in the East. It is not difficult to recognize the Plains Indian costumes in Robert Reid's mural "Boston Tea Party," in the State House, Boston, or in Edward Trumbull's "William Penn's Treaty with the Indians" in the Capitol at Harrisburg, both of which were executed in the first quarter of this century. So perhaps it should not seem strange to see 19th-century Plains Indians sitting at the feast in Jennie Brownscombe's appealing painting "The First Thanksgiving," which hangs in Pilgrim Hall, Plymouth, Mass.

THE PLAINS INDIAN AS A NATIONAL SYMBOL

It is a fact that every American coin bearing any resemblance to a representation of an Indian has strong Plains Indian associations. Both the Indian-head penny, first minted in 1859, and the $10 gold piece designed by Augustus Saint-Gaudens for issue in 1907 represent the artists' conceptions of the Goddess of Liberty wearing a feathered bonnet. A number of Indians have claimed they were the models for the fine Indian head on the famous "buffalo nickel." However, its designer, James Earle Fraser, in a letter to the Commissioner of Indian Affairs, dated June 10, 1931, stated: "I used three different heads: I remember two of the men, one was Irontail, the best Indian head I can remember; the other one was Two Moons, and the third I cannot recall."

Significantly, the two models remembered by the artist were Plains Indians. Two Moons, the Cheyenne chief, had helped to "rub out" Custer's force on the Little Big Horn. Strong-featured Iron Tail had repeatedly led the Sioux attack on the Deadwood Coach in Buffalo Bill's Wild West Show. For 25 years after this coin was first minted in 1913—during the days when a nickel would purchase a ride on the New York subway, a cigar, or an ice-cream cone—this striking Indian head in association with the buffalo on the opposite side of the coin served to remind Americans of the Plains Indians.

The only regular issue United States stamp to bear the portrait of an Indian is the 14-cent stamp issued May 30, 1923. Titled "American Indian," it bears the likeness of Hollow Horn Bear, a handsome Sioux from the Rosebud Reservation, South Dakota, who died in Washington after participating in the parade after President Woodrow Wilson's inauguration.

In the solemn ceremonies marking the burial of the Unknown Soldier of World War I in Arlington Cemetery on November 11, 1921, one man was selected to place a magnificent feather bonnet upon the casket as a tribute from all American Indians to their country's unknown dead. He was Plenty Coups, an aged, dignified war chief among the Crow Indians of Montana. This was one hundred years to the very month after the young Pawnee hero Petalesharro first appeared in the Nation's capital wearing a picturesque flowing-feather bonnet. During the intervening century the war-bonneted Plains Indian emerged as the widely recognized symbol of the North American Indian.

REFERENCES

American Turf Register and Sporting Magazine. 1829, Vol. I, No. 2. Baltimore.

Catlin, George. 1841. *Letters and notes on the manners, customs and condition of the North American Indians.* 2 vols. London.

Cooper, James Fenimore. 1828. *Notions of the Americans: Picked up by a traveling bachelor.* 2 vols. Philadelphia.

Custer, George Armstrong. 1872–73. "My life on the Plains." *The Galaxy.* Vols. 13–16. New York.

Darley, Felix O. C. 1843. Scenes in Indian life: A series of original designs portraying events in the life of an Indian chief. Drawn and etched on stone by Felix O. C. Darley. Philadelphia.

Ewers, John C. 1954. Charles Bird King, painter of Indian visitors to the Nation's Capital. Ann. Rep. Smithsonian Institution for 1953.

Frost, John. 1852. *The book of the Indians of North America, illustrating their manners, customs, and present state.* Hartford, Conn.

———. 1856. *Indian wars of the United States from the earliest period to the present time.* New York.

Goodrich, Rev. Charles Augustus. 1823. *History of the United States.* Hartford, Conn.

Goodrich, Samuel Griswold. 1844. *History of the Indians of North and South America.* Boston.

———. 1846. *The manners, customs, and antiquities of the Indians of North and South America.* Philadelphia.

———. 1847. *Parley's primary histories: North America or the United States and the adjacent countries.* Louisville.

———. 1860. *The American child's pictorial history of the United States.* Philadelphia.

Jackson, Donald. 1962. Letters of the Lewis and Clark Expedition, with related documents, 1783–1854. Urbana, Ill.

James, Edwin. 1823. Account of an expedition from Pittsburgh to the Rocky Mountains performed in the years 1819 and 1820. 2 vols. and atlas. Philadelphia and London.

Johannsen, Albert. 1950. *The house of Beadle and Adams and its dime and nickel novels.* Norman, Okla.

Keiser, Albert. 1933. *The Indian in American literature.* New York.

Linderman, Frank Bird. 1930. *American: The life story of a great Indian, Plenty Coups, Chief of the Crows.* Yonkers, N.Y.

Longfellow, Henry Wadsworth. 1856. *Song of Hiawatha*. London.

McKenney, Thomas L., and James Hall. 1836–44. *History of the Indian tribes of North America*. 3 vols. Philadelphia.

Moore, William V. 1856. *Indian wars of the United States from the discovery to the present time*. Philadelphia.

Morton, Samuel George. 1839. *Crania Americana, or a comparative view of the skulls of the various aboriginal nations of North and South America*. Philadelphia.

Parkman, Francis. 1849. *The California and Oregon Trail*. New York.

Peters, Harry T. 1931. *America on stone*. Garden City, N.Y.

Russell, Don. 1960. *The lives and legends of Buffalo Bill*. Norman, Okla.

Shaw, Avery. 1945. *A Micmac Glengarry*. New Brunswick Museum. Saint John, New Brunswick.

Smith, De Cost. 1910. "Jean François Millet's drawings of American Indians." *The Century Illustrated Monthly Magazine*. Vol. 80, no. 1, pp. 78–84.

Taft, Lorado. 1925. *The history of American sculpture*. New York.

Taft, Robert. 1953. *Artists and illustrators of the Old West, 1850–1900*. New York.

Webster, Noah. 1832. *History of the United States*. New Haven, Conn.

Wied-Neuwied, Maximilian Alexander Philipp, Prinz von. 1839–41. *Reise in das Innere Nord-America in den Jahren 1832 bis 1834*. Coblenz, Germany.

Chapter 3

Words *Can* Hurt

What's Correct? American Indian or Native American?

Arlene Hirschfelder

A debate persists over the proper designation for hundreds of nations of peoples who were (and are) the original inhabitants of the North American continent. The following excerpts suggest that Indian and non-Indian people hold differing opinions about the use of the general terms "American Indians" and "Native Americans." But there is agreement that, whenever possible, individual tribal names such as Mohawk, Menominee, Hopi, and Pomo should be used.

SAMPLE OPINIONS

"I thought it disgraceful to be called an Indian; it was considered as a slur upon an oppressed and scattered nation, and I have often been led to inquire where the whites received this word, which they so often threw as an opprobrious epithet at the sons of the forest. I could not find it in the bible, and therefore concluded, that it was a word imported for the special purpose of degrading us. At other times I thought it was derived from the term in-gen-uity. But the proper term which ought to be applied to our nation, to distinguish it from the rest of the human family, is that of 'Natives'—and I humbly conceive that the natives of this country are the only people under heaven who have a just title to the name . . ."

> —William Apes [Pequot], *A Son of the Forest: The Experience of William Apes, a Native of the Forest. New York:* Published by author, 1831.

"For too long now, the native peoples of this hemisphere have remained passive while the European invader does away with all of the ancient place-names, and then comes up with new names for the native people and their land. The white man has called us Savages, Redskins, Red Niggers, Indians, Inyuns, Amerinds, Tawney Serpents, Aborigines, Indigenes, Red Indians, Half-Breeds, Full-Bloods, Mestizos, Quarter Bloods, Breeds, Metis, and dozens of other names, most of them directly

Named
used
are
dehum
aracist

dehumanizing, and almost all of them foreign and racist. *This land is not Indian and we are not Indians.* Let's face it—the people of India have a right to keep their own name. . . . I would propose that we drop the use of Amerigo's name, and adopt a name in a native language meaning 'native land,' 'Indian land,' or 'Indian country.' Therefore I propose that we call this land *Anishinabe-weki* which means "Indian country" in the languages of the Algonquian speaking peoples (especially in the Chippewa, Algonkin, Ottawa, and Potawatomi languages). Of course, some people might object to using an Algonquian name for our continent; however, we have to choose a name from *one* of our many languages . . ."

—Jack D. Forbes [Powhatan], "It's Time to Throw Off the
White Man's Names." *Akwesasne Notes,* March 1972.

NA
itself
is harmless
use
to
the
problm

"The term Native American, in and of itself, is a seemingly harmless term, but it is used in a way that infers, however innocent its author, that native people are somehow exactly the same as other hyphenated Americans (Chinese-Americans, Polish-Americans, etc.). That would not be objectionable, except that native peoples are in fact members of their respective nations, and the denial of their rights as distinct and separate nations with their own territories, sovereignty, cultures, and power over their own lives has been the basis of much racialist policy in the Western Hemisphere. Because of that history, our own preferences lead us to use terms such as 'native people' rather than Native Americans because we feel that it is a more accurate term."

—*Akwesasne Notes,* editorial policy statement, late spring 1977.

AI

"You notice I use the term American Indian rather than Native American or native indigenous people or Amerindian when referring to my people. There has been some controversy about such terms, and frankly, at this point, I find it absurd. Primarily it seems that American Indian is being rejected as European in origin—which is true. But all above terms are European in origin; the only non-European way is to speak of Lakota—or, more precisely, of Oglala, Brule, etc. and of the Dine, the Micosukee and all the rest of the several hundred correct tribal names."

—Russell Means [Oglala Lakota], "Fighting Words on the Future
of the Earth." *Mother Jones,* December 1980.

"The names applied to native groups are very seldom the people's own names, in part because many groups depicted on maps were not self-conscious, named entities. But even when a native name has always existed, white writers have often persisted in using an alien term, as with Delaware (from Lord De La Warr), instead of Leni-Lenape, and Navaho (or Navajo) in place of Dine (Dineh). Indians themselves have gradually been forced to 'live with' or even to accept alien names because of the pressure stemming from white 'custom' (and occasionally, because of editors' demands for uniformity)."

—Jack D. Forbes [Powhatan], *Native Americans
of California and Nevada,* 1982.

"It has been suggested that (Columbus) named them Indios not because he imagined them to be inhabitants of India (which in the fifteenth century was still called Hindustan) but because he recognized that the friendly, generous Taino people lived in blessed harmony with their surroundings—una gente in Dios, a people in God."

—Peter Matthiessen, *Indian Country*, 1984.

". . . a growing number of American Indians and Alaska Natives are not comfortable with the term 'Native American' because it creates even greater confusion than the term it was once proposed to replace—namely, American Indian. American Indians are easily distinguished from Asian Indians by a single locational adjective, but 'Native Americans' include Hawaiian natives and the descendants of immigrants from all nations, along with American Indians, Eskimos, and Aleuts. A casual survey of recently published books and articles indicates that the term 'Native American' is falling into disuse and that 'American Indian' is preferable."

—C. Matthew Snipp for the National Committee for Research on the 1980 Census, *American Indians: The First of This Land*, 1989.

"How I loathe the term 'Indian' . . . Indian is a term used to sell things—souvenirs, cigars, cigarettes, gasoline, cars . . . 'Indian' is a figment of the white man's imagination."

—Lenore Keeshig-Tobias [Ojibway], *Stolen Continents: The Americas Through Indian Eyes Since 1492* by Ronald Wright, 1990.

"As the publisher of an Indian advocacy newspaper, the largest of its kind in America, we use American Indian, Indian, or Native American, but we prefer to use the individual tribal affiliation when possible. For instance, if the subject of an article is Navajo, we use that, or Lakota, Ojibwa, Onondaga, etc. We are, more and more, pulling away from using Native American because, as so many phone calls and letters have pointed out to us, and correctly so, anyone born in the Americas can refer to themselves as Native American. We realize the word 'Indian' is a misnomer, but for generic purposes, we are often forced to use it when speaking of many different tribes. American Indian is also acceptable in Indian country. Any politically correct thinker who believes Native American is the preferred identification tag for the Lakota or any other tribe is wrong. Most of us do not object to the use of Indian or American Indian. And as I said, Native American can be used by any American native to this land."

—Tim Giago [Oglala Lakota], December 4, 1991,
editorial in *Lakota Times*.

". . . the term 'First Nations' has been increasing in usage throughout North America to describe its indigenous people. . . . Why the term 'First Nations'? This term more accurately describes the Americas' indigenous people. In the United States alone, there are hundreds of differing tribes. Each tribe has a sovereign legal status (above that of a state's in most instances), each tribe has its own customs, language, and world view. In other words, each indigenous tribe is a separate nation."

—Yvonne Murry-Ramos, March 17, 1993,
editorial in *News from Indian Country*.

"Indian is the term of art that has made its way into U.S. and Canadian treaties, statutes, case law, governance documents, and modern English and French parlance. Indian replaced far less desirable names in popular North American culture, such as *Savage, Redskin,* or *L'Indian Rouge,* which are still considered fighting words. Compared to these, *American Indian, Canadian Native, Native American, Indian,* and *Native* seem mild, and are currently viewed as inexact and silly, rather than offensive. Most Native Peoples in North America use these imprecise and awkward terms interchangeably when referring to the race as a whole. With some 600 different Indian Nations in the United States and Canada, having nearly as many separate languages, histories, territories, religions, and cultures, more emphasis is placed on the tribal names than on the collective. . . . A greater priority now is on Indian national and personal names, and on substituting traditional tribal names for those imposed through the missionizing and colonizing processes. The Diné, for example, in the early 1990s, issued a formal call for all to use their traditional name, which means 'People' rather than the name by which they are widely known, Navajo. With the success of the movie *Dances with Wolves,* the general public is now more aware of the original and preferred names *Lakota* and *Dakota* over the imposed name *Sioux,* a French variation of an Anishinabe (Ojibwe or Chippewa) word meaning 'enemy.'"

—Suzan Shown Harjo [Cheyenne/Muscogee], Foreword to
North American Indian Landmarks by George Cantor, 1993.

"The terms indigenous and First Nations Peoples still generalize the identity of the more than 550 indigenous groups in the lower 48 and Alaska. However, I believe they are empowering 'generalized' descriptors because they accurately describe the political, cultural, and geographical identities, and struggles of all aboriginal peoples in the United States. I no longer use Indian, American Indian, or Native American because I consider them to be oppressive, counterfeit identities."

—Michael Yellow Bird [Sahnish (Arikara) and
Hidatsa First Nations], *Winds of Change*, Winter 1999.

What's Correct? Eskimo or Inuit?

Arlene Hirschfelder

A debate raged in Canada over which term to use for the circumpolar peoples popularly called "Eskimos." The word *Inuit*, which means "the people" in dialects across northern Canada and Alaska, has largely replaced "Eskimo," an Indian word seen as derogatory by many people in Canada. Indeed, since the 1970s, the designation Eskimo has been dropped from use throughout much of Canada and parts of Greenland, especially by government agencies, scholars, and the media.

The term "Eskimo" has been used since the 1600s to describe the people inhabiting coastal areas stretching across the circumpolar north—from Greenland across the Canadian Arctic to the North Slope, down to Bristol Bay and across much of Siberia. It has long been considered to have come from an eastern Canadian Algonquian term meaning "raw meat eaters." Some linguistic scholars debate whether the word Eskimo is actually derogatory. They argue the word originated with the Montagnais Indians and actually means "snowshoe netter."

The story is different in Alaska, however, where not everyone wishes to be called *Inuit*. The problem has to do with the fact that Eskimos in Alaska fall into two broad language and cultural groups: *Inupiaq*, people who live in the northwestern part of the state, and *Yupik*, people who live in the western part of the state. Both words mean "a real person." The plural forms are *Yupiit* and *Inupiat,* or "the real people." *Inuit* means the same thing in *Inupiaq* as it does in Canada— "the people." But the word *Inuit* does not exist in *Yupik*, the most widely spoken language in Alaska. *Inuit* is as foreign a word in Bethel, Alaska, as Eskimo. *Yupik* (from the base *yuk*, person, plus *pik*, real), or real person, is the preferred name for people living in western Alaska.

31

Eliminating the "S" Word

Paulette Fairbanks Molin

Because of the efforts of Anishinaabe (Ojibwe, Chippewa) high school students, the state of Minnesota enacted a law mandating the elimination of the term "squaw," or the "s" word, as the students and their supporters began calling it, from place names in the state. The Minnesota law, Chapter 53—S.F. No. 574, states:

> On or before July 31, 1996, the commissioner of natural resources shall change each name of a geographic feature in the state that contains the word "squaw" to another name that does not contain this word. The commissioner shall select the new names in cooperation with the county boards of the counties in which the feature is located and with their approval.

Two students from Minnesota's Cass Lake-Bena High School, Dawn Litzau and Angelene Losh, began a campaign in 1994 to change Leech Lake Reservation place names, Squaw Point and Squaw Lake. In letters to congressional representatives, tribal officials, and newspaper editors, they explained why the "s" term is offensive to Native American women. The high schoolers also sought support from other students by circulating petitions for them to sign. After receiving positive responses, a Name Change Committee was formed at their school.

Following the success of effecting a name change from "Squaw Point" to "Oak Point" locally, the Name Change Committee began extending its efforts statewide. Researching locations using the "s" word in place names, committee members identified sites via Minnesota's Department of Natural Resources. Among the Name Change Committee's supporters was Minnesota State Senator Harold "Skip" Finn, who sponsored the legislation to eliminate the use of the term from geographic features. Senator Finn, Anishinaabe, recalled as a child hearing his mother called a "squaw." Dawn, Angelene, and their advisor, Muriel Litzau, testified before both state Senate and House committees concerning the legislation. Their efforts paid off when the bill received overwhelming support in Minnesota's full Senate and House of Representatives. It was signed into law by Governor Arne H. Carlson on April 18, 1995. As of September 1, 1996, sixteen of nineteen place names in the state of Minnesota had been changed, with two counties failing to comply with the law.

33

The term "squaw" has extensive use in North America. Besides countless place names, including California's popular ski resort "Squaw Valley," it has been perpetuated in printed matter and public discourse since the colonial period. There is disagreement on the origin of the term. A number of scholars refer to a standard European-American source, *The Oxford English Dictionary*, which defines the term as "A North American Indian woman or wife" and cites the following as the source: "[a. Narragansett Indian *squaws*, Massachusetts *squa*, woman, with related forms in many other Algonquin dialects]." This dictionary indicates that the term first appeared in a publication in 1634. Another source attributes the origin of "squaw" to "a French corruption of the Iroquois word *otsiskwa* meaning 'female sexual parts,' a word almost clinical both denotatively and connotatively" (Sanders and Peek, p. 184).

Regardless of its origins, the term "squaw" has been universally applied to Native females in North America by Europeans and European-Americans and continues to be used as a generic label, a pejorative epithet. Dictionaries, such as the standard edition of *The American Heritage Dictionary*, cite the word as "offensive." Native women, who should have the primary voice on the issue, know from personal experience how degrading the word is. As journalist Avis Little Eagle points out, "Ask an Indian woman how she feels about being called a 'squaw,' and you might find yourself on the receiving end of a right cross" (*Indian Country Today*, April 7,1993). The word has negative connotations that stereotype indigenous women. On the one hand, "squaw" categorizes Native women as worn-out drudges who walk ten paces behind their men or, on the other, as women loose or promiscuous with their sexuality. For Native women, who are the victims of this disparaging labeling, it means constantly having to fight the stereotype on behalf of themselves and their sisters. For Native men, it means that their female relatives are treated with the utmost disrespect. > 34

In contrast to the use of a single (mis)appropriated word to label Native women in the English language, the reality is that there are hundreds of tribal nations with diverse languages. As Little Eagle points out, "Each tribe has its own word for women. In Lakota it is *winyan*, a far cry from 'squaw.'" In their original letter objecting to the use of the word "squaw" for place names, Dawn Litzau and Angelene Losh likewise state: "We suggest that the word 'squaw' be replaced with 'ikwe,' which means woman in Ojibwe, or '*nimaamaa*' meaning mother." Tribal languages representing differing cultures include rich, beautiful terminology related to gender and its associated status. In some tribal languages, for example, the word for mother or grandmother is the same as that for earth. There are also age-appropriate terms, such as those for baby girl, baby daughter, or baby sister, all the way to old age. Indeed, there are female versions of some tribal languages. In the colonizer's English language, "female," "girl," or "woman" are the appropriate terms for Native girls or women.

Although the Cass Lake-Bena High School students have obtained support from family, friends, and others since they began the effort to eliminate the "s" word, they have also encountered resistance. Representatives of Minnesota's Lake County, north of Duluth, proposed renaming its Squaw Creek and Squaw

Bay, Politically Correct Creek and Politically Correct Bay. The Department of Natural Resources responded that those politically motivated names were inappropriate. A demographics supervisor from the agency noted that of the over 900 uses of "squaw" in the United States, five of those names were attached to a slang word for a woman's breast, so "if there's any doubt in anybody's mind that it's used in a derogatory fashion, that puts it to rest."

Some tribal people, exposed to assimilationist teachings over the centuries and taught primarily by non-Indian teachers, have also internalized the use of the dehumanizing term. As Dawn Litzau eloquently writes, "Our people have been desensitized to the word, and when people have been put down so much, they are not even aware of the negative connotation and that makes me feel bad."

The Name Change Committee continues to work for change on this issue, using its experience in Minnesota as a model. Today, similar efforts are underway in several other states, including Arizona and California. As the tribal resolutions attest, numerous tribal governments support the effort to eliminate the "s" word. The committee's work has also attracted local, regional, and national media attention including the *New York Times*, ABC, and public radio. Dawn Litzau and Angelene Losh, who have both graduated from Cass Lake-Bena High School, were recipients of a 1997 Vision Award, an honor given to young women who have had a positive impact on others. They still serve on the Name Change Committee, which states: "We continue to strive for our goal of eliminating the word 'squaw' in place names throughout the United States. . . . We continue to educate people through news articles, letters, interviews, and conferences which will have an impact nationwide." Eliminate the "s" word.

1997 Resolutions in Support of Eliminating the "S" Word

The Mille Lacs Band of Ojibwe Indians, Minnesota, February
Bois Forte Reservation Tribal Council, Minnesota, April
Cedarville Rancheria Tribal Office, California, July
Upper Sioux Community Board of Trustees, Minnesota, December 1998
Fond du Lac Reservation Business Committee, Minnesota, January
Red Lake Band of Chippewa Indians, Minnesota, January
Shakopee Mdewakanton Sioux Community, Minnesota, January
Prairie Island Indian Community, Minnesota, February
Red Cliff Band of Lake Superior Chippewa, Wisconsin, February
Affiliated Tribes of Northwest Indians of the United States, Oregon, February
Minnesota Chippewa Tribe, Minnesota, March
Bay Mills Indian Community, Michigan, March
Fort Mojave Indian Tribe of Arizona, California and Nevada, April
Tribal Council of the Colorado River Indian Tribes, April
Uintah and Ouray Tribal Business Committee of the Ute Indian Tribe, Utah, April
Sault Ste. Marie Tribe of Chippewa Indians, Michigan, April
Lovelock Paiute Tribe, April

STATEMENT BY ANGIE LOSH

"Dawn and I started our cause in Mike Schmid's Social Studies and History class. We wrote a letter and sent it to our tribal council and our district Senator and House Representatives. We got positive responses and help from everyone we sent the letter to.

After we got their support, I started a petition in Squaw Point to see if anyone else was supportive of our cause. I needed at least 17 signatures, I got more than enough.

As the summer went on, we had many interviews by phone and some came out with cameras.

When the school year resumed, we added a few more students to our committee. They have helped by going with me to the elementary school to educate the younger students on how discriminating the word is.

On February 7, the Cass Lake-Bena High School Name Change Committee went in front of the Cass County Board of Commissioners and presented what we are trying to do. They passed a resolution unanimously to change 'Squaw Point' to 'Oak Point.'

We went to Squaw Lake to talk with the Local Indian Council and the town council to express our concerns and ask them to change the name of their town and lake. They said they would consider it.

Doing this has given me pride and has helped me to open up and speak instead of being shy. Everyone who knows me is very proud of me and I am proud of myself."

STATEMENT BY DAWN STAR LITZAU

"Boozhoo, my name is Dawn Star Litzau. I am a 1994 graduate of Cass Lake Bena High School. I am the daughter of Muriel Litzau. My mother comes from the town of 'S.' Lake, and has lived there throughout her childhood. My family's roots are deep within that town.

I've always been taught the term 'squaw' is a put down not a word meaning Indian woman, like the dictionary claims, or a word that I should be proud of. My mother told me when I was younger not to use that word on anyone and that it was demeaning term, even though that was the name of her home town. When I was older, I found out firsthand just how hurtful the word can be. My friend and I were walking down the street when a boy she knew called us 'dumb squaws.' Only then did I really know how completely demeaning and degrading this word is. People are shocked when other people call a black person 'nigger' or an oriental person 'chinc' but some of our own people are not shocked and say they are proud to be called that. Our people have been desensitized to the word, and when people have been put down so much, they are not even aware of the negative connotation and that makes me feel bad. That is why I am involved in this issue.

It started with Angie and I having something in common. She lived in the Squaw Point area and I had roots in Squaw Lake. We drafted a letter and the teachers, Mike Schmid and my mother, Muriel Litzau, suggested that we send our letter to the local papers, Native American papers, tribal council, the Senator and other people it might concern. We wrote to them hoping to educate them on the word and have their help in our efforts.

The papers loved the idea of two high school students fighting for what they believed in and that made everyone look twice at our letters. We were very surprised to be interviewed for television coverage. It still surprises us to see ourselves in the media. It was a whirlwind after that, meeting new people, visiting new places.

And with meeting new people, we got to meet Senator Harold Finn who drafted the bill to eliminate the word squaw from Minnesota geographical places. Skip had told us that he had experienced the word and what it meant firsthand when his mother was called squaw when he was very young.

Angie and I traveled to the state capital several times. Each time we had to testify on behalf of our cause and our feelings. All in all, we had to testify three times in front of committees of law makers and it was a scary experience. But, in the end our hard work paid off and the governor signed the bill. Yet that didn't mean our work was done.

There was opposition and still is. Many people think we are oversensitive, and have no idea what the word means because the dictionary says that it means an Indian woman. This opposition reared its ugly head when we went to the Squaw Lake School meetings to change its name. I could not believe the ignorance in that room but I couldn't blame them because they have lived there all their lives. Sq. Lake is not a big town, but this is the 20th century. There are going to be children who are going to be educated in that school but the people who are chosen to educate the children refuse to educate themselves about that derogatory term. It was frustrating for me just to be there. There were men telling me I should be proud to be called a 'vagina' and that it is an honor for my people. That is not the only the negative comment we have received.

Yet, there is a positive side to having negative comments. We have reached so many people by speaking out, and have had letters of support from people all over the country. There are people wanting to change the term in their state, such as Montana and Arizona. In Arizona there are two young women fighting to change that horrible term and they are using the Minnesota bill as an example to encourage lawmakers to make the change.

Angie and I didn't do all this work by ourselves. We had the support of our parents, teachers, tribal council, the Cass Lake-Bena School, people in the community, the Name Change Committee and many others.

The Name Change Committee has done much more than help change the name of squaw. They have spoken out against mascots; for example, they have addressed the Pequot Lake School about their feelings on the mascot issue. The

Pequot Lakes listened to the Committee and searched for another word. They have written letters to the Crayola Company and Disney Productions.

In these past years of fighting for justice and my beliefs, there is one thing I have learned, that is, *never compromise your beliefs and never let anyone tell you how you should feel."*

MINNESOTA CHIPPEWA TRIBE RESOLUTION 52-98

WHEREAS, the Minnesota Chippewa Tribal Executive Committee is the duly elected governing body of the Minnesota Chippewa Tribe, comprised of the six member reservations (Bois Forte, Fond du Lac, Grand Portage, Leech Lake, Mille Lacs, and White Earth), and

WHEREAS, the Name Change Committee from Independent School District #115 has undertaken a campaign to eliminate the use of the term "Squaw" in naming places, facilities, and its use in general; and

WHEREAS, the Minnesota Chippewa Tribe recognizes that the use and public acceptance of such a term carry derogatory connotations to Native American people and serve only to further negative stereotypes and attitudes by the non-Indian society; and

WHEREAS, the Minnesota Chippewa Tribe has determined that the efforts of the Name Change Committee are commendable and serve the best interests of the members of the Minnesota Chippewa Tribe.

NOW THEREFORE BE IT RESOLVED, that the Minnesota Chippewa Tribal Executive Committee does hereby support the Independent School District #115 Name Change Committee in their effort to eliminate the use of the term "Squaw" from the names of places, facilities, and its use in general.

We do hereby certify that the foregoing Resolution was duly presented and acted upon by a vote of 10 For, 0 Against, 0 Silent at a regular meeting of the Minnesota Chippewa Tribal Executive Committee, a quorum present, held on March 5, 1998, at Vermilion, Minnesota.

Norman W. Deschampe, President
THE MINNESOTA CHIPPEWA TRIBE

Eli O. Hunt, Secretary
THE MINNESOTA CHIPPEWA TRIBE

RESOLUTION
COLORADO RIVER TRIBAL COUNCIL

A Resolution to Support the Request to Change the Word Squaw and other Demeaning and Offensive Words that are used as Geographical Names

Be it resolved by the Tribal Council of the Colorado River Indian Tribes, in regular meeting assembled on April 11, 1998

WHEREAS, the Colorado River Indian Tribes ("Tribes") is a sovereign government recognized by the United States of America and organized pursuant to the Indian Reorganization Act of June 18, 1934 (48 Stat. 984), as amended by the Act of June 15, 1935 (49 Stat. 378); and

WHEREAS, American Indian students of the Minnesota Chippewa Tribe, in particular those attending the Cass Lake-Bena High School have formed a Name-Change Committee to bring awareness to derogatory and demeaning names used to describe geographical places in Minnesota and elsewhere; and

WHEREAS, the word "squaw" is a corruption of American Indian words and is used in a derogatory manner by non-Indians, whether intentionally or unintentionally; and

WHEREAS, the American Indian population, particularly the members of the Colorado River Indian Reservation are offended by the use of the word in public places and literature of the American public; and

WHEREAS, it is commendable to see our American Indian students rise up to confront issues and attempt to educate public officials and the general public about derogatory terms that are demeaning to American Indians.

NOW, THEREFORE, BE IT RESOLVED that the Colorado River Indian Reservation does hereby support the Cass Lake-Bena High School Name-Change Committee in their efforts to bring awareness and request change on all public places and literature where the offensive words are used.

The foregoing resolution was on April 11, 1998 duly approved by a vote of 7 for, 0 against and 0 abstaining, by the Tribal Council of the Colorado River Indian Tribes, pursuant to authority vested in it by Section 1. r. Article VI of the Constitution and By laws of the Tribes, ratified by the Tribes on March 1, 1975 and approved by the Secretary of the Interior on May 29, 1975, pursuant to Section 16 of the Act of June 18, 1934, (46 Stat. 984). This resolution is effective as of the date of its adoption.

REFERENCES

Chavers, Dean, "Doing Away with the 'S' Word," *Indian Country Today*, March 10–17, 1997, p. A5.

"Derogatory Use of "S" Word: The Full Story," *HONOR Digest*, vol. 8, no. 3 (May/June 1997):8–9.

Giago, Tim, "*Time* Owes Native Women Apology for Offensive Slam," *Indian Country Today*, June 22–29, 1998, p. A4.

"How to Change the 'S' Word on Geographic Locations," *HONOR Digest*, vol. 9, no. 2 (March/April 1998):10.

Johansen, Bruce E., "'Squawbles' in Minnesota," *Native Americas*, vol. xiii, no. 4 (Winter 1996):4.

Avis Little Eagle, "I Am a Woman, Hear Me Roar—I Am Not a Squaw!" *Indian Country Today*, April 7, 1993, p. 34.

Sanders, Thomas E., and Walter W. Peek, *Literature of the American Indian*. Beverly Hills, Calif.: Glencoe Press, 1973.

Lethal Consequences: Stereotyping American Indians in the Military

Paulette Fairbanks Molin

"An Indian Marine" by Jim Northrup

> I'm not Crazy Horse,
> I'm not Sitting Bull,
> I'm not Ira Hayes,
> I'm Me.
> Being called Chief
> is not an honor
> like you think
> "Hey, do you know this guy
> We called him Chief, he was
> Choctaw, Cherokee, Cheyenne
> or something."
> I'm not a code talker
> your schools robbed me
> of the language
> I used to have
> I'm no braver nor
> more of a coward than you
> But when I took the
> green uniform off
> I could be Indian again

As Anishinaabe veteran Jim Northrup states in his poem, "Being called Chief is not an honor like you think." Winnebago veteran Gerben Earth concurs, "Not in the past nor presently, does the term 'chief' convey any manner of respect. This term is comparable to a soldier using 'Jap' or 'Nip', to describe the Japanese soldier, or 'Kraut' to describe a German soldier." Earth points out that American Indian males are called "chief" by both officers and enlisted men although military personnel "are required to display their last name on virtually every article of clothing, from headgear to boots." The experience of being called "chief" is often coupled with another aspect of stereotyping, the non-Indian practice of calling

41

American Indians by the names of well-known figures, such as "Crazy Horse," "Sitting Bull," or "Ira Hayes." Northrup underscores the fact that this stereotypical practice, along with the failure to correctly identify the names of individuals or their associated tribal nations, denies American Indians the dignity of their own names, distinct tribal identities, or, in the case of the armed services, actual military rank.

Although American Indians have served in the armed forces of the United States from the colonial period to contemporary times, factual information about the nature and extent of that service is grievously lacking across the general population. The service contributions and experiences of American Indian service men and women are generally overlooked, thus rendered invisible. When they are considered, it is often in stereotypical ways. As in the terminology, "chief," stereotypes from the larger society have followed Native Americans into the military. These include the perception of tribal soldiers as instinctively and ancestrally "warlike and bloodthirsty," genetically prone to fighting. American Indians in the military also encounter widespread beliefs about their physical qualities, such as being attributed with keenness of sense and extraordinary dexterity. According to these beliefs, they possess vision that can penetrate the darkness, hearing that can detect approaching enemies from great distances, and the instinctive ability to soundlessly stalk enemies. Deemed to be "fleetfooted as a deer," to possess the skill of "swimming like a fish," and to have an unerring sense of direction in any environment, it is little wonder that the "Indian scout syndrome" has persistently besieged American Indian soldiers.

Northrup refers to another aspect of military service when he writes, "I'm not a code talker," referring to the American Indian servicemen who provided unique and valuable services during World Wars I and II transmitting messages via codes created from their own tribal languages. The best known code talkers, though not the first and only ones, were a specially trained unit of Navajo servicemen who were instrumental in U.S. marine victories in the Pacific during World War II. One of the Navajo code talkers commented, "When I was going to boarding school, the U.S. government told us not to speak Navajo, but during the war, they wanted us to speak it!" He refers to federal policies forbidding the use of tribal languages, as does Northrup, who writes, "your schools robbed me of the language I used to have."

For American Indians in the military, racist stereotypes have contributed to a preponderance of the most difficult and dangerous assignments, including scouting on long-range reconnaissance missions, walking point on patrols, and fighting in high casualty units during wartime. Besides having a disproportionately high number of soldiers in the armed services in relationship to tribal populations, American Indians have suffered high casualty rates in wars largely due to the nature of their service. Aspects of their role in the military are beginning to be examined, as in the reference materials that follow. These accounts, and others, address realities associated with the armed services, including the experiences of Native veterans.

Beyond racism and stereotyping, American Indians have rich histories associated with service in the military. The richness and complexity extend to both males and females as well as to tribal communities. Likewise, the role of American Indians in the military has a longer history than that associated with the United States. Among tribal nations there are ancient warrior traditions, including military societies, military preparation ceremonies, farewell ceremonies, cleansing or healing rituals, honoring ceremonies, song repertoires, dance customs, and/or honoring ceremonies for veterans. These traditions, which predate European colonization, continue to sustain American Indians and those tribal members who fight to safeguard national boundaries and give special poignancy to the meaning of survival.

> "Indians are not mascots—we are human beings"
> by Gerben D. Earth, Winnebago, Nebraska
> Letter to the editor of *Indian Country Today*, November 17–24, 1997
>
> To the editor:
> I served five and a half years in the U.S. Army and was always referred to as "chief" by officers and enlisted men. This name was never used in the manner as described in Webster's dictionary. Throughout my military service, many American Indians told me they were also called "chief," although Army personnel are required to display their last name on virtually every article of clothing, from headgear to boots.
> Not in the past nor presently, does the term "chief" convey any manner of respect. This term is comparable to a soldier using "Jap" or "Nip", to describe the Japanese soldier, or the term "chink" to describe the Chinese soldier, or "Kraut" to describe a German soldier. In Vietnam, it was "slope or gook." When soldiers of any nation run down or attempt to dehumanize a person, relegating that person to something less than a human, it makes it easier for them to kill and to justify doing so.
> Since the European invasion, they referred to American Indian males as chiefs and females as squaws, to make it easier to kill them and justify doing it. So is referring to enemy country as Indian country, and thus keeping the ideas alive that Indian people are still thought of as the enemy.
> No matter how subtle, things will never change as long as people do not speak up when racism occurs. American Indian people continue to fight racism no matter where it occurs. We American Indians must do this through the education process. Until the late 1970s, education was always a one way street—non-Indians trying to teach the Indians. This has changed; Indian people have begun to educate the non-Indians.

REFERENCES

Aaseng, Nathan. *Navajo Code Talkers*. New York: Walker and Co., 1992.

Bernstein, Alison R. *American Indians and World War II. Toward a New Era in Indian Affairs*. Norman, OK: University of Oklahoma Press, 1991.

Bixler, Margaret T. *Winds of Freedom: The Story of the Navajo Code Talkers of World War II.* Darien, CT: Two Bytes Publishing Co., 1992.

Britten, Thomas A. *American Indians in World War I.* Albuquerque, NM: University of New Mexico Press, 1997.

Calloway, Colin G. *The American Revolution in Indian Country: Crisis and Diversity in Native American Communities.* New York, NY: Cambridge University Press, 1995.

Civil War Times Illustrated, a bimonthly magazine published since 1959 in Harrisburg, Pennsylvania, has published articles about Indians in back issues.

Hauptman, Laurence M. *Between Two Fires: American Indians in the Civil War.* New York, NY: Free Press, 1995.

Holm, Tom. *Strong Hearts, Wounded Souls: Native American Veterans of the Vietnam War.* Austin, TX: University of Texas Press, 1996.

Navajo Code Talkers, a film by Tom McCarthy, distributed by Native American Public Telecommunications, P.O. Box 83111, Lincoln, Nebraska 68501 (30 minutes).

Northrup, Jim. *The Rez Road Follies: Canoes, Casinos, Computers, and Birch Bark Baskets.* New York: Kodansha International, 1997.

Chapter 4

Reading Is Fundamental for Truths or Stereotypes

Introduction to American Indian Authors for Young Readers*

Mary Gloyne Byler

American Indians have had to struggle for more than their physical survival. It is not only land that has been appropriated; it has also been a fight to keep mind and soul together, for along with the United States Cavalry, missionaries, educators and the "Americanizers," have come the writers of books about Indians.

Down through the years the publishing industry has produced thousands of books about American Indians—a subject that fascinates many. Fact and fiction—it is not always possible to tell which is which—have rolled off the presses since "frontier" days. But American Indians in literature, today as in the past, are merely images projected by non-Indian writers.

Most minority groups in this country have been, and are still, largely ignored by the nation's major publishing houses—particularly in the field of children's books. American Indians, on the other hand, contend with a mass of material about themselves. If anything, there are too many children's books about American Indians. There are too many books featuring painted, whooping, befeathered Indians closing in on too many forts, maliciously attacking "peaceful" settlers or simply leering menacingly from the background; too many books in which white benevolence is the only thing that saves the day for the incompetent, childlike Indian; too many stories setting forth what is "best" for American Indians.

There are too many stories for very young children about little boys running around in feathers and headbands, wearing fringed buckskin clothing, moccasins and (especially) carrying little bows and arrows. The majority of these books deal with the unidentified past. The characters are from unidentified tribes and they are often not even afforded the courtesy of personal names. In fact, the only thing identifiable is the stereotyped image of the befeathered Indian.

---

*Reprinted by permission from "Introduction," *American Indian Authors for Young Readers: A Selected Bibliography*, by Mary Gloyne Byler. New York: Association on American Indian Affairs, 1973, pp. 5–11.

This depersonalization is common in books for children. In *Good Hunting Little Indian* (Young Scott Books) the characters are referred to as Little Indian, Mama Indian and Papa Indian, calling to mind Mama Bear, Papa Bear and Baby Bear. But, in *Granny and the Indians* (Macmillan) the same author personalizes the "Granny" by giving her a name (Granny Guntry) while the other characters are simply "the Indians"—who are made to look silly and ridiculous both in the story and in the illustrations. The pictures in both of the books contain a baffling hodgepodge of Indian dress.) 47- 8

The device of repeatedly referring to people in this impersonal and anonymous way, and then reinforcing the anonymity with illustrations that are nondescript, creates the impression that one is not dealing with full-fledged human beings.

Many books parody Indian life and customs, holding them up to ridicule and derision. *Indian Two Feet and His Eagle Feather* (Childrens Press) is about a little boy (Indian Two Feet) and how he earns the right to wear an eagle feather. This makes a mockery of those tribes that consider eagle feathers symbolic of courage and honor, and it equates the process of earning them with child's play.

A much-used theme is that of a child in search of his "real" name. According to the jacket copy on *Little Indian* (Simon & Schuster), readers will "gleefully" discover that there is more than one way to acquire a name. This story distorts and makes fun of the name-giving practices of some tribes and makes of them whimsical, meaningless exercises to be viewed with humor.

The degree to which a non-Indian author's concept of things "Indian" is distorted and an example of how distortions are kept alive are demonstrated in a book called *Buffalo Man and Golden Eagle* (McCall Publishing Co.).

The book begins with that quaint old "Indian" expression, "Many moons ago." Why not simply say "a long time ago?" According to the story, Golden Eagle (also referred to as "the Indian") hunted six days a week, but on the seventh day he would don "his most beautiful headdress, put his peace pipe in his mouth, and stroll off into the hills."

The six-day work week is misplaced in the context of time; it did not exist for American Indians. The tribes that wore headdresses wore them only on special occasions, not to "stroll" around in. Peace pipes were smoked ritually and in the proper ceremonial setting. So while Golden Eagle, or "the Indian," adheres to the biblical injunction against working on the Sabbath, he is disrespectful towards ceremonial and religious articles that are particularly American Indian—all in five lines of text with a total of seventy-five words.

This book was originally published in Austria. The author was born in Germany, studied in Munich, now lives in Bavaria and raises riding ponies. The story is designed to convey a lesson about cooperation and friendship. The real message, however, is that publishing houses in the United States will go to Europe for books about American Indians but are hesitant to venture into Indian country here at home.) 48

It is one thing to write about imaginary beings from an imaginary time and place, but American Indians are real people and deserve the dignity of being presented as such. These little books with their "charming" stories, fanciful illustrations and cute little characters put Indians in the same category with witches, ogres, giants, fairies, and baby animals.

Some authors indulge in what amounts to acts of cultural vandalism. An example of this is in *Pink Puppy* (Putnam's). The setting is among the Cherokees in North Carolina.

The book opens with a wake for Cindy Standingdeer's mother. The author's understanding of a Cherokee wake and of the dynamics involved is highly superficial. Cindy, eight years old, feels that because people are singing they are happy. Since most Cherokee children are taken to wakes from the time they are infants, it is unlikely that an eight-year-old would so grossly misunderstand the hymn singing in this way.

The old "stoic Indian" cliché is thrown in when the author has Grandmother Standingdeer say to Cindy, "Cherokees don't cry, You'll have to learn the old Indian way—it's a good way." The school teacher (white) arrives and urges Cindy to cry, saying, "That's all right Cindy. Go ahead. You'll feel better." And later she adds, "I'll cry with you Cindy."

The author cannot have attended many Cherokee wakes or funerals or it would be obvious that Cherokees do indeed cry. However, if it were true that Cherokees do not cry, and if it is really the "old Indian way," then the teacher, in encouraging the child to cry, is interfering with behavioral and cultural patterns in a very direct way. She is undermining the grandmother's position and is saying, in effect, that the "old Indian way" is not a good way, after all.

Cindy is "glad her grandmother didn't come up close and put her arm around her the way the white people do." But she accepts the embrace of the teacher, "a young white woman," without a qualm.

Cindy becomes abstracted and it is alleged that "somebody had a medicine man conjure her." It is irresponsible of the author to introduce the subject of witchcraft and medicine men. Responsible scholars hesitate to make judgments about the extent to which present-day Cherokees in western North Carolina believe in or practice conjuration.

Whatever the Cherokees think or feel about conjuration, a medicine man is a figure to be respected and should not be equated with a capricious wicked witch who casts spells on innocent children.

Cindy's father keeps her home from school "day after day" because he is lonely. He agrees to take his family (three children and himself) to live with his mother because her house is "bigger and it's better built."

A book of this sort is all the more insidious because it is well meant and is not obviously bad. The language itself is not derogatory. It is the impressions the words convey that are objectionable: the grandmother is a cold person untouched by the death of her daughter; the father is an industrious but incompetent and selfish man who cannot provide his family with adequate shelter.

The teacher is the only person who comforts or sympathizes with Cindy. She is warm, understanding and concerned.

The book is supposedly about a young Cherokee girl, but it is really about the pretty young white teacher who copes with the problems created by the death of the girl's mother. The implication is that it is the non-Indian only who can solve problems and make decisions for American Indians because Indians are not capable of doing so.

This patronizing attitude is indicative of an arrogance that sometimes borders on the grotesque. In *Trading Post Girl* (Frederick Fell, Inc.), the following passage occurs:

> "Libby gave Barney a teasing glance. 'Red earth, white clouds and blue water—Daddy, are you patriotic!'
>
> 'Well, now, Punkin, I guess you're right. This really is a piece of our American life, right among the Indians. You wait and see, some day they'll be real fine American citizens.'
>
> 'Oh, Daddy, not those savages.'
>
> 'They've got a lot of things to learn, too, honey. Give them time. They've got lots of good in them.'"

The author, under the guise of fairness, is telling us that American Indians are not "patriotic," are not "real fine" citizens, and that they have "lots of good in them" in spite of the fact that they are "savages."

A number of authors have taken it upon themselves to establish the humanity of American Indians by presenting arguments for and against the idea. Humanness is not an arguable point.

One of the factors that significantly contributes to and nourishes this kind of arrogance is the way American Indians are portrayed in history books. This description of "the Indian" appears in *The French and Indian Wars* (American Heritage Junior Library): "To the Indians pity was a form of cowardice. Their captives were no longer persons but things to be exchanged for ransom or tortured for amusement according to their shifting savage moods. The custom of scalping was symbolic of the Indian mind, a mind so apart from that of the whites as to remain incomprehensible. So heedless were the red men of human suffering that the word cruelty seems inadequate to describe their ingenious tortures. Even the gentle Roger Williams called them 'wolves with the brains of men.'"

This description is in sharp contrast to the following statements from Hodge's scholarly *Handbook of Indians North of Mexico*: "From the days of Columbus to the present travelers have given testimony of customs and manners of Indians . . . which displayed a regard for the happiness and well being of others." "Abundant evidence might be adduced to show that Indians are often actuated by motives of pure benevolence and do good merely from a generous delight in the act." "Truth, honesty, and the safeguarding of human life were everywhere recognized as essential to the peace and prosperity of a tribe, and social customs enforced their observance." "The care of one's family was regarded as a social duty and was generally observed." "Honesty was inculcated in the young and exacted in the tribe."

Non-Indian writers have created an image of American Indians that is almost sheer fantasy. It is an image that is not authentic and one that has little value except that of sustaining the illusion that the original inhabitants deserved to lose their land because they were so barbaric and uncivilized. ＼ＳＯ－＼

This fantasy does not take into account the rich diversity of cultures that did, and do, exist. Violence is glorified over gentleness and love of peace. The humanistic aspects of American Indian societies are ignored in the standard book.

A book of "Indian stories" for young readers published in the 1930s proclaimed itself a "fine collection of exciting stories in which Indian war whoops fairly echo through the pages and painted savages peek out behind each word."

The world has changed a lot since then, but the publishing industry has not. In 1968 Harper & Row published *Indian Summer*, an "I CAN READ History Book" for children ages four through eight. According to the jacket copy it is "wonderful—geared to that important group, late first through third grade. . . . It is a perfect book."

The setting for the story is a log cabin in a Kentucky forest during the time when the American colonies were fighting to gain independence from Britain. While the man of the house is away fighting with the American forces, men of some unidentified tribe skulk around the cabin. The "pioneer" woman outwits them and they retreat hastily into the forest. The author in a fit of incredible cuteness has contrived to work the sound "ugh" into the story.

The message a child gets from this "history" book is that the settlers are good, peaceful people who love their homes and families, and that American Indians are menacing but stupid creatures called "redskins" who can be made fools of by a lone woman. The "pioneer" woman is bravely and courageously defending her home and children. The father is patriotic and dutiful. There is nothing in *Indian Summer* indicating that American Indians are also fathers and mothers with families and homes.

Undoubtedly it is accurate that settlers were threatened by, and afraid of, Indians, but Indians were equally, if not more, threatened by the settlers and they had much more to lose. The history books and story books seldom make it clear that Native Americans, in fighting back, were defending their homes and families and were not just being malicious.

It is rarely, if ever, mentioned that non-Indians scalped people, but scalping as an Indian practice is emphasized in most of the books about American Indians, including the textbooks used in schools throughout the country.

For example, in *Indian Summer* these statements occur: "Those Indians are after your scalps." "Then they could have scalped you a long way from the cabin. That's an old Indian trick." A book called *Tough Enough's Indians* (Walck, Inc.) has this to say, "'Injuns didn't go fussin' up their critters that-a-way.' Beanie said, 'They didn't have time. They were too busy huntin' and fishin' and beatin' drums and scalpin' other Injuns and white folks, cuttin' their skin and hair right off, somethin' terrible, and burnin' 'em up at stakes.'" *Pontiac, King of the Great Lakes* (Hastings House) contains this sentence, "A warrior had only to drop his canoe into the water and he was on his way to a council, a feast, or some scalp-taking expedition of his own."

The frequency with which non-Indian authors mention scalping, and the relish with which they indulge in bloody descriptions, would indicate that it is they, rather than Indians, who are preoccupied with scalps.

Contrary to what people have been led to believe, scalping was not a widespread custom among American Indians tribes. Scalping was practiced by the ancient Scythians as long ago as the fifth century B.C., but research shows that it was not a very old practice on the American continent, and was originally confined to an area limited to the eastern United States and the lower St. Lawrence region, excluding New England and much of the Atlantic Coast region.

According to the *Handbook of American Indians North of Mexico*, compiled in the late 1800s, "The numerous popular misconceptions in connection with the scalping practice may be recapitulated in a series of negatives. The custom was not general, and in most regions where found was not even ancient. The trophy did not include any part of the skull or even the whole scalp. The operation was not fatal. The scalp was not always evidence of the killing of an enemy, but was sometimes taken from a victim who was allowed to live. It was not always taken by the same warrior who had killed or wounded the victim. It was not always preserved by the victor. The warrior's honors were not measured by the number of his scalps."

The *Handbook* further states, "The spread of the scalping practice over a great part of central and western United States was a direct result of the encouragement in the shape of scalp bounties offered by the colonial and more recent governments. . . ."

The Puritans offered rewards for Indian heads. As early as 1641 New Amsterdam (New York City) paid bounties for Indian scalps, as did other colonies.

In 1755, Massachusetts paid 40 Pounds (about $200) for the scalp of an adult male Indian and 20 Pounds (about $100) for the scalps of women and children. The French and English, in addition to paying for Indian scalps, offered rewards for the scalps of white people. Many non-Indians took advantage of the opportunity to supplement the family income by collecting scalp bounties.

There were many tribes who never took scalps. In all fairness, a more balanced approach is needed. In 1972, in an obvious attempt to counteract such books as *Indian Summer*, *Tough Enough's Indians*, and *Pontiac*, Harper & Row brought out a book entitled *Small Wolf* in which Small Wolf, a young boy from an unidentified tribe, goes hunting on what is now Manhattan Island. He sees many strange sights including a man whose face is "all WHITE." He brings his father to the island and they are run off at gunpoint by an irate Dutchman. The settlers grow in numbers, occupying more and more land, repeatedly forcing Small Wolf and his family to pack their belongings and move.

While it is admirable that Harper & Row is willing to attempt to present an Indian point of view, the book is not without flaws. The man whose face is "all WHITE" is described as having " a fat jaw and cracks between his teeth," so that Small Wolf thinks he is wearing a "devil mask." The illustration shows a fat, ugly, leering man (Dutch). The implication is that "bad" people are physically unattractive—not to be confused with good, clean-cut Americans.

Historically the "devil mask" is misplaced; the devil is a Judeo-Christian concept, not an American Indian one.

This book fosters a common misunderstanding about American Indians and the concept of land ownership. "They [other Indians] had no right to sell the land. The land and the sky and the sea are all Mother Earth for everyone to use," says Small Wolf's father.

This bit of dialogue presents a simplistic and highly romanticized version of what were various practical concepts of land ownership. It leaves the impression that American Indians had *no* concept of land ownership at all.

The Native peoples of this country were not rootless wanderers drifting about the country helter skelter. Certainly, when the colonists landed, the people who owned the land did not have deeds and fee-simple titles to whip out and exhibit as proof of ownership; however the various tribes and bands did claim sovereignty over specific areas of land, dwelling, hunting, and farming within well-established boundaries.

The people who came here to establish colonies were, after all, in search of a piece of land to own. Historically and philosophically one rationalization for the seizure of Indian-owned lands is that nobody owned the land anyhow. Much book space has been, and is being, devoted to maintaining that myth. Apparently the producers of books feel that the American public and system of government can not stand the truth.

The ending of *Small Wolf* gives the impression that American Indians eventually just faded into the sunset. This denies the fact that there are American Indians around today.

While non-Indians are portrayed negatively, they ultimately come across as being strong and aggressive. Small Wolf and his family evoke a feeling of pity. American Indians want respect, not pity—it is demeaning and denies human dignity.

This book is a sincere effort to offset the negative images portrayed in books like *Indian Summer*. But both of these books exemplify a flaw common to most books about Indians: they are portrayed either as a noble superhumans, or as depraved, barbarous subhumans. There is no opportunity for them to behave like mere human beings.

A more direct assault is made upon the humanity of American Indians by the use of key words and phrases which trigger negative and derogatory images. Words such as savage, buck, squaw and papoose do not bring to mind the same images as do the words man, boy, woman and baby.

Descriptions of half-naked, hideously-painted creatures brandishing tomahawks or scalping knives, yelping, howling, grunting, jabbering, or snarling are hardly conducive to a sympathetic reaction to the people so described. Ethnocentric bias is translated into absurdities, i.e. making a point of the fact that American Indians could not read or write English when the Pilgrims arrived; they did not have clocks; they had no schools.

Broad generalizations are made, obliterating individuality. Such generalizations, while convenient, serve to foster and sustain stereotypic misconceptions. For example, in *The Indians of the Plains* (American Heritage Junior Library) this pronouncement occurs, "War was the Indian's career and hobby, his work and his play."

The author does not mention that some tribes considered warfare to be an expression of insanity. Others strove to maintain peace and harmony in all phases of their existence. Besides, it is doubtful that there was actually much inter-tribal "war" before the coming of the white men.

Extensive cultural bias is evidenced by the comparisons invited by authors in their descriptions of people. In *Something for the Medicine Man* (Melmont), the "Granny," a Cherokee woman, is described as having a face that is "dried up like a persimmon." The teacher (non-Indian) is "tall as trees," not "old like Granny," and has eyes "like blue flags"—the baby (Cherokee) has eyes "like a baby fox." The Cherokee family eats "like hungry dogs."

The non-Indian teacher in *My Name Is Lion* (Holiday House) is young, and smells "like too many flowers." A Navajo lady is described as "an old woman" who is sitting "huddled in a blanket." Lion, a Navajo boy who finds he does not "mind" the way the teacher smells, discovers that the Navajo woman "sure" does not smell "like that flower teacher." Lion's grandfather is drunk, dirty, and "whining in Navajo about money." The positive intent of both of these books is canceled by the negative aspects of the implied comparisons.

The repeated juxtaposition of man and animal serves to instill and reinforce the image of American Indians as being not only subhuman but also inhuman beings. In *Captives of the Senecas* (Hale & Co.), Senecas are described, "A ring of painted Indians was closing in on them, darting like huge weasles through the grass of the intervale." A later sentence reads, "Indians were coursing the ground like hunting dogs." *The American Indian* (Random House) has this to say, "The Indians hung around New Amsterdam, as the colony on Manhattan Island was called, and made themselves a nuisance. They were lazy, insolent, and thievish as monkeys." *The French and Indian Wars* (American Heritage Junior Library) puts forth this thought, "The Indian might turn gentle, but as with a tame wolf, it was a gentleness never to be trusted." *The Secret Name* (Harcourt Brace) has this statement, "Dad thinks Indians are like wild animals. . . . You can tame them a little bit, but not all the way."

It has been well established by sociologists and psychologists that the effect on children of negative stereotypes and derogatory images is to engender and perpetuate undemocratic and unhealthy attitudes that will plague our society for years to come.

It is time for American publishing houses, schools, and libraries to take another look at the books they are offering children and seriously set out to offset some of the damage they have done. Only American Indians can tell non-Indians what it is to be Indian. There is no longer any need for non-Indian writers to "interpret" American Indians for the American public.

Feathers, Tomahawks and Tipis: A Study of Stereotyped "Indian" Imagery in Children's Picture Books*

Robert B. Moore and Arlene B. Hirschfelder

The following article will attempt to demonstrate how all of the items below are interrelated to one another—and to children's books.

ITEM: MINEOLA, NY, 1976

In a Long Island courtroom a Blackfeet woman is being cross-examined. The white prosecutor says, "And when you lived here you lived in a whiteman's style domicile or residence, didn't you?" She answers, "I don't know what you mean by that question." He continues, "Well, did you live in a tipi, or did you live in a built house that whitemen live in?"

ITEM: RIDGEWOOD, NJ, 1976

A man in a business suit quietly enters the rear of an elementary classroom as the teacher tells the class that a Native American visitor will speak to them that day. Almost in unison, the children put their hands to their mouths and start whooping "like Indians." When the embarrassed teacher introduces the visitor, the children stare in disbelief. "But you don't look like an Indian," and "You're not dressed like an Indian," they say.

---

*Reprinted by permission from *Unlearning "Indian" Stereotypes* by the Council on Interracial Books for Children, 1841 Broadway, New York, NY, 1977.

ITEM: ST. LOUIS, MO, 1976

A white family is telling their five-year-old son about his adopted one-year-old sister's Native American heritage. She is a Winnebago and they tell him about her people and culture. Suddenly he interrupts and nervously asks if his baby sister "will kill us when she grows up?"

ITEM: ONCHIOTA, NY, 1971

John Fadden (Mohawk) works at the Six Nations (Iroquois) Indian Museum. He reports that time and time again children "refuse to come onto the grounds of the museum because of an intense fear of possibly meeting an Indian. Some actually cry and scream."

ITEM: MINNEAPOLIS, MN, 1971

Third and fourth graders write their impressions of Native Americans (spelling is original):

> Indians use to fight cowboys. Sometimes they fight with war paint on. . . . Indians live in Teepees.
> A hundred years ago they were bad, know there are some nice ones. They heurt lot of people in the world. Thousands of people were kild. They are different then us. Because they are a different color than us. The Indians didn't know about Amiraca.
> Some have red skin They fot in wars. . . . They were dirty rotton pigs thats what.
> Indians would be like us if they weren't dark and they talk different. sometimes there like savages.
> I think they are killers to americans. Indians wear war paint. Indians make war with americans.

ITEM: NEW YORK, NY, 1974

First graders describe the pictures of "Indians" they had drawn:

> It's an ugly Indian and he has a bow and arrow and the things he throws. He's a bad Indian and an ugly one. And he kills. He's a really bad Indian and he's a chief and he commands all of them. He throws really far and he kills.
> If an Indian moved to the city he'd kill people. He's not smart and would think people were cowboys and would kill dogs because he would think they were buffalo or fish.
> [A girl said she had seen Indians close-up when they surrounded a train she was on.] I saw Indians take off the girls' dresses and it scared me. It was something I saw outside the window of the train. There was a chief and the cowboys shot him. I was safe inside the train. The Indians were all around.

ITEM: WASHINGTON, DC, 1975

U.S. Bureau of the Census reports that Native Americans have the lowest income, life expectancy, and standards of housing and health, and highest levels of infant mortality, T.B. and suicide of any racial group in the U.S.

Anti-Native American attitudes and stereotypes are pervasive throughout U.S. society. The 1969 report of the U.S. Senate Special Sub-Committee on Indian Education states:

> [The U.S. is a] nation that is massively uninformed and misinformed about the American Indian, and his [sic] past and present. Prejudice, racial intolerance, and discrimination towards Indians [are] far more widespread and serious than generally recognized.[1]

Over the centuries of EuroAmerican interaction with native peoples, an enormous amount of myth, fiction, and stereotyping has developed within white society about "Indians." This pervasive, white-created image of "Indians" has generated much continuing interest, but neither the image nor the interest bear relationship to the reality of Native peoples. Alvin Josephy notes that:

> . . . from the time of the Europeans' first meeting with the Indians in 1492 until today, the Indian has been a familiar but little known—and, indeed, often an unreal—person to the non-Indian. What has been known about him [sic], moreover, frequently has been superficial, distorted, or false.[2]

Michael Dorris (Modoc) writes of a key negative generalization—called "Indian"—made by Europeans:

> With this generalization a new, artificial and completely invalid ethnic group emerged upon the world scene, the product of a myopic European imagination: The INDIAN was born.[3]

Generalized reference to "the American Indian" or to "Indian culture" obliterates the enormous diversity of ceremonies, world views, political and social organization, lifestyles, language, and art among the Chickahominy, Navajo, Menominee, Ojibway, Mohawk, Choctaw, Osage, Ute, Hopi and other Native peoples, both in the past as well as today.

An additional problem is the frequent portrayal of particular Native cultures as static and unchanging. Jack Forbes (Powhatan) writes:

> . . . it is technically incorrect to speak of "Navaho culture," "Quechan culture," or "Sioux culture" without a reference to a particular time period unless it is fully understood that one is speaking about a fluid, changing "tradition" which has only one basic, unifying element, that is, that it is associated with a particular people. "Navaho culture" before 1000 was very different from 1890, which in turn was different from 1960.[4]

A prime example of how the white-created "Indian" image subverts the diversity of Native cultures is the amalgamation by whites of particular aspects of the cultures of the Lakota (Sioux), Crow, Cheyenne and other nations of the Great Plains area (flowing-feathered headdress, tipis,* "war-dances," buffalo hunting) into a standard motif for the white-created "Indian." This process can be attributed to a variety of factors—the popular paintings of George Catlin in the mid-1800's; the determined resistance of Native nations in the Great Plains to the U.S. invasion in the latter 1800's; the sensationalized press accounts of those wars; and the enormous popularity of Buffalo Bill's Wild West Show. While these factors helped to create the white image of "Indians," it was left to Hollywood to concretize it and distribute it throughout the world.

Ralph and Natasha Friar, in *The Only Good Indian: The Hollywood Gospel*, analyze hundreds of the "several thousand" films about "Indians." They write that:

> No other race or culture depicted on film has been made to assume such a permanent fictional identity. . . . Thanks to the moving pictures, we can, let us say, lump the Apache tribes with the Mohawk Nation, call them "Indians" and assume not only a racial but an *ethnic* relationship as well. . . . Hollywood has continued to be a co-conspirator in committing cultural genocide by subverting the Native American's various ethnic identities and retaining him [sic] as a racial scapegoat.[5]

Children's** perceptions of Native Americans are formed from a variety of sources. Parents, peers and teachers help to mold attitudes. TV, movies, comics, advertisements, games and toys, food packages, and greeting cards contain stereotypes and caricatures which transmit the white-created "Indian" image.

Children's books play an important role in perpetuating these images. Mary Gloyne Byler (Cherokee) analyzed 600 children's books *about* Native Americans.[6] She found depersonalization, ridicule, derision, inauthenticity, and stereotyping in the vast majority. Native people were treated in patronizing ways, portrayed as fantasy, set in an unidentified past, or juxtaposed with animals.

When reading to our own children, the authors of this present study often spotted stereotypic images of Native Americans, even when the theme and text of the books were totally *un*related to Native people. We undertook this study to analyze the context in which such stereotyping occurs in picture and in picture-story

---

*"Tipi" will be the spelling used in this article in reference to the style of housing used by certain nations of the Great Plains area. This spelling derives from the Siouan "ti," meaning "to dwell" and "pi," meaning "used for."

**Derogatory stereotypes of Native Americans impact negatively on all children, Native American or other. Our discussion will deal with the effects of such stereotypes on non-Native American children, most of whom have no direct contact with Native people.

books for children under ten.* (This project was totally different from Byler's study because all books written *about* Native Americans, or any of the many books with content that could be *expected* to relate to Native Americans, such as Westerns or pioneer stories, were *not* included.) 758 ¬

We scanned books in children's libraries in Bergen County, New Jersey, and in the Donnell Library, New York City. We also checked book stores for books too new to be on library shelves. We found 75 books containing hundreds of illustrations portraying non-Native children and animals dressed up as "Indians," as well as caricatured illustrations of Native Americans. All of these characters in all of the illustrations wear a feathered headpiece. Some illustrations additionally include buckskin clothing, moccasins, tomahawks, tipis, etc. These images appear one or more times in each of the books. Many of these books were published in the 1950s and 60s, but many recently published books contain the very same images. We did not attempt to find out how many of the older books are still in print. More to the point is that these books are still on library shelves and are still read by children. Our sample is *representative* of an unknown, but *substantially larger* number of books with similar derogatory images.

No one illustration is enough to create stereotypes in children's minds. But enough books contain these images—and the general culture reinforces them—so that there is a cumulative effect, encouraging false and negative perceptions about Native Americans.

Stereotyping occurs when an entire group is characterized in specific ways and these characteristics are attributed to all individuals who belong to that group. Native American stereotyping occurs when particular characteristics are treated as distinguishing Native people from other people. What children learn from these books is: Native people always wear feathers or headdresses; they frequently brandish tomahawks; they live in tipis; the women usually have babies on their backs; the men are fierce and violent; they lurk behind trees; they spend much time dancing on one leg; and their existence is dependent on the proximity of cowboys. Native people are not men, women and children but "braves," "squaws" and "papooses." These attributes and behaviors epitomize the white-created "Indian" caricature ("an exaggeration by means of deliberate simplification and often ludicrous distortion of parts or characteristics"—*Webster's Dictionary*). In reality, these caricatures have no relation to Cherokee, Hopi, Passamaquoddy, Mohawk or other Native peoples.) 59

The white-created "Indian" imagery consists of inauthentic representations of Native American peoples and cultures. This imagery is used in these books for one or more of the following functions: for *humor*, by portraying "Indians" as

---

*Picture books for the very young include alphabet and counting books, "first" books and concept books. The pictures are synchronized with minimal text, enabling the child to comprehend the story independently of the text. In picture-story books the illustrations help to interpret the text, and are inseparable from it.

silly and laughable; for *fantasy*, by portraying animals or non-Native children as "Indians," or by placing "Indians" in a fictionalized, mystical past; for purely *decorative* purposes, as in the frequent addition of a headdress in a manner unrelated to the text; and for *symbolic* reasons, employed to suggest violence, danger or fear. Whether used for comical, fanciful, decorative or symbolic purposes, this "Indian" imagery degrades Native American people and cultures, and distorts non-Native children's perceptions of Native Americans.

The implications of this imagery are far more serious than would be stereotyped illustrations of German, Swedish or French people used for humor, or inaccurate depictions of Irish, Dutch or English cultures used for decoration. Young children see white ethnic groups in many dimensions in real life or in literature, films, advertisements, and TV. But *most* of the images children receive of Native peoples and cultures are—like the images in these books—stereotypic, distorted and unreal. And these images play a crucial role in distorting and warping non-Native children's attitudes toward Native Americans. To paraphrase Kenneth Clark and other investigators regarding children's attitudes about Black people, "Children's attitudes toward [Native Americans] are determined chiefly not by contact with [Native people], but by contact with the prevailing attitudes toward [Native people]. It is not the [Native person], but the idea of the [Native person] that influences children."[7]

SEVEN CATEGORIES

As we reviewed the books definite patterns emerged, both in the ways "Indian" imagery was used and in its repeated appearance in certain types of books. We have organized this article into seven categories:

1. Books with illustrations of children "playing Indian" (no reference to "Indian" in the text)
2. Books with illustrations of children "playing Indian" (reference to "Indian" in the text)
3. Books with animals portrayed as "Indians"
4. Books with illustrations supposedly depicting Native Americans
5. Alphabet and Dictionary books
6. Counting books
7. Hat books

1. Children "Play Indian"

The 27 books with illustrations of non-Native children "playing Indian" have been divided between those with no mention of the word "Indian" in the text and those in which the children are called "Indians." We found 19 books with non-

Native children wearing stereotyped clothing, without mention of any "Indian" in the text. Therefore, these images may reflect the ideas of the illustrator, rather than the author.

In *The Little Boy and the Birthdays* (Buckley and Galdone, 1965) a boy is pictured in nine illustrations wearing a headband and two feathers. In *Daddies* (Carton and Jacobs, 1963) a father sits in a chair reading a newspaper, while his son runs around with two feathers in his hair. *The Repair of Uncle Toe* (Chorao, 1972) has many illustrations of a little boy wearing a headband and feather. The cover of *You Can't Catch Me* (Bridgeman, 1976) shows a little girl wearing a headdress, and an illustration inside the book shows her in headdress again, this time with another child wearing a cowboy hat.

Books about Halloween frequently contain illustrations of children dressed as "Indians." For example, *How We Celebrate Our Fall Holidays* (Lucy Banks and John Hawkinson, 1961) contains an illustration of children trick-or-treating, with two of them dressed as "Indians." The title page of *Halloween Parade* (Lystad and Szekers, 1973) features a child, wearing a headdress, peeking around a door. And *Halloween With Morris and Boris* (Wiseman, 1975) contains five pictures of a girl hosting a Halloween party and wearing buckskins, moccasins and feathers.

Twelve other books in this "playing Indian" category include stereotypic items like tomahawks or bows and arrows along with "Indian" dress. And, more pernicious, all but two of these books associate "Indians" with violence.

Will I Have a Friend? (Cohen and Hoban, 1969) has five illustrations in which a boy in a group of children wears a headband and feather. In one, he carries a tomahawk, raises one foot and holds a hand to his mouth. This stance recurs in many books, suggesting a whooping, wild "Indian." *The Rooster Crows: A Book of American Rhymes and Jingles* (Maude and Miska Petersham, 1971) contains an illustration of three children running, one with headdress and tomahawk. This illustration accompanies the verse, "First's the worst, second's the same, last's the best of all the game."

One illustration in *The Day Busy Buzzy Stopped Being Busy* (Fringuello, 1970) shows "Busy Buzzy" wearing a headband and feathers. The caption reads, "Sometimes he would jump with the dog." The dog is cowering, paws over head, while "Busy Buzzy" jumps over him brandishing a tomahawk. *What's Good for a Four-Year-Old* (Cole and Ungerer, 1967) features children telling a neighbor what games they like to play. One illustration shows a boy holding balloons and floating in the air, while another boy, in headdress, prepares to shoot an arrow at the balloons. In *What's Good for a Five-Year-Old?* (Cole and Sorel, 1969) children tell what five-year-olds like to do. "Roughhouse" is one response, and four boys are shown. One—wearing headband and feathers—is fighting with another, a third whirls a lasso and a fourth carries a dagger in his mouth.

The Blackboard Bear (Alexander, 1969) contains numerous illustrations of boys playing cowboys and "Indians." The "Indians" are barefoot, wear headdresses or feathers, carry tomahawks, and shoot bows and arrows.

Ted, the central character in *Boy, Was I Mad* (Hitte and Mayer, 1969) is dressed as a cowboy. He runs away, meeting his friend Tom, who wears loincloth, buckskin shirt and headdress. In one illustration Tom is behind a tree, with hand formed into a gun pointing at Ted, who clutches his chest and falls. Another shows them sneaking after one another, around a large rock. The text incongruously states, "Tom and I did some stunts and things like standing on our heads. And I jumped farther than Tom, and we climbed around on some big rocks."

Five other books in the "playing Indian" category are less subtle in associating "Indians" with violence. Two involve sibling rivalry and three peer aggression. *If It Weren't for You* (Zolotow and Shecter, 1966) concerns an older brother's speculation of how wonderful it would be not to have his younger sibling always around. Throughout the book, the older brother is dressed as a cowboy, the younger protagonist as an "Indian," replete with moccasins, buckskins, headband and feather. In one illustration, the "Indian" sits astride a dog (again cowering with paw over head), whooping it up after shooting an arrow at his brother, who is trying to read a book.

The situation is reversed in *I'll Fix Anthony* (Viorst and Lobel, 1969), with a younger brother fantasizing revenge against an older brother. The title page shows the avenging youngster on horseback, wearing a blanket and headdress, brandishing a lance and chasing down a bewildered sibling.

The Two Reds (Lipkind and Mordvinoff, 1950) involves a red-headed boy and a red cat. One day the boy smells smoke, peeps through a fence hole, and sees "the Seventh Street Signal Senders ready to initiate a new member." Almost all of the fifteen or so members are wearing feathers, a couple have headdresses, and some carry lances or bows and arrows. In one illustration they have the initiate on hands and knees, and in another, tied to a tree. Spotting the red-headed boy, they give chase with guns, lances and knives but, through a bit of good luck involving the cat, he gets away. The image of the befeathered "Signal Senders" remains threatening and negative throughout the story.

A sequel, *Russet and the Two Reds* (Lipkind and Mordvinoff, 1962), adds Russet, a red-headed girl. The "Signal Senders" chase Russet, capture her, and shout "A squaw! A paleface squaw!" Red rescued her and, in the end, the two are invited to "Come back sometime and join our club."

An "anti-war book," *Bang Bang You're Dead* (Fitzhugh and Scoppettone, 1969) presents a somewhat confused message. Two groups of children "playing war" suddenly begin to actually fight with rocks and sticks, drawing blood and bruises. This results in their uniting to play together—at "play war." One child is dressed as a cowboy and one wears an enormous feathered headdress.

2. Children Become "Indians"

A second category of books with illustrations of children "playing Indian" includes text in which the word "Indian" *is* applied to non-Native children. Of the eight books we found in this category, one states that the children are *pretending* to be "Indians" while in the other seven, the non-Native children simply "are Indians."

Little Leo (Politi, 1951) is a book in which white children "playing Indian" is the central theme. Leo's father buys him "an Indian Chief suit"—moccasins, buckskins and headdress. After donning the outfit Leo runs into the yard and, "With his hand to his mouth he let out strange yells. Wa-wa-wa-wa-wah! . . . Leo danced, crept, crawled, and did everything he had seen Indians do in the movies." The twist of the story is that Leo and his immigrant family return to Italy, from whence they came. There, Leo and his "Indian Chief suit" become the envy of every village child and soon all wear similar outfits. "We can all play Indian" they said. With hands to mouths they let out "yells and strange cries." The once quiet little village "was full of lively little Indians."

What Can You Do with a Pocket? (Merriam and Sherman, 1964) suggests that with varying items in your pocket you can be a cowboy, princess, fisherman, squirrel, seal at the circus, orchestra conductor, etc. These all represent occupational roles or fantasy as animals. But, "with a FEATHER in your pocket you can be an INDIAN." This sentence is accompanied by a caricature with long headdress and a pipe.*

What Do You Do, Dear? (Joslin and Sendak, 1961) is a book on "proper conduct for all occasions." On one occasion "you are an Indian chief" who invited some cowboys to smoke a "peace pipe." But when it's your turn to puff, you swallow a lot of smoke. What do you do? "Cover your mouth when you cough." The illustrations show a child with a headband and feathers sitting outside a tipi. The cover shows the befeathered child smoking an elaborate pipe.

William Steig's *CDB* (1968) has an "Indian"-costumed child addressing another child. "I M N-D-N" says the first child. "O, I C," says the second. *Tom in the Middle* (Amoss, 1968) is about sibling rivalry. Tom has problems with both older and younger brothers but, in the end, they all get along well and "play Indian." Wearing the works, carrying a bow, arrow and tomahawk, they decide to "make a tent with John's blue blanket and be sleeping Indians."

Of the previously discussed books, twenty showed boys "playing Indian" as compared to three showing girls. All the latter were books of relatively recent copyright date—1973, 1975, 1976. This is one instance of stereotyped sex-role behavior that should not be sexually integrated, but ended altogether. However, three additional examples, from earlier times, were found showing that girls, as well as boys, can "play Indian."

The jacket of Phyllis McGinley's *Sugar and Spice: The ABC of Being a Girl* (1960) states that McGinley's "work reflects her deep understanding of the heart

---

*"Peacepipe" is a misnomer applied by Euro-Americans to a variety of pipes which serve a range of functions—from those used only to smoke tobacco to those sacred pipes used only ceremonially. The term "pipe" will therefore be used in this article.

of a woman." Hopefully, her understanding has changed over the last decade and a half, for the book is as sickeningly sexist as the title suggests. About the only non-sex-role stereotyped behavior is found under the letter "F":

> Felicia Frances is my firm fast friend.
> We have more fun
> Playing let's-pretend.
> Sometimes we're princesses, sometimes we're spies,
> Sometimes we're Indians, feathered to the eyes . . .
> Sometimes we're Eskimo, *fastened into furs,
> But she's always my friend
> And I am hers.

Colleen Browning's illustration shows a figure in a dress, wearing a headdress, holding a tomahawk high and in the "flamingo"—one-leg-in-the-air—stance. This whooping, dancing caricature is usually illustrated as a male.

I Wish I Had Another Name (Williams and Lubell, 1962) shows two children playing cowboy and "Indian." The cowgirl muses, "I'm Galloping Gertrude, the best in the West, with a pearl-handled gun and a star on my chest." The second child, of indeterminate sex, is creeping along with a headdress and tomahawk, saying, "And I'm Gitchee-Gumdrop, the Chief of the Utes; when my tomahawk flashes, you shake in your boots." In addition to yet another image of creeping, fierce "Indians," the name "Gitchee-Gumdrop" makes a mockery of Native American names. And, all of these insults are attributed to a specific Native people—the Ute.

A book that contains numerous "Indian" images is *A Child's Garden of Verse* (Stevenson and Fujikawa, 1977). Originally published in 1885, the 1977 printing carries a Grosset and Dunlap copyright of 1957. Although Stevenson was Scottish, and his work reflects a British perspective, children in the United States reading the book would not generally be aware of that. The endpaper illustrations of a child with headband, feather, bow and arrows are the most benign. A very racist verse, "Foreign Children," is accompanied by an illustration of six white children, five of them in varying national costumes. The girl who is reciting the verse wears contemporary dress. One barefoot boy wears a headdress and carries a bow and arrow, while a girl wears a headband and feather. The message to children in the United States is that Sioux, Crow and other Native children are "foreign" (as indeed they were to Stevenson) but the ethnocentrism and racism of the verse remain, even with that caveat:

> Little Indian, Sioux or Crow,
> Little Frosty Eskimo,

---

*Illustrations of Inuit ("Eskimo") people and of igloos were not included in this article, as that subject warrants a separate study. There are distinct cultural, linguistic and genetic differences between the Inuit of Alaska, Canada, Greenland, etc., and Native Americans.

Little Turk or Japanee,
Oh! don't you wish that you were me?

. . . Such a life is very fine,
But it's not so nice as mine;

. . . You have curious things to eat,
I am fed on proper meat;
You must dwell beyond the foam,
But I am safe and live at home.

"The Land of Storybooks" is illustrated with a little boy, with headband, two feathers and a gun, crawling behind a sofa:

> . . . Now, with my little gun, I crawl
> All in the dark along the wall
> And follow round the forest track
> Away behind the sofa back.
> . . . I see the others far away
> As if in firelit camp they lay,
> And I, like to an Indian scout,
> Around their party prowled about. . . .

In "The Gardener," a child muses about a gardener who is too busy to play. ". . . O how much wiser you would be, To play at Indian wars with me!" The illustration shows a little girl with a large headdress. Stevenson's book is a classic, fondly remembered by many an adult and still enjoyed by many a child. Yet it clearly reinforces stereotypes.

What's Wrong with "Playing Indian?" "Playing Indian" is a common play activity for children—in the United States as well as in other countries. For example, the fictionalized and stereotyped works of Karl May have been enjoyed by generations of German youth, including Adolf Hitler, who loved "playing Indian" as a boy.[8] Undoubtedly most, if not all, of us have seen children hopping up and down, patting a hand against their mouths and yelling "woo-woo-woo," or raising one hand shoulder high and saying "how" or "ugh." The perpetuation of these and similar white-created "Indian" behaviors reflects the influence of peer socialization, schooling and movies. They mock Native cultural practices and demean Native people as subhumans, incapable of verbal communication.

James W. Sayre, M.D. and Robert F. Sayre, Ph.D., write of the origins of this activity in their article "American Children and the 'Children of Nature'":

With the crowded conditions of late 19th century cities, along with nostalgia over lost frontier simplicity and vanished Indian glory, playing Indian therefore became a recommended form of recreation for white children. In 1902, the *Ladies Home Journal* began a series of articles by Ernest Thompson Seton, the nature writer, in a "new Department on 'American Woodcraft' for Boys." The series was so popular that "tribes" of "Seton's Indians" and "Woodcraft Indians" sprang up, and Seton responded to requests for reprints of the articles by republishing them in a pamphlet entitled *How to Play Injun*. In 1906, he enlarged his material into a small book, *The Birchbark Roll of the Woodcraft Indians*. In England, Sir Robert Baden-Powell . . . had meanwhile been building the Boy Scout Movement, an out-growth of his promotion of "scouting" as a military tactic. Seton's "Woodcraft Indians" merged with Baden-Powell's Boy Scouts and the Boy Scouts of America was born.[9]

The YMCA sponsors a nationwide parent–child program called the Y-Indian Guide and Y-Indian Princess program, in which fathers and sons/daughters take on "Indian" names, form themselves into "tribes," meet every other week and "play Indian." In 1975, the Executive Committee of the Congress of American Indians passed a resolution condemning "this activity of the YMCA or any organization" and called on such organizations "to stop and put an end to such activities deemed offensive by Indian people." An analysis of the YMCA program by Native people attacked specifically the abuse of sacred aspects of certain Native cultures. A more general charge was made about the concept of "playing Indian" itself:

> Many Indian people felt that . . . taking Indian names, tribal names, wearing head-bands, feathers and in general pretending like they are Indian is offensive and mocking the Indian person. This would not happen with any other group for you wouldn't have a parent/child group pretending like they are Catholic, Jews, Chinese, Blacks or Protestants for a night every two weeks. If there was an understanding of Indians, there would be no psychological need to imitate them.[10]

The most frequent occurrences of "Indian" imagery we found in our sample were illustrations of children "playing Indian," or becoming "Indian" simply by putting on a feather. There is nothing harmful in children dressing up to play clowns, witches, cowboys, or pilots. These are *roles* that can be taken on by people of any racial, religious or national group. *But being a Native American is not a role.* Native people are human beings with diverse cultures and distinctive national identities. Being Lakota (Sioux), Hopi, Navajo, etc., is an integral aspect of their human condition. To suggest that other people can *become* "Indian" simply by donning a feather is to trivialize Native people's diversity and to assault their humanity.

3. Animals As "Indians"

In 1972 the National American Indian Council protested an insulting act at a Las Vegas casino in which monkeys, gorillas, orangutans and chimpanzees were dressed as "Indians." Yet children's book continue to perpetuate the same insults. In this category we found 12 books containing illustrations of animals as "Indians," the most *de*humanizing of all portrayals, for it suggests that Native people are not fully human, but rather are creatures of fantasy such as witches or elves.

The character in *Clifford's Halloween* (Bridwell, 1967) is trying to decide what her dog can be for Halloween. One choice is an "Indian." The accompanying illustration shows the dog wearing a headdress, blanket, and "war-paint," with a pipe in his mouth.

Maurice Sendak's *Alligators All Around: An Alphabet* (1962) has two alligators "imitating Indians" under the letter "I." One, wearing a headdress, looks rather fierce as it brandishes a tomahawk and does the one-leg-in-the-air-stance. The other takes a stoic pose, eyes closed while puffing a pipe. The pose, the headband and two feathers, and the pipe all share a remarkable resemblance to the child on the cover of Sendak's *What Do You Do, Dear?*, mentioned earlier. The latter book has an illustration of a dog with headband and feather, looking out from a tipi. Similarly, *Whose Hat Is That?* (Kessler, 1974) shows a cat standing beside a tipi and wearing five feathers.

The Stupids Step Out (Allard and Marshall, 1974) contains five illustrations showing a dog wearing a headdress. Another of Marshall's books, *George and Martha Encore* (1973), is about two hippos. "George decided to dress up as an Indian" to fool Martha. Of course, his loin cloth, headdress and tomahawk do not fool the discerning Martha, who asks, "Why are you wearing that Indian costume?" However, when she sees that his feelings are hurt, she claims she only recognized him because of his bright smiling eyes. George felt much better, but one wonders how Native American children might feel reading the book (while probably not "dressed like an Indian"). The spider in *How Spider Saved Halloween* (Kraus, 1973) is having trouble disguising himself and has the same problem as George—he still looks like himself even when wearing a headband and feather.

Jenny's Birthday Book (Averill, 1954) is about a cat celebrating her birthday with cat-friends. One of them, Florio, "wears an Indian feather in honor of the birthday." A double-spread shows fifteen partying cats in a park. Fourteen are dancing while Florio, feather on head, *lurks* behind a tree. This image of stealthy, lurking "Indians" is another stereotype applied to Native Americans.

Richard Scarry's *Please and Thank You Book* (1973) has thirty-three baby chicks on the title page—one wears a headdress and another a single feather. His *Storybook Dictionary* (1974) contains a buffalo named Chief Five Cents and his daughter, Penny. While Chief Five Cents is never labeled an "Indian," he wears buckskin clothing and a large headdress, lives in a "smokey tepee," and carries bow and arrows. Scarry's *Best Word Book Ever* (1974) has, among numerous animal characters, three dressed as "Indians": papa bear is named "Indian," momma bear "squaw," and baby bear "papoose." Other bears are shown as "gold miner," "cowboy," "sheriff," and "policemen." "Indian" wears buckskins and a large headdress, "squaw" wears a buckskin dress, single feather and "papoose" strapped to her back. *ABC Word Book* (1971) contains a bear wearing a headdress ("Wild Bill Hiccup"); a befeathered, buckskinned cat labeled "squaw" (who carries a befeathered kitten on her back); and a mouse in a tipi.

What's Wrong with Animals As "Indians"? A student in a New York City public school wrote to Richard Scarry about the "Indian" bear in *Best Word Book Ever*:

> I did not like when you drew the Indian like a bear. Indians do not look like a bear and Indians do not put feathers on the heads, only on special occasions.

Scarry's response is enlightening:

> I am sorry that you don't like the Indian I drew in the *Best Word Book Ever*. I drew him as a bear because I LIKE bears and I LIKE Indians. Have you noticed that, in all my books there are only animals.
>
> The Doctor in my books is Dr. Lion. And I drew him as a lion. I have a family of pigs. And a family of bears. A policeman who is a dog. And all my firemen are pigs. . . .
>
> All of this because I prefer to draw animals. It's more fun for me. Everyone of these characters are real to me. I consider them friends. And if one of them does something a little giddy, like wearing his Indian feathers when there is no ceremony, he just does it because he feels proud to wear them. Or he does it just for fun.

Scarry claims that in his books there are "*only animals*," yet states "I am sorry that you don't like *the Indian* I drew," revealing a confusion of terms that is precisely the problem. While doctor, police officer and firefighters are all *roles* to be applied in fantasy to animals, "Indian" animals cannot be written off as "no harm done." Whether Scarry LIKES "Indians" or not is beside the point. One assumes he also LIKES Asian people, yet thankfully there are no animals in his books dressed in stereotyped outfits and labeled "Jap," "Coolie" or other terms as derogatory as "squaw."

4. Illustrations Supposedly Depicting Native Americans

A number of books without any *thematic* connection to Native American include illustrations supposedly depicting them.

Ho for a Hat! (Smith and Chermayeff, 1964) shows an "Indian" and his "Indian War-Bonnet" with this verse:

> See how he comes
> To the beat of the drums—
> Pow-wow-pom—
> Fire in his eyes
> Like the sun at sunrise,
> He dances around a feathered pole.
> His moccasins pound
> The dusty ground;
> He shakes a long stick, He rattles a rattle,
> And calls on the Sun for courage in battle.
> And the Indian, wearing his Indian War-Bonnet,
> Looks like that . . .

This verse belittles and mocks Native American religious and cultural traditions and implies the superiority of Euro-American religious and cultural practices. It seems to suggest a Sun Dance. Many Native American religious beliefs and world views are based on an understanding that all things are of the Creator, and therefore sacred—including the sun. Thus a dance with the sun as a central theme is a *spiritual* ceremony directed to the Creator, and not simple worship of the sun as suggested in the verse. When books show children doing "Indian" dances (or teachers have students do "Indian" dances) it is often insulting to native cultures, and is frequently sacrilegious. Just as books and schools would not have children play at High mass or Yom Kippur services, respect should be given to Native American religious ceremonies.

What Can You Do with a Pocket?, mentioned earlier as perpetuating the notion that a child with a feather can become an "Indian," also contains an illustration supposedly portraying Native Americans. Outside two tipis, "Indian" women—one with a baby on her back—sit around a fire, preparing food. A man sits by the fire, smoking a pipe. While aspects of the scene reflect traditional cultural practices of some Native nations, the image is stereotypic. And the verse that accompanies it is demeaning. "Walk tall, Indian brave. Cook meat by the campfire, Indian maid. Strap onto my back and sleep tight, little papoose." The image is of people of the past, suggesting to children that "Indians" do not exist in the present or that, if they do, they are less "Indian" today. Also, "brave," "papoose" and "squaw" are considered derogatory terms by most Native people.

Most of the books with illustrations supposedly depicting Native people manifest the same stereotypic treatment. *Elvira Everything* (Asch, 1970) is a fantasy unconnected to Native people. One illustration shows people wearing national dress from various countries. One has a feather on her head and carries a baby on her back. The baby wears a headdress. Similar illustrations are found in *The Christmas Tree Alphabet Book* (Mendoza and Bernadette, 1971) in which people around the world are shown celebrating Christmas. One illustration, captioned "Running Deer ties ribbons of red velvet," shows "Running Deer" with a feather in her hair and a baby on her back, standing outside a tipi and tying a ribbon around the neck of a deer. While many Native people *are* Christian and *do* celebrate Christmas, it is silliness to suggest they do so by standing outside a tipi, with a feather on their head, tying a red ribbon around a deer. If a book ignores the traditional religious beliefs of many Native people and chooses to show them celebrating Christmas, it should also ignore stereotypes and portray them as modern-day people.

Similar confusion between past and present exists in *The True Book of Communications* (Miner and Evans, 1960). A page discussing "SIGNS" is all in the present tense: "We *get* many messages without words. A friend *nods* his head, *smiles* or *waves* his hand to say HELLO . . . We *can tell* what kind of animal went by from his [sic] tracks in the sand or snow." While no mention is made of "Indian," the opposite page depicts a stereotyped "Indian" wearing moccasins, buckskins, headband and feather, and carrying a bow and arrows, following the tracks of an animal. The cover shows another "Indian," sending smoke-signals. And how did he start the fire? *Bennett Cerf's Book of Riddles* (1960) asks the question, "What is the best way to make a fire with two sticks?" And answers, "Make sure one of the sticks is a match." Innocent enough, but the illustrations show a befeathered "Indian" holding two sticks and then lighting the fire.

Cerf's *More Riddles* (1961) contains an image and verse that epitomize the detached nature of "Indian" imagery from the reality of Native people. "What has . . . Two legs like an Indian? Two eyes like an Indian? Two hands like an Indian? Looks just like an Indian? But is not an Indian?" The questions are accompanied by a headdressed, buckskinned, dancing caricatured "Indian." The answer to the riddle, on the next page, is "A picture of an Indian," and is illustrated with a child holding a picture of the same caricature. The "Indian" image in this and other books has no reality except as a white-created caricature of Native people, true only unto itself, and the answer to this riddle unwittingly reflects that fact.

Another riddle book is *Bill Adler's World's Worst Riddles and Jokes* (Malsberg, 1976). Q. "Why were the Indians the first people in North America?" A. "Because they had reservations." This is accompanied by a caricatured "Indian," with twelve feathers, standing before tipis and holding a sign reading "Massasoit Lodge, Reservations Necessary." A second riddle asks, "Why does an Indian really wear feathers in his hair? A. "To keep his wigwam." Here is another caricature with headdress and pipe.

Martha the Movie Mouse (Lobel, 1966) is a story about Martha—a mouse who lives in a movie theater:

> In wonder Martha watched the screen.
> She saw things she had never seen.
> Fierce Indians with painted faces
> Fought cowboys in great desert spaces.

The accompanying illustration shows an "Indian" on horseback, wearing a headdress, loincloth, moccasins and "warpaint," about to shoot an arrow at a cowboy. And, as expected, no suggestion is given that the "Indian" is fighting to protect his homeland.

The Circus in the Mist (Munari, 1969) is a fascinating book about a trip to the circus. The book was designed with various kinds of paper (including transparent), colors and cutout shapes, so that each page contains a part of the upcoming one, and leads ever closer to the circus. One page contains two "Indian" silhouettes. One—about to shoot an arrow—wears a large headdress; the second wears a single feather. The nonsensical caption reads, "The Indian is really from the next town and the little Indian boy is his uncle!"

Another book with illustrations based on shapes and colors is *Spectacles* (Raskin, 1968), the story of Iris and the images she saw before she acquired her eyeglasses. "Come and watch my Indian make funny faces," Iris says—and the illustration contains a figure with feather and tomahawk. But friend Chester sets Iris straight—the "Indian's" braids are part of a table cloth, the leather a TV antenna, the tomahawk a lamp, and the eyes—believe it or not—two cowboys on TV! While you may have to see it to believe it, the images work, mainly because our eyes and minds have been so conditioned to seeing certain shapes associated with "Indians."

Similar conditioning allows us to perceive the "Wild Indian" shape in *More Hand Shadows* (Bursill, 1971). While this book was originally published in the 1860's, its recent re-publication with this picture and caption is unwarranted. Another book of shapes is *Ed Emberley's Drawing Book of Faces* (1975) in which directions are provided on drawing shapes to produce an "Indian" face, two feathers and a headband.

5. Alphabet and Dictionary Books

"Indian" is so frequently found under the letter "I" that one wonders if there is a lack of other words beginning with that letter. Most of the same problems previously described in this article recur in the alphabet/dictionary books—stereotypic clothing, feathers and tomahawks; stomping, whooping and fierce poses. But two additional problems arise. The first is the objectification of Native peoples—treating them as objects rather than as human beings. No other group is similarly treated: the "I-Indian" is never followed by a "J-Jew" or a "P-Puerto Rican." Nor is it accompanied by an "I-Italian," even though the "I" in Indian and the "I" in Italian have the same sound. Rather, the "I-Indian" co-exists with *objects*—Igloos, Islands, Ink, etc. Not infrequently, "I-Indians" co-exists with Insects, a combination perhaps epitomized in *The Golden Picture Dictionary* (Ogle, Thoburn and Knight, 1976) which has two entries under the letter "I"— "Indians" and "Insects"—on facing pages. (The book also contains three pictures of white children "playing Indian," one of which appears on the "Contents" page, illustrating the letter "I.")

A second problem highlighted in alphabet and dictionary books is the anachronistic placement of past-tensed "Indians" with modern items or settings. Depictions of "Indians" living in tipis, dressed in buckskins, wearing headdress and "warpaint" are stereotypic not only because they generalize (e.g. "all Indians live(d) in tipis") but also because they confuse the *past* and present (tipis are rarely lived in today). For example, past-tensed, "I-Indians" eat *Ice* cream cones (*The Alphabet Book*, Eastman, 1974), walk around a modern city (*Applebet Story*, Barton, 1973), are shown with an electric *Iron* (*The Great Big Alphabet Picture Book with Lots of Words*, Hefter and Moskof, 1972) and are followed by an illustration of Satellites above the earth (*Everything: An Alphabet, Number, Reading, Counting and Color Identification Book*, Hefter and Moskof, 1971). These anachronisms can only lead to confusion and misconceptions about who Native Americans are and how they live and dress today.

My First Golden Dictionary (Reed, Osswald and Scarry, 1963) highlights the objectification, the past/present confusion, as well as the amalgamation of Native cultures into the white-created INDIAN. The cover portrays a one-leg-in-the-air, befeathered, tomahawk wielding "Indian" along with a fly, fish, rooster, boat, apple and crayon. Inside, accompanying an illustration of a buffalo, children read that "The buffalo *used to* roam the western plains." Five pages later, they read that "The Indian *lives* outdoors and *hunts* buffaloes." The accompanying illustration presents a grotesque caricature to children and the use of the present tense in the verse reinforces children's misconceptions of how Native people dress today (as well, one might add, how they dressed in the past). The verse could easily lead children to believe that all Native people hunted buffalo, rather than just those in the plains area. And it ignores the wide variety of housing developed by Native societies and suggests that the people lived "outdoors" in the wild.

But the "I-Indian," pervasive as it is, is not alone. Some alphabet books contain white-created "Indian" images under other letters. Children "play Indian," riddle and rhyme "Indian," and animals imitate "Indians" under many different letters of the alphabet:

"B"—*The Golden Picture Dictionary*—a two-page spread on Buildings shows a white boy wearing a headband and a feather, holding a tomahawk and dancing the "flamingo" outside a "tepee." Next to that illustration is one of a boy playing a cowboy inside a play fort, with three "Indian" figures attacking.

"C"—*Grosset Starter Picture Dictionary* (1976)—a canoe with a figure wearing a headband and three feathers.

"D"—*Richard Scarry's ABC Word Book*—a bulldozer, driven by a bear ("Wild Bill Hiccup") wearing a headdress and buckskins, is running amuck. "The dizzy, daffy, dopey bulldozer driver! What does he think he is doing? He is dangerous. He has knocked down the drugstore, and the druggist is good and mad."

"F"—*The Golden Picture Dictionary*—on a page about Feet and what we wear on them, "moccasins" is accompanied by a silhouette of a child wearing buckskins and headdress, carrying a bow and arrow, and holding a hand up to his mouth.

"F"—*Sugar and Spice: The ABC of Being a Girl*—Felicia Frances and her firm fast friend "play Indian."

"H"—*The Golden Picture Dictionary*—a page about Homes contains illustrations of an "adobe house," a "hogan," and a "tepee."

"I"—*Alligators All Around: An Alphabet*—two alligators "imitating Indians."

"I"—*Everything: An Alphabet, Number, Reading, Counting and Color Identification Book*—"nine strong and silent in the forest find the red-feathered indians."

"I"—*Richard Scarry's Best Word Book Ever*—mouse wearing a headdress and eating a large Ice cream cone.

"I"—*A for Angel, Beni Montresor's ABC Picture Stories* (1969)—"The Indian on Irma's Island"—headdressed, buckskinned "Indian" with hand to brow.

"I"—*Peter Piper's Alphabet* (Brown, 1959)—Peter Piper's looking at a wooden "Indian." The accompanying verse:

> Inigo Impey itched for an Indian Image:
> Did Inigo Impey itch for an Indian Image?

If Inigo Impey itched for an Indian Image,
Where's the Indian Image Inigo Impey itched for?

"I"—*The Alphabet Book*—"Indian" [wearing headdress, buckskins] with ice cream.

"I"—*The Great Big Alphabet Picture Book with Lots of Words*—a grotesque, war-painted, befeathered, buckskinned "Indian," along with an iron, igloo, infant, inchworm, ink and ivy.

"I"—*The Golden Picture Dictionary*—a page of "Indians" facing a page of Insects.

"I"—*The Happy Golden ABC* (Allen, 1975)—befeathered, buckskinned "Indian" sits on an igloo writing with ink.

"I"—*The Little Golden ABC* (DeWitt, 1976)—headdressed, buckskinned "Indian" with tomahawk stands on an iceberg eating an ice cream.

"I"—*Applebet Story*—headdressed, buckskinned "Indian" picks up an apple from a city side-walk.

"I"—*Zag: A Search Through the Alphabet* (Tallon, 1976)—an enormous, headdressed "Indian" wraps his arms around an island. "When I looked around I was on an island surrounded by an Indian."

"J"—*Applebet Story*—the "indian" tosses the apple to a Juggler.

"P"—*Teddy Bears ABC* (Gretz, 1975)—a bear wearing a headdress is "Painting a Picture" of a tipi and an airplane.

"Q"—*Richard Scarry's ABC Word Book*—"The Queen is playing croquet with her friends," one of whom is a cat wearing a single feather, headband and buckskin dress and carrying a baby—wearing a single feather—on her back. The cat is labeled "squaw."

"R"—*Teddy Bears ABC*—the two bears, carrying the remnants of the headdress, are "Running in the Rain."

"R"–*The Christmas Tree Alphabet Book*—Running Deer.

"T"—*Curious George Learns the Alphabet* (Rey, 1963)—"The small 't' is a tomahawk. George [a monkey] had a toy tomahawk. It was a tiny one. He took it along when he played Indian. He also had a tepee—an Indian tent." George is shown wearing three feathers and doing the one-leg-in-the-air-dance.

"T"—*Richard Scarry's ABC Word Book*—a mouse is sticking its head out of a "tepee."

"W"—*Zoophabets* (Tallon, 1971)—"WOB lives in Wooden Indians, Eats wampum, wigwams, heap big whitefish, woolen blankets, wagon wheels, warpaint."

"Z"—*The Christmas Tree Alphabet Book*—befeathered "Indian" in a scene showing Zachariah pinning up stockings.

"Z"—*Richard Scarry's ABC Word Book*—"bulldozer" still being driven by bear wearing headdress.

6. Counting Books

Counting books frequently include "Indian" imagery, particularly under the number "10," along with the rhyme "Ten little, nine little, eight little Indians . . ." This well known verse not only objectifies Native people as *things* to count, but also romanticizes the genocidal destruction of Native nations from the time Columbus arrived in the Americas. Estimated to have been at least 10 to 12 million in what later became the continental United States, the Native population was decimated to an estimated 232,000 by the turn of this century. In order to better understand why many Native people object to this rhyme, consider present-day German youth reciting, "Ten little, nine little, eight little Jews . . ." This comparison is significant, since Hitler not only was fascinated by "cowboys and Indians" as a child, but told associates that his genocidal plans against the Jewish people were molded in part on his admiration of the practices of the United States against Native people, particularly in forcing them onto reservations and starving them.[11]

Counting Rhymes (Seiden, 1959) contains the verse "Ten Little Indians" and is illustrated by rows of look-a-like faces of "Indians," each with a headband and feather. *Play on Words* (Provensen and Provensen, 1972) is not actually a counting book, but one illustration depicts 10 sullen, shifty-eyed "Indians" along with the words, "X means 10. How many are X little Indians?" *Numbers, Signs and Pictures: A First Number Book* (Robinson and Murdocca, 1975) contains repeated images of a befeathered "Indian" astride a totem pole. *Ten What? A Mystery Counting Book* (Hoban and Selig, 1974) innovates. Children reading this book get to count "ten Oriental acrobats," after they have counted six mice dressed as "Indians" and six tipis. *1 2 3 for the Library* (Little, 1974) has a picture of a girl with feather, headband and buckskins, dancing the one-leg-in-the-air-step under the number eight, while Dick Bruna's *I Can Count* (1975) contains a figure wearing a headdress with eight feathers.

Everything: An Alphabet, Number, Reading, Counting and Color Identification Book (Hefter and Moskof, 1971) teaches all it purports, plus stereotypes. On page nine, children learn the letter "I" and the number "9," and read, count *and* color-identify nine "strong and silent in the forest find the red-feathered indians." They see these nine "red-feathered [and war-painted] indians" lurking behind trees and in tall grass. *Hailstones and Halibut Bones* (O'Neill and Weisgard, 1961) merely teaches color identification—and stereotypes. "What Is Red?" Among the answers, "Red is an Indian." This is illustrated with a cigar-store "Indian" that is red from headdress to toe.

The Marcel Marceau Counting Book (Mendoza and Green, 1971) has photographs of Marceau wearing assorted headgear and miming a related behavior. Under number 19, he "is an Indian," wearing a long red, white and blue headdress, and shooting a bow and arrow.

7. Hat Books

Books on hats are another category that often include "Indian" imagery, primarily inauthentic representations of headdresses. *Whose Hat Is That?* (Kessler, 1974) includes a childlike drawing of a headdress with the words, "Lots of feathers in this hat. Whose hat is that? An Indian Chief's. Boom . . . Boom . . . Boom . . . Boom . . . Pow!" The opposite page depicts two white children wearing headdresses and warpaint and running around a tipi. The caption reads, "Here come the little Indians now."

Ho for a Hat! (Smith and Chermayeff, 1964) includes a cartoon-like head in a headdress, along with a verse (discussed in section 4) which ends, "And the Indian, wearing his Indian War-Bonnet/Looks like that . . ." *Hurrah for Hats* (Wagner and Eckart, 1962) includes an illustration of a cowboy trying to lasso a "Chief," who is wearing a headdress and carrying a tomahawk and bow. The introduction states, "Here are hats as children know them—ridiculous, useful, fascinating, revealing and even magic." One must wonder which of the above describes Native headdresses.

Because so many books use headdresses to project "Indian" imagery, some discussion of headdress is in order. *Jasper and the Giant* (Brennan, 1970)—epitomizing the use of headdress for purely decorative purposes—is a book about a lonely child and his fantasized playmate. Both wear enormous, colorful headdresses in every illustration, even though no mention is made of "Indians" or of headdress in the *entire* story.

What's Wrong with This Use of Headdress? That ever-present headdress, which is so uniformly applied by white society to *all* Native American cultures, resembles to varying degrees the headdress of the Lakota (Sioux) and some other nations of the Great Plains area. If it *is* supposed to be a Lakota headdress, did the illustrators *accurately* portray the materials and design of a Lakota headdress, the number and types of feathers, the sacred symbolism of each part and of the whole? And if the illustrator understood and carefully reproduced all this, then why is the headdress being worn by an animal or a child at play? Traditionally, headdresses were only worn in ceremonies by those people who had earned that privilege and honor. How would an illustration of a dog wearing a mitre and carrying a crucifix in its mouth be received? Ceremonial headdresses and pipes have similar religious and cultural significance to many Native peoples.

WHAT PURPOSE DO THESE DISTORTIONS SERVE?

Children's books are not merely frivolous "entertainment." They are part of a society's general culture. U.S. culture is white-dominated and racist. Children's books in the U.S. reflect our society, while at the same time reinforcing and perpetuating its racism. The ideology of racism against native Americans developed in colonial times to justify the physical destruction of Native peoples and nations, in order for Europeans to take over their lands. The ideology was later refined to justify the genocidal policies and the treaty abrogations of the U.S., as land continued to be taken away. As the Friars note in relation to movies, "By explicitly justifying the genocide perpetrated by our forefathers, Hollywood utilizes our ignorance to enforce our egoism."[12]

But much more is involved in the perpetuation of stereotypes about Native Americans today than white "egoism" about the nation's past. The struggle of Native nations to regain their sovereignty, independence and self-determination against the encroachment of the U.S. is as real today as it was in the past. The

land base held by Native nations today contains sizable amounts of valuable resources which the U.S. wants as much as it wanted the gold, coal, iron, copper,
timber and land itself one hundred years ago. The "energy crisis" has put a pre-
mium on these resources—coal, gas, oil, uranium—which abound on the remaining reservation and treaty land of Native nations today. The desire of expanding urban populations in the Southwest for land and water is continuing the
historical abuse of Native nations' rights and property. Meanwhile, across the
country, Native peoples are increasing their struggles to regain treaty lands and
rights illegally taken from them. ⟩ 75, 6

Whatever "positive feelings" or attempts at "understanding" underlie programs
like the YMCA Indian Guide and Indian Princess, they reflect romantic notions
that lack any connection to the reality of Native people. Genuine interest in the
uniqueness and diversity of native cultures can be met by studying the cultures,
without having to "play" them. And, genuine concern for Native people can best
be met not by "playing" them, but by actively confronting the policies and practices of the United States which directly oppress Native people.

It is within this context that one must examine racism in children's books. To
the extent that Native people continue to become inhuman, objectified "Indians"
in the minds of non-Native American children; to the extent that these children
believe that Native Americans are people of the past or creatures of fantasy; to the
extent that these children's attitude is that "all Indians are alike"; and to the extent that these children are taught to fear "Indians"—to that extent continued aggression against Native peoples is supported.

(As long as citizens of the United States are conditioned *not* to see Native
people as human beings with human aspirations, national interests, and cultural integrity, with a long history of struggle to maintain their treaty rights
guaranteed by the U.S. constitution and by international law—then the citizenry of today, like the citizenry of 100 years ago and 200 years ago, will pas-
sively condone or actively support continued aggression by the U.S. against
Native peoples.

Alvin Josephy writes: "If Indians are still about as real as wooden sticks to
many non-Indians, the facts concerning their present-day status in the societies of
the Americas are even less known."[13] The misperception of *who* Native Americans
are has a direct relationship to the misperception of their present-day situation.
One reinforces the other. The children's books in this study are part of the problem. Educators and parents, illustrators and editors, can be part of the solution. 76

GUIDELINES FOR ILLUSTRATORS AND EDITORS

(While there are frequent illustrations of non-Native children "playing Indian," we
did not find a *single* book in which Native American children were portrayed as
classmates or playmates of these children. Sensitive and skilled illustrators should

learn to portray a multi-racial group—including Native children—without relying on feathers. Editors should *insist* on this.

Accurate representations of *many* Native American cultures should appear in children's books. All children benefit from knowledge of cultural diversity. But illustrations must be drawn with knowledgeable respect and accuracy. The generalized use of "Indian" must give way to clear identification of national origin and accurate portrayal of clothing, housing, and lifestyles of the Lakota (Sioux), Navajo, Cherokee, or other Native peoples both as they existed at varying times in the past and as they have evolved to the present. If in-house expertise is lacking, editors should pay Native people for consultation.

GUIDELINES FOR PUBLISHERS AND TEACHERS

Avoid generalizations such as "Indians lived in tipis" when such cultural practices were not general among Native people but specific to certain cultures. One would not say that, "Europeans lived in windmills."

Avoid phrases such as "Mohawk Indians" which are as redundant as saying "French Europeans." Use instead "Mohawks" or "Mohawk people."

Avoid use of the terms "Indians," "Native Americans" or "Native peoples" if referring only to *one* people, such as the Seneca or the Cherokee.

If referring to Native peoples generally, use "Native peoples" and "Native Americans" as well as "Indian people."

If a story contains both Native Americans and Euro-Americans, do not use "Indians" to refer to the former and "people" to refer to the latter. Use "Indians" and "whites" or "Native people" and "white people."

Avoid terms such as "squaw," "brave" and "papoose." "Woman," "man" and "baby" are accurate.

Avoid stereotypic portrayals of Native people as fierce, violent, stealthy, stoic, etc.

Avoid phrases such as "acting like a bunch of wild Indians," "Indian giver," "going on the warpath," "let's have a powwow," "sitting Indian style" (cross-legged), "walking Indian file," "paleface," or "redskin."

Do not dress up animals, or children, as "Indians."

Do not use Native people as objects to be counted or alphabetized.

NOTES

1. U.S. Senate Subcommittee on Indian Education, *Indian Education: A National Tragedy—A National Challenge*, 1969, p. 21.

2. Alvin Josephy, *The Indian Heritage of America*, New York: Bantam Books, 1969, p. 3.

3. Michael Dorris, *Native Americans: 500 Years After*, New York: Thomas Y. Crowell Co., 1975, p. 4.

4. Jack Forbes, *Native Americans of California and Nevada*, Healdsburg, CA: Naturegraph Publishers, 1969, p. 134.

5. Ralph and Natasha Friar, *The Only Good Indian: The Hollywood Gospel*, New York: Drama Book Specialists, 1971, pp. 1–2.

6. Mary Gloyne Byler, *American Indian Authors for Young Readers*, New York: Association on American Indian Affairs, 1973, pp. 5–11.

7. Kenneth Clark, *Prejudice and Your Child*. Boston: Beacon Press, 1963, p. 25.

8. John Toland, *Adolf Hitler*, Garden City, N.Y.: Doubleday & Co., Inc., 1976, Vol. 1, pp. 12, 14–15.

9. James W. Sayre and Robert F. Sayre, "American Children and the 'Children of Nature,'" *American Journal of Diseases of Children*, Vol. 130, July 1976, p. 722.

10. Beatty Brasch, "A Review of the Y-Indian Guide and Y-Indian Princess Program," Lincoln, Nebraska: University of Nebraska-Lincoln, unpublished paper, pp. 38–39.

11. Toland, op. cit., Vol. 11, p. 802.

12. Friar, op. cit., p. 2.

13. Josephy, op. cit., p. 8.

PICTURE BOOKS USED IN THE STUDY

Adler, Bill. *World's Worst Riddles and Jokes*. Malsberg, ed., illus. Grosset & Dunlap, 1976.

Alexander, Martha. *Blackboard Bear*. Alexander, Martha, illus. Dial Press, 1969.

Allard, Harry. *The Stupids Step Out*. Marshall, James, illus. Houghton Mifflin Co., 1974.

Allen, Joan. *The Happy Golden ABC*. Allen, Joan, illus. Golden Press, 1975.

Amoss, Berthe. *Tom in the Middle*. Amoss, Berthe, illus. Harper & Row, 1968.

Asch, Frank. *Elvira Everything*. Asch, Frank, illus. Harper & Row, 1970.

Averill, Esther. *Jenny's Birthday Book*. Averill, Esther, illus. 1954.

Banks, Marjorie Ann. *How We Celebrate Our Fall Holidays*. Hawkinson, Lucy & John, illus. Benefic Press, 1961.

Barton, Byron. *Applebet Story*. Barton, Byron, illus. Viking Press, 1973.

Brennan, Nicholas. *Jasper and the Giant*. Brennan, Nicholas, illus. Holt, Rinehart & Winston, 1970.

Bridwell, Norman. *Clifford's Halloween*. Bridwell, Norman, illus. Scholastic Book Services, 1967.

Brown, Marcia. *Peter Piper's Alphabet*. Brown, Marcia, illus. Charles Scribner's Sons, 1959.

Bruna, Dick. *I Can Count*. Bruna, Dick, illus. Two Continents Publishing Group, Ltd., 1976.

Buckley, Helen E. *The Little Boy and the Birthdays*. Galdone, Paul, illus. Lothrop, Lee and Shepard, 1965.

Bursill, Henry. *More Hand Shadows*. Dover Publications, Inc., 1971.

Carton, Lonnie C. *Daddies*. Jacobs, Leslie, illus. Random House, 1963.

Cerf, Bennett A. *Bennett Cerf's Book of Riddles*. Random House, 1960.

———. *More Riddles*. Random House, 1961.

Chorao, Kay. *The Repair of Uncle Toe*. Chorao, Kay, illus. Farrar, Straus & Giroux, 1972.

Cohen, Miriam. *Will I Have a Friend?* Hoban, Lillian, illus. Macmillan Co., 1967.

Cole, William. *What's Good for a Five-Year-Old?* Sorel, Edward, illus. Holt, Rinehart & Winston, 1969.

————. *What's Good for a Four-Year-Old?* Ungerer, Tomi, illus. Holt, Rinehart, 1967.

DeWitt, Cornelius. *The Little Golden ABC.* DeWitt, Cornelius, illus. Golden Press, 1976.

Eastman, Phillip D. *The Alphabet Book.* Eastman, Phillip D., illus. Random House, 1974.

Emberly, Ed. *Drawing Book of Faces.* Emberly, Ed, illus. Little, Brown & Co., 1975.

Fitzhugh, Louise, and Sandra Scoppettone. *Bang Bang You're Dead.* Fitzhugh, Louise, illus. Harper & Row, 1969.

Fringuello, Judith. *The Day Busy Buzzy Stopped Being Busy.* Fringuello, Judith, illus. Troll Associates, 1970.

Gretz, Susanna. *Teddy Bears ABC.* Gretz, Susanna, illus. Follett Publishing Co., 1975.

Grossett Starter Picture Dictionary. Grossett & Dunlap, 1976.

Hefter, Richard, and Martin S. Moskof. *Everything: An Alphabet, Number, Reading, Counting & Color Identification Book.* Hefter, Richard, illus. Parents Magazine Press, 1971.

————. *The Great Big Alphabet Picture Book with Lots of Words.* Hefter, Richard, illus. Grosset & Dunlap, 1972.

Hitte, Kathryn. *Boy, Was I Mad!* Mayer, Mercer, illus. Parents Magazine Press, 1969.

Hoban, Russell. *Ten What? A Mystery Counting Book.* Selig, Sylvie, illus. Charles Scribner's Sons, 1974.

Joslin, Sesyle. *What Do You Do, Dear?* Sendak, Maurice, illus. Addison-Wesley Publishing Co. Inc., 1961.

Kahn, Joan. *You Can't Catch Me.* Bridgeman, Elizabeth, illus. Harper & Row, 1976.

Kessler, Leonard. *Whose Hat Is That?* Grosset & Dunlap, 1974.

Kraus, Robert. *How Spider Saved Halloween.* Kraus, Robert, illus. Parents Magazine Press, 1973.

Lipkind, William, and Nicholas Mordvinoff. *Russet & the Two Reds.* Mordvinoff, Nicholas, illus. Harcourt, Brace & World, Inc., 1962.

————. *The Two Reds.* Mordvinoff, Nicholas, illus. Harcourt, Brace & World, Inc., 1950.

Little, Mary E. *1 2 3 for the Library.* Little, Mary E., illus. Atheneum, 1974.

Lobel, Arnold. *Martha the Movie Mouse.* Lobel, Arnold, illus. Harper & Row, 1966.

Lystad, Mary. *The Halloween Parade.* Szekeres, Cyndy, illus. G. P. Putnam & Sons, 1973.

Marshall, James. *George and Martha Encore.* Marshall, James, illus. Houghton Mifflin Co., 1973.

McGinley, Phyllis. *Sugar and Spice: The ABC of Being a Girl.* Browning, Colleen, illus. Franklin Watts, Inc., 1960.

Mendoza, George. *The Christmas Tree Alphabet Book.* Watts, Bernadette, illus. World Publishing Co., 1971.

————. *The Marcel Marceau Counting Book.* Green, Milton H., photographer. Doubleday & Co., 1971.

Merriam, Eve. *What Can You Do with a Pocket?* Sherman, Harriet, illus. Alfred A. Knopf, 1964.

Miner, Irene S. *The True Book of Communication.* Miner, Irene and Evans, Katherine, illus. Childrens Press, 1960.

Montresor, Beni. *A for Angel.* Montresor, Beni, illus. Alfred A. Knopf, 1969.

Munari, Bruno. *The Circus in the Mist.* Munari, Bruno, illus. World Publishing Co., 1969.

Ogle, Lucille, and Tina Thoburn. *The Golden Picture Dictionary.* Knight, Hillary, illus. Golden Press, 1976.

O'Neill, Mary. *Hailstones and Halibut Bones—Adventures in Color.* Weisgard, Leonard, illus. Doubleday & Co., 1961.

Petersham, Maud, and Miska Petersham. *The Rooster Crows: A Book of American Rhymes & Jingles*. Petersham, Maud and Petersham, Miska, illus. Macmillan Co., 1971.

Politi, Leo. *Little Leo*. Politi, Leo, illus. Charles Scribner's Sons, 1951.

Provensen, Alice, and Martin Provensen. *Play on Words*. Provensen, Alice and Provensen, Martin, illus. Random House, 1972.

Raskin, Ellen. *Spectacles*. Raskin, Ellen, illus. Atheneum, 1968.

Reed, Mary, and Edith Osswald. *My First Golden Dictionary*. Scarry, Richard, illus. Golden Press, 1963.

Rey, H. A. *Curious George Learns the Alphabet*. Rey, H. A., illus. Houghton Mifflin Co., 1963.

Robinson, Shari. *Numbers, Signs & Pictures: A First Number Book*. Murdocca, Sal, illus. Platt & Munk, 1975.

Scarry, Richard. *Richard Scarry's ABC Word Book*. Scarry, Richard, illus. Random House, 1971.

———. *Richard Scarry's Best Word Book Ever*. Scarry, Richard, illus. Golden Press, 1974.

———. *Richard Scarry's Please & Thank You Book*. Scarry, Richard, illus. Random House, 1973.

———. *Richard Scarry's Storybook Dictionary*. Scarry, Richard, illus. Golden Press, 1974.

Seiden, Art. *Counting Rhymes*. Seiden, Art, illus. Grosset & Dunlap, 1959.

Sendak, Maurice. *Alligators All Around: An Alphabet*. Sendak, Maurice, illus. Harper & Row, 1962.

Smith, William J. *Ho for a Hat!* Chermayeff, Ivan, illus. Atlantic-Little, Brown, 1964.

Steig, William. *CDB*. Steig, William, illus. Windmill Books & E. P. Dutton, 1968.

Stevenson, Robert L. *A Child's Garden of Verses*. Fujikawa, Gyo, illus. Grosset & Dunlap, 1977.

Tallon, Robert. *Zag: A Search Through the Alphabet*. Tallon, Robert, illus. Holt, Rinehart & Winston, 1976.

———. *Zoophabets*. Tallon, Robert, illus. Bobbs-Merrill, 1971.

Viorst, Judith. *I'll Fix Anthony*. Lobel, Arnold, illus. Harper & Row, 1969.

Wagner, Peggy. *Hurrah for Hats*. Eckart, Frances, illus. Childrens Press, 1962.

Williams, Jay, and Winifred Lubell. *I Wish I Had Another Name*. Atheneum, 1962.

Wiseman, Bernard. *Halloween with Morris and Boris*. Wiseman, Bernard, illus. Dodd, Mead & Co., 1975.

Zolotow, Charlotte. *If It Weren't for You*. Schecter, Ben, illus. Harper & Row, 1966.

The Sign of the Beaver:
The Problem and the Solution

Sanda Cohen

The Sign of the Beaver is required reading in many elementary schools in the United States. Here is how one New Jersey teacher incorporated the novel, one she considered problematic, into her fifth-grade curriculum.

THE PROBLEM

For sixty years students at a New Jersey private school studied U.S. history using a textbook and chronological approach. They read a chapter, answered questions listed at the end, and memorized dates and names. The highlight of this curriculum approach culminated in a social studies fair held at the end of the year. After writing a research paper on a famous person in American history (not necessarily related to the era they had studied), the students attended the fair costumed as "their" person, acting out their historical parts before the faculty, other students, and the parents. The students loved the fair, and the school considered it the most successful aspect of the social studies curriculum.

Five years ago teachers decided to rewrite the social studies curriculum and to incorporate many of the more exciting aspects of the fair into the daily curriculum. The fifth grade team developed an experiential, theme-oriented, integrated curriculum, including eight field trips and an overnight campout. Teachers selected a new and less traditional textbook and a large selection of fiction related to American history. The result was a new and intellectually stimulating approach to American history. Fifth graders studied the development of the original thirteen American colonies by focusing on the history of New Jersey. As a member of the fifth grade team, I took part in the campout and field trips to various colonial sites designed to help the students understand the experience of the early colonial settlers.

After the field trips, the trouble started. The entire fifth grade began a thematic unit based on *The Sign of the Beaver,* a novel by Elizabeth George Speare that was awarded a 1983 Newbery Honor Book by the American Library Association and the Scott O'Dell Award for Historical Fiction. In 1989, Speare captured the Laura

81

Ingalls Wilder Award administered by the American Library Association. Given every three years to an author or illustrator who has made a lasting contribution to children's literature, this award honored Speare for *The Sign of the Beaver* as well as her other works. Recommended for classroom use by many well-known and well-respected publications, such as the *Horn Book* (1984), *Instructor* (March 1990), and *The Web: Wonderfully Exciting Books* (Winter 1984), the novel is also on videocassette, available through Random House Video, Newbery Video Collection. An illustrated version of the book is meant as an enrichment program to "help students to follow the plot, to visualize characters and setting and to practice important listening skills."[1]

The Sign of the Beaver is a story about Matt, a twelve-year old boy who leaves Quincy, Massachusetts, in 1768 with his father, ostensibly to build a homestead in the area of the Penobscot River in Maine. That summer Matt's father returned to Massachusetts to pick up his wife, daughter, and a baby born after Matt and his father had left for Maine. During his father's absence Matt was left alone in Maine and in a series of misadventures, Matt's rifle was stolen, his family's supply of flour lost to a bear, and his life almost ended by a swarm of bees. As a result of these adventures, he met Saknis, an Indian belonging to an unspecified tribe, and Saknis' grandson, Attean.

My students began to read the book and to write reflectively about the reading in their reading logs each night. Weekly vocabulary lessons were based on words taken from the text. Each night I chose a different word from the novel and the students were required to write a paragraph using the word as it related to their own lives. However, as we progressed in our classroom discussions, certain elements of the story began to disturb me; I was not sure what was nagging at me until page 74. There Attean kills a bear and tells Matt that the work of butchering the bear is "squaw work." Although I read the book before it was assigned to the students, I had never noticed the use of that word before. Now it struck me immediately that this obviously pejorative label would require many discussions about stereotypes and the way that stereotypes are accidentally reinforced, sometimes by well-meaning writers, teachers, parents and others who influence the way children view the world.

The worst was yet to come. This unit culminated with "The Sign of the Beaver Day," during which students were requested to dress either as "settlers" or as "Indians." No guidance was given to help them dress with any authenticity. (Although the school's library housed books that would have been helpful, I am not sure that any student actually used them for research.) After the students and faculty proceeded to the school brook, they participated in four different activities: writing treaties, storytelling, drawing, and games. The faculty made a great effort to be authentic about what it was teaching, and research was done to be sure that Indian ways were respected. But for me there was one overriding issue: I could not allow my class to dress up as Indians without feeling that I had done something wrong. Although I knew that in the previous year "The Sign of the Beaver Day" had been a huge success, I did not believe that the students' enjoyment justified the blatant stereotyping of American Indians. As Robert B. Moore and Arlene Hirschfelder state in *American Indian Stereotypes in the World Of Children: A Reader and Bibliography*:

> Genuine interest in the uniqueness and diversity of Native cultures can be met by studying the cultures, without having to "play" them. And genuine concern for the Native people can best be met not by playing them, but by actively confronting the policies and practices of the United States which directly oppress Native people.[2]

Further:

> . . . one cannot become a Native American by donning feathers, fringed buckskin, and moccasins because a Native person is not an occupation or a role to be played. It is a state of being, an ethnic identity. Having children dress up and play Indians encourages them to think Native Americans are nothing more than a playtime activity rather than an identity that is often fraught with economic deprivation, discrimination, gross injustice, and powerlessness.[3]

Because I agreed, I simply could not countenance students dressing up in "Indian" costumes at this time or in the future. This meant I had to change the way this unit was handled.

THE SOLUTION

After reading and rereading *The Sign of the Beaver* with great care, many more things bothered me. From the beginning, the reader becomes persuaded that the Indians did terrible things to white people as a matter of course. Matt thinks to himself: "His father had been assured by the proprietors that this new settlement would be safe. Since the last treaty with the tribes, there had not been an attack reported in this part of Maine. Still, one could not forget all those horrid tales."[4] As a Minnesota League of Women Voters study points out: "A distorted image of Indians as war-like has prevailed throughout American history. Indians defending their land against encroachment by European settlers have been termed 'blood thirsty savages' and their victories 'massacres.'"[5] At the end of the book, the Indian reasons for attacking settlers is explained. By then, the message transmitted to the students cannot be reversed.

Attean's relationship with Matt also reinforces stereotypes. Attean is not happy to spend time with Matt but his grandfather, Saknis, wants Attean to learn to speak and read English. However, throughout the book Attean speaks in pidgin English, the halting speech so often associated with American Indians, and reinforced in too many movies to mention as well as by the Random House video made specifically for children. Matt is clearly trying to give Attean something of value, in this case English, in exchange for what Attean has taught him about survival in the woods. But Attean resists. "The only thing Matt could teach him, Attean was set against learning. For Attean the white man's signs on paper were *piz wat*—good for nothing. Nevertheless, Matt noticed that in spite of himself Attean had learned something from the white boy. He was speaking the English tongue with greater ease. Perhaps he was not aware himself how differently he spoke."[6]

Although Attean did not value the "white man's language," the author was committed to having him learn to speak English correctly. Speare, however, did not make him smart enough to notice the difference in how he spoke or what he said. Further, although Matt said Attean was speaking better English his dialogue never improved and he never spoke proper English. Even at the end of the book, when Attean was ready to leave Maine, he spoke to Matt in pidgin English. "What for I read? My grandfather mighty hunter. My father mighty hunter. They not read."[7] Matt believes that Attean does not or cannot understand what he was trying to teach. Matt thinks to himself, "How could you explain, Matt wondered, to someone who just did not want to understand?"[8] This writing by Speare suggests that Attean is just not smart enough to understand. On three separate occasions, Matt says that Attean could never understand what Matt was trying to teach him. He could not understand the concept of land ownership, he could not understand Robinson Crusoe, and he could not learn to use a watch. But Matt is easily capable of understanding the complicated ideas of land ownership from the Indian perspective, as well as their language and customs. Once again, Matt is represented as much smarter than Attean.

Cultural stereotyping emerged again in Chapter 14 when Attean and Matt exchanged stories about religion. Matt told the story of Noah and the flood, and Attean told a story of the Beaver people, the story of Gluskabe and an Indian flood. Matt, who refused to accept this Beaver story as unique, could not understand how Attean could know about Noah and the Flood.

At the end of the story, Saknis and Attean leave the area and invite Matt, whose parents had not yet returned, to join them. Matt says that he prefers to wait for his parents but somehow the reader is left with the feeling that Matt is committed to the lifestyle he knows—as opposed to the Indian way of life.

During the school year when we began to plan "The Sign of the Beaver Day," we decided that the day would focus on what the lessons of this novel meant to the students. Because it is clear Speare created two unlikely friends who influenced one another, I set out to create the same scenario. Each student was told to plan to teach something he/she knew to another student. The students were broken into groups and each was assigned a partner. The students were not allowed to pick their own partners and the teachers made sure that each student was assigned a partner that he/she would not have chosen.

When the students came to my room, I began a lesson based on the meaning of friendship. I asked the students to tell me what qualities they felt a friend should have. After listing the traits on the board they voted and picked truthfulness and loyalty as the most important qualities. Then they were asked if they believed they had those same qualities to offer in friendship. The question surprised them. They were much more comfortable describing how someone else should behave as a friend rather than talking about whether they offered the same qualities. But the ensuing discussion was powerful. When a student tried to go back to the book in order to keep the discussion on a less personal level I redirected the conversation back to their feelings. I wanted them to internalize the lesson about friendship. I did not want them to think only about the relationship of two fictional characters who lived long ago. I wanted the story about two unlikely friends to have real meaning in their daily lives. They had plenty of interesting things to teach each other. One student taught another to play a tune on the piano, one shared his camera and took pictures around the school, one student taught another to weave a bracelet out of thread, one taught calligraphy, one taught clay modeling, one taught cartooning, one taught a card game, and one taught another how to play mancali (a complicated game played with marbles). To my astonishment the students thought of many things a teacher would not have imagined. They were interested and involved because they were all doing something they were good at and enjoyed. When the time allotted for this activity came to an end, the students all seemed sorry that the experience was over. Most chose to have lunch with their partners. Although I do not assume that permanent new friendships were formed that day, I do think that many of the students discerned interesting and wonderful qualities in peers they previously did not know well. Perhaps in the future they will be more likely to let new people into their lives.

The students enjoyed the day just as much as if they had dressed up and pretended to be either "settlers" or Indians. They learned a lot about friendship in a couple of hours without pretending to write "peace treaties" or make up fake Indian legends. Additionally, the lessons were learned without any child pretending he/she could "speak Indian." The students, (who seemed to have forgotten about Attean and Matt), were far more interested in what they had taught to their partners or what they had learned from theirs.

Hopefully the students have learned to make a connection between the concept of friendship expressed in *The Sign of the Beaver* and their own lives.

NOTES

1. Pamphlet published by American School Publishers, Random House Newbery Video Collection, 1988.

2. Robert B. Moore and Arlene B. Hirschfelder, "Feathers, Tomahawks and Tipis: A Study of Stereotyped 'Indian' Imagery in Children's Picture Books," in *American Indian Stereotypes in the World of Children: A Reader and Bibliography,* ed. Arlene B. Hirschfelder (Metuchen, NJ: Scarecrow Press, Inc.,1982), p. 73.

3. Arlene B. Hirschfelder, "Toys with Indian Imagery," in *American Indian Stereotypes in the World of Children: A Reader and Bibliography,* ed. Arlene B. Hirschfelder (Metuchen, NJ: Scarecrow Press, Inc.,1982), p. 171.

4. Elizabeth George Speare, *The Sign of the Beaver* (New York: Dell Publishing, 1984), p. 9.

5. League of Women Voters, "Children's Impressions of American Indians: A Survey of Suburban Kindergarten and Fifth Grade Children: Conclusions," in *American Indian Stereotypes in the World of Children: A Reader and Bibliography,* ed. Arlene B. Hirschfelder (Metuchen, NJ: Scarecrow Press, Inc.,1982), p. 9.

6. Speare, *Sign,* pp. 66, 67.

7. Speare, *Sign,* p. 116.

8. Speare, *Sign,* p. 117.

Chapter 5

What Your Teachers Never Told You (Maybe They Didn't Know)

Textbooks and Native Americans*

Council on Interracial Books for Children

NATIVE AMERICANS ARE THE
ORIGINAL INHABITANTS OF NORTH AMERICA

"It has often been said that the only native American is the Indian. Certainly it is true that the Indian has been native to America for a longer period of time than any other people. But even the Indian was an immigrant." [*The Pageant of American History*, p. 2]

Comment

Many textbooks refer to Native Americans as the first immigrants, or the "First Americans, "based on unproven theories linking them to people who migrated to Alaska over a "land bridge" from Asia. Assertions that Native Americans were merely the first among many groups of immigrants serve as subtle justification for European conquest, implying that they had no greater claim to the land than did later immigrants. Native Americans should be portrayed as the original inhabitants of the continent. In fact, evidence of "modern man" existing in the Americas over 70,000 years ago predates knowledge of such life in Europe.

References

Indians of the Americas. John Collier.
They Came Here First: The Epic of the American Indian. D'Arcy McNickle.
This Country Was Ours. Virgil Vogel.
"Coast Dig Focuses on Man's Move to New World," *New York Times*, August 16, 1976, p. 33.

---

*Reprinted by permission from "Native Americans, in *Stereotypes, Distortions and Omissions in U.S. History Textbooks*. in New York: Council on Interracial Books for Children (1841 Broadway, New York, N.Y. 10023), 1977.

PRE-COLUMBIAN NATIVE AMERICAN SOCIETIES
REFLECTED GREAT DIVERSITY AND COMPLEXITY

"The Eastern Woodland tribes lived in the region east of the Mississippi River, from Canada to Florida. . . . The Indians hunted for their food and clothing. . . . The Eastern Woodland Indians were farmers, too, and they grew corn, beans and squash. They lived in buildings called longhouses . . . which were rows of apartments, shared by several families. The men hunted and fished; the women tended the fields and gathered the fruit. They had money called wampum, which consisted of bits of seashells strung together like beads." [*The Challenge of America*, p. 111]

Comment

Textbook attempts to describe the social, political and cultural fabric of pre-Columbian Native American societies are grossly oversimplified and ethnocentric. In North America there were over 300 distinct languages and about 500 separate cultures. Societies ranged from the urban complexes of the "Mound Builders" and the multi-national political alliances of the Iroquois and of the Huron, to the small hunting bands of the Inuit. Art, science and oral literature flourished in every society. Well developed systems of trade existed between many of the nations.

Emphasis should not be placed on material objects—such as wampum, moccasins and baskets—but on the alternative social relationships and value systems that were (and are) predominant among Native American peoples. Native religions and spiritual practices should be described as equally valid as other religions. Native American cultures should be presented as dynamic and changing, rather than static and primitive. To discuss Native cultures only in terms of the pre-European past suggests that the cultures disappeared and denies their continuity with Native cultures today.

References

Indians of the Americas.
The Indian in Americas Past. Jack D. Forbes.
They Came Here First.

THE MYTH OF "DISCOVERY" IS BLATANTLY EUROCENTRIC

"In reality, Columbus 'rediscovered' the New World. Other Europeans had explored there many years before. The Norsemen were probably the first Europeans to reach the New World. . . . Other Europeans may also have 'discovered' the New World before Columbus. . . . However, after Columbus' voyage the Americas stayed discovered." [*Rise of the American Nation*, p. 101]

Comment

Evidence indicates that when Columbus arrived in the Americas, the Western hemisphere (North and South America) was occupied by 50 to 100 million people. While scholars may disagree over the exact numbers, it is Eurocentric to suggest that Europeans "discovered" a continent that had, perhaps, a larger population than did western Europe at that time. While the existence of the Americas may have been new information to Europeans, anthropological evidence suggests that Native Americans had previous contact with African and Chinese travelers, none of whom apparently claimed either "discovery" of—or rights to—the land.

References

Indians of the Americas.
Essays in Population History: Mexico and the Caribbean. Sherburne F. Cook and Woodrow Borah.
"The Tip of an Iceberg: Pre-Columbian Indian Demography and Some Implications for Revisionism." Wilbur R. Jacobs, in *William and Mary Quarterly*, January, 1974.
They Came Here First.

AT LEAST TEN TO TWELVE MILLION NATIVE PEOPLES MAY HAVE LIVED IN WHAT LATER BECAME THE U.S.

"When Europeans first came to North America, there were probably about 750,000 Indians living in the land that is now the United States." [*America: Its People and Values*, pp. 563–564]

"In 1492 the number of Indians in all of North America north of Mexico was about equal to the number of people in the city of Detroit today. . . . When Columbus landed in America, there was one Indian for every 150 persons who now live in the United States. At that time the Indians within the present boundaries of the United States were only slightly greater in number than the people who live in Baltimore, Maryland, today [less than two million]." [*Man in America*, pp. 31–32]

Comment

Most texts provide very low figures—ranging from less than one million up to two million—for the Native American population of North America before the arrival of Europeans. Such figures, when compared to the number of people in the U.S. today, suggest that the vast continent was underutilized and imply that European settlement was justified. Regardless of the number of Native Americans at the time, such implications are unfounded. The low figures in textbooks are based on research by scholars who utilized, in part, the writings of European explorers and settlers. Other scholars, using different methodology, believe that the Native population of North America was actually between 10 and 12 million. Three-quarters of the Native population is thought to have been wiped out by epidemic diseases such as smallpox, measles, cholera and syphilis brought to this continent by Europeans. Because Native Americans had developed no natural immunity to these foreign diseases, epidemics spread rapidly among them, carried into the interior by Native people who had contracted the diseases directly from Europeans. Thus, the population of many Native nations was drastically reduced before Europeans actually reached them and wrote of their encounters. While the transmission of these diseases was generally unintentional, occasionally a deliberate attempt at germ warfare was made by Europeans. One such device was to infect Native people by giving them blankets infested with smallpox.

References

"Estimating Aboriginal American Population: An Appraisal of Techniques with a New Hemispheric Estimate," Henry F. Dobyns, in *Current Anthropology*, VII, 1966.
"The Tip of an Iceberg: Pre-Columbian Indian Demography and Some Implications for Revisionism."
Chronicles of American Indian Protest. Council on Interracial Books for Children.

"ADVANCED CULTURE" IS AN ETHNOCENTRIC CONCEPT AND DOES NOT EXPLAIN OR JUSTIFY EUROPEAN CONQUEST

"A conflict of cultures. The Eastern Woodland Indians did not develop a highly advanced culture. But their culture did make it possible for them to live successfully in ways suited to their needs. . . . Beginning in the mid-1600's, the world of the Eastern Woodland Indians suddenly changed. The Indians faced Europeans, who were people with more advanced cultures. These Europeans had better weapons, better tools, and more advanced forms of political organization." [*America: Its People and Values*, p. 68]

". . . Indians were limited by their natural environment. Wasn't this a weakness—a minus—for the Indians?. . . Beginning in 1492, groups with a higher technology invaded the New World. These groups soon used their knowledge to overcome the Indians." [*Man in America*, p. 40]

Comment

"Advanced culture" is a highly relative term. Politically, most Native American societies were more democratic than those in Europe or the colonies. Decisions were generally made by consensus, women were usually actively involved and there was seldom a property requirement for participation. In fact, the colonies borrowed from the political organization of the six nations of the Iroquois Confederacy in designing their central authority. With few exceptions, Native American societies were more accepting of diversity, offered greater individual freedom, and were more "community" oriented and less competitive than European societies.

Prior to European contact, Native Americans utilized virtually all available medicinal plants and herbs. The enormous variety of foodstuffs cultivated by Native Americans—which Europeans came to depend on—demonstrates the agricultural knowledge of many of the societies. It was not until the development of the cartridge rifle that Euro-American technology "overcame the Indians." The previous muzzle-loading, one-shot arms had been too slow and cumbersome against bows and arrows.

European survival in North America was heavily dependent on the technology and skills of Native Americans in agriculture, medicine, transportation and hunting. That Europeans prevailed over Native societies is attributable not to "advanced culture," but to epidemics, which had a tremendously disruptive and weakening effect on Native societies, and to the land greed of the Europeans. Neither of these factors reflects "advanced" culture.

References

Indians of the Americas.
God Is Red. Vine Deloria, Jr.
The Patriot Chiefs. Alvin Josephy.
They Came Here First.
The Great Law of Peace of the People of the Longhouse. White Roots of Peace. Authentic factual source of the social and political structure of the Mohawk Nation.

WAR AND VIOLENCE WERE NOT CHARACTERISTIC OF NATIVE NATIONS

"War was part of the way of life of these southeastern Indians." [*Man in America*, p. 36]

"The Iroquois were a fierce and warlike people." [*America: Its People and Values*, p. 68]

Comment

Descriptions of Native American nations as "warlike" must be treated with caution. Much of the available information on Native Americans was written by Europeans who naturally viewed those defending their lands and communities against European invasion as warlike. Native American nations had many non-violent, well-ordered processes for solving their international problems. While there were conflicts prior to the European invasion, they were generally for limited objectives rather than for total victory or conquest, and loss of life was minimal.

European encroachments forced some societies to move from their traditional lands into those of others. In some instances this caused conflicts (as when the Sioux moved into the territory of the Crow), while in other instances the new arrivals were assisted by the original inhabitants (as when the Sioux moved into the territory of the Mandan).

References

Indians of the Americas.
Who's the Savage? A Documentary History of the Mistreatment of the Native North Americans. D. R. Wrone and R. S. Nelson.

NATIVE AMERICAN TECHNOLOGY AND KNOWLEDGE WERE ACHIEVEMENTS IN THEIR OWN RIGHT

"The Indian gave us the snowshoe, the canoe, and the moccasin. He gave us buckwheat cakes and maple syrup, root beer and sarsaparilla, pumpkins and pineapples, chicle (chewing gum) and tobacco. His skills as a naturalist and his knowledge of the environment are contributions the Indian made to America." [*The Pageant of American History*, p. 7]

Comment

Textbooks commonly discuss "contributions of the Indians." The implication is that the sole value of Native Americans lies in what they "gave" to the U.S.

A much less ethnocentric implication would result if texts were to state that Europeans—of necessity—adopted much of Native American technology and knowledge for their own survival. Native American achievements in agriculture, transportation, medicine and social and political practices were admirable in their own right and should be an integral part of the discussion of Native American societies and cultures, apart from their value to white people. Also, this textbook's use of the male pronoun denies the primary role of Native women in agricultural achievements.

MISSIONARY ACTIVITIES WERE AN INTEGRAL PART OF EUROPEAN CONQUEST

"From the beginning, there were a few settlers who made friends with the Indians and tried to understand them. . . . Churches sent missionaries to teach their religion to the Indians, cure their sicknesses, and try to teach them new ways. The missionaries accomplished much, but there were never enough of them or of other settlers who wanted to help the Indians." [*America: Its People and Values*, p. 564]

Comment

Missionary efforts principally benefited the Europeans by providing them with free labor in developing missions and farms, and with a source of converts. For the most part, missionaries operated from the perspective that Native Americans were "savages" in need of uplifting from "heathen" beliefs. European powers and the U.S. government encouraged missionaries to break down traditional Native American customs, beliefs and societies.

Under the administration of U.S. President Grant, reservations were parceled out among various religious denominations whose members were appointed as agents to supervise the Native people under their control. The missionary lobby succeeded in having Congress declare Native American religious practices illegal, a situation which existed until 1934. The fact that the traditional religious practices and beliefs survive attests to their vitality and importance to Native American people.

References

Akwesasne Notes. Vol. 7, No. 5. Early Winter, 1975.
Custer Died for Your Sins. Vine Deloria, Jr.
God Is Red.
The Indian in America's Past.
A Pictorial History of the American Indian. Oliver La Farge.

NATIVE NATIONS MADE ALLIANCES WITH EUROPEAN NATIONS FOR THEIR OWN STRATEGIC PURPOSES

"[George Rogers Clark] set out in 1778 to end once and for all the attacks by Indians who had been stirred up, apparently, by the British at Detroit." [*The Free and the Brave*, p. 208]

"Indians! Along the frontier, from Maine to New York, the Indians are attacking. And English colonists fight back to defend their houses and their lives. . . . The Indian attacks along the frontier are part of a larger conflict. A bitter struggle is going on between England and France. Most of the Indians are fighting on the side of France. . . . The French encouraged the Indians to make many of these attacks . . ." [*America: Its People and Values*, p. 127]

Comment

Textbooks often describe Native Americans as being "stirred up" by one European group to attack another. The impression is that they were pawns, manipulated by Europeans. Native nations were struggling to maintain their communities and lands and, like other people in similar circumstances, made whatever alliances seemed to offer them assistance. Alliances with various European nations need to be placed in the perspective of Native American survival objectives.

References

Bury My Heart at Wounded Knee. Dee Brown.
Chronicles of American Indian Protest.
To Serve the Devil. Vol. I: Jacobs, Landau and Pell.
The Patriot Chiefs.
The American Indian Wars. John Tebbel and Keith Jennison.
This Country Was Ours.
Red Man's Land, White Man's Law. Wilcomb E. Washburn.
Who's the Savage?

CONFLICTING EUROPEAN AND COLONIAL ECONOMIC INTERESTS IN NATIVE LANDS HELPED TRIGGER THE U.S. REVOLUTION

". . . [The French] had to drive off a little force of Virginia militiamen com-manded by a colonel named George Washington. . . . Washington and other Virginians believed the future lay in the rich, unsettled lands of the West.

"The government in London quickly moved to clean up the wreckage of the war and pay its huge costs. Among the first steps was a 1763 ruling to forbid set-tlement west of a 'Proclamation Line' running down the Alleghenies. The procla-mation would hold back pioneers until an Indian policy could be worked out. This seemed especially necessary after a gifted Indian named Pontiac united many tribes in a rebellion in 1763 that took a year to subdue. But the measure angered the colonists." [*The Impact of Our Past*, pp. 146 and 150]

Comment

Pontiac and the 18 nation confederacy he led almost defeated the British, and the Proclamation of 1763 resulted. While the Proclamation "angered the colonists," most texts omit information about its effect on the financial interests of George Washington and other wealthy colonists—an effect that, in part, led to their anger with Britain. Large plantation owners, like Washington, were frequently in debt to British merchants and often speculated in western (Native American) lands to make quick profits. Thus, the Proclamation was a major irritant to these speculators.

Washington was paid for his services in the French and Indian War with thou-sands of acres of Native land beyond the Appalachians. And, immediately before the Proclamation of 1763, he had invested heavily—along with Patrick Henry, Benjamin Franklin and other businessmen—in land speculation schemes involving millions of acres of that now forbidden Native American territory. It is clear that he had a pressing personal stake because he hired his own surveyor to locate addi-tional lands in that legally untouchable territory. The surveyor had written instruc-tions to maintain the utmost secrecy. Washington, at the time of his death, "owned" over 40,000 acres of those disputed Native American lands west of the Alleghenies.

References

The American Revolution 1763–1783. Herbert Aptheker. See pp. 29–30 discussing Plantation owners, land speculation and the Proclamation of 1763.

An Economic Interpretation of the Constitution of the United States, Charles A. Beard. See pp. 144–145 discussing Washington.

Chronicles of American Indian Protest. See pp. 36–48 for discussion of land speculation and and Proclamation of 1763.

"The Revolution and the American Indian Frontier," Steve Talbot, in *WASSAJA*. August, 1976, p. 9.

NATIVE NATIONS FOUGHT THE INVADERS TO MAINTAIN THEIR COMMUNITIES AND LANDS

"The Old Southwest had everything—a rich soil, a mild climate, and plenty of wild animals. There were Indians, too, and other dangers. But what were dangers compared with opportunities?

"East and West Florida were now American territory. But trouble with the Indians slowed down the process of settlement." [*America: Its People and Values*, pp. 287 and 292]

"Traders and pioneers who crossed the plains on their way to California and the Pacific Northwest reported that much of the plains country was good for settlement. But a tremendous obstacle to settlement remained—the Plains Indians." [*Rise of the American Nation*, p. 440]

Comment

While many Euro-American settlers did view Native Americans as "obstacles," creating "dangers" that "slowed down" settlement, it is Eurocentric for textbooks to present this one perspective as fact. It is not sufficient remedy for the newer books to state—in one section—that Native people were fighting for their lands and way of life, if—in another section—Native people are still characterized as "trouble," "dangers," or "obstacles."

Textbooks should include information on the reactions of Native people within various nations to the threat of invasion. Such information would offer an alternative perspective and provide the human dimension necessary to counteract the objectified image of "the Indian."

References

Bury My Heart at Wounded Knee.
Chronicles of American Indian Protest.
To Serve the Devil. Vol. 1: Natives and Slaves.
The Patriot Chiefs.

The American Indian Wars.
This Country Was Ours.
Red Man's Land, White Man's Law.
Who's the Savage?

LAND HAS A SPECIAL SIGNIFICANCE
TO NATIVE AMERICANS AND HAS BEEN
THE CENTRAL ISSUE OF CONFLICT WITH THE U.S.

"As the settlers pushed inland, they found the Indians living in the areas the set-
tlers wanted. The Indians did not understand the settlers' idea of land ownership.
They thought the land belonged to all people who needed to use it . . . [*America:
Its People and Values*, p. 564]

Comment

This quote reflects a textbook tendency to "blame" Native Americans for not understanding European concepts of land ownership. It does not discuss the failure
of Europeans to respect the Native American concept of communally using—but
not individually owning—land, just as people use—but do not own—air. It should
be noted, however, that Native nations did have defined, territorial areas for their
peoples' use. The Euro-American "respect" for land ownership is applied with a
double-standard. Even when Native title to land is clearly defined by legal treaty,
Euro-Americans have no compunction about disregarding "ownership" or about
taking over the land of others.

References

Of Utmost Good Faith. Vine Deloria, Jr.
This Country Was Ours.
Red Man's Land, White Man's Law.

IT IS EUROCENTRIC TO CATEGORIZE NATIVE
AMERICANS AS EITHER "FRIENDLY" OR "UNFRIENDLY"

"A friendly Indian named Squanto helped the colonists. He showed them how to
plant corn and how to live on the edge of the wilderness. A soldier, Captain Miles
Standish, taught the Pilgrims how to defend themselves against unfriendly
Indians." [*American: Its People and Values*, p. 73]

Comment

Sacajawea, Squanto and other Native Americans are portrayed as "friendly"
because they assisted the invaders, while Metacom ("King Philip"), Goyathlay

(Geronimo) and other Native Americans are often portrayed as "unfriendly" because they attempted to defend their communities. All nations define a "patriot" as one whose allegiance is toward his or her own people. Consequently, true Native American heroes are those who fought to preserve and protect their people's freedom and land.

References

Bury My Heart at Wounded Knee.
The Patriot Chiefs.

U.S. POLICIES TOWARD NATIVE AMERICANS REFLECT MANY POLITICAL AND ECONOMIC FACTORS WITHIN U.S. SOCIETY

"How Did Jackson deal with the Indians? As a westerner Jackson knew what it meant to fight Indians. His Indian policy as President is a dark chapter in his administration. Under Jackson it became the official policy of the administration to remove the Indians from any and all lands east of the Mississippi. The Removal Act of 1830 gave the administration the right to force the Indians to move from their homelands to tracts of land set aside for them in the far West. . . . In Georgia, the people of that state were eager to have the lands on which the Cherokee Indians lived." [*The Pageant of American History*, p. 174]

Comment

If events related to the relations between the U.S. and specific Native nations are discussed, they are usually presented in a void, often labelled "trouble with the Indians." Texts describe all the interest groups, ideologies and political considerations associated with Jackson's actions regarding the Bank of the United States, but provide no more than simplistic reasons for his removal policies toward Native peoples. Jackson's policies were not merely a "dark chapter" in his administration but a consistent part of the ongoing U.S. policies toward Native Americans. These policies are an integral part of the political and economic dynamics within U.S. society at any given time, and need to be discussed within that context. For example, the long and enormously expensive U.S. war against the Seminoles was fought, in large part, because slaveholding interests, heavily represented in the national government, wanted to destroy the sanctuary that the Seminoles provided for escaped slaves.

References

Chronicles of American Indian Protest. See pp. 110–152 and 153–161.
Removal of the Choctaw Indians. A. H. DeRosier, Jr.

The Black West. William Katz. Black involvement in Seminole War.
This Country Was Ours. See pp. 107–136 for Jackson and removal.
Redskins, Ruffled Shirts and Rednecks. Mary E. Young. Socio-political background of Jackson's policies.

TEXTBOOK TERMINOLOGY IS EUROCENTRIC, IGNORING NATIVE AMERICAN PRESENCE AND PERSPECTIVES

"The purchase of the Louisiana Territory was one of the greatest real-estate bargains in history. The vast and empty territory . . . was mostly unexplored." *[The Challenge of America* p. 230]
"Daniel Boone in Kentucky. Among the first men to make their way through the Appalachian Mountains and look longingly at the land to the west was Daniel Boone. . . . But he did not start the first settlement there. James Harrod did that . . . in 1774. . . . Thanks to the efforts of Daniel Boone and others like him, Kentucky soon became safe for settlement." *[America: Its People and Values,* p. 289]
"In 1889 Oklahoma—once supposed to be preserved as Indian Territory—was opened to homesteading. . . . Overnight, Oklahoma got a population and tent-and-shack towns. . ." *[The Impact of Our Past,* p. 451]

Comment

Native Americans are often relegated to special sections of textbooks and ignored outside of those sections. This invisibility is often accomplished through use of specific terminology. Areas outside European settlements were not *"empty"* or *"unexplored"* but were inhabited for centuries by Native peoples. Boone may have been among the first *"white people"* to enter the Appalachian Mountains, but was certainly not among the first *"men."* From a Native American perspective— particularly those who were settled there long before 1774—Boone's exploits cannot be thanked for making Kentucky *"safe for settlement."* Similarly, the territory that became Oklahoma got a *"white"* population in 1889. It already was home to a large Native American population (both those indigenous to the area and others forced into the area from their homelands east of the Mississippi).

LEGALLY BINDING TREATIES ARE CENTRAL TO THE RELATIONS BETWEEN NATIVE NATIONS AND THE U.S.

"The government policy toward the Indian was a confused one, to say the least. Few people in authority understood the Indian and his way of life. The Indians, in their turn, did not understand the terms of the treaties or agreements that the tribes had made with the government." *[The Pageant of American History,* p. 315]

"With the reservation system, the Indians became wards of the United States government. The tribes were no longer to be treated as nations with whom the United States would make treaties." [*America: Its People and Values*, p. 505]

Comment

Most textbooks do not take the treaties seriously, discussing them as unimportant curiosities of the past or omitting any reference to them. There is no basis to the frequent claim that Native Americans "did not understand the terms of the treaties," for the treaties were generally quite specific. It has been the U.S. government that has consistently reneged on these documents.

Article III of the United States Constitution states: ". . . all treaties made, or which shall be made, under the authority of the United States, shall be the supreme law of the land . . ." Treaties with Native American nations are of equal legal standing as are treaties with European nations. This interpretation has been repeatedly confirmed by federal courts, most importantly by the 1832 Supreme Court decision of *Worcester vs. Georgia*. They are U.S. law and are binding under international law.

In 1871, the period the second quote refers to, Congress passed the Indian Appropriation Act which stated: "No Indian nation or tribe within the territory of the United States shall be acknowledged or recognized as an independent nation, tribe or power with whom the United States may contract by treaty . . ." However, since 372 legally ratified treaties previously existed, the Act also stated: ". . . but no obligation of any treaty lawfully made and ratified with any such Indian nation or tribe prior to March 3, 1871 shall be hereby invalidated or impaired." While a few documents concluded after that date were called "treaties," most were called "agreements" and were ratified by both houses of the U.S. Congress and not just the Senate.

References

Handbook of Federal Indian Law. Felix Cohen.
Behind the Trail of Broken Treaties. Vine Deloria, Jr.
Indian Affairs, Laws and Treaties. Charles Kappler.
This Country Was Ours. See pp. 124–132 for text of *Worcester vs. Georgia*. See pp. 162–165 for text and discussion of 1871 Act.

THE 1887 DAWES ACT RESULTED IN THE LOSS OF THREE-QUARTERS OF THE REMAINING LAND OF NATIVE AMERICANS

"The [Dawes] act grew out of a growing concern by many that America's policy toward the Indian was unjust. . . . [It] tried to improve Indian life. One of its basic provisions in policy matters was that of treating Indians as individuals rather than as tribal nations. It provided that land be distributed to individual families." [*The Pageant of American History*, pp. 317–318]

Comment

U.S. President Arthur proposed the Dawes Act in 1887 to provide allotments of land "to such Indians . . . as desire it," but Congress made allotments compulsory. The stated intent of the Act was to "civilize" Native Americans by making them private property owners—a concept contrary to Native beliefs and practices. In reality, the Act was designed to take away "excess" Native lands, and it resulted in the loss of more than three-quarters of the remaining land held by Native Americans at that time. This "surplus" land was sold or given to white home-steaders, industrialists and ranchers.

A Native American head of household was allotted 160 acres. While provision was made for lesser allotments to single people and orphaned children, no provision was made for descendants to receive additional land. Native Americans were usu-ally allotted the poorest parcels. Some boycotted the allotment procedures to protest the Act, and the government used troops to force them to take an allotment. The Act provided that Native Americans who received allotments could gain citizenship if they farmed the land for 25 years and adopted "the habits of civilized life."

The Dawes Act was illegal, given the Constitutional status of treaties which had guaranteed the lands to Native nations, rather than to individuals within those nations.

References

Behind the Trail of Broken Treaties.
100 Million Acres. Kirke Kickingbird and Karen Ducheneaux.
The American Indian Today. Stuart Levine and Nancy O. Lurie (eds.).
This Country Was Ours. See pp. 174–181.

THE CITIZENSHIP ACT OF 1924
WAS NOT A BENEVOLENT ACTION

"A turn for the better in the Indians' lives came after 1910. . . . In 1924, Congress declared that all Indians were full citizens of the United States." [*America: Its People and Values* p. 507]

Comment

This 1924 action was, in part, a recognition of the numbers of Native Americans who fought in WWI. It did not confer "full citizenship" rights upon Native Americans because existing laws and practices denied many such privileges.

Eight Native nations protested to Congress that the Act was illegal and, when no relief was forthcoming, took their appeal to the League of Nations. The Act was part of federal policy to "Americanize" and "civilize" Native people by assimilation into white society. As part of this policy, Bureau of Indian Affairs officials and federal troops forcibly cut the long hair of Native American men.

Reference

This Country Was Ours. See pp. 194–195.

THE REORGANIZATION ACT OF 1934 HEIGHTENED NATIVE AMERICAN ALIENATION AND POWERLESSNESS

"Congress made another shift in policy by passing the Indian Reorganization Act in 1934. The main purpose of this act was to allow Indians to use their own culture . . . it encouraged tribes to set up self-governing constitutions on their reservations . . . [and] made funds available for loans to the tribal governments and for Indians' education. Surplus government lands were returned to the tribes, to be used for conservation purposes. . . . [The Act] guaranteed freedom of religion to the Indians. Under the Indian Reorganization Act, tribal governments were formed. Indian leaders gained confidence as they gained experience." [*Man in America*, p. 546]

Comment

The Reorganization Act of 1934 was the only major government act with a benevolent intent. Yet many Native Americans view it as one of the most disastrous laws ever passed regarding Native Americans.

Prior to 1934, most Native Americans were not allowed to openly practice their religions, speak their languages or hold meetings of more than three people (although the latter restriction was relaxed in the 1920's). Although traditional governments had no legal standing, they nevertheless functioned, providing secret religious ceremonies and secret teaching of their own languages. The Act imposed an alien form of government based on U.S. practice—an elected "tribal chairman" and elected "tribal council." Traditional forms of government are almost always more democratic, with leaders chosen by consensus—not by majority rule or election. Because it is an alien system, most Native Americans do not vote in the tribal elections.

The 1934 law reversed the Dawes Act and allowed Native Americans to own land communally and—as "tribes"—to reaccumulate land that had been lost, but only through purchase rather than recognition that it was rightfully theirs. The Act strengthened control by the Bureau of Indian Affairs and gave the Secretary of the Interior extraordinary power. The BIA maintains trusteeship of the land and exercises total veto power over any decisions that the chairpersons or councils make. Native people are forced to deal with this white bureaucracy because the U.S. channels health, education and welfare funds through it.

To say that "Indian leaders gained confidence as they gained experience" is paternalistic and condescending. It implies that Native Americans did not govern themselves prior to the 1934 Act and had no confidence in governing themselves until given permission.

References

Our Brother's Keeper: The Indian in White America. Edgar S. Cahn.
Behind the Trail of Broken Treaties.
A Pictorial History of the American Indian.
This Country Was Ours.
The Way. Shirley Hill Witt and Stan Steiner. Discusses traditional government.

THE TERMINATION POLICY OF THE 1950s
RESULTED IN THE LOSS OF MORE LAND
AND THE ABROGATION OF TREATIES

". . . in the 1950s, Congress announced a policy of 'termination,' that is, ending government support for certain reservations. Termination caused hardship for some tribes. Among them were the Paiutes in Utah and the Menominees in Wisconsin." [*Man in America*, p. 546]

Comment

Six nations were terminated, each by a specific act of Congress. While the policy as a whole was subsequently dropped, the six acts remained in force. Termination was not simply the ending of "government support for . . . reservations." A "terminated" nation no longer legally existed and the nation's land became federal or state land. The Menominees were the first to be terminated and their land became a county of Wisconsin. Thus, they no longer "owned" the land, land that they had been allotted individually through the Dawes Act and had then reaccumulated communally after the Reorganization Act.

The Menominee immediately incorporated to run their land as a company, but local and state taxes forced them into bankruptcy. While terminated, the Menominee sued the U.S. for not honoring treaty provisions concerning hunting rights. The Supreme Court ruled that the treaty was valid, but dealt only with hunting rights, and skirted the issue of termination. After years of litigation, the Menominee were reestablished as a reservation in 1973, but the new lands were smaller and poorer than those held before 1953.

References

Our Brother's Keeper.
This Country Was Ours.
Who's the Savage?

THE BIA IS A CORRUPT AND INEFFICIENT BUREAUCRACY CONTROLLING THE AFFAIRS OF ONE MILLION PEOPLE

"Today, the Bureau [of Indian Affairs] is trying to help the Indians to build new ways of life that they themselves want." [*America: Its People and Values*, p. 565]

Comment

The Bureau of Indian Affairs has a history of Congressional politicking, mismanagement, internal corruption, and general non-responsiveness to Native people's concerns. Numerous Congressional studies over the years have condemned the BIA for inefficiency and outright cruelty. For example, BIA schools are notorious for their failure to educate Native American youth. The schools frequently exclude Native languages, values and customs from the curriculum and overemphasize Euro-American values and customs. Teachers' lack of knowledge of Native American values and heritage combined with teacher prejudice and textbook bias drive large numbers of students out of the schools.

The BIA is a bureaucracy that controls the affairs of a million people. No other group of people in the U.S. has a special bureau controlling its affairs. Until such time as the people control their own lives, the BIA must be held responsible for the dismal living conditions of Native Americans today.

References

Our Brother's Keeper. Documented information that exposes the BIA's policies and practices.
Behind the Trail of Broken Treaties.
Indian Education: A National Tragedy—A National Challenge. U.S. Senate. Most condemning report ever issued on the education of Native Americans. Gov't. Printing Office claims out of print. Can be obtained through office of Senator Edward Kennedy.
This Country Was Ours. See especially pp. 233–238.

OPPRESSIVE CONDITIONS LEAD TO PROPORTIONATELY LOWER POPULATION INCREASE FOR NATIVE AMERICANS

"No one today is certain of how many Indians there are in the United States. Vine Deloria . . . estimates the number at about one million. If so, this is close to the number that lived here when Columbus landed in America. For centuries the number of Indians decreased, but now the Indian population is increasing." [*Man in America*, p. 546]

Comment

There are approximately one million Native Americans in the U.S. today. While the Native American population has risen since the turn of the century, it was—and still is—rising much more slowly than the population as a whole. Native Americans have a life expectancy of 64 years compared to 71 for whites. Twice as many Native American infants die during their first year as do infants as a whole. Native Americans suffer the highest incidence of suicide, TB, and alcoholism of any group in the U.S. And an estimated 25–35 percent of all Native children are removed from their families and placed in foster or adoptive homes or institutions. These figures are symptoms of the oppressive conditions under which Native Americans exist.

References

Our Brother's Keeper.
Fact Sheet on Institutional Racism. Foundation for Change.
Indian Family Defense. Association on American Indian Affairs. This quarterly newsletter
   demonstrates the national scope of the Indian child-welfare crisis.

RESERVATIONS REPRESENT
A PARADOX FOR NATIVE AMERICANS

"Today, Indians may choose whether or not they want to live and work on reservations. However, most of them still live there. . . . Indian reservations are now owned by the Indians who live on them." [*America: Its People and Values,* p. 565]
    "Fewer than half the Indians in the United States live on reservations. Those who do may leave if they wish. Today they are as free to move about as other Americans." [*Man in America*, p. 546]

Comment

On the one hand, reservations are perceived as concentration camps and are a constant reminder of the loss of land and of sovereignty. Yet reservations—as bad as they are—represent the only land Native Americans have left. Land is an integral aspect of Native American cultures, and, despite widespread poverty, reservations provide Native Americans with a sense of community and attachment to the earth.

Traditional Native American communities are communal, noncompetitive and nonalienating. Outside these communities, Native Americans are forced to participate in a competitive system that discriminates against them and denies them necessary skills and education. The resources of reservations are exploited by white ranchers and corporations, with little or no profit to Native people, many of whom are forced to seek jobs off the reservations. Many return whenever possible and consider the reservation to be "home." Less than 20 percent live outside the reservations permanently.

Given Native American legal and cultural ties to the land, it is misleading for textbooks to state that Native people are as "free to move as other Americans." It is also misleading to state that "Indian reservations are now owned by the Indians who live on them" without discussing other factors. Native American do, in fact, own reservation land as well as vast other areas of the country under legal treaties. But the BIA maintains control over their land and Native Americans cannot make decisions without BIA approval.

References

Indians of the Americas.
Our Brother's Keeper.
Behind the Trail of Broken Treaties.
The Way.
A Pictorial History of the American Indian.

TREATY RIGHTS, SOVEREIGNTY, SELF-DETERMINATION AND THE RETURN OF LAND ARE THE MAJOR GOALS OF NATIVE AMERICANS

"... the Indians are increasingly demanding their rights as American citizens." [*The Pageant of American History*, p. 318]

"Dramatic confrontations against the white establishment . . . brought concerted action and support from tribes across the country. Yet Indian nationalism is essentially tribal nationalism, with each tribe having separate needs. Disputes between tribes and between young and old leaders within tribes have characterized Native American development." [*The American Experience*, pp. 642–643]

Comment

While there have been minor disputes between Native nations, Native American "development" has been mainly "characterized" by disputes with the U.S. Each reservation has been confronted by specific hostile actions of federal or state governments. Although the "needs" of each reservation are thus defined by its particular struggle, major Native American organizations are united on the overall need to redress the cause of oppression through treaty rights, sovereignty, self-determination and the return of land. These—and not rights as American citizens—are the central goals of the modern Native American movement.

Native Americans do not all share the same viewpoints, but there has never been a "generation gap." A basic characteristic of Native American cultures is strong cross-generational ties and respect. The occupation of Wounded Knee was an example of the involvement of people of all ages in the struggle for self-determination.

References

Akwesasne Notes.
Chronicles of Indian Protest.
Behind the Trail of Broken Treaties.
The American Indian Today.
WASSAJA.
The Way.

THE STRUGGLE TO MAINTAIN LAND CONTINUES TODAY

"A long, and often bloody, conflict began over the land. It did not end until the settlers had spread their farms and ranches and cities from coast to coast and from Canada to Mexico." [*America: Its People and Values*, p. 564]

"Much of the land in the Last West is *public domain*; that is, it is owned either by the national government or by a state government. Millions of acres are still held as reservations for Indians. Valuable timber, coal, oil and natural gas resources lie on or under parts of these lands. Who shall decide how they will be used?" [*Man in America*, pp. 373–374]

Comment

Textbooks frequently imply that the conflict over land ended long ago. Native Americans continue to struggle to regain lost land that legally still belongs to them. And land continues to be taken from them. Federal, state, local and corporate efforts to take over and/or exploit the resources of Native American lands are a constant source of concern and struggle.

Reservations contain almost all of the known reserves of uranium, huge oil and gas reserves, and ⅓ of the low-sulphur coal within the U.S. According to the Federal Energy Administration, over $2.7 billion of oil and gas; $187 million of coal; $349 million of uranium and $434 million of non-energy mineral resources have been produced from Native lands through 1974. Additionally, there are important fresh water reserves, timber and other resources. Yet the exploitation of these resources by private corporations, through arrangements

with the BIA, has resulted in high profits for the corporations and very low return of revenue to Native peoples.

The second quote gratuitously asks who shall decide how the land will be
used—continuing the long tradition of ignoring Native American treaty rights and
sovereignty.

References

Akwesasne Notes, Vol. 8, No. 1, Early Spring, 1976. See pp. 22–23.
100 Million Acres.
The American Indian Today.
This Country Was Ours. See pp. 214–233.
U.S. News and World Report, August 2, 1976, pp. 29–30.
WASSAJA, October, 1976, p. 8.

THERE IS A RELATIONSHIP BETWEEN
THE PAST EXPERIENCES AND THE
PRESENT REALITY OF NATIVE AMERICANS

"In the spring of 1973, the second Battle of Wounded Knee broke out. AIM took
over the town of Wounded Knee on the Pine Ridge Indian reservation in South
Dakota. They held the town for several weeks. There was occasional gunfire and
some people were wounded. Buildings were burned in Wounded Knee and other
damage was done. Arrests were made after the AIM Indians gave up Wounded
Knee and left town." [*History of the American People*, pp. 400–401]

"Still another hazard to white settlement on the Plains was the Indians. . . .
They attacked isolated settlements, seeking to protect their land. They fought
pitched battles with soldiers sent West to help white settlers. Sometimes the
Indians won. The Sioux massacred Colonel George Armstrong Custer and over
two hundred men at the Battle of the Little Big Horn, in Montana, in 1876. But
usually the Indians lost. Farther and farther west they were pushed, and herded
onto reservations." [*History of the American People*, p. 221]

"Gold discoveries opened other areas to Americans . . . gold strikes were made
in the Black Hills of South Dakota. Once again the rush was on." [*History of the
American People*, p. 210]

Comment

Each of these three quotes from the same textbook refers to the Sioux Nation. No
connection is made between the discovery of gold in the sacred Black Hills of the
Lakota Nation (the richest gold strike in U.S. history) and the invasion of U.S.
troops (including Custer). This invasion was not to protect white settlements but
to force the Lakota to give up the Black Hills which had been guaranteed to them

in the 1868 Fort Laramie Treaty. The text provides no information on the terms of the Treaty and the repeated actions of the U.S. which directly contravened the Treaty—such as the application of the Dawes Act to the Lakota in 1902 or the imposition of an alien form of government in 1934.

Without such background information, students have little chance of understanding the reasons for the occupation of Wounded Knee in 1973 (which was initiated by traditional Lakota residents of the reservation, lasted for 71 days, and resulted in the death of two Native Americans). The book does not mention the demands that reflected the grievances of the Lakota: a U.S. Presidential Treaty Commission to discuss treaty rights and abuses; an investigation of the BIA and of the corrupt "tribal" government; and the establishment of a traditional government for the Lakota Nation. Without a cohesive presentation of the experiences of Native Americans, students can develop little understanding of their history or of their present reality.

References

Akwesasne Notes, Vol. 5, No. 6, Early Winter, 1973. See pp. 10 and 11 for discussion of provisions of 1868 Fort Laramie Treaty.

Voices from Wounded Knee, 1973. *Akwesasne Notes*. Excellent discussion of the background and events of the 1973 occupation of Wounded Knee.

Bury My Heart at Wounded Knee. See particularly pp. 102–142 discussion of the history of Sioux-U.S. relations up to the massacre at Wounded Knee, 1890.

Chronicles of American Indian Protest. See pp. 209–233 for historical background.

Misrepresentations of the Alaskan Natives in Social Studies Texts Currently in Use in the United States Including Alaska: A Preliminary Report*

Department of Education,
University of Alaska College, Alaska,
March 14, 1969

This report is of a preliminary study on the coverage of Alaskan Natives** in social study texts used in elementary and high schools throughout the country, including the Alaskan classrooms. The study is far from complete in that it covers only current editions of texts which were available through the North Star Borough school District Administration Offices at Fairbanks, Alaska. Several interesting problems arise in the discussion of Alaskan Natives in these texts. These problem areas are summarized below, with specific illustrations of gross misrepresentations in the lists following. A list of texts which were reviewed and in which the representation of the Eskimo was acceptable is also included even though the texts failed to mention even the presence of the Indian population in the state. It was interesting to discover that many elementary social study series did not even include information on the state of Alaska, much less the Natives: such books are also listed on the following pages.

Not only today, but also throughout history, there have been several distinct differences between the Eskimos of Canada and those of Alaska. These differences

---

*Reprinted from Hearings Before the Subcommittee on Indian Educ. of the Committee on Labor and Public Welfare, U.S. Senate, Ninety-First Congress 11, Part 1. U.S. Govt. Printing Off., Washington, D.C., 1969.

**The Native people of Alaska prefer to be called collectively Alaska Natives (Eskimos, Indians, and Aleuts).

are rarely brought forward in social studies texts. The Canadian Eskimo has historically been more nomadic than the Alaskan. A few Canadian Eskimos even today still live as their ancestors did—traveling hundreds of miles by dog-sled, building snow houses, and tenting in the summer. The vast majority of Canadian Eskimos, however, are now settled in towns and are supplied by train, plane, or ship with their necessities for life. The Alaskan Eskimo, on the other hand, has had very little nomadic history, and today it can be guaranteed that no Alaskan Native builds a snow house or nomadically travels hundreds of miles with his family in search of food. Today's Alaskan Eskimo uses kerosene, oil or electricity for heat and light; he lives in established communities with schools, stores, airstrips, and, in some cases, an electricity generating facility. The villages have regular mail service and have radios, whereby they maintain contact with other villages and cities. All native children have access to schools of one type or another, either in the villages or in central locations. Hunting and fishing are still an important occupation of many Natives; however, most Natives get their food and supplies through stores which are supplied by airfreight or ship. Many Natives are employed in Defense jobs, oil, mining, and fishing operations.

While realistic for a very small minority of people living in another country, stories of the Eskimo travelling for miles hunting seals and caribou, building snow houses and tents, and such activities are highly misleading when application of the story to the Alaskan Native is implied. This is probably the most serious problem in the presentation of the Alaskan Native. In reading these stories, one is often led to believe that due to arduous travels the Eskimos do not stop long enough to educate their children, to learn about the existence of electricity, to communicate with the outside world, or for that matter, to even know of another world. Stories of this kind are highly prejudicial against the Alaskan Eskimo of today. While such tales may have had some validity for Eskimos of past generations, they are commonly used today in texts with no accompanying explanation of the fact that these modes of living are now long gone, only to be found in museums. This problem of confusing history with the present, and confusing Canadian modes with Alaskan modes so far only includes consideration of Alaska's Eskimos, a fact which leads to another basic problem in coverage of the Alaskan Native in social study texts.

This problem in the treatment of the Alaskan Native is that in only one or two of all the texts reviewed was there even mention of the Indians. Alaska's native population is made up of both Eskimos and Indians. While there is a geographic difference in the distribution of these two cultures in the state, there is very little morphological difference in the people, and their communities often have very similar characteristics. While some of the texts give very good treatment of the Eskimo they are almost universally discriminatory in that they do not even mention the Indian who has played a very important role in the settling of Interior and Southern Alaska. While on the surface little difference can be seen between these two Alaska native groups, their cultural modes are certainly different enough to bear separate coverage in texts. The fact that all native Alaskans are called Eskimos is highly insulting to the Alaskan Indian who has a well deserved pride in his distinct culture.

It must be stressed that this report represents only a cursory survey of curriculum materials on hand. The misrepresentations and discriminatory statements are in some cases so gross that the background, or reference material, may also be suspected. No research has been done to date on coverage of the Alaskan Natives in common reference material. Another area which is known to be heavily loaded with discriminatory material is the children's literature on the Eskimo: as is the case with the reference material, no formal search has been made in this area. Although the scope of this report is limited for the present to include only the latest editions of texts in use, mention must be made of the fact that many schools are still using older editions of social studies texts which in many cases contain even grosser discriminatory passages against the Alaskan Natives.

The following list of books are current elementary school social study readers in which there is no mention of Alaska Natives at all; and, in some cases, no mention of the state of Alaska. Although there are some high school texts which also neglect to mention Alaska Natives, they are not included in the list.

Burnette, O. Lawrence, Lettie Lee Ralph, and T. J. Durell. *Basic Social Studies*. New York: Harper & Row, 1964. Grade 5. No mention of Alaska Natives.

Cutright, Prudence, John Jarolimek, and Nae Knight Clark. *Living in America Today and Yesterday*. New York: Macmillan, 1966. No mention of Alaska Natives.

Dederick, Nelle, Josephine Tiegs, and Fay Adams. *Your People and Mine*. Boston: Ginn, 1965. No mention of Alaska.

Goetz, Delia. *At Home in Our Land*. Boston: Ginn, 1965. No mention of Alaska.

Hagaman, Adaline P., and Thomas J. Durell. *Basic Social Studies*. New York: Harper & Row, 1964. Grade 4. No mention of Alaska.

———. *World Cultures Past and Present*. New York: Harper & Row, 1965. No mention of Alaska Natives.

Hanna, Paul R., Clyde F. Kohn, and Robert A. Lively. *In All Our States*. Chicago: Scott, Foresman and Company, 1965. No mention of Alaska Natives.

Hunnicut, C. W., and Jean D. Grombs. *We Look Around Us*. Chicago: L. W. Singer Company, 1963. No mention of Alaska Natives.

Jarolimek, John, and Elizabeth B. Carey. *Living in Places Near and Far*. New York: Macmillan, 1966. No mention of Alaska Natives.

King, Frederic M., Dorothy K. Bracken, and Margaret A. Sloan. *Regions and Social Needs*. River Forest, Illinois: Laidlaw Brothers, Inc., 1968. Grade 3. No mention of Alaska Natives.

Lally, Laura, Ernest W. Tiegs, and Fay Adams. *Your Neighborhood and the World*. Boston: Ginn, 1966. Does not even include a map of Alaska in map of our country.

McClellan, Jack, Grace Dawson, Ernest W. Tiegs, and Fay Adams. *Your World and Mine*. Boston: Ginn, 1965. No mention of Alaska Natives.

McGuire, Edna. *The Story of American Freedom*. New York: Macmillan, 1967. No mention of Alaska Natives.

Pierce, Mary Lust, and Euphrosyne Georgas. *The Community Where You Live.* Boston: Allyn and Bacon, 1965. No mention of Alaska.

Preston, Ralph C., and Eleanor Clymer. *Communities at Work.* Boston: D.C. Heath, 1964. No mention of Alaska Natives.

Preston, Ralph C., and John Tottle. *In These United States and Canada.* Boston: D.C. Heath, 1965. Only mention of Eskimos is Canadian. No mention of Alaska Natives in chapter on Alaska.

Wann, Kenneth D., Emma D. Sheehy, and Bernard Spodek. *Learning About Our Families.* Boston: Allyn and Bacon, 1967. Grade 1. No mention of Alaska.

Wann, Kenneth D., Jane D. Vreeland, and Marguerite A. Conklin. *Learning About Our Country.* Boston: Allyn and Bacon, 1967. Grade 3. No mention of Alaska except one reference as to size.

Wann, Kenneth D., Frances C. Wann, and Emma D. Sheehy. *Learning About Our Neighbors.* Boston: Allyn and Bacon, 1967 Grade 2. No mention of Alaska.

Wann, Kenneth D., Henry J. Warmon, and James K. Confield. *Man and His Changing Culture.* Boston: Allyn and Bacon, 1960. No mention of Alaska.

The following list of books includes elementary and high school social study texts in which the materials on Alaskan Eskimos are acceptable: only a few mention Indians.

ELEMENTARY

Brown, Gurtrude S., Josephine Tiegs, and Fay Adams. *Your Country and Mine.* Boston: Ginn, 1965.

Carls, Norman, Phillip Bacon, and Frank E. Sorenson. *Knowing Your Neighbors in the United States.* New York: Holt, Rinehart and Winston, 1966

————. *Knowing Our Neighbors in the U.S. and Canada.* New York: Holt, Rinehart and Winston, 1966.

Coons, Frederica, and John Prater. *Trains to Freedom in American History.* Boston: Ginn, 1967.

Cooper, Kenneth S., Clarence W. Sorensen, and Paul Todd Lewis. *The Changing New World.* Morristown, N.J.: Silver Burdett and Company, 1967.

————. *Learning to Look at Our World.* Morristown, N.J.: Silver Burdett and Company, 1967.

Crabtree, Ester, Josephine Tiegs, and Fay Adams. *Understanding Your Country and Mine.* Boston: Ginn, 1965.

Cutright, Prudence, and John Jarolimek. *Living in Our Country and Other Lands.* New York: Macmillan, 1966.

Drummond, Harold D., and Fred A. Sloan. *A Journey Through Many Lands.* Boston: Allyn and Bacon, 1964.

————. *Journeys Through the Americas.* Boston: Allyn and Bacon, 1964.

————. *The Western Hemisphere.* Boston: Allyn and Bacon, 1966.

Gross, Herbert, Dwight W. Follett, Robert E. Gobler, William L. Burton and Ben F. Ahlschwede. *Exploring Regions of the Western Hemisphere.* Chicago: Follett, 1966.

Hanna, Paul R., Helen F. Wise, and Livey Kohn. *In the Americas.* Chicago: Scott, Foresman, 1965.

King, Frederick M., Dorothy K. Bracken, and Margaret A. Sloan. *Communities and Social Needs*. River Forest, Illinois: Laidlaw Brothers, 1968.

Polansky, Lucy, Kenneth D. Wann, and Henry J. Warman. *The Changing Earth and Its People*. Boston: Allyn and Bacon, 1967.

Rickard, John A. *Discovering American History*. Boston: Allyn and Bacon, 1965.

Townsend, Herbert. *Our America*. Boston: Allyn and Bacon, 1964.

Wann, Kenneth D., Edith Stull, and Henry J. Warman. *Our Changing Nation and Its Neighbors*. Boston: Allyn and Bacon, 1967.

Whittemore, Katheryne T., and Melvin Svec. *The United States and Canada*. Boston: Ginn, 1966.

HIGH SCHOOL

Anderson, Vivienne, and Laura M. Shufelt. *Your America*. Englewood Cliffs, N.J.: Prentice-Hall, 1967.

Casner, Mabel B., and Ralph H. Gabriel. *Story of the American Nation*. New York: Harcourt, Brace and World, 1967.

Cutright, Prudence, and John Jarolimek. *Living as World Neighbors*. New York: Macmillan, 1966.

Holt, Sol. *World Geography and You*. Princeton, N.J.: Van Nostrand Co., 1964.

Koller, Marvin R., and Harold C. Couse. *Modern Sociology*. New York: Holt, Rinehart and Winston, 1969.

Resnick, Mariam R., and Lillian H. Nerenberg. *American Government in Action*. Columbus, Ohio: Charles E. Merrill, 1969.

Smith, Harriet Fuller, Ernest W. Tiegs, and Fay Adams. *Your Life as a Citizen*. Boston: Ginn, 1967.

Van Cleef, Eugene, and John L. Finney. *Global Geography*. Boston: Allyn and Bacon, 1966.

The following is a list of texts in which are contained passages which either make a false statement about Alaskan Natives, or which by implication give a false representation of these people.

ELEMENTARY

Carls, Norman, Elaine M. Templin, and Frank E. Sorenson. *Knowing Our Neighbors Around the Earth*. New York: Holt, 1966.

The only reference to Eskimos in the entire book occurs after mention of the diet of Asiatics: "Eskimos also eat seaweed," p. 94. This is true of such a small minority of Eskimos that it is hardly worth mentioning, especially when it is the only reference to these people.

Clark, Thomas D., Roy Compton, and Amber Wilson. *America's Frontier*. Chicago: Lyons and Carnahan, 1965.

In this text there is only a brief reference to the Eskimos as Alaska's natives; they also mention that "The Eskimos will not starve so long as there are reindeer," p. 385. This statement puts the Eskimos on a very simple-minded status as compared with the common American Middle Class status. The situation of adequate food supply for the natives is far more complex than merely having enough reindeer. Granted that many Eskimos raise reindeer for the meat market where they realize sufficient income to purchase their food supplies. No Eskimo, however well adapted, though, can avoid starvation by eating reindeer meat alone.

Cutright, Prudence, and John Jarolimek. *Living in the Americas.* New York: Macmillan, 1966. "Hunting is especially important to the Eskimos living in the tundra region of Alaska. They depend on the walrus, seal, whale, Arctic fox and other wild animals. To the Eskimos these animals mean food, clothing and shelter." p. 395. Again one sees a highly simplified picture of the Alaskan Native.

Hamer, O. Stuart, Dwight W. Follett, Ben Ahlschwede, and Herbert H. Gross. *Exploring Our Country.* Chicago: Follett, 1962.
"At the Eskimo village everyone rushes to greet us. We tell the American schoolteacher and his wife that we have come to see how the Eskimos live. The first Eskimo home we visit is a skin tent. This is a summer house. . . . Inside the house is a seal oil lamp used for light and heat and cooking." p. 364. This is probably the worst case of discrimination against the Eskimos encountered. Why do the authors differentiate between the American schoolteacher and the Eskimos; are not the Eskimos also Americans? This story is supposed to have taken place at Point Barrow, Alaska. In this large, hustling town, Natives are more likely to cook on conventional stoves. Despite a later insinuation in the text, these people know of electricity, telephones, and normal canned and dried foodstuffs. They buy a great many of their clothes and household items through mail order houses. They do not depend entirely on whales, walruses, and seals as the authors would have the reader believe.

Isreal, Saul, Norma H. Roemer, and Loyal Durand, Jr. *World Geography Today.* New York: Holt, Rinehart and Winston, Inc., 1966.
"For the most part, the Eskimos of the North American tundra make a scant living by fishing, trapping and hunting." pp. 498–499.

Patterson, Franklin, Jessamy Patterson, C. W. Hunnicut, Jean D. Grambs, and James A. Smith. *Man Changes His World.* Chicago: L. W. Singer, 1963.
This text includes two stories about Eskimos. Both of these stories have illustrations accompanying the text in which the Eskimos are building snow igloos in the winter and tents in the summer. The stories follow a sequence on cave men, in which the cave men were dressed in shaggy skins and chasing animals over the snow with spears. The pictures of the Eskimos show men dressed in furs with similar spears chasing seals and caribou. The fact that at the end of the story there is a picture of a modern Eskimo classroom hardly compensates for the misrepresentation of Eskimos in the stories. A quip about the clever Eskimos of today who can take apart an outboard motor also falls short of demonstrating the depth of understanding and adaptation now occurring in the villages and cities among the Native population.

Preston, Ralph C., Caroline Emerson, P. E. Schrader, and A. F. Schrader. *Four Lands, Four Peoples.* Boston: D.C. Heath, Inc., 1966.
In the only mention of people in the Arctic the text says: "Eskimos and other wandering peoples can live in the Arctic by hunting and fishing." p. 31.

Senesh, Lawrence. *Our Working World.* Chicago: Science Research Associates, 1964.

Thralls, Zoe A., Edward L. Biller, and William Hartley. *The World Around Us.* New York: Harcourt, Brace and World, 1965.
In this beautifully illustrated text pictures of Canadian Eskimos in tents and snow houses are shown as examples of Alaskan Eskimos. "Some Eskimos winter in sod huts; others build igloos of snow and ice." p. 21.

Townsend, Herbert. *Our Wonderful World.* Boston: Allyn and Bacon, Inc., 1963.
"People (Eskimo) dress in furs and hunt seal, walrus and polar bear for food and clothing. Some live in huts made of earth and skins, but others build homes of frozen snow, called igloos. When the Eskimo wants to travel, he harnesses up his sled dogs, called huskies." p. 146.

HIGH SCHOOL

Bollens, John C. *Communities and Government in a Changing World.* Chicago: Rand McNally, 1966.
"Many Eskimos of Alaska maintain a way of life not too different from that of generations of Eskimos that lived before them." p. 158.

Bradley, John Hodgdon. *World Geography.* Boston: Ginn, 1968.
"The primitive Eskimo eats fish and seal meat not because he is too stupid or too lazy to raise corn and cows, and not necessarily because he prefers wild to cultivated food. He eats fish and seal meat because his physical environment will not provide enough hay for cows and heat for corn." p. 37. Although the author qualifies his statement about the Eskimos, the insinuation is still there, by mere mention of the words stupid and lazy. The author implies that Eskimos do other things because of stupidity and laziness. The use of the word "primitive" to modify Eskimo is unforgivable in this context.

Caughey, John W., John Hope Franklin, and Ernest R. May. *Land of the Free.* New York: Benziger Brothers, 1967.
"The hunting people of the Alaskan interior (Indians) are not particularly notable, but the Eskimo along the coast had made remarkable adjustment to a forbidding climate." p. 44.
"In a few remote places the Indians still possess the land and maintain the old way of life, as do the Eskimos." p. 49.

Cole, William E., and Charles S. Montgomery. *High School Sociology.* Boston: Allyn and Bacon, 1967.
"Primitive Eskimos in Asia and North America had only themselves and their environment from which to make their living and from which to fashion a culture. Consequently they built their houses of blocks of snow and ice and skins. They subsisted largely upon sea animals, and used the fat, or 'blubber' of these animals for light and heat. Today they may have radios and cigarette lighters." p. 201.

Kolevzon, Edward R., and John A. Heine. *Our World and Its Peoples.* Boston: Allyn and Bacon, Inc., 1967. There is no differentiation between Canadian and Alaskan Eskimos. "Sometimes dome-shaped igloos are built from blocks of hard-packed snow." p. 74.

Packard, Leonard O., Bruce Overton, and Ben D. Wood. *Geography of the World.* New York: Macmillan, 1959.
"Primitive peoples take from the earth what happens to be found in the regions in which they live. The Eskimos and the Lapps obtain all the necessities of their simple lives from the animals of the locality. To this they may add a crude shelter of stones or skins or blocks of snow." p. 58

Sorenson, Clarence W. *A World View.* Morristown, N.J.: Silver Burdett, 1964.
"And the simple stone or snow houses of the Eskimo are heated and lighted by burning seal fat." p. 49.

The Treatment of Iroquois Indians in Selected American History Textbooks*

Arlene B. Hirschfelder

Many American Indian organizations[1] and concerned individuals are currently trying to inform the American people about the cultures, histories, and contributions of American Indians.[2] They are also informing people about the mistreatment of Indians by non-Indians throughout the history of the United States. Few Americans have a complete and realistic picture of the part played by Indians in American history. Contributing to this lack of knowledge concerning Indians are the authors of American history textbooks.

A close examination of the treatment of individual Indian tribes, particularly the Iroquois, illustrates the inadequate, inaccurate, misleading, and lackluster textbook writing on American Indians. The Iroquois tribes warrant some space in textbooks both for the different and complex life styles they have led and for the relationships they have had with Euro-Americans throughout the course of American history.

Twenty-seven American history textbooks, published in the late fifties and sixties, have been examined for their treatment of Iroquois Indians. They are:

Bailey, Thomas A. *The American Pageant: A History of the Republic.* Boston: D. C. Heath and Company, 1966.

Blum, John M.; Catton, Bruce; Morgan, Edmund S.; Schlesinger, Arthur M., Jr.; Stampp, Kenneth M.; and Woodward, C. Vann. *The National Experience.* New York: Harcourt, Brace and World, Inc., 1963.

Boller, Paul F., Jr., and Tilford, E. Jean. *This Is Our Nation.* St. Louis: Webster Publishing Company, 1961.

Bragdon, Henry W., and McCutchen, Samuel P. *History of a Free People.* New York: Macmillan Company, 1964.

*Reprinted by permission from *The Indian Historian*, Vol. 8, No. 2, Fall 1975, pp. 32–39. Published by The Indian Historian Press, Inc. 1451 Masonic Ave., San Francisco, Calif. 94117. Copyright, 1975 by the American Indian Historical Society. All rights reserved. No part of these contents may be duplicated in any manner without written permission of the publisher.

Brown, Richard C.; Lang, William C.; and Wheeler, Mary A. *The American Achievement.* Morristown, N.J.: Silver Burdett Company, 1966.

Casner, Mabel B.; Gariel, Ralph H.; Biller, Edward L.; and Hartley, William H. *Story of the American Nation.* New York: Harcourt, Brace, and World, Inc., 1962.

Caughey, John W.; Franklin, John Hope; and May, Ernest R. *Land of the Free: A History of the United States.* New York: Benziger Brothers, Inc., 1966.

Craven, Avery O., and Johnson, Walter. *American History.* Boston: Ginn and Company, 1961.

Current, Richard N.; DeConde, Alexander; and Dante, Harris L. *United States History.* Glenview: Scott, Foresman, and Company, 1967.

Gewehr, Wesley M.; Gordon, Donald C.; Sparks, David S.; and Stromberg, Ronald N. *The United States: A History of the United States.* New York: McGraw-Hill Book Company, Inc., 1960.

Graff, Henry F. *The Free and the Brave.* Chicago: Rand McNally, 1967.

Graff, Henry F., and Krout, John A. *The Adventure of the American People: A History of the United States.* New York: Rand McNally and Company, 1963.

Hofstadter, Richard; Miller, William; and Aaron, Daniel. *The American Republic.* Vol. I. Englewood Cliffs, N.J.: Prentice-Hall, Inc., 1964.

————. *Structure of American History.* Englewood Cliffs, N.J.: Prentice-Hall, Inc., 1964.

————. *History of a Republic.* Englewood Cliffs, N.J.: Prentice-Hall, Inc., 1957.

Liebman, Rebekah R., and Young, Gertrude A. *The Growth of America.* Englewood Cliffs, N.J.: Prentice-Hall, Inc., 1959.

McGuire, Edna, and Portwood, Thomas B. *Our Free Nation.* New York: Macmillan Company, 1961.

Moon, Glen W., and Cline, Don C. *Story of Our Land and People.* New York: Holt, Rinehart and Winston, Inc., 1964.

Muzzey, David Seville. *Our Country's History.* Boston: Ginn and Company, 1961.

Muzzey, David Seville, and Link, Arthur S. *Our American Heritage.* Boston: Ginn and Company, 1963.

Perkins, Dexter, and Van Deusen, Glyndon G. *The United States of America: A History.* Vol. I and Vol. II. New York: Macmillan Company, 1962.

Reich, Jerome R., and Biller, Edward L. *Building the American Nation.* New York: Harcourt, Brace and World, Inc., 1968.

Savelle, Max. *A Short History of American Civilization.* New York: Dryden Press, 1957.

Steinberg, Samuel. *The United States: Story of a Free People.* Boston: Allyn and Bacon, Inc., 1964.

Todd, Lewis Paul, and Curti, Merle. *Rise of the American Nation.* New York: Harcourt, Brace and World, Inc., 1964, 1966.

Wilder, Howard B.; Ludlum, Robert P.; and Brown, Harriet McCune. *This Is America's Story.* Boston: Houghton Mifflin Company, 1960, 1966.

Winther, Oscar O., and Cartwright, William H. *The Story of Our Heritage.* Boston: Ginn and Company, 1962.

Textbooks written by the same author or authors are viewed as different books in this study. Textbooks of two-volume length are treated as one book. The books have been chosen on the basis of their availability in university curriculum libraries and because they are generally representative of United States textbooks in secondary school use.

Textbooks, according to one scholar,[3] are a major educational tool because they are so universally and consistently used throughout a child's school career. History textbooks, in particular, are important because they are so widely used at the primary and secondary levels. A serious problem involving the use of such books is that many of them are unreliable sources of information. They often put forth as fact controversial theories, and they present biased, misleading, inaccurate, and unrealistic material relating to American Indians, especially the Iroquois. Many students who read these books are unlikely to question the information they find on the printed page. They regard such content as inviolable. Since these students are not equipped to make the required value judgments concerning the merits of the material they are reading, the authors unwittingly give an intellectual and historical basis to the collection of stereotypes and myths young people have acquired about Indians, principally from the mass communications media.[4]

Jeannette Henry, a Cherokee Indian scholar, has discussed the analogy that an unreliable textbook, like a defective automobile, is a potential danger to individuals and should be retired:

> A textbook is an instrument of learning, which may be compared to an automobile as an instrument of transportation. An automobile which has defective brakes or is otherwise not dependable, is recalled by the manufacturer, so that lives may not be endangered. But a textbook which is defective, inaccurate, and unreliable, is not retired despite the possibility that minds may be endangered.[5]

A textbook usually remains in a school for three to seven years. If allowed to remain in schools, these texts will endanger not only one classroom of students but succeeding ones as well. Therefore, it is important that textbooks not be taken for granted but reviewed periodically for their reliability. In the context of this article, *a reliable textbook* is defined as one that contains accurate, unbiased, realistic, balanced, and sufficient information about American Indians.

Of the twenty-seven books examined for information on the Iroquois Indians, three historians do not mention them at all[6] and another three writers briefly refer to them once.[7] Essentially then, six authors ignore the Iroquois in their textbooks.

In terms of fundamental descriptive information about Iroquois Indians, the textbooks have presented an array of misinformation, misconceptions, omissions, and ethnocentricity. The Iroquois are generally introduced into books as "greatly feared by their enemies . . . and respected by their friends";[8] "the most famous of the Eastern woodland Indians";[9] "more advanced"[10] than other tribes; "best known of the East Indians;"[11] and "one of the most important groups of Eastern Indians."[12] Only one author, however, mentions the names of the tribes that compose the Iroquois, and this information is conveyed not in the main body of the text, but in a picture caption: ". . . the Finger Lakes of New York bear the proud names of the five original tribes—Mohawk, Seneca, Oneida, Cayuga, and Onondaga. After 1700 when the Tuscaroras of North Carolina joined the Confederation, the Five Nations as they were called, became the Six Nations. . . ."[13] The only other references that the Iroquois were (and are) a group of tribes are so oblique that it would be virtually impossible for uninformed readers to understand the formally organized, multitribal organization of the Iroquois: "five (later six) tribes joined together to form the League of the Iroquois";[14] "the Iroquois . . . brought five, later six tribes or nations into an effective confederacy";[15] "Five Nations home valley in New York";[16] a caption to a map locating the Iroquois tribes—"Iroquois formed League of Five Nations. . . .";[17] and finally, "the Iroquois were divided into five nations, or groups of Indians."[18] All except one of the writers omit, then, even a rudimentary explanation of Iroquois structure, and all fail to explain that the tribes' cultural and linguistic similarities make confederation possible.

Only one author goes into adequate detail explaining the territory of the Iroquois tribes avoiding the inappropriate textbook map label of "Eastern Woodland Indians":[19]

> The heart of the Iroquois empire extended across the rich central valley of present day New York State, from the Hudson River to the Genesee. . . . No more strategic terrain was to be found in all North America. . . . At its peak in the eighteenth century, the Iroquois empire spread some 800 miles between the Appalachians and the Mississippi, southwesterly from the Five Nations' home valley in New York . . . immensely rich fur empire.[20]

There are no other textbook comments regarding the region that the Iroquois occupied. One author, however, cites an observation of Francis Parkman on the attitude of the Iroquois toward their land empire. In Parkman's judgment, it "gave the . . . Iroquois confederates advantages they perfectly understood and by which they profited to the utmost. . . ."[21] If the other authors had each devoted one paragraph to the rich nature of the Iroquois land possessions, it would have helped to explain the subsequent struggles among the Iroquois, French, British, and American colonials for possession of the area.

The few authors who want to convey some notion of the behavior of the Iroquois describe it in warlike terms: "The Iroquois whose tribes were the most warlike in the eastern parts of North America."[22] "These Indians (Iroquois) were constantly at war with other tribes. They fought so often that the leaders began to fear that there would not be enough young men to protect their homes. For a while they kept the strongest of the enemies whom they captured and made them members of their tribes to replace their own warriors who had been killed."[23] One author quotes a Jesuit, Lafitau, who "knew the Iroquois at the peak of their prosperity toward the end of the seventeenth century"[24] to document his point: "They (Iroquois) have taken the ascendant over the other nations, divided and overcome the most warlike, made themselves a terror to the most remote. . . ."[25] To push his point even further, the same historian quotes from Francis Parkman: "Among all the barbarous nations of the continent, the Iroquois of New York stand paramount . . . ferocious vitality, which, but for the presence of the Europeans, would probably have subjected, absorbed, or exterminated every other Indian community east of the Mississippi and north of the Ohio."[26] At another point in his narrative, the above author refers to "Iroquois warriors."[27] Two textbooks contained identical references that the Iroquois were constantly on the warpath. . . .[28] One of the preceding authors pursues the matter with "They had such noble qualities as dignity, courage, and endurance, but they often tortured captured enemies."[29] Although the last part of the previous statement is accurate in that the fate of Iroquois prisoners who were not adopted was a cruel one according to modern standards, it is nevertheless deceptive, because torturing one's enemies was an accepted code of behavior among Indians and non-Indians. A misimpression that Iroquois were particularly brutal to enemies has been created by the omission of pertinent data regarding the similar behavior of non-Indians.

It is evident that none of the textbook authors provide accurate and balanced information on Iroquois behavior. Iroquois men, before contact with non-Indians, were hunters as well as warriors, the former being an extremely important job in their lives. They were also craftsmen, physicians, politicians, dancers, and religious leaders. These roles of Iroquois men are ignored, however, in favor of stressing their "warlike" behavior.

None of the authors compare or contrast pre-Columbian Iroquois attitudes about sexual roles with contemporary European and colonial American attitudes. The role of women (early seventeenth-century Iroquois and contemporary European and colonial American) is a topic that provides important cross-cultural information. One author includes an illustration of Iroquois women and one caption: "Women in front of the storage building at the right are busy preparing food."[30] Iroquois women were the farmers in their culture as well as clothesmakers, dispersers of herbal remedies, cooks, and dancers in ceremonials. They also had an important political role because of their power to name and remove Confederacy Chiefs. One scholar believes that "There is no question but that at the time of the European contact, the Iroquois woman occupied a higher, freer, and more influential place in her society than did the European woman in hers . . . the Iroquois woman's position was securely based on her leadership in the family and in agriculture."[31]

In terms of the settlement patterns of Iroquois Indians very little material can be found in textbooks. One author mentions the subject in a caption to a picture: "Iroquois Indians (Senecas) about 1500 A.D. in a community in what is now Western New York State" and further describes: "The permanent Iroquois villages were impressive. Each was made up of a series of houses solidly built and surrounded by a low earthen wall. On or inside the wall a wooden stockade was constructed."[32] The same author describes an illustration of a longhouse, "the typical Iroquois dwelling,"[33] and another author mentions that Iroquois "lived in large, bark-covered houses, known as 'long houses'"[34] but they both fail to indicate *when* the tribes lived this way and *why* they chose the longhouse for living quarters. The answer lies in the cultural structure of the Iroquois which the writers fail to describe. By not describing whether or not these settlement patterns have persisted into the twentieth century, both textbook authors have created misconceptions. Young readers may be left with the notion that Iroquois Indians are still leading a sixteenth- and seventeenth-century style of life.

Two textbooks contain the same statements about Iroquois attitudes toward land. "They were constantly . . . shifting their hunting grounds. They knew nothing about the white man's idea of private ownership of property."[35] "They were constantly shifting their hunting grounds. They knew nothing about the white man's idea of private ownership of property. Hunting grounds were claimed in common by the tribe or a group of tribes."[36] Both authors describe the Iroquois concept of land in terms of the Indians' ignorance of non-Indian thought on the subject. These textbook statements obscure the knowledge from readers that non-Indians were equally ignorant of tribal concepts of land. Negative descriptions about Iroquois Indians do not permit students to know that the tribes had different but equally valid conceptions of land ownership and property rights.

THE IROQUOIS CONFEDERACY AND ITS IMPACT

Textbook material on Iroquois political organization is meager although scholars have studied and found the Iroquois Confederacy to be an important political system. One author presents a brief and reasonably informative account of the Confederacy:

> . . . the Iroquois added a spectacular achievement in government. They brought five, later six tribes or nations into an effective confederacy. Each tribe kept a measure of independence, but they acted together on broader matters. The Iroquois also showed a genius for tying other peoples in as conquered tribes, allies, or immigrants.[37]

Two authors, however, refer to the Iroquois form of government as a "crude sort of government"[38] while another two convey the opposite opinion: "Tribes like the Iroquois in Upper New York were highly organized politically"[39] and "The Iroquois . . . had achieved remarkable success in government."[40]

Only three authors discuss (and one other hints at) the existence and founding of the Iroquois Confederacy, also known as the Iroquois League. The first one writes:

> The Iroquois . . . League or Confederation has been known as "The Great Place" when it was first brought together in the middle of the sixteenth century by the imaginative chieftain, Hiawatha. The purpose of the League had been to end warfare among the Five Nations of New York Valley, and, by presenting a united front, to discourage the surrounding tribes from aggression.[41]

This author writes that the Iroquois Confederacy "was first brought together in the middle of the sixteenth century by the imaginative chieftain, Hiawatha," and presents this information as though it were verified as fact. This author and others who have the same ideology have not alerted their readers to the fact that what information exists about Iroquois has been embodied in orally transmitted history, part of the heritage brought down from one Iroquois generation to another. It is important to remember that "The myth itself is not . . . an historical record. We do not know whether its heroes, Deganawidah and Hiawatha, actually lived. But the myth probably reflects in a general way what did happen."[42] It is also evident from the preceding quotation that this textbook author ignores the role of the legendary Deganawidah in the formation of the Confederacy—one of the two great heroes in the Iroquois culture. Moreover, no authority has determined the precise time the Confederacy was formed:

> When white men first became conscious of it, the Iroquois already thought of it as ancient. Since the Iroquois had no method of dating years accurately, and since their time sense was different from ours, we cannot know what "ancient" means. Some authorities have set the date in the middle of the sixteenth century, some in the middle of the fifteenth. Some modern Iroquois believe that the Confederacy was founded as early as the end of the fourteenth century.[43]

The second author who discusses the existence and founding of the Iroquois Confederacy writes:

> According to legend, the Iroquois Confederation was organized by two great leaders—Deganawidah and Hiawatha. For more than two centuries, the Confederation was highly successful. The legendary Deganawidah was a man of magnificent vision. He dreamed of a day when the Confederation would include all Indians, war would be abolished, and peace would reign across the face of the earth. We catch a glimpse of this noble ideal in the Iroquois "constitution" passed on by word of mouth from generation to generation: "I, Deganawidah, and the Confederated Chiefs, so uproot the tallest pine tree, and into the cavity thereby made we cast all weapons of war. Into the depths of the earth, deep down into the underneath currents of water flowing to unknown regions, we cast all weapons of strife. We bury them from sight and plant again the tree. Thus shall the Great Peace be established." Deganawidah's ideal was shattered when the Europeans began to settle the New World. Allied with the British, the organization that had been created as an instrument of peace, became, for a time, a formidable instrument of war.[44]

This author has adequately explored the role of Deganawidah in the formation of the Confederation and has sketched the relationship of Europeans to the League, but he has been remiss in not citing the sources of his information.

The third author who deals with the topic of the origin of the Iroquois Confederacy writes: ". . . to save the lives of the young men, the tribes banded together into a league. They formed a council of leaders who were elected by the people of the different tribes. The council made laws which put a stop to wars. The League made the Iroquois the strongest group in the eastern part of North America."[45] This author's simplistic interpretation of the Confederacy's formation barely reflects Iroquois legend or the research that has been done by Iroquois scholars.

A fourth author suggests the existence of the Confederation with the statement: "Because the five Iroquois nations agreed to fight together against any enemy, they became the strongest Indians living in the eastern woodlands of North America."[46]

Scholars have recognized and studied the impact of the Iroquois Confederacy on American political organization. Not all historians have agreed it was one of the models on which the United States Constitution has been based. One renowned anthropologist has felt "There is some historical evidence that knowledge of the League influenced the colonies in their first efforts to form a confederacy and later to write a constitution."[47] One textbook author has treated this subject in his book: "It was from the great League of the Iroquois that the founders of our government got some of their ideas for making our democracy."[48] However, the evidence that the Confederacy impressed the white settlers has been omitted by all the other writers.

THE IROQUOIS CONFEDERACY AND THE ALBANY CONFERENCE OF 1754

The significant role of the Iroquois Confederacy in the Albany Conference of 1754 is another subject that has been ignored by the textbook writers. Historians have established that the presence of the Iroquois stimulated the British Crown and some colonists to work at formal union of the disparate colonies to improve relations with the Confederacy and to improve colonial defenses against the French and their Indian allies, the latter of which were enemies of the Iroquois. Several authors who include information on the Albany Conference omit mentioning the presence of the Iroquois at the talks. Perhaps the writers were unfamiliar with existing data that the Board of Trade in London summoned an intercolonial conference at Albany, New York in the summer of 1754, conveniently close to Iroquois country, for the purposes of improving relations with the Iroquois and strengthening colonial defenses. One textbook writer notes: "In 1754, English officers called a meeting at Albany, attended by Commissioners of seven colonies, to discuss ways of creating such an organization (union of colonies)."[49] A second one states: "In 1754, it was decided to have a meeting in Albany, New York to consider plans for defense. The colonies were asked to send representatives to the meeting and seven colonies did so. . . . The Albany Plan is of interest now because it shows that some colonial leaders understood the need for united action."[50] Both writers have omitted the attendance of well over one hundred Iroquois as well as the reason for the Indians coming to the Albany Conference. Another author, who asserts that the Conference "was attended by over one hundred fifty Indians and by delegates from seven of the colonies,"[51] does not give any information about the tribes that attended the Conference and their reasons for doing so.

Twelve textbooks contain material on the role of the Iroquois in the Albany Conference. Five of the authors mention the Iroquois in connection with the conference but never clearly state that these Indians were participating members:

colonial delegates assembled at Albany . . . to try to make a common peace with the Indians and to win support of the Iroquois in the coming war with France."[52] "A meeting was called at Albany. . . . The major purpose of the meeting was to work out a treaty with the Iroquois tribes that would keep them on the side of the English."[53] ". . . conference called by the British Government. This colonial conference was held in Albany, New York close to Iroquois Indian country. The Iroquois were enemies of the Algonquins, who were allies of the French. The English hoped to keep the Iroquois as allies, and this was one reason for the Albany Conference."[54] ". . . representatives . . . convened . . . to seek a joint agreement with the Iroquois to fight on their side."[55] Only one author asserts that "delegates . . . met at Albany, New York to discuss common measures of defense against the French and their Indian allies. They were joined there by Indian representatives of the Six Nations."[56] A seventh author presents an ethnocentric description: "In 1754, nineteen delegates . . . rode into Albany to confer with Iroquois chieftains. As the Iroquois listened, the white men went through the formalities that Indians demanded in all negotiations: the grandiloquent declarations of esteem, the ceremonial presentation of gifts . . ."[57] This comment ignores the reasons for the careful attention given to gift-giving and certain procedures by the Indians, obscures the knowledge that the Iroquois were quite skilled at diplomacy and negotiation, and disregards the fact that the white men probably insisted on certain procedures that must have seemed equally peculiar to the Iroquois.

The remaining authors who have anything to write about the Albany Conference and the Indians' role in it present inaccurate or misleading statements. Two authors are mistaken in writing: "At the Albany Conference, the colonies promised to help Great Britain and the Iroquois Indians also agreed to help the British troops fight against the French."[58] "The meeting at Albany . . . accomplished two important tasks: it made peace with the Iroquois Indians and at least partially secured their neutrality in the war that was coming. . . ."[59] There is no evidence that the Iroquois delegation made any commitments at the Albany Conference. The two preceding statements are inaccurate. A third author imparts that same misinformation but also includes an uncalled for pejorative phrase: "The immediate purpose was to keep the *scalping knives of the Iroquois tribes* on the side of the British in the spreading war, and this objective was gained when the chiefs were harangued and presented with gifts."[60] (Emphasis mine.) A fourth author writes that the colonists conferred at Albany for the purpose of making an alliance with the Iroquois, but misleads his readers into believing it was accomplished by adding: "Besides making an agreement with the Iroquois. . . ."[61]

THE IROQUOIS AND BENJAMIN FRANKLIN

Not one textbook author refers to the impact of the Iroquois Confederacy on the thinking of Benjamin Franklin. Scholars have discovered that Mr. Franklin learned about the organization and operation of the Iroquois League while attending Indian Councils and these experiences may have suggested to him the pattern for a United States of America. Regarding his proposed Albany Plan of Union, he wrote in a letter:

> It would be a very strange thing, if six nations of ignorant Savages should be capable of forming a Scheme for such a Union, and be able to execute it in such a Manner, as that it has subsisted ages, and appears indissoluble; and yet that a like Union should be impractical for ten or a Dozen English colonies, to whom it is more necessary, and must be more advantageous; and who cannot be supposed to want an equal understanding of their ignorance.[62]

CONTEMPORARY IROQUOIS AFFAIRS

Although textbook material on Iroquois political organization is meager, the situation worsens when trying to find information on contemporary affairs of Iroquois Indians. There are only two small textbook references to the present existence of those portions of Iroquois tribes living on reservations in New York that managed to evade the Removal Act of 1830.[63] The first author who mentions contemporary Iroquois in New York has distilled all of the complex political and social realities of the six tribes into one cheerless statement: "The Iroquois League lasted three hundred years, and vestiges of its traditions are still sustained by the few thousand tribesmen who continue to occupy the grounds of their vanished glory."[64] Neither the locations of the reservations nor the nature of the traditions have been mentioned. The other author writes: "The powerful Iroquois Confederacy that had blocked the path to white settlement in central and western New York has broken up. . . . The remnants of the tribes in the Confederation gave up their New York state lands and were settled on small reservations."[65] This statement suggests that the Iroquois tribes were settled outside New York State, which has not been the case. The author also fails to explain why the tribes "blocked the path to white settlement," and creates the impression that the Iroquois had no rights to their land. It is not surprising that many Americans, both young and old, are not aware that Iroquois reservations exist in upstate and western New York because a basic source of information, American history textbooks, has omitted this information.

CONCLUSIONS

It is evident from the preceding analyses that it would be virtually impossible for students to get a clear understanding of the Iroquois tribes culturally and historically as well as an understanding of the impact of the Confederacy on American political organization. Textbook information is inaccurate, ethnocentric, misleading, insufficient, or altogether missing from the narrative. If this sort of textbook writing continues to be published, large numbers of young readers will continue to be harmed. As one scholar warns:

It is hardly necessary to expand . . . on the consequences of . . . deformed history; the creation or reinforcement of feelings of racial arrogance, and the disgorgement from our schools of students with a warped understanding of their cultural heritage, with no comprehension of the revolutionary changes taking place in the world, and no intellectual equipment for dealing with the problems of race relations here and abroad.[66]

Damaging myths, inaccuracies, misconceptions, and omissions involving Iroquois Indians (as well as other tribes) must be eliminated. Instead, knowledge about the precise nature of Iroquois thought and actions in American history and in contemporary times should be truthfully recorded.

NOTES

1. Among those organizations actively engaged in informing and educating the American people concerning the histories and cultures of American Indians, Aleuts, and Eskimos are the American Indian Historical Society, Association on American Indian Affairs, many tribes and Indian education agencies.

2. ". . . Columbus's name for . . . Indians is to this day understood by many to refer to a single people. Despite the still commonly asked question, 'Do you speak Indian?' there is neither a single Indian people nor a single Indian language, but many different peoples, with different racial characteristics, different cultures, and different languages." Alvin M. Josephy, Jr., *The Indian Heritage of America* (New York: Bantam Books, Inc., 1969), p. 9. This author will use the plural form—Indians or Natives—throughout the paper.

3. Lloyd Marcus, *The Treatment of Minorities in Secondary School Textbooks* (Anti-Defamation League 1963), p. 3.

4. Several years ago, the National Congress of American Indians, an all-Indian organization located in Washington, D.C., created the American Indian Media Service (AIMS) Committee to help eliminate the false, derogatory, and harmful Indian stereotypes ("bloodthirsty savage" and "slovenly lazy drunk") that often appear in the communications media: television, newspapers, magazine ads, and radio.

5. American Indian Historical Society, *Textbooks and the American Indian* (San Francisco: Indian Historian Press, 1970), p.11.

6. Gewehr, Gordon, Sparks, and Stromberg, *History of a Democracy*; Hofstadter, Miller, and Aaron, *Structure of American History*; Wilder, Ludlum, and Brown, *This Is America's Story.*

7. Brown, Lang, and Wheeler, *The American Achievement*; Perkins and Van Deusen, *The United States of America: A History*; Reich and Biller, *Building the American Nation.*

8. Todd and Curti, *American Nation*, p. 50.

9. Reich and Biller, *Building the Nation*, p. 25.

10. Muzzey, *Our Country's History*, p. 24; Muzzey and Link, *Heritage,* p. 12.

11. Graff, *The Free and the Brave.* p. 9.

12. Liebman and Young, *Growth of America*, p. 50.

13. Todd and Curti, *American Nation*, p. 50.

14. McGuire and Portwood, *Our Free Nation*, p. 263.

15. Caughey, Franklin, and May, *Land of the Free*, p. 43.

16. Hofstadter, Miller, and Aaron, *American Republic,* p. 126.

17. Wilder, Ludlum, and Brown, *America's Story*, p. 114.

18. Reich and Biller, *Building the Nation*, p. 25.

19. Jack D. Forbes, well-known scholar, deplores the use of map labels such as "Eastern Woodland Indians." *Native Americans of California and Nevada: A Handbook* (Berkeley: Far West Laboratory for Educational Research and Development, 1968), pp. 121–122.

20. Hofstadter, Miller, and Aaron, *American Republic*.

21. Ibid., pp. 123–124.

22. Wilder, Ludlum, and Brown, *America's Story*, p. 119.

23. Liebman and Young, *Growth of America*, pp. 48–49.

24. Ibid., 123.

25. Ibid.

26. Ibid.

27. Ibid., 126.

28. Muzzey, *Our Country's History*, p. 24; Muzzey and Link, *Heritage*, p. 12.

29. Muzzey, *Our Country's History*, p. 24.

30. Graff, *The Free and the Brave*, p. 9.

31. Hazel Hertzberg, *The Great Tree and the Longhouse: The Culture of the Iroquois* (New York: The Macmillan Company, 1966), p. 73.

32. Graff, *The Free and the Brave*, p. 9.

33. Ibid.

34. McGuire and Portwood, *Our Free Nation*, p. 263.

35. Muzzey and Link, *Heritage,* pp. 12–14.

36. Muzzey, *Our Country's History*, p. 24.

37. Caughey, Franklin, and May, *Land of the Free*, pp. 124–125.

38. Muzzey. *Our Country's History*, p. 24; Muzzey and Link, *Heritage* pp. 12–14.

39. Hofstadter, Miller, and Aaron, *History of a Republic*, p. 20.

40. Graff, *The Free and the Brave*, p. 9.

41. Hofstadter, Miller, and Aaron, *American Republic*, pp.124–125.

42. Hertzberg, *Culture of the Iroquois*, p. 86.

43. Ibid. , 85.

44. Todd and Curti, *American Nation*, p. 50.

45. Liebman and Young, *Growth of America*, p. 49.

46. Reich and Miller, *Building the Nation*, p. 25.

47. Clark Wissler, *Indians of the United States: Four Centuries of Their History and Culture* (New York: Doubleday and Company, Inc., 1940), p. 112.

48. Liebman and Young, *Growth of America*, p. 49.

49. Graff and Krout, *Adventure*, p. 82.

50. McGuire and Portwood, *Our Free Nation*, p. 132.

51. Muzzey and Link, *Heritage*, p. 59.

52. Hofstadter, Miller, and Aaron, *American Republic*, p. 65; Hofstadter, Miller, and Aaron, *History of a Republic*, p. 139.

53. Moon and Cline, *Land and People*, p. 138.

54. Brown, Lang, and Wheeler, *The American Achievement*, p. 53.

55. Hofstadter, Miller, and Aaron, *Structure of American History*, p. 40.

56. Todd and Curti, *American Nation*, p. 51.

57. Blum, Catton, Morgan, Schlesinger, Stampp, and Woodward, *National Experience,* p. 76.

58. Reich and Biller, *Building the Nation*, p. 146.

59. Savelle, *American Civilization*, p. 115.

60. Bailey, *American Pageant*, p. 154.

61. Graff, *The Free and the Brave,* p. 154.

62. Stuart Levine and Nancy O. Lurie, *The American Indian Today* (De Land, Florida: Everett/Edwards, 1965), p. 148.

63. An act signed May 28, 1830, which enabled the United States President, Andrew Jackson, through treaties, to remove Indians living east of the Mississippi to areas west of it. This act made it possible for land-hungry whites to take over Indian lands.

64. Hofstadter, Miller, and Aaron, *American Republic*, pp. 124–125.

65. Perkins and Van Deusen, *History*, p. 314.

66. Virgil J. Vogel, "The Indian in American History Textbooks," *Integrated Education,* Vol. VI, No. 3 (May/June, 1968), p. 16.

Arctic Survival—Inaccurate Textbooks Create Igloo Myths in Alaska*

Howard Rock

For great many years there has been an erroneous image in connection with the snow igloo in Alaska. It persists because educators have not bothered to correct certain textbooks used in schools in the United States. It is disconcerting to say the least, for an Eskimo pupil in Alaska to read in his textbook that he lives in snow igloos. The Eskimo student has never seen a snow igloo. It is also likely that his parents or grandparents have never seen a snow igloo unless they have traveled east in Canada.

It is no wonder that tourists from the lower states are often disappointed in finding out that the Eskimos in Alaska have never lived in snow igloos. The common remark has been, "But I read in my geography book that you live in snow igloos."

No Snow Igloos

Although Alaskan Eskimos have never lived in snow igloos, there are other Eskimos who do. These are Canadian Eskimos. They are nomadic and out of necessity use snow igloos. Their economy depends on moving with the animals they hunt for subsistence. They use the snow igloo as a temporary dwelling.

When a hunter or traveler in Alaska is caught in a storm or cannot make the distance home, he makes temporary shelter for the night. Not knowing how to make a snow igloo like his Canadian cousin, he digs into a bank of snow. Some Alaskan Eskimos who are close to the Canadian border do know how to build snow igloos because they have learned the art of making them from Canadian Eskimos.

---

*Reprinted by permission from *Tundra Times*, Nov. 19, 1962; reprinted by *Tundra Times*, Jan. 23, 1974, p. 7.

Florida Igloo

When Paul Tiulana of King Island was asked by a tourist if he had ever seen a snow igloo, he replied, "Only once." "Where was that?" the tourist asked. "In Florida," was Tiulana's reply. He had seen the igloo while on a tourist promotional tour in one of the warmest of the states.

The sod igloo is, and was, a permanent type home in Alaska; permanent homes and villages were a necessity. Villages were picked because of their strategic economic value. There was no need to be nomadic. Animals were plentiful and nature provided a succession of animals; that is, when one specie left, a different specie migrated to take its place and in turn was hunted.

To take advantage of these excellent hunting conditions the ancient Eskimo in Alaska devised a home that was ideal for the climate of the Arctic—the sod igloo. This is how he builds it.

Long before the igloo is to be built, usually in late spring, the family who wishes to build cuts sod in one-foot squares about 5 or 6 inches thick. As the squares are cut out they are piled in tiers so the wind and sun can dry them out. The cutting and drying of these sod squares may be done a year earlier from the time the igloo is to be built. The reason: dry sod is necessary for a warm igloo. When sod is put on wet and fresh off the ground, it freezes when cold and is hard to heat.

Building Igloo

But even when it is applied fresh off the ground, in time it dries out thoroughly from the internal heat of the igloo and by the sun and wind on the exterior. It then becomes a perfect conductor of heat and cold. A dry and seasoned sod igloo is easy to heat and slow to cool. After the sod pieces have been cut and set to dry the flooring and frame of the igloo is begun. The man of the house takes driftwood that has been washed ashore, smoothes the sides flat with his jade adze. After sufficient driftwood pieces have been prepared, the Eskimo is ready to erect the igloo on his chosen site.

He digs into the ground a desired foundation about 2 feet deep. He then lays the flooring upon which he builds the frame of the igloo. The igloo, almost in all cases, faces south. The roof is built somewhat of a dome shape with about a three foot square skylight. A small ventilator on the roof is built on. When the frame of the main room and the frame of the long hallway or tunnel has been built, it is ready for sod covering. All around the base, sod is applied two feet thick about three quarters of the way up the walls. This is to prevent the sod from falling off the walls and to provide added warmth to the igloo. The rest of the wall is covered with a foot thickness of sod.

Sod Slabs

The sod squares are applied in bricklaying fashion so the sod will adhere solidly to the walls. When the sod has been applied flush with the walls, a different operation is begun to cover the roof. Sod slabs with fine grass surfaces and strongly interwoven with fine grass roots, and which are hard to tear, are used to cover the roof.

These slabs are roughly two and a half feet in diameter and about 3 inches thick. They are cut with a hoe-like tool that slices into the grassy surface. The blade of the tool is made out of a whale rib that flares out at the blade end, tapered flat and sharpened.

For the final operation the same sod slabs are applied with the grassy side to the weather. Care is taken that cracks or seams are overlapped so rain and snow will not leak through the roof. The ancient igloos usually had long, low hallways to warm the frigid air somewhat before it entered the igloo.

Long Hallways

The ancient igloo had a novel entrance which is no longer used today. It was a round hole, or trap entrance, to the front edge of the room. The hallway or tunnel, dipped rather sharply to this entrance to allow room for persons entering. The reason for this type of entrance was, again, to warm the air. Frigid air, being heavier than warm air, tends to stay more or less, immobile and only limited cold air enters the room. The evidence of this principal can be seen in very cold weather. Steam forms at a trap entrance where warm air comes in contact with cold air. Cold air does not rush in to cool the igloo. When desired, the entrance was covered to give added warmth.

The long hallway of the ancient igloo had small chambers or rooms, two usually, on each side. One was for storage of meat for immediate use and the other was the kitchen. Here, the woman of the house cooked the meals for her family and brought the meals into the house when done. The cooking chamber had simply a small hole in the roof for smoke to escape from an open fire over which the woman of the house cooked.

Prior to the whaling culture that started some 2,000 or 2,500 years ago, driftwood was apparently used for hallway frames. Later, whale ribs, jawbones, and shoulder blades were used for hallways. Apparently, this was done to conserve wood which has always been scarce on the Arctic Coast. There were two entrances into the hallway of the ancient sod igloo: one, at the front end on the ground level, usually a small door; the other, on the roof of the outer end of the hallway. This roof entrance was about two and a half feet square to which led a ladder for means of entering and leaving. This entrance was necessitated by heavy blizzards that would sometimes bury the ground level entrance.

The Kalagee

There was another type of igloo the ancient Eskimo did not do without. He needed it for social affairs. This was a Kalagee or recreation hall. The Kalagee

was a huge igloo. It accommodated many people. It was used for Eskimo dancing, games, feasts, performances of medicine men, and for story-telling sessions.

A Kalagee was built about the same way the resident igloo was built but many
times larger. Stationary benches were built all around the floor surface. Sometimes another bench above the other was built to accommodate more people. For
heating and lighting of the Kalagee, as well as the ordinary igloo, whale oil lamps
were used. In the case of the Kalagee several of them were required, placed at regular intervals.

Although a few sod igloos are still in use in Alaska, they are disappearing. In
places where a few igloos are still in use Eskimos are stubbornly trying to keep
them in existence under pressure of civilization. Sod igloos have been under subtle but relentless attack. One way this was done was by instructors in schools who
expounded the superiority, in appearance, of the frame igloo.

Subtle Attack

It has been the experience of this writer, while attending school, that he was made
to feel ashamed of the sod igloo without really knowing how it happened. A con-
scientious construction engineer once expressed his feelings while building frame
dwellings for Eskimo families who had been persuaded to vacate their sod igloos.
He said he had been told to move the Eskimos from their warm and snug but
crowded houses, to larger, roomier, but colder ones, where they would probably
catch colds and other diseases.

The sod igloo, while it may not have been an eye-catching structure, served its
purpose extremely well in the survival of the Eskimo in the Arctic. It was easy to
heat where fuel was scarce. It stood up extremely well under the rigors of the
Arctic climate and was comfortable. It was carefully thought out and built ac-
cordingly. Once finished, the sod igloo lasted for many, many years.

Chapter 6

Still Playing Cowboys and Indians after All These Years?

Toys with Indian Imagery

Arlene B. Hirschfelder
with illustrations by Leslie Frank McKeon

For children to develop positive attitudes toward racial and cultural groups different from their own they "need to be exposed to a variety of experiences, information, and images about each cultural group in order to develop an understanding of rich cultural patterns and diversity."[1] Children get their information and images about Native Americans from a variety of sources which includes adults—particularly teachers, museum displays, food packages, advertisements, television, radio, movies, books, and toys. Many of these sources frequently transmit unfavorable stereotypes and inaccurate information about Native Americans thus preventing children from developing a realistic picture of past and contemporary Native life. As Moore and Hirschfelder argue in "Feathers, Tomahawks, and Tipis: A Study of Stereotyped 'Indian' Imagery in Children's Picture Books,"[2] no one illustration is sufficient to create stereotypes in children's minds. However, too many books, advertisements, movies, and toys have these images—and the general culture reinforces them—so that there is a cumulative effect which encourages false perceptions about Native Americans.[3] Thus, it is to be expected that young children who continuously assimilate the stereotyped portrayal of Native Americans in their books, television programs, movies, and toys eventually develop attitudes toward them that are not only unrealistic but also negative.

Native American children who frequently encounter stereotyped images of Indians[4] are hindered in developing a feeling of pride in their heritage and in developing a healthy self-image and racial identity. The attitudes toward Native Americans revealed through the media, books, toys, and other sources of information

> are among the most potentially hazardous, for these can easily be internalized—particularly by the "minority" child. Such internalized attitudes profoundly affect self-concept, behavior, aspiration and confidence. They can inhibit a child before he or she has learned to define personal talents, limits or objectives, and tend to become self-fulfilling prophesies.[5]

The National Congress of the American Indians (NCAI) wrote years ago that "The continued insensitive projection of false stereotypes has resulted in untold harm to, and discrimination against, the American Indian. Such portrayals have resulted in real socioeconomic handicaps and loss of self-esteem among members of the Indian population."[6] A Native American educator assesses the impact of stereotyping on Native people in this way:

> It is time for Indian people to begin approving of and accepting themselves as human beings. For too long we have allowed ourselves to be guided by other people's standards and ideals. We must begin discarding archaic stereotypes of who and what Indians are. All across Indian country, this is one of the major concerns: to change and improve the image of the North America Indian in the eyes of Indians and non-Indians alike. Up until the present day, the American public has been fed, and has accepted as fact, inaccurate information about Native Americans. . . . The damage that can be done by attributing stereotyped characteristics to another, or to oneself, is immeasurable. When looked at through image-colored glasses, an individual is never seen as an individual; he is not seen for what he is but for what he "ought" to be. All stereotypes and prejudgments only get in the way of allowing people the freedom to be who they are . . . considerable work is yet to be done among non-Indians, as well as among ourselves, to rid us all of this nonproductive activity called Stereotyping. The first step is to assist non-Indians in ridding themselves of their negative concepts about who and what we are and to assist them in seeing us as human beings.[7]

Studies have been done on the treatment of Native Americans and other racial groups in school textbooks, children's storybooks, literature, magazine cartoons, movies, and television. Little if any research has been done, however, on the imagery of racial groups in the everyday playthings of children. This is surprising because play is an important means by which children learn. According to Geraldine L. Wilson, former director of the New York City Regional Training Office at New York University, play develops creative thought, problem solving, and other related skills; helps develop positive attitudes about self and others; and can build positive attitudes toward people who are different racially and culturally.[9] Toys are, very often, the "tools" of the play but they are not merely playthings to amuse children according to Public Action Coalition on Toys (PACT), a New York based public-interest organization seeking to encourage the development and securing of safe and sensible, quality toys for children and working to discourage the production of toys that exploit, injure, or limit a child's growth, safety, or welfare. PACT explains that toys

> play an important role in advancing a child's social, emotional, physical and intellectual development. Even very young infants are attracted by bright mobiles and crib toys, which increase the strength of their eye muscles and help to develop their hands and arms as they watch and reach up to touch the bright objects. . . . Older children derive a wealth of experience from toys. Toys are tools through which both social roles and intellectual skills are learned and outlets provided for emotions. . . . Toys help children to grow emotionally. Mastery through play gives children that sense of pleasure and accomplishment so important to the development of a positive self-image. Toys provide props and models for role-playing. Toys enable children to try on the world, to test what they think and feel about themselves and others. . . . Since toys

play such an important role in the development of children it is immediately apparent that they can also be quite harmful. Toys that are unsafe, racist, sexist, violent or anti-creative can be as negative to development as the toys described earlier as positive.[9]

Children who play with toys are not equipped to make value judgements concerning the merits of the toys with which they are playing. They do not stop to consider whether the toys are unsafe, racist, sexist, or violent. They assimilate the "content" of toys with little conscious thought. This is because children have limited cognitive skills and have not mastered the ability to evaluate information. They simply believe what they see. And what they see quite often are toys that convey derogatory and false images of Native Americans.

From 1975 to 1980, the author collected toys and toy-related items which have particularly insensitive, unauthentic, and damaging images of Native Americans. These toys misrepresent Native Americans to non-Indian children. In addition, they can undermine the self-esteem of Native children. The toys and toy-related items were purchased in neighborhood candy shops, discount and retail toy stores, novelty shops, drug stores, and similar retail operations in Bergen County, New Jersey and New York City. It is safe to assume that the same toys or similar ones can be found in stores around the country. Because New York City is the "capital of the United States toy industry," it has a fair sampling of toys that are merchandised around the country. The toys range in price from forty-nine cents to over fifteen dollars—with the majority costing well under five dollars. They have all been sold in the United States over the past five years. These toys share certain characteristics that convey incorrect and often offensive images of Native Americans. Seven characteristics of these toys have been selected and carefully examined and illustrated in the pages that follow. These include: 1) Indians-with-Headdresses; 2) Indians-of-the-Past; 3) Indians-as-a-Mixture; 4) Indians-as-Animals-Cartoons-Objects; 5) Indians-as-Occupation-or-Role; 6) Cowboy-and-Indian; and 7) Indian-Toy-Language. Fifteen line drawings of representative toys illustrate the characteristics. Other toys that also illustrate certain categories are described and discussed. Many of the toys, of course, demonstrate several characteristics of the Indian image[10] but only one is selected to represent and prove a point. Whenever it is possible, the names and addresses of the toy manufacturers are supplied. Some toys are not identified.

INDIANS-WITH-HEADDRESSES

The most prevalent characteristic of Indian imagery in toys is either the headband-with-one-feather or the headdress containing numerous feathers which resembles, in varying degrees, a Plains war bonnet.[11]

Sometimes, the headdresses are toys themselves as illustrated by the "Big Chief Authentic Indian Headdress" (Rollin Wilson Company of Memphis, Tennessee 38107) (Fig. 1) or TWA's Chief Twanta Headband Kit (Cal Industries, Inc.). The

Fig. 1

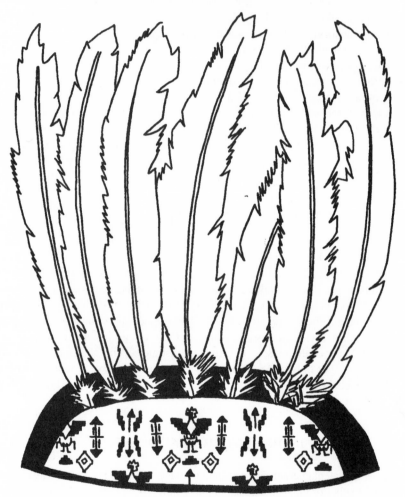

ten individual feathers that fit into this headband are decorated with animals, fish, and birds. Several years ago, the Horchow Catalogue offered a collection of four children's play hats which included an "Indian feathered bonnet." The idea of children "playing Indians" with these headdresses will be discussed later.

Hi Flier Manufacturing Company (Decatur, Illinois) which calls itself "The World's Largest Kite Mfrs" has offered in its line an inexpensive triangular-shaped paper kite with an enormous graphic design of an Indian face with a head-dress consisting of twenty feathers. One of the puzzles in the Junior Guild Jigsaw Puzzle line (Whitman Company) is "Indian Hunter and His Dog." The puzzle is a color photograph of a young boy dressed in a striped teeshirt and a war bonnet with a bow and his dog beside him. On the September 1977 "It's Time for School" cover of Sesame Street magazine, Grover is pictured wearing a head-dress. The cover of "Yankee Doodler, It's Fun to Draw and Scribble," a pad of paper (Prudential Paper Products Company, Inc. of Glendale, New York 11227) shows doodles of everyday objects together with a boy bedecked in a headdress (Fig. 2). Another pad of paper designed for school use (Westab of Dayton, Ohio 45402) is entitled "Big Chief" and sports a face of an Indian man looking off into the distance (Fig. 2). The cover of a small "Peanuts Memo Pad" (Butterfly Originals by Plymouth, Inc. of Bellmawr, New Jersey 08030) contains a photo-graph of an authentic Plains tipi with Snoopy and Woodstock superimposed over it. Snoopy is wearing a multifeathered headdress and holds a peace pipe while Woodstock strolls around in a one-feathered headband. In 1980, Rose Art Industries (of Passaic, New Jersey 07055) offered for sale an "Indian Beads" set to make bracelets, necklaces, and belts. The plastic beads are encased in a trans-parent headdress.

Everybody and everything from children to animals as well as cartoon charac-ters are bedecked with anywhere from a single feather to a multifeathered head-dress even though the toy or toy-related item has nothing to do with Native Americans. It is no wonder, then, that non-Indian children are greatly surprised when they learn that Native Americans do not habitually wear feathered head-dresses or war bonnets on their heads. On the contrary, headdresses and particu-larly the war bonnet were only worn during war dances, battles, or raids, and on special ceremonial occasions. The large eagle feather war bonnet was worn only by certain men, and rarely by young men or women, who belonged to tribes that lived on the Plains, between the Mississippi River Valley and the Rocky Mountains and from Canada south to the Mexican border.

There are several varieties of war bonnets. Most are of the "swept back type" with the feathers on the cap leaning toward the rear, but some are of the "straight-up" type which lacks a cap and results in the feathers standing upright from a wide headband. In a third type, the feathers slope out evenly all the way around the headband. There were also many other headdresses that varied in shape, de-sign, and style that were worn traditionally by Indian tribes in other parts of America. The war bonnet was worn only as a privilege, a symbol of recognition

Fig. 2

of skill, success in war, and leadership ability and was often considered to possess a magic protective power. A youth had to earn his right to wear such a bonnet through his warlike deeds. According to Jake Herman, a Sioux cowboy, storyteller, and writer:

> To the Oglala Sioux of South Dakota, the war bonnet was a symbol of pride, honor, and leadership. . . . A young warrior, in order to qualify the wearing of the eagle headdress, had to: Excel in the field of medicine, perform an act of bravery in war, be generous and his lodge must be open to his people, hunt and provide for women and children or the older people who were unable to hunt, be honest and loyal to his country and his tribe. When a young warrior became a good hunter, he could wear a single eagle feather. Then, as he became a scout and warrior performing an act of bravery in battle, he could wear two eagle feathers. Then he had to capture enemy horses and bring back enemy scalps. When a warrior had fulfilled all these obligations, the leaders or chiefs would investigate his deeds at the council fire. . . .[12]

Headdresses consist of several parts: a skull cap, decorative brow band, large eagle feathers, occasionally a trail, and other decorative accessories. The main feathers, ranging in number from sixteen to thirty-eight, are attached to the edge of the cap. The Plains war bonnet is so widely known and publicized because of television, movies, comics, and other visual media that many tribes

> which never wore it in former times now appear in Plains war bonnets. It is worn by men and women alike without regard for the old rules, almost like an official uniform. The war bonnet . . . has steadily increased in size, fanciness, use of garish color and trimming. Except for the very oldest Plains people it has lost all meaning and now is merely a vague general symbol of the Indian. An Indian has to wear one to convince tourists that he is an Indian! Tribes which never even heard of war bonnets now greet their visitors in them; and "Princesses" in war bonnets smile from every Sunday rotogravure.[13]

Toy manufacturers who use war bonnet motifs indiscriminately in toys rarely portray the shape, design, or style with any accuracy. Further, the manufacturers put the bonnets on children who were never privileged to wear them. Adding bonnets to animals and cartoon characters demeans and belittles the handsome and highly esteemed eagle feather war bonnet. Neither non-Indian nor Native children can benefit from perverting objects that are significant to some Native American cultures.

INDIANS-OF-THE-PAST

Children are confused about who Native Americans are, how they live, think, behave, and dress. Toy manufacturers contribute to this confusion by juxtaposing Indians of the past with contemporary items or settings. Toys with language arts themes illustrate this best. "Grosset Reading Blocks" (Grosset and Dunlap, Inc., New York) (Fig. 3) show a male Indian-of-the-past (I), a man (M), a girl (G), and

Fig. 3

a nurse (N)—all in contemporary dress—and an umbrella (U), nail (N), and an urn (U)—all modern-day objects. Besides associating the Indian man with animals, food, and other objects, and treating him as a separate category from other human beings (Indians after all are men and women), these reading blocks, with the anachronistic placement of past Indians with contemporary items, confuse children about contemporary Native American lifestyles. The I-J-K-L block of "Dolly Toy's Sof-Pla Blocks" (Dolly Toy Company, Tipps City, Ohio), created for infants of six months to children of four years, is cast in the same mold. A forbidding looking Indian-of-the-past wearing a war bonnet, buckskin leggings, and breechcloth, and brandishing a tomahawk is depicted near jam and bread, a smiling lion and mouse, and a cheerful kitty carrying an umbrella and a purse. Nine cloth cubes, manufactured for ages one and a half to three and a half years by Creative Playthings (a company which has been bought by Gabriel of New York, N.Y.), are decorated with a baby carriage, boat, animals, rocking horse, a building resembling a church with a steeple together with a tipi. The tipi, a dwelling of the past which is rarely used today, associated with contemporary objects such as a baby carriage and a church-like building certainly confuses the past and the present. Several years ago, Magran Industries (Vernon, California 90023) produced "AlphaTiles: Pre-School Wooden Alphabet Set" for children over three. The tile with the ubiquitous I-for-Indian-with-a-headdress is followed by a J-for-jet-plane tile.

These toys misinform young, impressionable children about who Native Americans are today by their inappropriate placement of Indians-of-the-past with contemporary objects. Natives today do not dress or live the way they are pictured on these language arts toys. Nor did they ever dress or live in the uniform way the toy companies have presented them. These companies, like most Americans, picture "real" Indians as they imagined them to be rather than as they really were or are now.

Traditional Indian clothing materials, hairstyles, and headdresses varied from tribe to tribe. The Iroquois largely dressed in deerskin, the Haidas and other Northwest Coast groups used cedar bark clothing, the Hopis and other Pueblos wore cotton dress, the Eskimos kept warm in seal skin and caribou skins, and the Plains peoples mostly used buffalo skins. Today, Native Americans rarely wear traditional dress except for ceremonies, Indian fairs, rodeos, powwows, or the like. Most Native American people dress exactly or nearly the same as other Americans.

The style of clothing of Native American women varied. Women from the Northwest Coast wore the wrap-around dress. Women from different parts of the West wore fore-and-aft aprons. Pueblo women wore folded cloth rectangles. Plains women wore long skin dresses; Eastern Native women wore wrap-around skirts, and Native women along the Canadian-United States border, but mostly in Canada, wore slip-and-sleeve dresses, and Eskimo women wore tailored costumes.

Tribes lived in dwellings that varied considerably. The buffalo skin tipi, which so many people consider the typical mode of existence of all Native Americans, was a dwelling of Plains Natives (Blackfeet, Crows, Sioux, Cheyennes, etc.) in a certain phase of their history. The Iroquois lived in longhouses, Chippewas in wigwams, Wichitas in grass houses, Eskimos in sod houses, and Kutenais in birchbark tipis. Seminoles lived in thatched houses, Navajos in hogans, Pueblo groups in adobe houses, California Natives in shingled round, mud, bark, plank, and brush houses, Mandans and others in earth lodges, and Haidas in plank dwellings with totem poles. There were also sweat houses, houses for the dead, food shelters, kivas, and ceremonial houses. Today, many Natives live in frame houses, although some traditional forms such as peyote tipis, Pueblo kivas, sun dance lodges, and others have survived in a ceremonial context.

Native American cultures were and are extremely diversified and cannot be typified by the outdated and inaccurate Indian-of-the-past image so often used in toys.

INDIANS-AS-A-MIXTURE

Toy manufacturers further create confusion about Native cultures by combining elements from different Native groups into a manufacturer-created Indian village. When the toy companies create a mix, they almost always combine visual characteristics of Plains culture with elements from either the Southwest or Northwest Pacific Coast groups. Whitman, a subsidiary of Western Publishing Company, Inc. (Racine, Wisconsin 53404) offers "Play Indian Village" (Fig. 4). This village combines elements from the cultures of the Plains and Southwest Native groups (Navajos and Pueblos). For example, this village contains four Plains tipis, one of which has Southwest painted symbols on it; some Plains men, women, and children; some dancers and other figures that appear to be a cross between Plains and Southwest people; a Navajo-looking woman scraping a Plains buffalo skin; a Pueblo-looking man with his characteristic woven robe wrapped around him wearing a Plains two-feathered headband (Pueblo men wear a narrow band of folded cloth on the head to keep the hair in place); a Pueblo-looking woman making southwestern pottery; a Navajo-looking woman weaving southwestern fiber baskets (Plains people did not weave baskets or make clay receptacles. They used buffalo hide containers to hold food and other items). The colorful 26" by 30" playsheet features a creek and desert-like area with corn growing. This amalgamation of several Native cultures into one Indian village frankly violates the integrity of the cultures of Plains Natives, Navajos, and Pueblo groups. Furthermore, ceremonial dancing is not a routine activity and it is inappropriate to put fully-dressed dance figures in an everyday scene.

"How the West Was Won: Indian Village" (Fleetwood Toys, New York, New York 10010) (Fig. 5) combines elements from a toy-created version of a Plains village and a totem pole, an object from Pacific Northwest Coast groups. Like the tipis, the monumental totem poles with their column of carved animals and birds, one above another have become "a visual symbol, like a trademark, for all American Indians among white men in many parts of the world"[14] despite the fact that the totems were only displayed in villages along the Pacific Northwest Coast.

Fig. 4

play Indian village

Fig. 5

HOW THE WEST WAS WON

INDIAN VILLAGE

Several years ago, Hubley Division, Gabriel Industries, Inc. (Lancaster, Pennsylvania 17604) produced a Lone Ranger kit entitled "The Adventure of the Hopi Medicine Man." The kit included a Hopi Kachina doll, two Hopi masks, a drum, rattle, beaded jewelry, and a Plains war bonnet. Caran D'Ache of Switzerland includes with its set of various colored blocks of clay, an illustrated brochure with suggestions for modeling. One of the clay dioramas shows a tipi, three Plains-looking men, one of whom is in a creeping position with tomahawk in hand, a cactus, and a totem pole complete with feathers on its top.

In 1980, a Marx Fort Apache Playset consisted of a "complete 16 Section Frontier Post with Command Post Building, plus 36 Assorted Cavalry troopers and Indians, 3 Horses, a Teepee, Totem Pole, Log Fire, Water Well, Flag Pole, and 5 Stockade Accessories." This toy, a departure from the others, combines the Southwest (Apache), Northwest (totem), and Plains ("teepee").

The widespread and mistaken notion that all Indians are alike has allowed toy manufacturers to pick and choose Native cultural elements, particularly tipis and totems, as though they were all pieces of the same puzzle. Those toy manufacturers that lump together bits of Plains, Southwest, and Pacific Northwest Coast groups with little concern for regional and tribal differences have never even considered the idea that groups WITHIN regional areas can vary in religion, customs, dress, decoration, and world view. The groups of Plains Indians, who lived in historic times between the Rocky Mountains and the Mississippi River Valley, and from southern Texas to the Saskatchewan River Basin in Canada, lived in one of two distinct subcultures existing in different parts of the area. There were semi-agricultural, village-dwelling tribes on the eastern fringe of the Plains and mobile, horse-mounted peoples west of these sedentary groups. The Northwest Pacific Coast groups, although they shared many cultural traits, also exhibited various tribal differences. The same existed with the Pueblo groups that both shared cultural features and also differed from one another.

It is time that toy companies develop some concern for tribal differences that exist in dress, housing, customs, decorations, etc. and refrain from lumping Native Americans into one large unit labeled "Indian Village."

INDIANS-AS-ANIMALS-CARTOONS-OBJECTS

One characteristic of toy Indian imagery that particularly offends Native Americans is the practice of toy companies putting war bonnets and headbands on animals and cartoon creatures, thus associating or equating them with Natives in the minds of children. "Big John, the Chimpee Chief" manufactured in Japan (distributed by Willis Imports of Farmingdale, New York 11735) and priced anywhere from $16.99 to $29.95 typifies this practice (Fig. 6). The cover of the pad entitled "Fun Pad" (Prestige Books, Inc. of New York) (Fig. 7) depicts three cartoon-like animals wearing feathers and carrying weapons associated with Native Americans.

Fig. 6

Fig. 7

Jaymar Specialty Company (Brooklyn, New York 11232) has manufactured a puzzle with Walt Disney characters to include Donald Duck, in a war bonnet, and two young ducks in single feather headbands, all brandishing tomahawks, who appear to be ready for Mickey Mouse, who is wearing a fur cap and carrying a rifle in combat position. Cartoonarama (Reseda, California 91335) manufactures paint sets in which children "paint on transparent cels, the same way cartoon studio artists do to create animated films." The company which has created a kit with authentic-looking Native American faces has associated them with Woody Woodpecker and friends, Pink Panther, Mighty Mouse, and other cartoon characters. Child Guidance has created "Wild West Wheelies: Cowboy and Indian" (Fig. 8). Not only does this toy offer children the opportunity to play cowboy versus Indian (another characteristic of toy Indian imagery that is discussed later) but it also presents children with an image of a distorted, silly-looking Indian.

These and other toys which present animals dressed as Indians are "the most dehumanizing of all portrayals, for it suggests that Native people are not fully human, but rather are creatures of fantasy such as witches or elves."[15] Mary Gloyne Byler points out in her study of children's books about Indians[16] that "American Indians are real people and deserve the dignity of being presented as such."[17] Big John, the Chimpee Chief, Wild West Wheelies, the Fun Pad, and other toys like these are insulting and instill and reinforce the image of Indians "as being not only subhuman but also inhuman beings."[18]

Besides treating Native peoples as animal or cartoon creatures, toy manufacturers often treat Native peoples as objects rather than as human beings. No other ethnic group in America is subject to such dehumanizing treatment. Children can

Fig. 8

put their coins in a bank shaped like an Indian head (Fig. 9) or they can get Pez candy out of a dispenser that is topped with an Indian head wearing a war bonnet (Fig. 10) or one can decorate gifts or Christmas trees with the "Indian Brave" (Fig. 11). Toys that treat Natives as things do not encourage children to view Native Americans as human beings.

Fig. 9

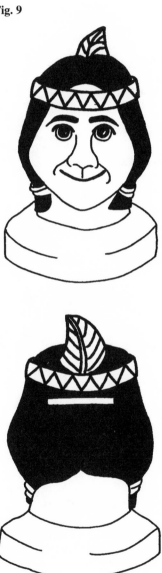

Fig. 10

Fig. 11

MINIATURE HANDMADE
SAFE SOFT STUFFED
INDIAN BRAVE

• Charming replica of the antique original.
Lovely little gift, for mini scenes,
collectors, gift tie ons, favors, tree
decorations, etc. With loop for hanging.

INDIANS-AS-OCCUPATION-OR-ROLE

Another characteristic of toy Indian imagery is the treatment of Native Americans as an occupation or role rather than as an ethnic identity. Years ago, Spartan Sales (Yonkers, New York) offered an "Instant Indians" set. Their promotion pitch read: "Turn a suburban spread into an Indian village! Six-foot wigwam assembles with rubber-capped poles; tots turn into squaws and braves; rubber tomahawks, bow and arrow, headdress, war paint, all harmless." Over the past few years, the New York FAO Schwarz Holiday Gift Selections catalogue has included "Indian Chief and Squaw costumes" alongside costumes for nurses, ballerinas, special forces, and police. The Horchow catalogue mentioned previously has offered playhats including an Indian feathered bonnet, a red felt cowboy hat, a black felt top hat, and a red straw fire chief's hat. During the 1981 Halloween season, the Topstone Rubber Company, Inc. (Danbury, Connecticut 06810) offered masquerade wigs. The line offers, among others, pirate, colonial man, witch, and Indian wigs. In addition, Topstone sells a "Make Up Kit" which includes make-up sticks and "stick-um scars" to "Be a clown, Indian pirate, gypsy, devil, weirdo, etc." Both the Topstone packages picture cartoon-like Indians besides clowns, devils, gypsies, witches, pirates, etc. Herman Iskin and Company Inc. (Telford, Pennsylvania) has manufactured Play Suits and includes in its line "Indian outfit" with a headdress, of course. Several years ago, Transogram, a subsidiary of Miner industries, Inc. (New York, New York 10010) offered an Indian playset "featuring Bow, Arrows, Knife, Tom-Tom, Head-dress, and Tomahawk."

Schaper Manufacturing Company (Minneapolis, Minnesota 55440) epitomizes the treatment of Indians as a role or occupation with its "Discovery Set," an introductory set to "Playmobile Systems," ten sets of plastic figures and their accessories. The "Discovery Set" (Fig. 12) informs one that three figures and sixty-four accessories can be used to create a cavalry figure, a vacationer, a police officer, a construction worker, a knight, a cowboy, a farmer, a doctor and nurse, a fire fighter, and an Indian. (Each of these ten figures and their corresponding accessories can be purchased separately. For example, Indians are available in "Deluxe, Special Deluxe," "Super Deluxe," and Accessories sets).

This concept of a Native American representing an occupation or a role to be played is illustrated by a gift wrapping paper (Drawing Board Greeting Cards, Inc., Dallas, Texas) (Fig. 13). In a spin-off of the small child's fortune telling rhyme and Leonora Speyer's poem "Oberammergau" a "Rich Man, Poor Man, Beggar Man, and Thief" line up with a "Doctor, Lawyer, Merchant, and Chief" as well as with a "Tinker. Tailor, Soldier, and Sailor." None of the figures pictured on the wrapping paper or in the "Discovery Set" have an ethnic identity except for the Indian.

Cavalry, police, construction workers, knights, ballerinas, farmers, cowboys, tinkers, tailors, soldiers, and sailors are occupations. Members of each of these occupations usually wear certain kinds of clothes that identify their work. A person of any race can wear these clothes. Children of any race can don appropriate clothing and play the role of being a doctor, a fire fighter, or a farmer. They can dress up as a pirate, a witch, a devil, or rich or poor person and role-play these characters. But one cannot be come a Native American by donning feathers, fringed buckskin, and moccasins because a Native person is not an occupation or a role to be played. It is a state of being, an ethnic identity. Having children dress up and play Indians encourages them to think Native Americans are nothing more than a playtime activity rather than an identity that is often fraught with economic deprivation, discrimination, gross injustice, and powerlessness.

Fig. 12

Fig. 13

COWBOY-AND-INDIAN

A popular characteristic of toy Indian imagery is the one that portrays the antagonistic cowboy and Indian relationship and the more benign but less frequently used variant, the relationship devoid of conflict. Examples of the hostile cowboy-Indian motif can be seen in a mobile for infants (Fig. 14), manufactured in Japan, which contains cowboys and fierce-looking Indians that float menacingly at each other armed with tomahawks, guns, bows and arrows, and lances. There are the ever-present sets of two- to three-inch plastic cowboys and Indians which can be found in most neighborhood candy shops, drug, or dime stores. In 1980, Miner Industries, Inc. (New York, New York 10010) offered twenty cowboys and Indians, "Unbreakable action figures" "realistically detailed," and "not recommended for children under three years old." Multiple Toymakers offers "Buckaroos and Braves," dress-up cowboys and Indians with snap-on accessories. Arco Industries, Ltd. (New York, New York 10010) promotes a "Big 50 Cowboys, Indians, and Horses."

Presto MagiX Dry Transfer Game, distributed by the Gillette Company, Paper Mate Division (Boston, Massachusetts 02199) has a "Stagecoach Attack" in its series. Pictures of Indians, mostly in the attack position, can be peeled off backing paper and positioned on the background scene which contains a southwestern desert with a fleeing stagecoach on the right hand side and three menacing Indians on the far left side. A note to parents reads: "Presto MagiX allows children of all ages to use creativity and a sense of relationships to produce an endless variety of scenes." What sense of relationship and variety can be achieved by children positioning attacking Indians on a background with a fleeing stagecoach? In fact, children are playing out a particular manufactured scenario that has shown little variation over the past hundred years. What kind of relationship between Native Americans and non-Natives can be achieved by children playing cowboy and Indian with the "Trick Arrow Through Head" manufactured in Hong Kong? (Fig. 15)

In 1975 Ward International, Inc. (North Bergen, New Jersey) offered "Cowpokes and Little Folks," a set containing a wagon train with cowpoke and "two attacking Indians." Children can still buy Marx Company's Fort Apache Playset, complete with a "16 Section Frontier Post with Command Post Building, plus 30 Assorted Cavalry Troopers and Indians, 3 Horses, a Teepee, Totem Pole, Log Fire, Water Well, Flag Pole, and 5 Stockade Accessories." In 1980, H-G Toys, Inc. (Long Beach, New York 11561) offered "Big Frontier Raid: Wild West Cowboy and Indian Playset" with over seventy pieces. The box reads: "The Drama of the Old West Comes Alive with 2 Covered Wagons, Log Cabin, Tepees, Terrain, Cowboys, Indians, Western Fort Diorama, and Accessories."

Fig. 14

COWBOYS AND INDIANS MOBILE

Fig. 15

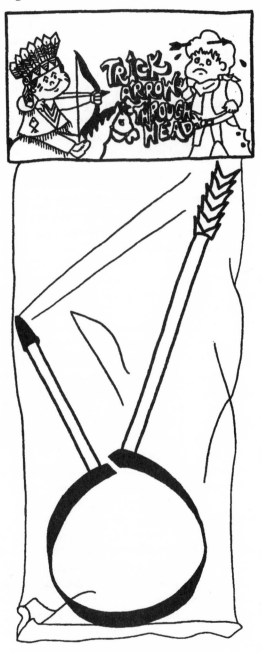

Ed-U-Cards of Easton, Pennsylvania has sold two mini-card games, one entitled "Cowboys and Indians" and the other "Daniel Boone: Concentration Game." The Indians that are illustrated on one side of the cards in the "Cowboys and Indians" card game are drawn from Plains Indian life. If you flip the deck over, put the thirty-five cards in numerical order, and riffle the top of the deck with a thumb, a "flip-movie" is created which shows a bare-chested Indian, shooting off an arrow in one direction, suddenly reverse his position, and run off in the other direction, chased by a cowboy wielding a gun which lets off a shot. The graphics of the Indians in the other game, "Daniel Boone" are menacing. Some of the cards are entitled "Ambushed," "Indian Fight," "Captured," and "Under Siege." "Daniel Boone" is really a game of visual recall, which is a favorite card-matching game of young children. It is hardly necessary for youngsters to try to remember scenes of Daniel Boone being tied to a tree by two bare-chested Indian men, firing off a rifle at Indians or being ambushed by them on horseback, or attacked by a lion, and fighting hand-to-hand combat with a knife-wielding Indian.

One variation of the cowboy-Indian motif is the more benign relationship with almost all conflict deleted. "Birthday Child" gift wrap paper manufactured by Rust Craft Greeting Cards (Dedham, Massachusetts 02026) has a design of squares containing child-faced, smiling cowboys twirling lassos, riding rocking horses, or shooting off guns. The other squares show either a stage coach, Indian drum, or the full figure of a young Indian, with a smiling face, braids, and a war bonnet with trail, arms crossed over a bare chest wearing breeches and long pants. Allan Industries, Ltd. (High Wycombe, England) which designs and manufactures "Fuzzy-Felt" sets offers "Fuzzy-Felt Wild West." A note to purchasers reads: "You can make exciting Wild West pictures with these lively cowboys and Indians living on the plains with their horses and wild animals." The set includes five felt Indian men, one Indian woman, all identified by fringing, two cowboys, two shapes that become a tipi, a rifle, one buffalo, two horses, cows, and assorted geometric shapes.

The cowboy-Indian motif is fraught with meaning for children. They have been programmed from many sources to see the cowboy as the hero and the good guy and the Indian as the enemy and the bad guy, an ongoing hazard always encountered and eventually overcome. Children who sit through old motion pictures on television, who go to see current movies, who listen to old radio programs, who read "Wild West" comics root for cowboys, settlers, cavalry, or similar good guys to wipe out the Indians. The Indian-white relations that children see on the screen and hear on the radio or read about in books are seldom peaceful and rarely accurate. Children who play with plastic cowboy-and-Indian playsets, dry transfer figures, trick arrows through the head, or similar toys reenact the violent and aggressive scenes they have seen or heard about, without having the slightest idea what was involved in the relationship between whites and Indians in the East and in the West—which did involve some prolonged violent conflicts. Children rarely know and understand that Native Americans were defending their homelands and their ways of life. As Mary Gloyne Byler states:

> Undoubtedly it is accurate that settlers were threatened by, and afraid of, Indians, but Indians were equally, if not more, threatened by the settlers and they had much more to lose. The history books and story books seldom make it clear that Native Americans in fighting back, were defending their homes and families and were not just being malicious.[18]

Another serious problem with these cowboy-and-Indian toys is that they are linked to warring and violence in which the act of killing is glorified. The cowboy-and-Indian toys are loaded down with weaponry—bows and arrows, tomahawks, lances, and rifles. Impressionable children, conditioned to books, movies, television, and playing with cowboy-and-Indian toys may indeed decide someday as adults to use aggression as a way to resolve conflict. PACT considers:

> Think whether any parent really wants his or her child to grow up to use violence and aggression as a way to solve conflicts. This seems a ridiculous proposition, yet guns, monster toys, and games which depict war and fighting continue to sell well. [One could add cowboy-and-Indian toys to this list as well.] Apparently parents do not appreciate the extent to which these toys have a direct influence on how children resolve conflicts. One does not have to observe a group of children too long before one sees a war game with shooting and killing, and Kung Fu with kicking and beating. . . . A gun's only message to a child is shoot. Without the stimulus of violent toys, children will find more constructive ways to express anger and aggressive feelings, ways which are healthier for them and their friends.[20]

If one doubts the impact playing cowboys and Indians can have, consider Colonel Edward G. Lansdale, an American Air Force officer and Senior CIA operative, who often played cowboys and Indians with the children of Ngo Dinh Nhu of South Vietnam.[21] He was given to using Wild West figures of speech.

> Wherever he went, to the Philippines and later to Indochina, peasant guerillas were of course the Indians, the merciless savages all, with their "savage" attacks, their campaign that "continued savagely for months and years, " their "ruthless savagery," . . . and their terror that "was the old nightmare of savagery with murders and kidnappings." As for the Company cowboy, Lansdale was ever the man with the gun (or guns) who pointed more than his finger. . .[22]

History has shown of course that war and killing are not glorious. More proof may come someday that playthings that condone, promote, or glorify violence or killing eventually do psychological damage to children. There are several physicians who have taken stands against war toys, which include the cowboy-and-Indian toys, games, and weapon accessories. Dr. Jerome F. Frank of The Johns

Hopkins University School of Medicine (who unequivocally states that "Research has shown that the mere sight of a gun will increase violent behavior. . ."[23]) feels that the only way to discourage violence is

> to keep guns out of the environment from childhood on. Children learn mainly from their parents and attitudes formed in childhood last throughout life. By giving our children toys of peace instead of war we show them that we disapprove of violence. This discourages them from resorting to it and may lead them as adults to search for new non-violent ways of resolving conflicts that do not endanger human survival in the nuclear age.[24]

INDIAN-TOY-LANGUAGE

Some of the words associated with Indian toys are loaded and carry attitudes of contempt or demeaning characterizations that unconsciously affect the self-image of Native American children and offend Natives in general. Two studies have been done, the "Vocabulary of Prejudice" and "Racism in Language,"[25] which deal with racism in language and how it affects thought. Cohen does a semantic analysis of certain disparaging words some people use "such as the common contemptuous or patronizing terms, nigger, coon, darkie, redskin, paleface, chink, Jap, wop, etc."[26] He looks at "innocent" repetition, repelling associations, the irrelevant adjective, what words reveal, and the existence of two vocabularies. Moore looks at terminology, symbolism, politics, ethnocentrism, and "loaded words" and explains how these aspects of racism in language shape thought. Both of these scholars conclude, however, that "consciousness of the influence of language on our perceptions can help to negate much of that influence"[27] or "The technique of semantic analysis will not of itself eliminate human prejudice. But it may help us to uncover the inarticulate value premises of ourselves and others. Such understanding may itself lead to greater tolerance of cultural diversity."[28]

In the context of Indian toys, words such as "Indian Chief and Squaw," "Big Chief," "Indian Brave," and "Big Chief Authentic Headdress" are loaded and have negative or insulting overtones. Mary Gloyne Byler concurs:

> A more direct assault is made upon the humanity of American Indians by the use of key words and phrases which trigger negative and derogatory images. Words such as savage, buck, squaw, and papoose do not bring to mind the same images as do the words man, boy, woman, and baby.[29]

Words that mock Native American names should be abolished. Big John, the Chimpee Chief, and Chief Twanta ridicule Native names. The omnipotent word "Indian" (as in "Indian outfit," "Instant Indian," "Indian Hunter," and "Play Indian Village") erases all tribal distinctions and conveys a distorted picture of Native Americans.

Toy companies must become aware of the influence of language in the perceptions and attitudes of children and consider the effects of using words such as "squaw," and "chief." Toy manufacturers should completely eliminate terms that degrade Native Americans and use language that reflects sensitive and accurate portrayals.

CONCLUSION

This sample of toys used for discussion in the previous pages no doubt represents a substantially larger number of toys with similar Indian imagery that conveys false or offensive pictures of Native Americans. Toy manufacturers should consider the harm they may be doing to Native American and non-Native children who either play with the toys or see them in stores or advertised in the media. It would be difficult for non-Native children playing with the toys that have been discussed to develop positive attitudes toward Native Americans and it would be exceedingly difficult, if not impossible, for Native children to feel good about their identity when confronted with so many toys that belittle their cultures. Not only does the lack of responsibility in the manufacture of Indian toys lead to damaged self-concepts among Native Americans, it also reinforces the stereotypes which will help to make racist adults of white children.

Toy companies should produce toys that portray diverse racial identities with dignity. Several years ago, Childcraft of New York distributed contemporary hand-made rag dolls featuring Black, Asian, and Native American children dressed in typical play clothes. This represents a clear effort to reflect ethnic diversity with dignity.

Until toy companies manufacture toys that portray Native Americans with accuracy and respect, adults and children should stop buying Indians, animals, and cartoon figures indiscriminately decorated with feathers that are either locked into the mid-nineteenth century, quasi-Plains mold, mixed up into one Indian cultural bag, or inextricably bound to cowboys and weaponry. After all, as Michael Dorris points out so well:

> Protecting children from racism is every bit as important as insuring that they avoid playing with electrical sockets. Poison is poison, and ingrained oppressive cultural attitudes are at least as hard to antidote, once implanted, as are imbibed cleaning fluids. No one gains by allowing an inequitable and discriminatory status quo to persist. It's worth being a pain in the neck about.[30]

NOTES

1. "Suggestions for Developing Positive Racial Attitudes," *Interracial Books for Children Bulletin*, vol. 11, no. 4, 1980: 10.

2. See Chapter 4 for the full text of this study.

3. See Chapter 4 for Mary Gloyne Byler's study of how children's books play an important role in perpetuating negative images of Native Americans. Also see the bibliography for studies of the imagery of Natives in movies, textbooks, television, art, literature, etc.

4. "Indians" refers to the manufactured or stereotyped image of Native Americans, the actual peoples.

5. Michael Dorris, "Why I'm NOT Thankful for Thanksgiving," *Interracial Books for Children Bulletin*, Vol. 9, no. 7, 1978: 7.

6. *NCAI Sentinel*. Letters to the Editor. August 1969. p.3.

7. JoAnn Morris, "Stereotypes: 'Neither Side Is Open or Free,'" *Talking Leaf*, vol. 40, no. 7 (August 1975): 13.

8. Geraldine L. Wilson, "Toys Are Political, Too: A Guide to Gift-Giving the Year 'Round," *Interracial Books for Children Bulletin*, vol. 11, no. 7 (1980): 10.

9. Public Action Coalition on Toys, *Guidelines on Choosing Toys for Children* (New York: The Children's Medical Center of New York Fund, 1977), pp. 1–3.

10. "Indian" refers to the manufactured toy image rather than to the actual peoples, the Native Americans.

11. The quintessential image of Native Americans to most Americans is a generalized version of the Plains Native. See Chapter 2 for a discussion of the emergence of the Plains Indian as the symbol of Native Americans.

12. Jake Herman, "Eagle Feathers and the American Indian," WASSAJA, vol. 2, no. 6 (July 1974): 9.

13. F. H. Douglas, "War Bonnets," Denver Art Museum Leaflet 110 (December 1951) p.40. See this leaflet for more for more information on war bonnets.

14. Alvin M. Josephy, *The Indian Heritage of America* (New York: Bantam Books, 1969), p.77.

15. Robert B. Moore and Arlene Hirschfelder, "Feathers, Tomahawks and Tipis: A Study of Stereotyped 'Indian' Imagery in Children's Picture Books," In *Unlearning 'Indian' Stereotypes* (New York Council on Interracial Books for Children, 1977), p. 13.

16. See Chapter 4.

17. Mary Gloyne Byler, *American Indian Authors for Young Readers: A Selected Bibliography*, (New York: Association on American Indian Affairs, 1973), p. 6.

18. Ibid., p. 11.

19. Ibid., p. 8.

20. Public Action Coalition on Toys, *Guidelines*, p. 4.

21. Richard Drinnon, *Facing West: The Metaphysics of Indian-Hating and Empire-Building* (New York: New American Library, 1980), p. 414. "Now and then, Thuc or Nhu would be with Diem when I arrived for a meeting with him, but would excuse themselves after we exchanged greetings. I saw Nhu's children more often, since they had the run of the palace, and I often stopped for a brief game of cowboys and Indians with them. . . ." Edward Geary Lansdale, *In the Midst of Wars*, 1972.

22. Ibid., p. 395.

23. Public Action Coalition on Toys, *Guidelines*, p. 11.

24. Ibid.

25. Felix S. Cohen, "The Vocabulary of Prejudice," in *The Legal Conscience: Selected Papers of Felix S. Cohen*. Edited by Lucy Kramer Cohen (New Haven: Yale University

Press, 1960). Robert B. Moore, *Racism in the English Language* (New York: Racism and Sexism Resource Center for Educators, 1976).

26. Cohen, *Vocabulary*, p. 480.
27. Moore, *Racism*, p. 14.
28. Cohen, *Vocabulary*, p. 435.
29. Byler, *Authors*, p. 10.
30. Dorris, *Not Thankful*, p. 9.

Why One Can't Ignore Pocahontas

Cornel Pewewardy

As an Indian parent, a former kindergarten teacher, a principal, and now as an educational consultant preparing future teachers for diverse classrooms, I am constantly approached with questions about American Indians—the overwhelming majority of which are sparked by the movie industry's blitz of Indian myths and stereotypes. This year, the challenge centers around the movie *Pocahontas.*

Disney is not always an easy target. *Pocahontas*, for example, can be easily caricatured as politically correct yet historically incorrect, sexist yet feminist, and both ethnographically sensitive and ethnographically suspect. Yet the overwhelming nature of the Disney juggernaut—a cultural onslaught that includes not just the animated film but spin-off books, toys, dolls, and kid's clothes—compels teachers to tread into this difficult terrain.

The motion picture industry has probably taught more Americans about American Indians than any other source in the teaching and learning process of American children. And this includes many Indians. Apathy and lack of self-esteem are all too common in the school lives of American Indian children, and a key reason is the negative portrayal of Native Americans in movies and television shows.

Children's self-images are very pliable and susceptible to external forces. Unfortunately, young Indian students who are treated as though they are less than human—whether in movies, children's books, sports mascots, or phenomenon such as the "tomahawk chop"—will tend to assume they are, indeed, inferior to white children. And this has a profound educational impact. Some educators, in fact, contend that American Indians remain the least educated ethnic group in the nation. For example, only 55 percent of Indian students graduate from high school, compared to 83 percent of their white peers. Of those who do graduate, only 17 percent enter college, the lowest percentage of any ethnic group.

The most common criticism of *Pocahontas* revolves around its historical inaccuracy, so let's set the story straight. Pocahontas was the daughter of Tidewater Virginia's legendary chief Powhatan. She married a tribal member in her early teens. Several years later, when she was eighteen, she was lured aboard a British ship in the Jamestown area and held captive for more than a year. She was dressed in the English fashion and took religious instruction, becoming baptized as a Christian. In 1614, Pocahontas married British colonist John Rolfe. In 1616, as part of a plan to revive support for the Virginia colony, the couple traveled to England with their infant son. There Pocahontas met King James I and Queen Anne. Just as she and Rolfe were setting sail back to America the following March, Pocahontas died, perhaps because of smallpox, perhaps because of the foul English weather. She was buried in an English churchyard.

None of this is reflected in *Pocahontas*. In the movie, Pocahontas disobeys her father and goes to meet Captain John Smith. This probably would not have happened during the time period portrayed in the movie, as it was a cultural norm for tribal members to adhere to any strict orders from their leaders, especially during a time of war.

Then there is the question of Disney's portrayal of Pocahontas' appearance. The type of dress worn by the Disney Pocahontas would have been very sexist during her time in history. Further, she has a Barbie-doll figure, an exotic model's glamour, and an instant attraction to a distinctly Nordic John Smith. Yet historians agree that Pocahontas and John Smith had no romantic contact. In short, Disney has abandoned historical accuracy in favor of creating a marketable New Age Pocahontas who can embody dreams for wholeness and harmony. But unlike Pocahontas, there is a large segment of American Indians who have not melted into the mainstream of American society, nor have they been totally eradicated by or assimilated into white culture.

This New Age Pocahontas is in line with shifts in stereotypes about Native Americans. For half a century or more, the dominant image of Indians was that of "savages," of John Wayne leading the U.S. Cavalry against the Indians. Today the dominant stereotype has shifted to that of the *noble savage*, which portrays Indians as part of a once great but now dying culture that could talk to the trees like Grandmother Willow and the animals like Meeko and Flit that protected nature. Such contradictory views of Indians, from terrifying and evil to gentle and good, stem from a Eurocentric ambivalence toward an entire race of people they attempted to destroy.

Pocahontas, meanwhile, is rooted in the "Indian princess" stereotype, which is typically expressed through characters who are maidenly, demure, and deeply committed to some white man. As writer Gail Guthrie Valaskakis notes, "The dominant image of the Indian princess appeared in the 1920s. She is a shapely maiden with a name like Winona, Minnehaha, Iona—or even Hiawatha. She sits posed on a rock or in a canoe, seemingly suspended, on a mountain-rimmed, moonlit lake, wearing a tight-fitting red tunic and headband with one feather; and she has the perfect face of a white female. Disney's *Pocahontas* is a 1990s version of the red tunic lady. She combines the sexually alluring qualities of innocence and availability."

Perhaps the most obvious manifestation of the racism in *Pocahontas* is in the movie's use of terms such as "savages," "heathens," "pagans," "devils," and "primitive." These terms reflect something wild and inferior, and their use implies a value judgment of white superiority. By negatively describing Native lifestyle and basing the movie on a "we-they" format, there is a subtle justification of the subjugation of Indian tribes by so-called "advanced" cultures in the name of progress. The movie makes little reference to the European greed, deceit, racism, and genocide that were integral to the historical contacts between the Indians and Jamestown settlers.

The song "Savages-Savages," despite its context of seemingly criticizing the values portrayed by the Europeans, contains brutally racist lyrics:

> What can you expect
> From filthy little heathens?
> Their whole disgusting race
> is like a curse
> Their skin's a hellish red
> They're only good when dead
> They're vermin, as I said
> And worse.
> They're savages! Savages!
> Barely even human. Savages!
> Savages!
> Drive them from our shore!
> They're not like you and me
> Which means they must be evil
> We must sound the drums of war!

Regardless of the movie's context, such lyrics are offensive to American Indian people. For Indian children, it becomes a nightmare when they come home in tears because school children or playmates sing "Savages-Savages" to them.

As an Indian educator, part of what I find discouraging about *Pocahontas* is that it takes time away from so many pressing issues. Many Indian educators would like the American public to take a quantum leap and come up to speed on cultural matters, so that we can begin better addressing issues such as the federal Indian budget, tribal sovereignty, loss of tribal languages, land claims, access to higher education, standardized tests, environmental exploitation and degradation of Indian lands, treaty rights, repatriation of artifacts, protection of burial sites, and return of Indian remains—the list goes on and on.

Protecting children from racism is a year-round responsibility and must extend beyond the school year. The producers of *Pocahontas* carefully chose the summer season to release its recreation of their invented Indian princess character—a time when most American youth are out of school and thirsty for movie entertainment. The question is, entertainment at whose expense? Since Disney won't, it is up to educators to help children answer such questions.

American Indian Mascots in Sports

Paulette Fairbanks Molin

For nearly thirty years, protests against American Indian mascots and the nicknames and antics associated with them have resulted in hard-won changes on the part of American Indian protestors and their supporters. During this period, both college and public school teams have adopted new names and eliminated mascot figures. Others, in an effort to clean up their half-time acts, have made cosmetic changes in sports logos or behaviors. Some teams have gone so far as to shop for Indian-made regalia in tribal communities in an effort to authenticate their mascots. Teams have also modified logo images to make them less "savage" looking. Further, individuals playing the role of mascot have attempted better theatrics. New clothes and tape-studied dancing aside, however, these teams still appropriate what isn't theirs and make it profane. As one sports writer observed of Chief Illiniwek's ersatz Indian dance, "sort of M. C. Hammer meets Richard Simmons meets Biff the town idiot." (Jeff Pearlman, *Sports Illustrated*, vol. 87, July 14, 1997, pg. 19) Nonetheless, these practices are institutionalized and applauded all the way from athletic stands to boards of trustees to legislatures to tomahawk-chopping presidents of the United States.

For American Indians, who represent less than 1 percent of the U.S. population, the elimination of appropriated nicknames and war-whooping mascots has been an uphill struggle, garnering powerful opposition, including arrests and lawsuits. Those who favor such nicknames, logos, and mascots (the majority) use a number of arguments and tactics to justify these practices. Among them is the claim of "honoring" American Indians. This claim is so pervasive that Jay Rosenstein entitled his 1996 documentary on the issue, "In Whose Honor? American Indian Mascots in Sports." Those who see nothing wrong with these stereotypical practices also frequently conduct polls with foregone conclusions, since the respondents are generally non-Indians uninformed about American Indians. Some fans attempt to validate their approval of Indian nicknames, logos, and mascots by claiming American Indian descent, although as a rule, they have neither set foot in a tribal community nor have an affiliation with recognized tribal groups. Still another tactic is to play "Good Indian, Bad Indian," finding an Indian person to agree with and justify their point of view (Good Indian) and disparaging those who disagree (Bad Indian).

Schools that have changed their names have been subject to challenges by individuals or groups unwilling to relinquish cherished nicknames, logos, and mascots. One of the most recent, a lawsuit by a group of alumni opposing the Los Angeles Unified School District's ban against American Indian-themed names and mascots, claims violation of First Amendment rights. As the following chronologies indicate, however, changes continue to occur despite overwhelming odds. The recent vote by the University of Illinois Senate to eliminate Chief Illiniwek may help sway the University of Illinois board of trustees to reverse their long-standing support of the mascot. As educator Cornel Pewewardy observes, "the critical mass of Indian educational associations and tribal governments want to eliminate Indian mascots and logos." It is imperative that they be heeded.

A CHRONOLOGY OF THE MASCOT ISSUE: COLLEGES, UNIVERSITIES, AND PROFESSIONAL TEAMS

1970   Dartmouth College in New Hampshire replaces its "Indians" team name with "Big Green."

1971   Marquette University in Wisconsin retires its mascot, "Willie Wampum." Stanford eliminates its "Indians" nickname and "Chief Lightfoot" mascot. Minnesota's Mankato State College drops its American Indian mascot but retains its "Indians" team name.

1972   The Cleveland Indian Center files suit in Ohio's Cuyahoga County Common Pleas Court, in objection to "Chief Wahoo," the baseball team mascot of the "Cleveland Indians."

1973   The University of Oklahoma eliminates its "Little Red" mascot.

1978   New York's Syracuse University eliminates its "Saltine Warrior" mascot.

1988   Saint John's University in New York drops its American Indian mascot but retains the team name, "Redmen."
Northeastern State University in Oklahoma drops its mascot, but votes to keep "Redmen" as a nickname.
Saint Mary's College in Minnesota changes its "Redmen" nickname to the "Cardinals."
The American Indian Registry for Performing Arts calls for protests against an ABC-TV program, "The Wonder Years," for presenting American Indians as mascots on the show's high school team.
Bradley University in Illinois drops its American Indian mascot.
The Michigan Civil Rights Commission calls for the elimination of American Indian symbols from the state's sports teams.

1989   Siena College in New York replaces "Indians" with "Saints" as its team name. New Jersey's Montclair State College eliminates both its American Indian nickname and mascot.

1990   University of Illinois trustees vote to keep "Chief Illiniwek" as the school's mascot. See sidebar, page 182.

1991   American Indians protest against the Atlanta Braves during World Series competition with the Minnesota Twins.

The National Congress of American Indians, the oldest and largest national tribal organization in the country, passes a unanimous resolution denouncing the use of American Indian nicknames.

Eastern Michigan University changes its team name from "Hurons" to "Eagles."

1992   American Indians protest against racism in sports outside the Super Bowl XXVI. The National Coalition on Racism in Sports and the Media is founded.

William Hilliard, editor of the *Portland Oregonian*, announces he will no longer publish the team names: "Redskins," "Redmen," "Braves," and "Indians."

A minor league affiliate of the Cleveland Indians in Columbus, Georgia, changes its team name from "Indians" to "Redsticks."

Michael Douglass, manager of District of Columbia radio stations WTOP and WASH, announces that the stations will not use offensive names, such as "Redskin," when referring to American Indians.

Don Shelton, assistant sports editor of the *Seattle Times*, announces that "Redskins," "Redmen," and "Red Raiders" will no longer appear in headlines, photo captions, or quotes made larger from a story. Such names will be avoided, when possible, or used sparingly.

The Wambli Ota Indian Club at Fort Lewis College in Colorado drafts a resolution to have students vote on revoking the mascot at their school, a cavalry soldier charging on horseback.

1993   The Great Lakes Inter-Tribal Council unanimously passes a resolution condemning American Indian mascots as "offensive, disrespectful, racist and demeaning."

Bradley University in Illinois announces that it will keep the name "Braves" for its athletic teams, but not use an American Indian mascot.

The Athletic Board of the University of Wisconsin, in response to the Great Lakes Inter-Tribal Council resolution on mascots, adopts a policy against scheduling teams with Native American mascots unless they're traditional rivals, such as the "Fighting Illini" of Illinois or a tournament opponent. See sidebar.

Boston McKinley, athletic director at the University of Minnesota, condemns the use of American Indians as mascots as racist and makes the decision to be sensitive to scheduling games with schools that have such mascots.

The Florida American Indian Movement and the National Coalition on Racism in Sports and Media sponsor a protest against Florida State University's "Seminole" mascot. Three protesters are arrested and a near riot ensues.

Arkansas State University replaces its "Spirit Joe" mascot with "Chief Big Track" and changes its school logo, but not its "Indians" nickname.

Senator Jeff Johnson, D-Cleveland, introduces a bill in the Ohio Senate seeking to prohibit public money from being used at public places that display or disseminate material "that is demeaning to a recognized ethnic or racial group." The bill would affect the Cleveland Indians and other Ohio teams with American Indian nicknames and mascots.

1994   The University of North Dakota Senate votes to change UND's "Fighting Sioux" nickname.

Marquette University announces a new nickname, "Golden Eagles," to replace "Warriors."

St. John's University in New York announces plans to replace its "Redmen" with "Red Storm," effective during the 1994–1995 school year.

The University of Iowa Board in Control of Athletes approves a policy banning visiting teams from bringing "any mascot that depicts or represents Native Americans." The policy also bans "music, dance and other behaviors that represent Native American culture in trivial, negative or stereotypical ways."

Eastern Michigan University objects to the Huron Restoration Alumni Chapter's use of the school's old logo, "Hurons," on clothing and promotional materials. The alumni group's attorney argued that the university had given up any claim to the logo by removing it from use and stated that the dispute may have to be settled in federal courts.

The University of Southern Colorado drops its American Indian mascot. *Indian Country Today* publisher Tim Giago and his staff boycott the Unity '94 journalism conference because it is held in Atlanta, Georgia, home of the Atlanta Braves and the "tomahawk chop." This newspaper, the country's largest American Indian weekly, has long opposed the use of American Indians as mascots.

1997   Members of the Cleveland Institute of Art's board of directors refuse to install or fund a billboard with a drawing of the Cleveland Indians' mascot Chief Wahoo, and the words "Smile for Racism." The billboard was designed by Cheyenne artist Edgar Heap of Birds as a protest against such mascots.

1997   The University of Tennessee changed its Indian logo, Chief Moccanooga, after complaints from American Indian activists that it was offensive. The new logo is a mockingbird, the state bird of Tennessee.

Miami University of Ohio dropped its Redskins nickname in favor of Redhawks out of concern that it might be derogatory toward the Miami Tribe. The decision affected the school's main campus in Oxford.

1998   The Wisconsin Senate Committee on Education held a public hearing on February 28 on SB341, which prohibits school boards from using an American Indian name, nickname, logo, or mascot if the state superintendent of public instruction considers its use a violation of the pupil antidiscrimination law. A vote by committee members will determine whether the bill, which has companion legislation in the Assembly, will go to the full Senate.

A CHRONOLOGY OF THE MASCOT ISSUE: SELECTED PUBLIC SCHOOLS

1978 Pekin High School in Illinois changes its derogatory nickname "Chinks" in favor of "Dragons."

1985 Steve Jerome-Wyatt, director of the Affiliated Obsidian Nation, and other supporters are instrumental in getting the Plumas Unified School District in California to change the name of "Injun Jim Elementary School." Activists also plan to mount a campaign to change the Colusa High School "Redskins" name and mascot.

1988 Southwest High School in Minneapolis changes its team name from the "Indians" to the "Lakers," following objections from an American Indian parent group.

1989 The *Chicago Sun-Times* reports "51 high schools in Illinois offer war whoops and paint. There are Redskins, Indians, Indianettes, Injuns, Blackhawks, Comanches, Braves, Mohawks. . . ."

The Lakota Times reports that the Minnesota Civil Liberties Union had a lawsuit under consideration against fifty-four schools with American Indian–theme team names "despite a state Board of Education resolution asking them to be dropped." The publication indicated that "twenty-two of the schools were called 'Indians,' the third most popular name in the state. Fourteen were called the 'Warriors,' six the 'Braves' and two the 'Chiefs.' Assorted others had names like 'Mohawks' and 'Redmen.'"

San Francisco School Superintendent Ramon Cortines orders Lowell High School to phase out its American Indian mascot.

1991 The Menomonie School Board (unrelated to the Menominee Nation of Wisconsin) appoints a task force to help ensure appropriate use of the district's American Indian name and logo.

1992 Rock County Circuit Judge John Lussow in Wisconsin rules that the Department of Public Instruction does not have the power to prohibit Milton High School's use of the term "Redmen" to refer to its sports teams.

The Shawano-Gresham School Board in Wisconsin, one of fifty-eight high schools with a team name associated with American Indians in the state, votes 6–3 to drop the American Indian name and mascot of Shawano High School.

Wisconsin Attorney General James Doyle issues a statement that American Indian nicknames may create "an intimidating or offensive environment, thus perpetuating past discrimination."

The school board of Naperville Central High School in Illinois votes to eliminate the name "Red Skins" and students of that school vote to replace it with the "Redhawks."

The National Indian Education Association denounces the use of the name "Injun" by the West Seneca West High School in Buffalo, New York, a school that also calls its cheerleaders, "Lady Injuns."

1993   Students at Longfellow Elementary School in Columbia, Maryland, vote to change the school's mascot from an American Indian to an eagle.

Colorado's Arvada High School Principal Jim Melhouse faces angry opposition from parents and students over his decision to change the school's athletic team's "Redskins" nickname.

The Wisconsin assembly passes a resolution urging public schools to consider dropping American Indian nicknames, logos, and mascots that could be offensive to American Indians.

Park View Middle School in Mukwonago, Wisconsin, votes to replace its Indian name and logo with a bulldog.

Sheboygan South High School in Sheboygan, Wisconsin, abandoned its Indian-head logo and the nickname "Redmen."

West Junior High in Rapid City, South Dakota, changes its mascot from the "Warriors" to the "Wolves."

The Washington state board of education votes to have the state's 296 school districts review the use of nicknames for sports teams and mascots.

1994   Milaca High School in Minnesota changes its nickname from "Indians" to "Wolves."

Watertown High School in South Dakota drops its school logo depicting an American Indian.

1995   Shawnee High School in Louisville, Kentucky, announces that its American Indian mascot is being replaced by a golden eagle.

1997   The Los Angeles Unified School District Board of Education, the second largest in the country, votes 6–0, with one abstention, to require three high schools and one junior high school to drop American Indian–themed names and mascots effective this school year.

In Denver, Colorado, the face of an Indian used as a mascot at Montbello High School will be painted over. The school's mascot will remain the Warriors, but the mascot will be represented as a "futuristic warrior."

1998   Jim Pitillo, an alumni of Birmingham High School in Los Angeles, files suit against the Los Angeles Unified School District and its officials on the grounds that the district's ban against American Indian–themed names and mascots restricts his first amendment right to free speech. Pitillo's activities include selling T-shirts, adorned with: "Save the Braves, 44 years of Pride."

U.S. District Court Judge Audrey B. Collins upheld the Los Angeles Unifed District's decision to do away with American Indian–themed names and mascots.

A state appeals court in Wisconsin rules that Mosinee High School's nickname, with a logo featuring a chief in a headdress, does not discriminate against American Indians.

Students at Enterprise High School in Enterprise, Oregon, voted to keep their nickname, the Savages, despite the school board's repeal of the politically incorrect mascot last year. But the accompanying Indian logo will be changed to either a fiery muscular man or axe-wielding monster.

Washington Redskins

"Ye firste Meetinge House was solid mayde to withstands ye wicked onsaults of ye Red Skins." 1699. Quoted in H.E. Smith, *Colonial Days* (1900). The American Heritage Dictionary defines "redskin" as "offensive slang" for Native Americans.

1992   Lakota legal scholar Vine Deloria, Jr.; Suzan Shown Harjo, Cheyenne-Arapaho director of the Morning Star Foundation; and five other prominent American Indian leaders file a petition on September 10 with the U.S. Patent and Trademark Office, *Harjo, et al. v. Pro-Football, Inc.* to cancel seven federal trademark registrations for various offensive nicknames and logos used by the Washington Redskins football organization. The petition asserts violation of the Lanham Act of 1946, which stipulates that trademark registrations cannot "falsely suggest a connection with persons, living or dead, institutions, beliefs, or national symbols, or bring them into contempt or disrepute."

1993   Senator Ben Nighthorse Campbell, the only Native American in the U.S. Senate, introduces a bill that would allow the federal government to transfer land to sports franchises only if they refrain from "derogatory or offensive ethnic and racial stereotypes." Representative Bill Richardson, D-New Mexico, sponsors the House version of the measure. The Washington football franchise seeks to build a new stadium on federal land.

1994   The U.S. Patent and Trademark Office's trial and appeal board rules in favor of the American Indian petitioners (and against Pro Football, Inc.) contesting the Washington football team's "Redskins" registration as illegal, thus allowing further litigation of the case.

        A county zoning officer rejects the Washington football team's plan to build a new stadium in southern Maryland.

1997   Dorsey & Whitney, a national law firm, files a "trial memorandum" with the Trademark Trial and Appeal Board. The "Conclusion" states "*Redskin(s)* is a racial slur. The record evidence overwhelmingly demonstrates that *redskin(s)* is today and always has been one of the most derogatory and offensive racial slurs for Native Americans."

1998   The Trademark Trial and Appeal Board plans to hear oral arguments in the case to cancel federal protection of the trademark of the Washington "Redskins."

1999   A three-judge panel of the U.S. Patent and Trademark office cancels seven registered Redskins trademarks for being disparaging to Native Americans. Redskins officials plant to appeal the decision in federal court.

University of Illinois

1989   American Indian groups and a small number of students, including art student
       Charlene Teters of the Spokane tribe, call for the elimination of the Chief
       Illiniwek mascot at the University of Illinois. Ms. Teters presented her concerns
       to the minority affairs committee of the student government, which drafted a
       resolution calling the mascot discriminatory and asked the administration to in-
       vestigate the matter further. The student government adopts an amended reso-
       lution, deleting paragraphs describing the mascot as a racist symbol.
       Senator Paul Simon of Illinois signs a petition calling for the elimination of
       Chief Illiniwek.
       The University of Illinois asks its pep club, cheerleaders, and marching band
       to refrain from wearing "war paint" at athletic events.

1990   University of Illinois trustees vote seven to one to retain Chief Illiniwek as
       the university's mascot.

1991   The Student Government Association at the University of Illinois adopts a
       resolution calling for the removal of Chief Illiniwek and offers a declaration
       of apology and reconciliation to Native Americans.
       The outgoing Alumni Association president of the University of Illinois an-
       nounces that alumni will be polled concerning the Chief Illiniwek mascot issue.

1994   Representative Rick Winkel of the Illinois House of Representatives intro-
       duces a bill to protect Chief Illiniwek as an "honored symbol" of the Univer-
       sity of Illinois. Race discrimination complaints are filed with the U.S. De-
       partment of Education, Office of Civil Rights against the University of
       Illinois by several staff members and students at the university.
       The Illinois Department of Human Rights dismisses three counts of discrim-
       ination filed against the University of Illinois by Michael Haney, American
       Indian leader and activist, who sought to force the university to eliminate the
       Chief Illiniwek mascot and the Fighting Illini nickname.

1995   The House of Representatives votes 80–26 in favor of the Winkel bill to pro-
       tect Chief Illiniwek.
       The University of Illinois student government association votes 45–19
       against submitting a referendum on student government election ballots ask-
       ing "Do you support Chief Illiniwek as the official symbol of the University
       of Illinois at Urbana-Champaign?"
       The newly established American Indian Council of Illinois calls on Illinois
       Governor Jim Edgar to veto Representative Rick Winkel's bill seeking to
       make Chief Illiniwek the symbol of the school forever.
       The U.S. Department of Education rules that the Chief Illiniwek mascot does
       not create a hostile environment for American Indians at the University of
       Illinois.

1998   The University of Illinois Senate, composed of 200 faculty members and 50
       students, votes March 9 in favor of eliminating Chief Illiniwek. The vote is
       advisory, with the university's board of trustees having final say on the issue.
       The National Coalition on Racism in Sports and the Media holds the first
       Conference on the Elimination of Racist Mascots from April 3–4 at the Uni-
       versity of Illinois in Champaign-Urbana.

"Redskin" Plates Prohibited in Utah

In 1999 the Utah State Tax Commission revoked three license plates imprinted with variations of the word "Redskin." The four-member commission reversed its 1996 decision allowing the personalized plates "Redskin," "Redskns," and "Rdskin." The reversal stemmed from a Utah Supreme Court ruling that the commission should have considered what an "objective, reasonable" person would find offensive. Utah law prohibits license plates that, among other objectionable wording, "express contempt, ridicule, or superiority of a race, deity, ethnic heritage, gender, or political affiliation." Guided by the court, the commission members, three of whom were new to the panel, ruled that a reasonable person "would be led to the inescapable conclusion" that the word is "derogatory or expresses contempt for a race or ethnic heritage."

Dallas, Texas, Public Schools

With the elimination of American Indian mascots from all of its schools in 1998, the Dallas Public Schools became a model for other districts in the country to follow. Spearheaded by representatives and supporters of the American Indian Education Program in the Dallas Public Schools, complaints were lodged against the district for its use of Indian mascots.

Using the district's own policies and philosophy affirming the value of a student's heritage, the opponents of the mascots began a process of education about the harmfulness of the practice. Phase I centered around the elimination of mascot names in the Dallas Public Schools, followed by Phase II, the removal of mascot imagery from school property, including athletic and cheerleading uniforms.

The process of education and change culminated in a powwow held by the American Indian Education Program on September 24, 1998, to recognize and honor the ten schools in the district that had eliminated their American Indian mascots and logos.

Clyde A. Erwin High School, Buncombe County, North Carolina

1996   The Buncombe County Native American Intertribal Association asks the Buncombe County School Board to eliminate American Indian mascots at Erwin High School outside Asheville, North Carolina. This high school has used the terms "warriors" and "squaws" since the 1950s to refer to its male and female athletic teams.

1997   Protests against the mascots at Erwin High School continue.

1998   The Buncombe County School Board puts the mascot issue to a vote by Erwin students in May 1998. Forty-one percent of the students vote to keep the mascots, thirty-three percent vote for change, and the remainder either vote "not concerned" or do not vote. The Intertribal Association opposes the vote, noting: "You don't vote on racism and sexual harassment."

On August 10, the first day of school, Intertribal Association members protest the Erwin mascot, holding a news conference and seeking support for a "Resolution of Respect for American Indian Culture," to be delivered to the Buncombe County School Board.

1999   The U.S. Department of Justice, after investigating the Buncombe County School mascot issue, determines that the school's elimination of the word "squaw" and religious items is sufficient to end its investigation. This determination stipulates that a 25-foot statute and two totem poles on school grounds do not have to be removed. The Justice Department authorizes Chief Joyce Dugan of the Eastern Band of Cherokee Indians to decide which religious items should be removed. Dugan approves retaining the American Indian warrior mascot.

Stanford Removes Indian Symbol:
Student Petition Gains Support*

We the Native American members of the Stanford University community, denounce the use of the symbol of the Indian which is used to represent the Stanford athletic teams, and the caricatures of the Indian accompanying the symbol as illustrations for posters and fliers which announce and advertise University events. We urge that the use of the Indian symbol be permanently discontinued. We also urge the University to fulfill its promise to the students of its Native American program by improving and supporting the program and thereby making its promise to improve Native American education a reality.

This petition is made necessary by the fact that the non-Indian members of the Stanford University community are insensitive to the "humanness" of their Native American counterparts. The name, the "Stanford Indians" displays this lack of understanding.

This distortion, which is an insult to the Native American student and professional community, and in fact to all Indians, is apparent in the following ways:

The usage of the name, "Stanford Indians," as the name of the athletic teams of the school. No one would show such ignorance by choosing the name "The Jews," or "The Negroes," for a school team. Stanford has exploited the name of a *race* of people for its entertainment. So long as the name of the team remains unchanged, the ignorance of non-Indians remains as deep as ever. There is little chance that those who regard the term "Indian" as suitable for a team name will ever realize the importance of the socio-economic problems, the traditional life styles, and the religious practices which are central to an understanding of today's Indian people. There will continue to be a failure to understand the human side of being Indian, so long as people are permitted to choose instead to see only the entertaining aspects of Indian life.

*Reprinted by permission from *The Indian Historian*, vol. 5, no. 1, Spring 1972, pp. 21–22. Published by The Indian Historian Press, Inc., 1451 Masonic Ave., San Francisco, Calif. 94117. Copyright, 1972 by the Indian Historical Society. All rights reserved. No part of these contents may be duplicated in any manner without written permission of the publisher.

A major part of the objectionable symbol's use involves "Prince" Tim Williams "Lightfoot," and the Stanford "Dollies." Neither Lightfoot, the mascot, nor the cheerleaders wear traditional dress. Their performances are an obscene parody degrading and highly objectionable to the Indian population of the Stanford community.

Lightfoot is especially insulting to the Plains Indian students, for the mascot's dances and costume are improperly designed after their traditional practices and dress.

These students have been raised to have a deep regard for their traditional dances, and a great deal of respect for those dancers who have *earned* the right and the honor of performing tribal rites. Lightfoot's actions on the football field make a mockery of these religious practices. Dancing to the marching band is not traditional, not Indian. The fact that Lightfoot wears a pseudo-traditional costume while dancing with the band shows that the code of respect that each wearer of the costume must follow has been ignored by him. The headdress is a sign of great honor and is presented to its wearer as a reward for decided right living. Putting a "hex" on the opposing team, as Lightfoot does, is a prostitution of the Eagle dance of the Plains Indians, the dance which the mascot's spell-casting motions most resemble. Because Lightfoot's performances are completely false, we insist that they are ethically wrong, and that they reinforce the ignorant Hollywood stereotype of Native Americans. That Lightfoot performs in this fashion out of ignorance and not out of malice, is certainly obvious. The very fact that he has dubbed himself "Prince" displays such ignorance. There was no such royalty among the Native peoples. Such a royal appellation is symptomatic of an entirely different social system, a system of social relations relevant to the monarchy, which in turn was in force as a result of an entirely different type of political organization and economic conditions than that existed all over the North American continent at the time of European intrusion upon our land and life.

Though the Stanford "Dollies" do not pretend to be traditional, their dress is offensive, and the image transmitted by their dress is totally unreal as well as degrading. Indian women are never allowed to act as the "Dollies" do when they are dressed in the Hollywood Indian image. This sort of conduct will never accommodate an understanding of real Indian living.

Publications by the Associated Students of Stanford University, and printed decals, pennants, dolls sold in the Stanford bookstore, habitually prostitute the use of the Indian in order to announce and advertise University events. Certainly anyone can see these representations are designed to capitalize on the facial characteristics which non-Indians stubbornly and ignorantly maintain are the patterns for facial characteristics of all American Indians. These products are physically unattractive. They seem to insist that the race upon which they are fashioned are also unattractive. We are well aware that the Stanford bookstore sells them only on request, but the fact remains that the distorted images continue to be sold. We feel that such cartoons and representations are wrongly used. They should not be made available for sale or distribution.

In removing the Indian as Stanford's symbol, the University would be renouncing a grotesque ignorance, which it has previously condoned. We appreciate the long history of Stanford's Indian symbol, and we are well aware that certain Indians themselves have either accepted it or even approved it. That fact does not obliterate the justification for our position, nor does it diminish one whit the strength of our demand for removing the symbol. We cannot, and we will not accept the demeaning, insulting ways in which the "Stanford Indian" symbol distorts the image of our people, and transforms into obscenity the religious aspects of all the Native Tribes in general. By retracting its misuse of the Indian symbol, the University would be displaying a progressive concern for the American Indians of the United States, and the Indian population of this University specifically.

* * *

In a decision reached by Dr. Richard W. Lyman, president of Stanford University, it was decided to abolish the "Stanford Indians" symbol, to end the idea of the mascot and the "dollies," and to eliminate the production, sale, and distribution of the decals, posters, and other advertising materials referring to the objectionable "Indians" symbol. In a statement from Lois S. Amsterdam, University Ombudsman, the following should be noted:

"I cannot add to the obvious force of the petition's statement on the demeaning exploitation of a race of people as a symbol for sport and entertainment. Whether it be a team name, 'mascot,' or dollie, all must be condemned as the progeny of an offensive use.

"I do feel impelled however to speak on a tangential problem. I have heard and read of the possible adverse reaction of our alumni to the abandonment of the Indian symbol. It is true that the symbol has been utilized for many years, and has therefore been nostalgically incorporated into some alumni activity and thought. The alumni are attached and committed to a University, and to the men and women who represent the traditions, goals, and aspirations of that University. They do not revere a symbol for its own sake, but rather take pride in the students who do their best to represent Stanford in competitive sport and intellectual endeavor. The alumni will be proud when their University removes any vestige of a symbolic use which degrades and insults members of our community. Surely we do not expect less from our alumni than we do from ourselves; and we should not disparage the alumni by assuming that they would cling obstinately to a symbol of the past whose present inappropriateness has become plainly apparent. . .

"It does appear that the Native American Program as presently operated has serious deficiencies which both handicap our Native American students in benefiting from the educational potential of the University and handicap the University in realizing its commitment to the Native American group. There is a problem, for example, in the absence of adequate supporting personnel; and there appears to be a need for special academic programs and support.

"I am presently exploring these and other problems further, and I plan to make recommendations to you concerning them within another ten days or two weeks. . ."

Recapturing Stolen Media Images: Indians Are *Not* Mascots or Logos

Cornel Pewewardy

Why bring Indian mascots, logos, nicknames, and the tomahawk chop to the attention of millions of loyal sports fans all over the nation who enjoy America's favorite pastime—baseball? My response has always been because these trappings and seasonal insults offend tens of thousands of other Americans—the indigenous peoples of North America. These invented media images prevent millions of Americans from understanding an authentic human experience—that of people called American Indians or Native Americans, both long ago and today.

Let's spread the fun around. If we can have the Washington Redskins, why can't we have the Los Angeles Yellowskins? And if we can have the Cleveland Indians—whose grinning-injun logo, Chief Wahoo, is to American Indians what Stepin Fetchit is to African Americans—why can't we have the San Diego Chicanos?

Many schools around the country exhibit Indian mascots, logos, nicknames, and do the tomahawk chop in sports stadiums in unauthentic representations of indigenous cultures. Still many school officials across the country think that they are honoring Indians and insist that their school's sponsored activities (ballgames, pageants, band, etc.) are not offensive, but rather a compliment to Indians. I want to argue otherwise, and contend that these racist activities are a form of cultural violence.

Why would anyone, especially educators, allow students to uncritically adopt a cartoon version of a people's culture as an Indian mascot or logo? Students need to be educated about the negative effects of racist Indian mascots and logos portrayed by sports teams. Some students have told me that they don't see the Indian mascot issue as important as those of alcoholism and child abuse. Some even say it's "too much fuss over team names" or "what's the point?" They don't see the connection, simply because they are not close to the issues. What a lot of people do not see is the mimicking and protesting that goes on in sporting arenas. They are not going to see the problem if they don't think there is a problem. I see the root cause of this negative portrayal of Indian mascots as "dysconscious racism."

This is a form of racism that tacitly accepts dominant white norms and privileges. The way in which Indian mascots and logos are used today is racism in American sports culture. It's as "American as apple pie and baseball." 189-90

The problem arises when the persons, symbols, or behaviors project a negative or stereotypical image. Sports mascots, logos, and related paraphernalia too often reflect stereotypes rather than authenticity. Various mascot sponsors have invented Indian characters that have nothing to do with the reality of indigenous people's lives, past or present. These mascots and logos, and the images that they convey, homogenize hundreds of indigenous cultures, robbing them of their distinctive identities and distorting their roles in U.S. history.

Many Native people take the Indian mascot, logos, nicknames, and tomahawk chop, as well as all the antics, as an insult. As an educator, I try to get teachers to see that the Indian mascot and logo issue is just one cause for low self-esteem in Native children. To make my point clear, I refer to the American Indian Mental Health Association of Minnesota and their position statement concerning Indian mascots in 1992 that says:

> Using images taken from the myths associated with American Indians throughout history and using those images to promote team spirit is a form a racism. It is NOT a way to show honor to us as a people. Anyone who promotes this falsehood has not done their research, and are more concerned with promoting their own agenda than with representing Native people.

Furthermore, I show students all the resolutions I have compiled over the years that have attempted to eliminate this racist practice in schools. All the resolutions to eliminate negative Indian images came from grassroots people—mostly Indian parents. Resolutions to ban Indian mascots and logos from schools normally originate from educational associations (National Indian Education Association, National Education Association, Wisconsin and Minnesota State Departments of Education), tribal governments (Governor's Interstate Indian Council, United Indian Nations of Oklahoma, Great Lakes Inter-Tribal Council, Oneida Nation of Wisconsin, and more), and Indian organizations (National Congress of American Indians, American Indian Movement).

To prove their point and defend the need to retain Indian mascots and logos, I've witnessed that many people will search up and down and find some Indian person that will gladly speak in favor of using them. Although some Indian people will even say they are honorable, the critical mass of Indian educational associations and tribal governments want to eliminate Indian mascots and logos from schools. 190

Who should decide what is demeaning and racist? Clearly, the affected party determines what is offensive. It is not for unaffected members of society to dictate how the affected party should feel. Many indigenous people do not feel mascots and logos such as those of the Cleveland Indians and Washington Redskins promote authentic representations of their respective cultures. Despite Indians' protests against using their images as sports mascots, dozens of teams continue to use unflattering, stereotypical symbols. ⟩ ١٩٥ -١

Advertising characters such as "Little Black Sambo" and the "Frito Bandito" are no longer acceptable in society because African American (especially the NAACP and the Urban League) and Mexican American and Latino/na populations (LULAC, MALDEF, National Council of LaRaza) have let it be known that such expressions carry racist overtones. But for some reason, we permit racism to continue when we see Indian mascots and logos displayed in American sporting events. These slogans cannot be more offensive to African Americans and Mexican American and Latino/na than "redskin" is to American Indians. With regard to being overly sensitive, how can American Indians be "just too sensitive" to a word defined in terms equally as demeaning as other racist terms? And how can they be "just too sensitive" to a word whose history conveys so many painful memories and intergenerational unresolved grief? And please don't associate this imperative with political correctness—the desire to appease every constituency that finds insult and injustice in the world, no matter how slight.

A few newspapers have started to implement policy when writing about Indian mascots, logos, and nicknames. The *Star Tribune* of Minnesota, the Portland *Oregonian,* and the *Seattle Times* of Washington State, as well as some smaller presses, have led the way in cleaning up the negative headlines and commentary about Indian mascots, logos, nicknames, and sports teams.

While the Cleveland Indians, Atlanta Braves, Washington Redskins, Kansas City Chiefs, and Chicago Blackhawks have resisted the pressure to change, scores of colleges, universities, and high school teams have adopted new names over the years: Stanford changed from "Indians" to the "Cardinals," Dartmouth changed from "Indians" to "The Big Green," and Ohio's Miami University "Redskins" became the "Red Hawks." Other institutions, including the University of Illinois' "Fightin Illini" and Haskell's "Fightin Indians" can make changes as well. In the Big Ten Conference, athletic departments of the University of Wisconsin and University of Minnesota established policies on Native American logos, and names. Many more colleges, universities, high schools, and junior high schools have dropped their racially insulting Indian mascots, logos and nicknames, but no professional sports team has felt enough heat—or, perhaps, has enough conscience or respect—to take a similar step. They should be able to do so without ugly alumni and student backlashes that either smear Indian protestors as troublemakers or gadflies or physically threaten them.

Many American Indian people, individually, are quiet about the mascot issue; often it is a silence born of disgust. It's only now that the mainstream media has picked up on the news because more Americans are being educated about the issues. People will not speak when there is no audience of patient, intelligent listeners. For many Indian and non-Indian people, this issue has become very old because they have been fighting this battle of Indian mascots and logos in schools for many years.

A genuine leadership role by school officials would seek to instruct the parents, teachers, and students about cultural and intellectual fallacies with regard to the use of Indians as mascots and logos. They should research the matter and discover that the indigenous people of North America would never have associated sacred practices with the hoopla of a pep rally or half-time entertainment, and the tawdry allegiances to a team or a public school. This serves as a valuable educational teaching lesson. This could help to deconstruct the fabricated images of Indians that most school-age children have in their psyche. The moment is ripe for illumination, but be cautious because "inaction is action."

Finally, my challenge is to educators. Where is the intellectual school leadership that will teach our communities about these issues?

From Subhuman to Superhuman: The Evolution of American Indian Images in Comic Books

Cornel Pewewardy

From subhuman to superhuman may sound strange to someone who is not familiar with the portrayal of American Indians in U.S. history and literature. Those grounded in the history of Indian-white relations in the United States know how American Indians have been portrayed in early American history as something less than human—subhuman. It took an 1879 court case, *Standing Bear v. Crook,* to prove American Indians were, indeed, real human beings. Decades later, writers of scientific fantasy viewed Indians primarily as superhuman.

Each new generation has reinvented the Indian in the image of its own era. Over the past hundred years, creators of comic books, products of their respective generations, have reflected the shift in the image of Indians from subhuman to superhuman.

In the past ninety years, comics, a unique form of American popular culture, have gone from a gimmick to boost newspaper circulation to a cultural institution read daily by millions of Americans. Once dismissed as vulgar doodles for children, they now provide a great deal of pleasure for millions of readers, adults and children alike. In the process, these daily offerings of sight gags, one-liners, and on-going sagas have offered a fascinating index of changing American notions and attitudes about ethnicity, class, and gender.

With antecedents in both the European tradition of picture stories and American graphic humor, the American comic strip grew out of a newspaper war in the closing decades of the nineteenth century (when the large urban daily papers were fighting to increase their circulation). One historian contends that the immediate genesis was the competition in the 1890s between William Randolph Hearst's New York *Journal* and Joseph Pulitzer's New York *World.*[1]

The comics have always reflected people's likes and dislikes, preferences, and prejudices, employing ethnic stereotypes, both negative and positive. It should not be a surprise that the history of comics reveals a wide range of attitudes toward ethnic minority groups. From the early years of this century, comic strips were suffused with crude, even gross stereotypes. Indeed, Blacks, Jews, Italians, Chinese, and American Indians were all maligned and mistreated.

Early in the century, ethnic characters were considered to be great comic material. The "funny" characteristics of the newly arrived European immigrants, as well as of "older" groups (indigenous peoples), were popular targets for the slapstick, and the often cruel, humor of the times. Falling down the stairs, getting electrocuted, having an eye poked out by a goat's horn were typical gags, and, more often than not, bumbling ethnic characters, with heavy, slurred accents, stoic-broken English dialects, big-nosed figures were the victims. Today, these insensitive and often blatantly prejudiced images shock our society, yet, during their time period in history, they were generally accepted and even encouraged by millions of Americans.

Crude stereotyping of ethnic characters became less prevalent as the first half of the century progressed. Syndication, which transformed the comic book industry in the 1920s, resulted in the use of fewer ethnic images. Also, the assimilation of certain immigrant groups into American society altered the way that these ethnic groups were portrayed in the comics.

While the 1920s saw in comics the rise of domestic and pretty girl strips, the 1930s were invigorated with illustrated adventure stories, pioneered in 1929 with the appearance of "Tarzan" and "Buck Rogers." Modeled after movie serials, these new strips were episodic and, influenced by contemporary advertising art and traditional illustration, were drawn with greater realism than the older gag strips. Soon endless Westerns, science fiction fantasies, melodramas, and action adventures set in exotic locales appeared side by side with the traditional funnies. Many of the new action adventure strips carried what in retrospect appears to be a naively ethnocentric American image of the world. In strips ranging from "Jungle Jim" and "The Phantom" to "Smilin' Jack" and "Terry and the Pirates"— the strip credited with pioneering "social usefulness"—the lone American hero matched his wits and muscle against a host of jungle-dwelling African savages and sinister, scheming Asians.[2] In strip after strip, derogatory racial stereotypes of the world's peoples were positioned against mythic images of so-called American physical, moral, and intellectual superiority.

In the decades following the end of the Second World War, the naïve worldview of the 1930s action-adventure comics, increasingly distant and archaic, came under attack. "Tarzan" was criticized by African delegations at the United Nations for presenting an image of Africa as a continent consisting solely of jungles and uneducated natives while at home, the NAACP protested the continuing racist humor of certain strips, a protest that gathered momentum during the Civil Rights era.[3] Racial humor had never been controversial enough to undergo the sanitation and social reconstruction that swept the social universe of the comics after syndication in the 1920s, as witnessed by its enduring popularity throughout the first half of the century. Characters of African, Asian, East Indian, and

American Indian heritage continued to be depicted in servile or stock, stereotyped roles as late as the 1960s.

By the mid-1940s, African Americans began to disappear from the pages of the nation's comic strips. A 1962 study that sampled comics illustrated between 1943 and 1958 provides telling evidence of American attitudes toward ethnicity during this period.[4] Of the 532 characters identified, there was one African American and no Jewish characters. Most characters came from Anglo-Saxon and Nordic racial backgrounds. While comic strip characters were found to be predominately white middle class, minorities and foreigners were less likely to be employed than the Anglo characters, and when employed, were most often in subordinate labor of service positions, sidekicks, or faithful Indian companions. They were more often portrayed in villainous roles and lower-status social positions, expressed a greater desire for power and revenge, a lower interest in material success, and a lower desire for love and affection.

As the century progressed and the country became more sensitive toward ethnic minorities, society—and the comics—began modifying their ethnic images in the comics. The stereotypes in comic strips have not only lessened, but cartoonists, responding to their readers and to the Civil Rights movement, have consciously introduced a wide range of classy new ethnic characters into their work. These new characters—ethnic minorities—radiate grace, pride, and intelligence.

Changes in ethnic images in the comics have resulted not only from the assimilation of certain groups and from the Civil Rights movement, but also from economic changes. The growing sophistication and increased economic power of ethnic minorities have resulted in a new concern for their interests and tastes.

A 1979 study attempted to illustrate the nature and varieties of stereotyping of Blacks and Native Americans that occurred in the first twenty years (1954–1973) of the popular magazine *Playboy* and to identify any changes in the content and frequency of that stereotyping over time.[5] The study found that among Native Americans the key traits were nose aquilinity, skin color, cheekbone structure, and hair style (bangs or braids). While Blacks began to be perceived as members of American society, Native Americans continued to be viewed largely as an "irrelevant minority" or one not conceived of in anything but romantic, historical, or primitive terms.

Today, a field trip to the comic book store reveals a major transformation in the portrayal of ethnic characters. Once subhuman, they now appear as superheroes. Superman, Captain Marvel, and Batman, all of Anglo heritage, have been joined by Black Panther (African), White Tiger (Puerto Rican), Kitty Pryde (Jewish), Banshee (Irish), Colossus (Russian), Firebird (Mexican), and more. No longer the butt of jokes, ethnic characters in the comics today are, with some important exceptions, treated positively and with increasing sensitivity. American Indian characters continue to carry on with the "back to the future" comic themes and traditions in a new comic book series called, *Tribal Force*.

Bill Jones wrote an article about *Tribal Force: Native American Superheroes Star in Comic Book Series* in the late March 1997 edition of *News from Indian Country*.

The year is 2006, and the United States of America is engaged in a civil war with the United Tribes of America. The United States wants to confiscate reservation land on which something valuable was discovered. But the land is sacred to the tribes, who will protect it with their lives if necessary. To help them in their struggle, the tribes have called upon their own team of superheroes who can do all your basic superhero feats. They can see, hear and fight better than any mortal—and, of course, some can fly. What distinguishes these idols from the like of Superman, Batman and Spider-Man is that they are Native Americans.

Together, they represent the little characters in *Tribal Force*, the first comic book featuring Native American heroes created by Native American talent. Artist Ryan Huna Smith and writer Jon Proudstar, both 28-year-old Tucson residents, were inspired to produce *Tribal Force* in part from a dissatisfaction with the way Native Americans are portrayed in comic books.

If they are depicted at all, Native Americans are usually "trackers, or they wear bone necklaces and lots of fringe, or have a cloud of mysticism and an eagle hanging around them," Smith said.

The one comic-book Native American hero Proudstar liked was *Thunder Bird*, in the X-Men series, but this hero was killed off shortly after his first appearance.

Proudstar, whose ancestry includes Mayan, Yaqui and Hispanic blood, had been kicking around a story about Native American heroes since he was 18. The opportunity to make his idea a reality came when he saw a drawing he liked hanging on the wall of a comic-book store. Proudstar asked the shop owner how to get in touch with Smith. Soon, writer and artist were collaborating on *Tribal Force*.

Smith, who is of Navajo and Chemehuevi descent, said they found private investors to kick in $50,000 to launch their comic-book brainstorm. *Tribal Force*, the first of the series, was produced by Mystic Comics. For Smith and Proudstar, it was important to retain control over all aspects of their project, even the possibility of future merchandising.

Some of their characters wear authentic tribal symbols, Smith said, "such as the Ghost Dance symbol." But just because tribal leaders gave them permission to use such symbols in a comic book doesn't mean they would permit the symbols to be displayed on toys.

"Jon and I needed to have the authority to say 'no' to that," Smith said. It was also important that they retain creative control over the characters and story. What's unique about the *Tribal Force* superheroes is that they represent different tribes as well as different social problems.

"One of our heroes was molested as a child," Smith said. "Another was born with fetal alcohol syndrome. So even though they are super-beings, they still deal with true-to-life issues."

Proudstar said the primary inspiration for *Tribal Force* was to provide Native children with contemporary heroes of their own. "Children today have no contemporary heroes to identify with," he said. "All our role models are from the past."

With *Tribal Force*, Smith and Proudstar are filling that demand, and then some. Besides entertaining kids, each book in the mini-series will dedicate one of its 22 pages to some aspect of Native culture. In the first issue, the history of the Ghost Dance is explained.

With *Tribal Force*, Smith and Proudstar have created the comic book that was missing from their childhood. Comic book #2 in the *Tribal Force* series is ready to go. Smith and Proudstar are looking for a publisher.

Negative stereotypes, as blatantly racist as those at the turn of the century, can still be found today, though such stereotyping more often targets new immigrants who are associated with American immigration policy disputes than old immigrant ethnic groups. There was never any question that comic characters portrayed as wartime heroes were battling the forces of evil, which, if left unchecked, threatened to destroy the American way of life. America was seen as a haven requiring protection by the strong, white hero (and occasional heroine), no matter what means were employed to do it.

The increasing sophistication of the comic book audience has been accompanied by more sophisticated comic book characters. Today cultural equality and acceptance seem to have replaced the self-conscious liberal depiction of social injustices typical in the late 1960s and 1970s. One study advocates that Marvel Comics' *New Mutants* are complex individuals, their personalities being formed in part by their different ethnic backgrounds.[6] Though still somewhat stereotypical—there is the dashing, womanizing Hispanic, the nature-loving Native American, and the repressed, Calvinist Scotswoman—their ethnic identities are more fully explored than the simpler depiction of the past. Indeed these series focus on the characters' personalities. While the *New Mutants* still battle evil, often the evil stems from within the heroes themselves.

With the increased emphasis on complex characterization, questions still remain whether or not the model of the comic book superhero actually has changed. Consider the case of Dani, the *New Mutants'* Native American leader. Dani successfully integrates contemporary American culture with her adherence to traditional Cheyenne ways. The cultural choices and compromises she makes are handled with sophistication, and her tribal traditions are portrayed with respect. Yet she still wields her powerful Cheyenne chants as easily as Captain Marvel utters the magic word "Shazam!" In this instance, at least, meaningful Cheyenne traditions are reduced to yet one more super power to be wielded by the proper hero.

Despite the mixed results, there is an encouraging trend toward the increasingly sensitive portrayal of ethnic characters in the comics. Evidence exists that cartoonists are going beyond the positive images so prevalent in the depiction of today's ethnic heroes and superheroes. A few ethnic characters are now full participants in their comic world, not just tokens.

Students in America cannot truly understand the realities of contemporary American Indian lifestyles and worldview without understanding the popular

Indian images of the past, present, and future. Understanding the contemporary images and perceptions of American Indians in comic books is extremely important, not only for Indian people but also for the mainstream culture.

Comic strips, like other mass media, at first portrayed a homogenous world of white Americans in which the great cultural myth of an equal chance for all Americans, regardless of race, color, place of origin, or social class, could be played out without disturbing contradictions. In the past decades, however, comics began to reflect America's shifting attitudes and values. Studying them provides a record of Americans' evolving attitudes toward ethnicity, class, and gender.

NOTES

1. Charles Hardy, "A Brief History of Ethnicity in the Comics," in *Ethnic Images in the Comics,* eds. Charles Hardy and Gail F. Stern (Philadelphia: Balch Institute for Ethnic Studies, 1986), pp. 7–10.

2. Ibid.

3. Ibid.

4. Ibid.

5. John R. White, "Playboy Blacks vs. Playboy Indians: Differential Minority Stereotyping in Magazine Cartoons," *American Indian Culture and Research Journal,* vol. 3, no. 2 (1979): pp. 39–55.

6. Amy Rashap, "You've Come a Long Way, Baby: Ethnic Superheroes in Comic Books," in *Ethnic Images in the Comics,* eds. Charles Hardy and Gail F. Stern (Philadelphia: Balch Institute for Ethnic Studies, 1986), pp. 31–36.

REFERENCES

Brown, Dee. *Bury My Heart at Wounded Knee.* New York: Holt, Rinehart and Winston, 1970.

Freedman, Theodore. "Foreword." In *Ethnic Images in the Comics,* ed. Charles Hardy and Gail F. Stern. Philadelphia: Balch Institute for Ethnic Studies, 1986.

Jones, Bill. "Tribal Force: Native American Superheroes Star in Comic Book Series." *News From Indian Country* (late March 1997): p. 13B.

Hardy, Charles. "A Brief History of Ethnicity in the Comics." In *Ethnic Images in the Comics,* ed. Charles Hardy and Gail F. Stern. Philadelphia: Balch Institute for Ethnic Studies, 1986.

Rashap, Amy. "You've Come a Long Way, Baby: Ethnic Superheroes in Comic Books." In *Ethnic Images in the Comics,* ed. Charles Hardy and Gail F. Stern. Philadelphia: Balch Institute for Ethnic Studies, 1986.

White, John. R. "Playboy Blacks vs. Playboy Indians: Differential Minority Stereotyping in Magazine Cartoons." *American Indian Culture and Research Journal,* vol. 3, no. 2 (1979): pp. 39–55.

The Y-Indian Guide
and Y-Indian Princess Program*

Beatty Brasch

PREFACE

In writing this paper, many American Indian people have been consulted and many of the available books on the subject have been reviewed. I am personally not speaking for the American Indian people but instead have tried to synthesize the available material on the Sioux people. Some native Indian people were interviewed as this work was begun and their feelings were incorporated into an original draft. That draft was later reviewed and criticized by American Indians. Where it was considered to be helpful to the reader, comments of these critics have been inserted in parentheses. ⟩ ₁ ٩ ٩

The organization The Council of American Indian Students, University of Nebraska, Lincoln, and the following people—Pat Menard, Corrina (Bobby) Drum, Galen Buller, Karen Buller, and Frank Black Elk have read this paper and generally agree with the content, the tone, and the changes that are necessary in the Y manual. Their comments on the manual are incorporated into the paper.

INTRODUCTION

In about 1970, a Y-Guide** Task Force was organized so that the Y-Indian Guide fathers-sons-mothers-daughters could gain a better understanding of Indian culture. This was done because "Charles Kujawa, national consultant to the Y-Indian

---

**Y refers to YMCA.

Guides, and others, became concerned about the criticism leveled at the program for its handling of the Indian lore."[1] The Y-Guide Task Force goal was to "take a close look at their practices, and if they were wrong, to change them."[2]

It appears that the Y-Indian Guide leaders who comprised the Manual Revision Committee[3] did not have on their committee people from the Plains Indian culture on which the manual was based.[4] If they had had American Indians from the Dakota tribes or "Sioux," as they are commonly called, there would have been further revisions of the manual. ("The people in the manual did not know anything about Sioux Indians and the bibliography is very poor."— Webster Robbins.) In the following discussions of the "Y-Indian Princess Manual," we will be discussing the material as it relates to the Teton Sioux, which includes Western Nebraska and North and South Dakota. Most of the following discussion relates to the Siouan speaking tribes, but because of cultural differences it is impossible to generalize.

To understand why certain symbols and prayers are offensive to many Sioux people it is necessary to have some understanding of their religion. Unlike the Christian religion, in which only certain symbols and images are sacred and to be treated with respect, the Sioux culture demands that "reverence runs through every aspect of life."[5] The Indian person "lives in a world of symbols and images where the spiritual and the common place are one."[6] The Sioux religion "encompasses the Indian's whole view of the world and his place in the universe."[7] To "him all life is sacred."[8] It is this "love and respect for all life, that preserved the balance of man and nature for so many centuries before the white man came."[9] The Indian religion brought into harmony all living things. The key to the Indian's whole being is a deep spirituality that permeates his whole life. "Indian religion is more than mere power for healing and for clairvoyance. It is the skein that binds the culture and makes life meaningful. Reverence runs through every aspect of life."[10]

The Y-Indian Princess book tries to be sensitive to the deep religious beliefs of the Indian people. The manual states that "prayers are sacred and meaningful to individual tribes."[11] ("If this is so why do the fathers and children pretend like they are Indians in their prayers."—Corrina Drum.) The manual further states that one should "refrain from using religious ceremonies that include sacred masks, dances, and symbolism."[12] It also states that "misrepresentation would constitute a grave injustice to the American Indian."[13] Why then in the manual do they suggest using such things as the peace pipe or gourds? Why do they suggest that one should pray to the Four Directions or the Great Spirit? ("Why do the Y-Indian Princesses feel a need to pray to the Four Directions or the Great Spirit? I would need to know their spiritual interpretation of the Four Directions and their theological explanation of their term 'Great Spirit'."—Webster Robbins.)

The following is a list of things that most American Indians feel is offensive in the book. It cannot be stated that all Indian people would be offended as it is "especially important to understand that all Indians are not the same. They cannot be glibly categorized as a single unified minority. There are important differences among the tribes, pueblos and bands. Variations are frequently marked in customs, beliefs and values between: a) urban and reservation Indians; b) traditionalist, Christian and Native American Church members; and c) full blood and mixed blood heritage."[14]

The following is an explanation of the meaning that certain objects and images have for the traditional Sioux people. By understanding the meaning to the traditional Sioux one can understand why it is offensive to many, and may be sacrilegious. Furthermore, the manual often does not use these objects or images in an authentic manner.

ITEMS IN THE Y-INDIAN PRINCESS MANUAL
ACCORDING TO WESTERN PLAINS LITERATURE

Great Spirit

In the Y-Indian Princess book they use the word 'Great Spirit' in the ceremonies, pledges, songs and prayers. For example, the Y-Indian Princess pledges "to seek a world pleasing to the eye of the 'Great Spirit'."[15] Although the term 'Great Spirit' is used by many Christians, their view of God and the American Indians' view differ. The term 'Great Spirit' is what the Native American people speak of when they talk about their God. ("Indian theology does not appease the Great Spirit. The world you realize is the way it is."—Webster Robbins.) The Indian person's "beliefs must be accepted with respect and reverence."[16] It is thus questionable for Christian people to be using the word Great Spirit in their ceremonies.

The "Great Spirit is not like a human being, like the white god. He is a power. That power could be in a cup of coffee."[17] Let me explain this further.

There was, and is, and will be Wakan Tanka, the Great Mystery. He is one, yet many. He is the Chief God, the Great Spirit, the Creator, and the Executive. He is the Gods both Superior and Associate and He is the Gods-Kindred, both the subordinate and the Gods-like. He is the good and evil gods, the visible and invisible, the physical and immaterial, for He is all in one. The gods had no beginning and they will have no ending. Some are before others; some are related as parent and child. Yet the gods have no mother or father, for anything that has birth will have death. Since the gods were created, not born, they will not die. Mankind cannot fully understand these things, for they are of the Great Mystery.[18]

Thus the Great Spirit is one; yet, he is many. He is part of the moon and the moon is part of him. The gods are separate beings but they are united in the Great Spirit. The Great Spirit split himself up into trees, stones, insects making them all holy by his ever-presence. But in turn all these things that make up the universe flow back to their source, the Great Spirit. "Everything significant or important, whether it is understood or not, is part of Wakan Tanka (Great Spirit). Wakan

Tanka is the highest god force. Wakan Tanka is really sixteen (16) gods. Anything, whether it be visible or invisible, material or without material, human or animal, can be represented as a god."[19]

Peace Pipe

In the induction ceremony of Y-Indian Princess the Chief of the New Tribe says "O Big Chief, I speak for these braves and their daughters who have heard the call of the Great Spirit, the Master of Life. They have seen the power of the peace pipe and wish to become a part of our . . . nation."[20] ("How have they seen the power of the peace pipe?"—Webster Robbins.) Later in the ceremony the induction Chief (holding pipe forward, above his head), "Great Spirit, take the pipe, the symbol of peace, council, and brotherhood."[21]

The use of the word "peace pipe" to most non-Indians means any pipe of Indian design or manufacture. However, it would be more accurate to describe all Plains Indian pipes as "ceremonial pipes." The peace pipe, or sacred pipe, as the Sioux refer to it is the "most important sacramental object in Sioux belief."[22] The sacred pipe "constitutes the prerequisite stage for the true spiritual realization."[23] The sacred pipe is "always at the center of the hoop of our nation, and with it the people have walked and will continue to walk in a holy manner."[24] "This pipe is Wakan (holy). We all know it cannot lie. No man who has within him any untruth may touch it to his mouth."[25]

The following quote in the book *Black Elk Speaks* helps to explain what the sacred pipe means to the Sioux people. Also, please notice in the prayers the use of the Four Directions (West, North, East, and South), and the meaning.

> So I know that it is a good thing I am going to do; and because no good thing can be done by any man alone, I will first make an offering and send a voice to the Spirit of the World, that it may help me to be true. See, I fill this sacred pipe with the bark of the red willow; but before we smoke it, you must see how it is made and what it means. These four ribbons hanging here on the stem are the four quarters of the universe. The black one is for the west where the thunder beings live to send us rain; the white one for the north, whence comes the great white cleansing wind; the red one for the east whence springs the light and where the morning star lives to give men wisdom; the yellow for the south, whence comes the summer and the power to grow.
>
> But these four spirits are only one Spirit after all, and this eagle feather here is for that One, which is like a father, and also it is for the thoughts of men that should rise high as eagles do. Is not the sky a father and the earth a mother, and are not all living things with feet or wings or roots their children? And this hide upon the mouthpiece here, which should be bison hide, is for the earth, from whence we came and at whose breast we suck as babies all our lives, along with all the animals and birds and trees and grasses. And because it means all this, and more than any man can understand, the pipe is holy.[26]

The sacred pipe is not any Indian pipe or any medicine pipe; it is the link uniting earth and sky, the Holy of Holiness of Sioux religion.

Four Directions

In the Sioux religion the Four Directions, or Four Powers of the world, embraced all that is in the world and all that is in the sky. Consequently, by circling the pipe to the Four Directions, the offering is made to all the gods. Ogalala Sioux begin with the holy man filling a sacred pipe with kinnekinnik (tobacco) and praying to each of the Four Directions.[27] He thanks them for their bounty and blessings to man and to the world. You will notice in Black Elk's prayer to the Four Directions, as the Sioux do in all rites with the peace pipe, he first offered the pipe to the West and then the North, then the East, and last of all to the South. This clockwise movement is almost always used by the Sioux.[28] In the induction ceremony of the Y-Indian Princess the prayer first offered to the North, then the South, then the East is and then the West. This would be regarded as blasphemy.

The meaning of the Four Directions to the Sioux and the way it is used in the Y-Indian Princess manual is completely different. For example, the Chief of the North says, "The Spirit of the North speaks to you. All true explorers know that to keep in mind the north is to keep them on the true course. . . ."[29] Actually, the north is not an explorers' or true course but the direction from which pain and purification come.

Gourd Shaker[30]

"Gourd dance, dance done to celebrate Custer's defeat. Only members of the Tia Piah Society can participate. The gourd dancers wear a special uniform made up of a sash, a blanket and beads, all colored blue and red, which represent cavalry uniforms. They carry a fan and a gourd."[31] For further information read "To the Singing to the Drums" by N. Scott Momaday in *Natural History Magazine*, Vol. LXXXIV No. 2, February '75.

Gourds[32]

The manual suggests that the Y-Indian Princess make a gourd rattle. The gourd, the holy rattle, is also a sacred object to the Sioux people. As Lame Deer said in his book, in the gourd there "were 40 small pieces of flesh which my grandmother had cut from her arm. . . . Someone dear to me had undergone pain, given me something of herself, part of her body, to help me pray and make me strong hearted."[33]

The gourd also has 405[34] little stones in it, "tiny fossils picked up from an ant heap. These little stones are supposed to have a power in them."[35] The "sound from the rattle is not music. . . . These rattles talk to you."[36]

Circle

One of the aims of the Y-Indian Princess program is to "love the sacred circle of my family."[37] Whereas the family is important in Indian culture, it is never represented by a circle. The circle is used to represent broader concepts; the tribe, the people, the universe. To the American Indian person the circle symbolized many things.

There is "much power in the circle."[38] Black Elk says in his book, *Black Elk Speaks*, "everything an Indian does is in a circle and that is because the 'Power of the world always works in circles and everything tries to be round.'"[39] The circle is "beautiful and fitting, symbol and reality at the same time, expressing the harmony of life and nature. Our circle is timeless, flowing; it is new life emerging from death—life winning over death."[40]

Council Fire[41]

The Y-Indian Princess manual suggests making a Council Fire on page 25. Fire to the Sioux "represented the great power of the Wakan Tanka."[42] "The fire purified them so they may live as Wakan Tanka wills."[43]

Drum and Drum Beater

It states in the Y-Indian Princess manual that "The Indian ceremony always began and ended with the beat of a tribal drum. The drum is an indispensable piece of equipment for the Y-Indian Princess tribe. Every tribe should make its own drum . . . the tribal drum becomes a symbol of the unity of the tribe. . . . An Indian effect is obtained by painting the drum in symbolic designs. . . . The tribal drum can establish the spirit of the Indian council for your tribal meetings. The Drum Beater should be shown how to beat the drum."[44]

"The drumbeat that is generally used in depicting Indian ceremonies by Indian dancers is not an Indian drum beat. It is a stereotype drum beat created by Hollywood musicians. I would recommend that anyone interested in American Indian music be prepared to spend at least 10 years in learning about it on the reservation."—Webster Robbins.

The manual does not explain what the drum meant to the Sioux.

The drum is often the only instrument used in our sacred rites. I should perhaps tell you why it is especially sacred and important to us. It is because the sound from the drum represents the whole universe and its steady strong beat is the pulse, the heart, throbbing at the center of the universe. It is as the voice of Wakan Tanka.[45]

Tipi

The Y-Indian Princess Book suggests making a tipi.[46] Also on the headband it is stated that grouped tipis symbolized "happy work in the community and the single tepee denotes happy work in the home."[47]

For the Sioux, every "tepee is the world in an image."[48] "The tepee is the universe, the cosmos."[49]

Thunderbird[50]

It is not certain whether the YMCA authors know that the design suggested on page 22 is the design of the "Thunderbird." The Thunderbird is regarded with such reverence in this part of the country that the Indian people seldom speak to a white person about the Thunderbird.

The Thunderbird is the protector of the sacred pipe, for the pipe like the lightning is the axis joining heaven and earth.[51] "The thunderbird is one of the most important and profound aspects of the Siouan religion. . . . His symbol is a zigzag red line forked at each end."[52] ("No suggestion whatsoever would suffice in the incorporation of the 'Thunderbird' in the Y-Indian Princess manual."—Webster Robbins.)

The Omaha Tribal Prayer

The Y-Indian Princess manual suggests on page 100 that the Omaha Tribal Prayer should be sung and may be used reverently in closing a tribal meeting.

The translation in the book is "Father, a needy one stands before thee: I that sing am he." The Y manual states this prayer was written by Alice C. Fletcher in the book *Indian Story and Song*. In Alice Fletcher's book the translation is "here needy he stands; and I am he."[53]

There is no explanation in the prayer of what this prayer meant to the Omaha people. The following is Mrs. Fletcher's explanation:

> In preparation for a rite which was to bring the Omaha youth into direct communication with the supernatural powers the youth was taught the Tribal Prayer. He was to sing it during four nights and days of his vigil in some lonely place. As he left his home, his parents put clay on his head; and, to teach him self-control, they placed a bow and arrows in his hand, with the injunction not to use them during his long fast, no matter how great the temptation might be. He was bidden to weep as he sang the prayer, and to wipe his tears with the palms of his hands, to lift his wet hands to heaven, and then lay them on the earth. With these instructions the youth departed, to enter upon the trial of his endurance. When at last he fell into a sleep or trance, and the vision came, of bird, or beast, or cloud, bringing with it a cadence, this song became ever after the medium of communication between the man and the mysterious power typified in his vision; and by it he summoned help and strength in the hour of his need.[54]

Many Omaha people I have talked to reported that they were offended that this prayer was in the manual and they felt it must be deleted. ("This is a religious prayer of my people and it is sacrilegious for the Y-Guide program to use it."—Corrina Drum.)

Benediction or Closing Prayers[55]

("It is sacrilegious and tacky."—Galen Buller.) ("The Indian people have more taste than that. The shooting of the bow and arrow at the end is not authentic, and the manner in which it is done offends me deeply."—Karen Buller.) ("How can you symbolize a request for peace by using a symbol of war? I do not know of any Indians that use sign language for prayers. People who have an oral language have little or no use for sign language especially at religious ceremonies."—Webster Robbins.)

The Lord's Prayer[56]

The Lord's Prayer concept of evil is one where Christians separate evil from good. The Sioux concept is to integrate evil with good into human life and to understand how they function together. ("This is a good example of how the manual wants to remain Christian but tries to incorporate Indian religious symbolism and Indian religious structure into it."—Galen Buller.) ("The manual is trying to incorporate a white man's way with the Indian tradition. They do not go together."—Webster Robbins.)

Symbols and Images in the Manual That in General Are Not Siouan

In the magazine *YMCA Today* (Summer 1975), it states the program had been founded on Plains Indian culture. However, the list appended below includes things not found in the Plains Indian culture. (In the Guide for Better Understanding of the American Indians, pp. 124, 125, it states many colorful and very meaningful customs were observed by Indians of various tribes, each adhering to their own culture and intellect. Misrepresentation would constitute a grave injustice to the American Indian. The Guide further states that strict authenticity is important. Why then is the manual taking and mixing customs from many different tribes in the U.S.?)

Totem Pole

The Y-Indian Princess Manual suggests that the group make a totem pole.

The tribes from the Northwest Coast generally used totem poles. The name totem pole is a poor one, "since what are carved on them are not technically speaking, totems, but crests and insignias. They are part of the procedure by which they validate their importance."[57] "An individual's ancestry and certain other experiences gave him the right to certain insignia or 'crests' as are carved on the so-called totem pole."[58]

Corn

In the Y-Indian Princess ceremony it says, "From this ear of corn the staff of life of the real Indian, I give each of you a kernal to use as a symbol of your sacrifice."[59]

Who is the real Indian? "Corn was as important and sacred to the Ree as is the pipe to our people."[60] The staff of life to the Sioux was the cottonwood tree.

Sachem[61]

The term "sachem," which is Algonquin, is used for those chiefs who sat at the tribal council and helped rule the tribe.[62]

Wampum Collector and Wampum Bearer[63]

The word wampum is the Algonquin Indian word for shell beads. It was a term used by the Indians of the New England States. . . . Iroquois people used wampum for official purposes as well as for religious ceremonies. . . . Wampum came to be regarded as something sacred.[64]

Longhouse

The longhouse people are Iroquois and their buildings were often referred to as "longhouses."[65] No longhouse exists in Plains culture. The Winnebago medicine lodge is not a longhouse.

Shields

The Y-Indian Princess book suggests, as a project, to make a shield. The book states, "The shield was a very significant and often sacred instrument to some American Indian tribes."[66] The Sioux people had shields but they were not as important to their culture as they were to the Cheyennes.

In the Cheyenne culture the Personal Shields of Men were first constructed and given to them after their Vision Quest.[67] The symbolic figures drawn on the shields "represented the individual Medicines and Clan Signs of the men who carried them."[68]

Princess

("Most Indians are offended by the concept of 'Princess' combined with 'Indian.' The concept of Princess is a Western European concept that had nothing to do with Indians."—Galen Buller.) ("In the Indian society there was no such things as monarchy [king, queen, prince, princess, etc.]."—Corrina Drum.) ("The concept of Princess, Big Chief, Braves have nothing to do with the Indian or with the societal structure of an American Indian and it seems to be completely European in origin as well as in name."—Webster Robbins.)

Some modern Indians may use these phrases, but they are not indigenous to Plains culture and have been taken over from white descriptions.

Calendar[69]

("It is not a Sioux calendar, but it could be a translation of some other tribe." —Galen Buller.)

STATEMENTS FROM AMERICAN INDIANS ON THE Y-INDIAN PRINCESS AND Y-INDIAN GUIDE PROGRAM

Frank Black Elk, great grandson of Black Elk, a holy man of the Ogalala Sioux, former executive director of the Lincoln Indian Center:

> If they are going to depict the Indian way of life they should not be using the ceremonies the way they do. If they are going to expose traditions, ceremonies it should be the Indian people doing it, not themselves. Calling themselves Indian guides should be taken out. There is a difference between acting like an Indian and making other people aware of the Indian culture. Tepees, gourds, drums—instruments of ceremonies—shouldn't be used.
>
> The whole program needs to be reevaluated according to the times. Not all American Indian people feel the way I do but because of the traditional and religious background my family comes from I feel I have valid grounds for saying this.

A Rosebud Sioux who wished to remain anonymous, Oct. 27, 1975:

> The book stereotypes the American Indian and is trying to imitate them. They are trying to imitate American Indian rituals and the white people wouldn't like it if we were running around pretending like we were priests or using their sacred objects. It makes a mockery of the Indian people. I couldn't understand some of the material in the book and I couldn't understand where they were getting it from.

Karen Buller, Comanche, Indian Center Board of Directors 1974; Former Indian Counselor at UNL; State Board Member of League of Women Voters:

> This book is the third biggest proponent of Indian stereotypes in America today. The first is the public school system, and the second is Hollywood movies. I want to see it mandatory for each individual Y group to be forced to study a local tribe of its area. Indian tribes have the right not to be misrepresented.

Reginald Cedar Face, Director, Lincoln Indian Center:

> My contention of the Y manual is that it is exactly what it is. A manual (recorded) that indicates dominance. We all know that Indian history was and is verbal. The very reason that the history of Indians (Sioux) and any Indian society is verbal is indicative that our Indian cultures are progressive and related to the present. By recording we have a tendency to keep progress at a standstill and sometimes keeps us from progressing.
>
> The purpose of Y-Indian Guide programs of getting father and son/daughter together to foster companionship is excellent. I would suggest though, that there should be people in the organization who are more knowledgeable about Indian culture.

I think portions of the manual need to be changed, especially the ceremonies such as the pipe ceremony. The ceremonies lead to stereotyping. The children and fathers need to have more knowledge of what they are doing and what it means to the Indian people. I feel the taking of Indian names and calling themselves by a Tribe gives the fathers and son/daughter a chance to learn more about the Indian people. The program as it is now does not give them an understanding of the Indian people. There needs to be more Indian input.

Webster Robbins, a Lincoln Indian. Faculty advisor to Council of American Indian Students—UNL said:

I seriously question the "expertise" which apparently was utilized to write and to develop the Y-Indian Guides Manual. I fail to see any relationship between the Y-Indian Guide program and American Indian culture both past and present.

The approach to the study of American Indian culture is superficial to say the least, and very poorly researched to say the most. After examining the manuals for authenticity as well as for general information, I have failed to satisfy both academic quests. The support given to this project by American Indian citizens is noteworthy, but only to the extent that a program such as this needs American Indian identification to be valid, if in name only. The support given by Indians must not be construed to mean what materials utilized are valid.

The manuals are in need of authenticity, if authenticity can contribute to a respect for the American Indian. I must seriously question the value of such a program.

Pat Menard, a Rosebud Sioux, who helped develop the Sioux opera Hamblecheya, was formerly on the Indian Center Board, and has also worked at the Indian Commission, as well as with American Indian prisoners at the penitentiary, had this to say:

The purpose of getting the father and son/daughters together in the YMCA Guide program is excellent, but for a group to pretend like they are Indians is very offensive. The taking of Indian names, wearing headbands, using tribal names to me is mocking the Indian people. If the Y-Guide Program wants to study Indian lore, they do not need to pretend like they are Indians. It is matter of respect to American Indian people that they do not have this program.

Some Indian people especially urban Indians may not agree with me, but I feel it is for the following reasons:

1. Many Indian people have been so assimilated into white culture that they feel no disgrace in allowing the white to Americanize the Indian person.
2. Many Indian people are and have been so dependent on the whites for their well-being that they would never say anything against such a program and would pretend like they agree with it while in fact they would feel it is very demeaning.
3. In order not to be disrespectful to another person, often American Indians will not openly admit what they actually believe; for example, in the company of a white person they would say one thing and in the company of an Indian person they would say another. The Sioux who frequently say one must help others as much as possible may help to account for this.

Even the goals of the Y-Guide program to foster understanding and companionship between father and son/daughter are not Sioux goals which are to strive for the virtues of generosity, bravery, fortitude, and wisdom. In the "Sioux belief, a man must know and accept his place in the nature of things, the great life, before he can receive understanding."[70]

Alfred Menard, Rosebud Sioux, declared:

I do not think it is right to dress up as an American Indian, or pray to the Four Directions. It would be like dressing up as a priest. If you are going to use Indians then the money the YMCA makes should go to Indian families. I realize that you had Indian consultants to help write the manual, but in my opinion the persons whom they consulted with do not know anything about their cultures. We went to the Convention of the National Congress of American Indians in Oregon, and it was not just us but the whole group felt that way. It is a very touchy subject, for some YMCA money does go to Indian people.

Corrina (Bobby) Drum, Omaha Indian, Student, UNL, explained:

Words do not come easy to me as I am angered that the YMCA Indian Guide program exists. There is a lot of misrepresentation. Also, very religious rituals and sacred customs are being used by not so well meaning people—in other words, whites. It is not only distasteful but undeniably sacrilegious to the Native American People.

I believe that you (the YMCA) should adhere to your own religion in regards to bringing about the togetherness of father and son or father and daughter relationships and forget about using Ours—the native people of this land.

You may say that you are only trying to secure our religion for us so that it will not disintegrate, but I believe we have been doing fine these past centuries, and we will continue to do so. We need no help from the outside because we have what it takes within.

In so saying I believe that the Y-Indian Guides and Y-Indian Princess Program should be completely done away with.

I hope you have taken into consideration (at the least) what I have just written and I also hope you will take immediate action.

Galen Buller, instructor in American Indian literature, UNL, 1973—May, 1975; faculty advisor to the Council of American Indian students:

The manual generalizes about American Indians and they do this by combining concepts of different tribes. What's wrong with this is what made Indian tribes unique in their different religions, language customs and life styles. If the manual is going to generalize almost by definition, the manual is going to be wrong. Every time you borrow a concept from one tribe and another concept from another tribe then that marriage results in a non-Indian. There is no respect for the Indian nationhood. The one thing Indian people have even after genocide is affiliation with a tribe and that affiliation makes them unique.

Mr. Buller also stated that what a group does with the book is important for it would be very easy for the parent/child group to misuse it and then the book would be a tool of irresponsibility.

RESOLUTION INTRODUCED AT THE
NATIONAL CONGRESS OF AMERICAN INDIANS

The following resolution was accepted and passed by the Resolution Committee at the 32nd annual convention of the National Congress of American Indians. Since there was not time for the entire convention to vote on it, it has been referred to the Executive Committee. Mrs. Menard was told that there would be no problem and that she should be congratulated on what she was doing. The resolution was introduced by Myron Long Soldier, Patricia A. Menard, and Alfred Menard. The Executive Committee is expected to vote on this within the next month. There were about 2,500 people and more than 300 tribes represented at the Convention from all over the country.

Resolution NCAI-75-13

WHEREAS, the Indians of Nebraska are being misrepresented in a program organized by a National Christian Organization, the YMCA. The program is called the Indian Y Guides and Indian Princess Program. The groups are seeking a better understanding of the Indian culture.

WHEREAS, this misrepresentation has offended many people in the Nebraska area. At the expense of our religious symbols, dances, and beliefs, this program has greatly exploited our culture.

WHEREAS, the group has such practices as the taking of Indian names, tribal names, wearing headbands, the use of feathers and in general pretending that they are Indians, which is mocking the Indian way of life. For one night of the week we have whites banding together in their tribes pretending they are Indians.

WHEREAS the use of the peace pipe and praying to the four directions in an induction service. And the singing of songs such as Ten Little Indians is included in their ceremony. The making of drums and tipis have no reverence behind them. The use of the sacred symbols used on them like the thunderbeing, being painted on the side of the drum.

WHEREAS, the Indian Y Guides and Indian Princess manual states "No one shall use the sacred dances or symbolism in their program," but this is not what has actually happened. These programs are in fact very detrimental to the Indian people all over the country, not just in Nebraska.

THEREFORE, BE IT RESOLVED THAT THE NATIONAL CONGRESS OF AMERICAN INDIANS, meeting in Portland, Oregon, November 10–14, 1975, condemn this activity of the YMCA or any organizations to stop and put an end to such activities deemed offensive by the Indian people.

A GUIDE FOR BETTER UNDERSTANDING
OF THE AMERICAN INDIAN[71]

On pages 124 and 125 of the Y-Indian Princess Manual there is a guide written to help the parent/child program leaders deal more effectively with the Indian lore in the back. "It is essential that YMCA lay and staff leaders in all YMCA centers and communities represent accurately and positively the American Indians' contribution to American life and history."[72] The guidelines are positive and many American Indian people would agree with them. The problem is that often the manual is inconsistent with the guidelines.

Please refer to the guidelines for a complete listing of them, for this paper will only be dealing with certain parts of it.

An American Indian Is a Human Being

In this guideline it states that scripts and youth groups that deal with the American Indian should "consider whether their works are befitting any human race. The Indian, as a member of the human race, should be portrayed with this thought in mind."[73]

Often in dealing with American Indians we forget this. The image we usually receive from TV or books is that of the vanished Indian. We usually treat Indians as a vestige of a past era. The Y-Indian Princess manual states that the Parent/Child program needs to acquaint members with the current plight of American Indians. However, the manual seems to give the idea to the children that Indians are extinct and do not really exist today. "The tragedy of American Indians is the Indian Americans love and love to read about, no longer exists except in the pages of books."[74]

If the manual treated American Indians as people of today then why do they have in the manual the song "10 Little Indians"[75] or the game, "draw the feather on the Indian?"[76]

Why does the manual use the American Indians' sacred religious symbols and objects such as the peace pipe, the gourd? Why does it have the children praying to the Indians' god?

I cannot imagine any other group of people being treated the same way. I think we have all been too sensitized. Can you imagine a group of non-Christian children pretending they are Catholic for an evening once every two weeks; the group of non-Christian children and their fathers taking Catholic holy names such as Jesus Christ, Saint Paul, or the Pope. Can you imagine non-Christian children taking communion, making a crucifix, or saying Hail Mary? ("It seems to me that such people making a mockery of another religion need to sit down and look at themselves and their own religion. Also, if we [Indians] put on robes of a priest and nun and paraded around, whites would become angered and sooner or later we [Indians] would wind up in jail for inciting a riot."—Corrina Drum.) It is not like a Sunday school class learning about another religion and perhaps even making some of their sacred symbols for a learning experience.

The manual doesn't explain what these symbols meant to the Indian people. We would not have a group of parents and their children pretending that they are Black, painting their faces black, wearing kerchiefs on their head, and singing "one little, two little, three little blacks."

Although the manual does not intentionally mock the American Indian and tries not to be offensive, this is actually what comes through. It is not just the Y-Indian Guide program but most scripts, films, programs, pageants and youth groups dealing with American Indians treat them as an extinct culture and forget that they are people living today. The American Indian is a human being who lives today. In materials, there is usually little recognition of the lives and contributions of these citizens at the present time.)ᘀᘁ-ᘐ

Sioux Religion Is Sound

The guideline states that each tribe's religious beliefs were sacred and meaning-ful and these beliefs must be accepted with respect and reverence.

No one would intentionally be disrespectful, but it is hard to take someone's belief and treat it with respect and reverence, when one does not understand its meaning. ("The Sioux religious beliefs are too complex, too intellectual, too so-phisticated, and too philosophical for most non-Indian people to understand."—Webster Robbins.)

Because of this lack of understanding, what a white person would do that he thinks would be non-offensive, might be very offensive to an American Indian. For example, the beating of a drum (see Drums for explanation of meaning) seems very innocuous and would not be insulting to many American Indian peo-ple, but to some traditional Sioux Indians it would be. The act of beating a drum is not offensive but doing this when one is pretending he or she is an Indian can be resented.

Since the Sioux religious beliefs are sacred and meaningful, it is sacrilegious for a white person to try to imitate these beliefs. Also the manual takes these be-liefs such as the Four Directions and assigns whatever meaning to it that fits into the aims and purposes of the Y-Indian Princess Program. The Sioux religious be-liefs are not being treated with reverence and respect.

Sioux Customs Have Special Meaning

The guideline states misrepresentation would constitute a grave injustice to the American Indian.

There are many examples in the book where customs and symbols have been misrepresented, for example, the peace pipe, the circle, the gourd and the Omaha Tribal Prayer. The manual has borrowed different customs from many different tribes; for example, Longhouse (Iroquois), Totem Pole (N.W. coastal Indians), Peace Pipe (Plains Indians) and Omaha Tribal Prayer (Omaha Indians).

Galen Buller said "this manual is ultimately helping Indian genocide by break-ing down tribal identity and affiliation. In the manual there is no respect for Indian nationhood. The one thing Indian people have had even after genocide is affiliation with a tribe and affiliation makes them unique."

The Language of the American Indian Is Graphic

The guideline states it would be advisable to portray the American Indian using the English language. Today few understand the Indian language. Why then do they suggest singing the Omaha Tribal Prayer?[77] Why in the Benediction or the Closing Prayer[78] do they use sign language?

The guideline states that words such as "ugh" and "how" should be avoided. Then why was a yellow brochure handed out this September at Gateway Mall? The brochure has on the front cover the word "How" and one of the suggested games is "Ugh." ("Ugh is a word made up by people like Hollywood producers to make the Indian look stupid and to make our language seem inferior."—Corinna Drum.) There are many other offensive things in the brochure such as the TomTom beater and medicine man. ("No white man can ever become an American Indian holy man [medicine man]."—Webster Robbins.) This pamphlet badly needs updating.

Indian Dances Are Highly Expressive

The guideline states that dances were always used with great discretion and ceremony.

In the manual when it discusses basic Indian dance steps it doesn't say to which tribe they are basic as tribal dances were very individualist. These basic steps are generally correct for the Sioux but they would not have dancers start in a circle and do each step eight times in one direction, then reverse.[79] ("Also, the manual does not explain the difference between social dances and religious dances."—Karen Buller.) ("It is very questionable that the contributors to this portion of the manual concerning dancing had any expertise in one of the Siouan fine arts, namely tribal dancing. Few people residing in the Northeastern U.S. have taken an academic degree in Lakota dancing or are confirmed graduates of the American Indian University of Fine Arts."—Webster Robbins.)

Many of the Y-Indian Guide and Y-Indian Princess groups go to see the Wacisa dancers. Wacisa dancers do not do authentic Indian dances and some of their dances are very sacrilegious such as the dying eagle dance. The costumes and songs also are not authentic.—Pat Menard and Webster Robbins. ("About these 'authentic' dances the Wacisa dancers do, it's a lot of bunk. They are about as aut-thentic as a basket of plastic fruit."—Corrina Drum.) ("I would much prefer to watch a 10th century European ceremony performed for people of European ancestry and replete with authentic costumes of the time on Halloween."—Webster Robbins.) Why aren't the kids instead encouraged to go to the powwows sponsored by the various Council of Indian Students that are held in the spring or to the reservations for the powwows held in August?

The Indians' Costumes Were Symbolic

They should be depicted with strict authenticity. It would be hard for a white person to make a costume that is authentic without being sacrilegious as some of the costumes have deep religious meanings. A person would have to have great understanding of the culture in order to understand what is acceptable and what isn't. Also, many of the materials that the Indian person used in his costumes are not available today.

There Is Real Danger in Stereotyping

The sketches in the manual of American Indians show how they existed a long time ago. There are not any sketches of how they live today. The American Indian today "dresses much the same as every other person, attends pretty much the same schools, works at many of the same jobs, and suffers discrimination in the same manner as do other racial minorities."[80] By not stressing how American Indians live today the Y-Guide manual is perpetuating the stereotype of the Indian as shown in the cowboy and Indian movies.

Most children's image of the Indian person is of an Indian who lives in tipis, beats a drum, rides horses, scalps white people, is a savage, a drunkard, and is untrustworthy. This is how he was portrayed in the movies and the Y manual does little to dispel this myth. In order for children to change their stereotypes, programs such as Y-Guides will have to work hard, and stress that Indians are people with many of the same feelings, wants and desires as they have, but at the same time, they do have a beautiful culture that needs to be respected.

Stereotyping does exist in the book. An example is on page 117 of the manual. It states that "the daughters can end this dance by sitting cross-legged, still in the circle, and raising each hand alternately 12 times."[81] Karen Buller states "this is a gross and blatant case of stereotyping and not part of Sioux dances." Also such games as draw the feather[82] on the Indian and the song "Little Brave Chopping"[83] leave a stereotyped image of the American Indian in the children's mind. ("These are viewed as extremely insensitive methods in teaching children about a highly sensitive and intelligent people."—Webster Robbins.)

Names Should Engender Respect

The Y-Indian Princess manual states that:

The selection of a name for daughter and father should be done with respect and ceremony, even as it is for the American Indian.[84] In all cases one must be discreet in the choice of title, considering all aspects pertaining to the well being of, and respect for, the American Indian.[85]

Lame Deer said in his book:

Words, too, are symbolic and convey great powers, especially names. Not Charles, Dick and George. There is not much power in those. But Red Cloud, Black Elk, Whirlwind, 2 Moons, Lame Deer—these names have a relationship to the Great Spirit. Each Indian name has a story behind it, a vision, a quest for dreams. We receive great gifts from the source of a name; it links us to nature, to the animal nations. It gives power. You can lean on a name, get strong from it. It has a special name for you alone—not a Dick, George, Charles kind of thing.[86]

Since one's name to the Sioux people is very important and has a lot of religious significance it is debatable if the parent/child should be giving each other Indian names when they have no idea of the meaning of the name and they "could be using a sacred name that has been retired and never to be used again"[87] (such as Crazy Horse[88]).

("Rather than using Indian names, it would be advisable if groups in search of a name for themselves would seek or intellectually research the meaning of their own European names."—Webster Robbins.)

CONCLUSION

The purpose of the Y-Indian Guide and Y-Indian Princess program of fostering understanding and companionship between the parent and child is praiseworthy. Both manuals, especially the Y-Indian Guide manual have attempted to remove material offensive to American Indian people. The problem is that in having a program that is based on Indian lore, it is probably impossible to avoid including material that would be offensive to one tribe or another.

What would be offensive to the Northwest coastal Indians probably would not be to the Sioux. Every tribe is different, with different histories, different languages, different cultural values and different religions. The Indian people are offended because the manual took practices, customs, and cultures from different tribes and mixed them together. They felt this manual was aiding the cultural genocide of the tribes.

The Y manuals were mainly based on the culture of the Plains tribes with concepts from other tribes thrown in, for example wampum, longhouse, and totem pole. Many Indian people felt this was offensive.

The manual is also offensive to the Sioux people, especially the traditionalist. The Sioux traditionalist lives in a world of symbols and images where the spiritual and commonplace are one. To the white man symbols are just words, spoken or written in a book. To the Sioux they are part of nature, part of themselves, the earth, the sun, the wind and the rain, stones, trees, animals, even little insects like ants and grasshoppers.[89]

An example of the difficulty in distinguishing what is religious and what is not can be found in the Y-Indian Princess Manual on page 22. They suggest, for a design, to put a Thunderbird on a drum. For a white person to paint a Thunderbird on a drum would be offensive to many Sioux people. The Thunderbird is one of the most important and profound aspects of the Siouan religion.[90] ("Why not paint a dollar bill on a snare drum as representative of a psychological need to interpret power in accordance with European tradition?"—Webster Robbins.)

It is suggested that symbols be painted, for example, on the drum and the tipi; however, how would the Y-groups know which symbols are offensive and which aren't? It would be necessary for each group to do an indepth study of a particular tribe. They would soon realize that the Sioux religion is completely interwoven with the culture and customs, and that they are impossible to separate. The "Sioux's reverence runs through every aspect of life,"[91] and the "Indian person's deep spirituality, permeates his life and is the key to his whole being."[92]

Even the making of such objects as a drum or a tipi could be offensive to the traditional Sioux for, as Lame Deer stated, "Everything we do during our ceremonies has a deeper meaning for us and in one way or the other, symbolizes the universe, the powers of nature, the spirits, all of which are ever present in our minds."[93]

As Frank Black Elk said, "The whole program needs to be re-evaluated according to the times for when the Y-Program first started; the American Indian people back then had been more or less instituted into the American way of life, but now they are getting back more and more of their traditional ways."

Obviously in today's world we see many Indian people who have been well integrated into the white society, who have lost all of their traditional beliefs. But, for those American Indians who do have their traditional beliefs, many aspects of the manual would be sacrilegious. Today there is a strong surge by many younger Indian people to learn more about their culture and religion.

Many Indian people felt that even having the parent/child groups pretending they were Indians was offensive. To them taking Indian names, tribal names, wearing headbands, feathers and in general pretending that they are Indian is offensive and mocks the Indian person. This would not happen with any other group for you wouldn't have parent/child groups pretending they are Catholic, Jewish, Chinese, Black or Protestant for a night every two weeks. ("If there was an understanding of Indians, there would be no psychological need to imitate them." —Webster Robbins.)

It is stated by many people that the Y-Indian guides are trying to help understand the Indian culture. ("You cannot learn anything about American Indian culture by following this guide."—Webster Robbins.)

There are many sacrilegious and offensive things in the Y-Indian Princess manual which need to be deleted immediately such as the induction ceremony where they used the peace pipe and pray to the Four Directions. Also songs such as "Ten Little Indians" must be deleted. The Guide for a Better Understanding of the American Indians is good, but "unfortunately the white man did not take the time to learn and appreciate the ways of the Indian."

NOTES

1. "YMCA Today," Vol. 51, No. 2 (Summer 1975), p. 8.
2. Ibid. , p. 9.
3. "The Father and Son Y-Indian Guide Manual," YMCA, Association Press, 1973, p. 6.

4. Loc. cit., p. 8.

5. Burnette, Robert and John Koster, *The Road to Wounded Knee* (Bantam, 1974), p. 109.

6. Lame Deer, John (Fire), and Richard Erdoes, *Lame Deer, Seeker of Visions* (Simon and Schuster, 1972), p. 35.

7. Lame Deer, loc. cit., p. 19.

8. Burnette, loc. cit., p. 122.

9. Lame Deer, loc. cit., p. 35.

10. Lame Deer, loc. cit., p. 35.

11. La Farge, Oliver, *A Pictorial History of the American Indian* (New York: Crown Publishers, Inc.), p. 99.

12. "The Father and Daughter Y-Indian Princess Manual," YMCA, 1974, p. 55.

13. Ibid., p. 124.

14. "Father and Daughter Y-Indian Princess Manual," p. 50.

15. Y-Indian Princess Manual, p. 2.

16. Ibid., p. 124.

17. Lame Deer, p. 39.

18. "Lakota Stories," edited by Leo American Horse and Joseph Cress, copyright 1970 by Red Cloud Indian School, Inc., Pine Ridge, South Dakota, 57770, p. v.

19. Ibid.

20. Y-Indian Princess Manual, p. 109.

21. Y-Indian Princess Manual, p. 110.

22. Burnette, loc. cit., p. 26.

23. Brown, Joseph Epes, *The Sacred Pipe* (Black Elk's account of the seven rites of the Ogalala Sioux), (Penguin Books, 1973), p. 69.

24. Ibid., p. 69.

25. Ibid., p. 13.

26. Neihardt, John G., *Black Elk Speaks* (Bison, 1961), pp. 2–3.

27. Brown, loc. cit., pp. 20–21.

28. Brown, loc. cit., p. 5.

29. YMCA Indian Princess Manual, p. 111.

30. Ibid., p. 114.

31. *Tonic Handbook* (Tutors of Nebraska Indian Children, 1973), p. 39.

32. YMCA-Indian Princess Manual, p. 67.

33. Lame Deer, loc. cit., p. 13.

34. Ibid., p. 114.

35. Ibid., p. 15.

36. Ibid., p. 192.

37. Y-Indian Princess Manual, p. 24.

38. Brown, loc. cit., p. 92.

39. Neihardt, loc. cit., p. 198.

40. Lame Deer, loc. cit., p. 112.

41. Y-Indian Princess Manual, p. 25.

42. Brown, loc. cit., p. 32.

43. Ibid., p. 31.

44. Y-Indian Princess Manual, p. 21.

45. Brown, loc. cit., p. 69.

46. Y-Indian Princess Manual, p. 80.

47. Ibid., p. 80.

48. Brown, loc. cit., p. 23.

49. Ibid., p. 23.

50. Y-Indian Princess Manual, p. 22.

51. Brown, loc. cit., p. 39.

52. Ibid., p. 39.

53. Fletcher, Alice C., *Indian Story and Song* (Boston: Small, Maynard and Company, 1970), p. 28.

54. Fletcher, loc. cit., p. 27.

55. Y-Indian Princess Manual, p. 101.

56. Ibid.

57. La Farge, loc. cit., p. 210.

58. Ibid., p. 204.

59. La Farge, loc. cit., p. 112.

60. Brown, loc. cit., p. 92.

61. Y-Indian Princess Manual, p. 19.

62. La Farge, loc. cit., p. 53.

63. Y-Indian Princess Manual, p. 19.

64. Tehanetorens, *Wampum Belts* (Onchioto, New York: Six Nations Indian Museum), p. 3.

65. La Farge, loc. cit., p. 44.

66. Y-Indian Princess Manual, p. 83.

67. Burnette, loc. cit., p. 9.

68. Brown, loc. cit., p. 9.

69. Y-Indian Princess Manual, p. 54.

70. Educational packets for Hamblecheya, p. 7.

71. Y-Indian Princess Manual, p. 124, 125.

72. Ibid., p. 124.

73. Ibid., p. 124.

74. Deloria, Vine, *God Is Red* (New York: Delta, 1975).

75. Y-Indian Princess Manual, p. 95.

76. Ibid., p. 72.

77. Y-Indian Princess Manual, p. 100.

78. Ibid., p. 101.

79. Ibid., p. 116.

80. Deloria, loc. cit., p. 19.

81. Y-Indian Princess Manual, p. 117.

82. Ibid., p. 72.

83. Y-Indian Princess Manual, p. 95.

84. Ibid., p. 53.

85. Ibid., p. 125.

86. Lame Deer, loc. cit., p. 117.

87. Frank Black Elk.

88. Another example is "Sitting Bull's" Lakota Indian name, Tatianka, which has many sacred connotations. Educational packets for Hamblecheya, p. 25.

89. Lame Deer, loc. cit., p. 109.

90. Brown, loc. cit., p. 39.
91. Burnette, loc. cit., p. 20.
92. Ibid., p. 35.
93. Lame Deer, loc. cit., p. 178.

BIBLIOGRAPHY

Brown, Joseph Epes. *The Sacred Pipe*. Penguin Books, 1973.
Burnette, Robert, and John Koster. *The Road to Wounded Knee*. Bantam, 1974.
Deloria, Vine. *God Is Red*. Delta, 1975.
Fletcher, Alice C. *Indian Story and Song*. Small, Maynard and Company, 1970.
La Farge, Oliver. *A Pictorial History of the American Indian*. Crown Publishers, Inc., 1956, revised 1974.
Lame Deer, John (Fire), and Richard Erdoes. *Lame Deer, Seeker of Visions*. Simon and Schuster, 1972.
Neihardt, John G. *Black Elk Speaks*. Bison, 1961.

Periodicals

YMCA Today. Vol. 51, No. 2 (Summer 1975).

Unpublished Material

Fargo-Moorhead Project, Bridge Education Committee. Comments on images of Indians Presented in Current History Texts—For classroom teachers, 1973.
Feraca, Stephen, and James H. Howard. *The Identity and Demography of the Dakota or Sioux Tribe*.
Educational packet for the opera Hamblecheya—a Sioux musical drama.

Other Sources

American Horse and Joseph Cress. *Lakota Stories*. Copyright, 1970, by Red Cloud Indian School, Inc., Pine Ridge, South Dakota.
Tehanetorens. *Wampum Belts*. Onchioto, New York: Six Nations Indian Museum.
Tonic Handbook (Tutors of Nebraska Indian Children), 1973.
White, James (editor). *Angwamas Minosewag Anishenabeg* (Time of the Indian). Sponsored by Poets in Schools Program. St. Paul Council of Arts and Sciences. Vol. 1.
YMCA. "The Father and Daughter Y-Indian Princess Manual," 1974.
YMCA. "The Father and Son Y-Indian Guide Manual," Association Press, 1973.

Chapter 7

Holidays Are Not
Always for Celebrating

Columbus in the Classroom

Bill Bigelow

Most of my students have trouble with the idea that a book—especially a text-book—can lie. When I tell them that I want them to argue with, not just read, the printed word, they're not sure what I mean. That's why I start my U.S. history class by stealing a student's purse.

As the year opens, my students may not know when the Civil War was fought, what James Madison or Frederick Douglass did, or where the Underground Rail-road went, but they do know that a brave fellow named Christopher Columbus discovered America. Okay, the Vikings may have actually *discovered* America, but students know it was Columbus who mapped it and *did* something with the place. Indeed, this bit of historical lore may be the only knowledge class members share in common.

What students don't know is that year after year their textbooks have, by omission or otherwise, been lying to them on a grand scale. Some students learned that Columbus sailed on three ships and that his sailors worried whether they would ever see land again. Others know from readings and teachers that when the Admiral landed he was greeted by naked, reddish-skinned people whom he called Indians. And still others may know Columbus gave these people little trinkets and returned to Spain with a few of the Indians to show King Ferdinand and Queen Isabella.

All this is true. What is also true is that Columbus took hundreds of Indians slaves and sent them back to Spain, where most of them were sold and subsequently died. What is also true is that in his quest for gold, Columbus had the hands cut off any Indian who did not return with his or her three-month quota. And what is also true is that on one island alone, Hispaniola, an entire race of people was wiped off the face of the earth in a mere forty years of Spanish administration.

So I begin by stealing a student's purse. I announce to the class that the purse is mine, obviously, because look who has it. Most students are fair-minded. They saw me take the purse off the desk, so they protest: "That's not yours, it's Nikki's. You took it, we saw you." I brush these objections aside and reiterate that it is mine, and to prove it I'll show them all the things I have inside.

223

I unzip the bag and remove a brush or a comb, maybe a pair of dark glasses. A tube, or whatever it's called, of lipstick works best: "This is my lipstick," I say. "There, that proves it is my purse." They don't buy it and, in fact, are mildly outraged that I would pry into someone's possessions with such utter disregard for her privacy. (I've alerted the student to the demonstration before class, but no one else knows that.)

It's time to move on: "Okay, if it's Nikki's purse, how do you know? Why are you all so positive it's not my purse?" Different answers: We saw you take it; that's her lipstick, we know you don't wear lipstick; there is stuff in there with her name on it. To get the point across, I even offer to help in their effort to prove Nikki's possession: "If we had a test on the contents of the purse, who would do better, Nikki or me?" "Whose labor earned the money that bought the things in the purse, mine or Nikki's?" Obvious questions, obvious answers.

I make one last try to keep Nikki's purse: "What if I said I *discovered* this purse, then would it be mine?" A little laughter is my reward, but I don't get any takers; they still think the purse is rightfully Nikki's.

"So," I ask, "why do we say that Columbus discovered America?" Now they begin to see what I've been leading up to. I ask a series of rhetorical questions which implicitly make the link between Nikki's purse and the Indians' land: Were there people on the land before Columbus arrived? Who had been on the land longer, Columbus or the Indians? Who knew the land better? Who had put their labor into making the land produce? The students see where I'm going—it would be hard not to. "And yet," I continue, "what is the first thing that Columbus did when he arrived in the New World?" Right: he took possession of it. After all, he had discovered the place.

We talk about phrases other than "discovery" that textbooks could use to describe what Columbus did. Students start with the phrases they used to describe what I did to Nikki's purse: he stole it; he took it; he ripped it off. And others: he invaded it; he conquered it.

I want students to see that the word "discovery" is loaded. The word carries with it a perspective, a bias; it takes sides. "Discovery" is the phrase of the supposed discoverers. It's the conquerors, the invaders, masking their theft. And when the word gets repeated in textbooks, those textbooks become, in the phrase of one historian, "the propaganda of the winners."

To prepare students to examine critically the textbooks of their past, we begin with some alternative, and rather unsentimental, explorations of Columbus's "enterprise," as he called it. The admiral-to-be was not sailing for mere adventure and to prove the world was round, as my fourth-grade teacher had informed her class, but to secure the tremendous profits that were to be made by reaching the Indies. From the beginning, Columbus's quest was wealth, both for Spain and for himself personally. He demanded a 10 percent cut of everything shipped to Spain via the western route—and not just for himself but for all his heirs in perpetuity. And he insisted he be pronounced governor of any new lands he found, a title that carried with it dictatorial powers.

Mostly I want the class to think about the human beings Columbus was to "discover"—and then destroy. I read from a letter Columbus wrote, dated March 14, 1493, following his return from the first voyage. He reports being enormously impressed by the indigenous people:

> As soon as they see that they are safe and have laid aside all fear, they are very simple and honest and exceedingly liberal with all they have; none of them refusing anything he may possess when he is asked for it, but, on the contrary, inviting us to ask them. They exhibit great love toward all others in preference to themselves. They also give objects of great value for trifles, and content themselves with very little or nothing in return. . . . I did not find, as some of us had expected, any cannibals among them, but, on the contrary, men of great deference and kindness.[1]

But, on an ominous note, Columbus writes in his log, "Should your Majesties command it, all the inhabitants could be taken away to Castile [Spain], or made slaves on the island. With fifty men we could subjugate them all and make them do whatever we want."[2]

I ask students if they remember from elementary school days what it was Columbus brought back with him from his travels in the New World. Together students recall that he brought back parrots, plants, some gold, and a few of the people Columbus had taken to calling "Indians." This was Columbus's first expedition and it is also where most school textbook accounts of Columbus end—conveniently. Because the enterprise of Columbus was not to bring back exotic knickknacks, but riches, preferably gold. What about his second voyage?

I read to them a passage from this fine book, Hans Koning's *Columbus: His Enterprise:*

> We are now in February 1495. Time was short for sending back a good "dividend" on the supply ships getting ready for the return to Spain. Columbus therefore turned to a massive slave raid as a means for filling up these ships. The brothers [Columbus and his brothers, Bartolomé and Diego] rounded up fifteen hundred Arawaks—men, women, and children and imprisoned them in pens in Isabela, guarded by men and dogs. The ships had room for no more than five hundred, and thus only the best specimens were loaded aboard. The Admiral then told the Spaniards they could help themselves from the remainder to as many slaves as they wanted. Those whom no one chose were simply kicked out of their pens. Such had been the terror of these prisoners that (in the description by Michele de Cuneo, one of the colonists) "they rushed in all directions like lunatics, women dropping and abandoning infants in the rush, running for miles without stopping, fleeing across mountains and rivers."
>
> Of the five hundred slaves, three hundred arrived alive in Spain, where they were put up for sale in Seville by Donjuan de Fonseca, the archdeacon of the town. "As naked as the day they were born," the report of this excellent churchman says, "*but with no more embarrassment than animals. . . .*"
>
> The slave trade immediately turned out to be "unprofitable, for the slaves mostly died." Columbus decided to concentrate on gold, although he writes, "Let us in the name of the Holy Trinity go on sending all the slaves that can be sold."[3]

Certainly Columbus's fame should not be limited to the discovery of America: He also deserves credit for initiating the trans-Atlantic slave trade, albeit in the opposite direction than we're used to thinking of it.

Students and I role-play a scene from Columbus's second voyage. Slavery is not producing the profits Columbus is seeking. He still believes there is gold in them thar hills and the Indians are selfishly holding out on him. Students play Columbus; I play the Indians: "Chris, we don't have any gold, honest. Can we go back to living our lives now and you can go back to wherever you came from?" I call on several students to respond to the Indians' plea. Columbus thinks the Indians are lying. How can he get his gold? Student responses range from sympathetic to ruthless: Okay, we'll go home; *please* bring us your gold; we'll lock you up in prison if you don't bring us your gold; we'll torture you if you don't fork it over, etc. After I've pleaded for awhile and the students-as-Columbus have threatened, I real aloud another passage from Koning's book describing the system Columbus arrived at for extracting gold from the Indians:

Every man and woman, every boy or girl of fourteen or older, in the province of Cibao (of the imaginary gold fields) had to collect gold for the Spaniards. As their measure, the Spaniards used . . . hawks' bells. . . . Every three months, every Indian had to bring to one of the forts a hawks' bell filled with gold dust. The chiefs had to bring in about ten times that amount. In the other provinces of Hispaniola, twenty-five pounds of spun cotton took the place of gold.

Copper tokens were manufactured, and when an Indian had brought his or her tribute to an armed post, he or she received such a token, stamped with the month, to be hung around the neck. With that they were safe for another three months while collecting more gold.

Whoever was caught without a token was killed by having his or her hands cut off. There are old Spanish prints . . . that show this being done: the Indians stumble away, staring with surprise at their arm stumps pulsing out blood.

There were no gold fields, and thus, once the Indians had handed in whatever they still had in gold ornaments, their only hope was to work all day in the streams, washing out gold dust from the pebbles. It was an impossible task, but those Indians who tried to flee into the mountains were systematically hunted down with dogs and killed, to set an example for the others to keep trying. . . .

Thus it was at this time that the mass suicides began: the Arawaks killed themselves with cassava poison.

During those two years of the administration of the brothers Columbus, an estimated one half of the entire population of Hispaniola was killed or killed themselves. The estimates run from 125,000 to one-half million.[4]

It's important that students not be shielded from the horror of what "discovery" meant to its victims. The fuller they understand the consequences of Columbus's invasion of America, the better they'll be equipped to critically reexamine the innocent stories their textbooks have offered through the years. The goal is not to titillate or stun, but to force the question: Why wasn't I told this before?

Students' assignment is to find a textbook, preferably one they used in elementary school (but any textbook will suffice) and write a critique of the book's treatment of Columbus and the Indians. I distribute the following handout to students and review the questions aloud. I don't want them to merely answer the questions one by one, but to consider them as guidelines in completing their critiques:

—How factually accurate was the account?
—What was omitted—left out—that in your judgment would be important for a full understanding of Columbus? (For example, his treatment of the Indians, slave trading, his method of getting gold, the overall effect on the Indians.)
—What motives does the book give to Columbus? Compare those with his real motives.
—Who does the book get you to root for, and how do they accomplish that? (For example, is the book horrified at the treatment of Indians or thrilled that Columbus makes it to the New World?)
—What function do pictures play in the book? What do they communicate about Columbus and his "enterprise"?
—In your opinion, why does the book portray the Columbus/Indian encounter the way it does?
—Can you think of any groups in our society that might have an interest in people having an inaccurate view of history?

I tell students that this last question is tough but crucial. Is the continual distortion of Columbus simply an accident, repeated innocently over and over, or are there groups in our society that could benefit from everyone's having a false or limited understanding of the past? Whether or not students are able to answer the question effectively, it is still important that they struggle with it before our group discussion of their critiques.

The subtext of the assignment is to teach students that text material, indeed all written material, is to be read skeptically. I want students to explore the politics of print, that perspectives on history and social reality underlie the written word and that to read is not only to comprehend what is written, but also to question why it is written. My intention is not to encourage an "I-don't-believe-anything" cynicism,[5] but rather to equip students to bring the writer's assumptions and values to the surface so that they can decide what is useful and what is not in any particular work.

For practice, we look at some excerpts from a textbook that belonged to my brother in the fourth grade in California, *The Story of American Freedom* (Macmillan 1964). Students and I read aloud and analyze several paragraphs. The arrival of Columbus and crew is especially revealing—and obnoxious. As is true in every book on the "discovery" I've ever encountered; the reader watches events from the Spaniards' point of view. We are told how Columbus and his men "fell upon their knees and gave thanks to God," a passage included in virtually all el-

ementary school accounts of Columbus. "He then took possession of it [the is-
land] in the name of King Ferdinand and Queen Isabella of Spain."[6] No question
is raised of what right Columbus had to assume control over a land which was obviously already occupied by people. The account is so adoring, so respectful of
the Admiral, that students can't help but sense the book is offering approval for
what is, quite simply, an act of naked imperialism.

The book keeps us close to God and church throughout its narrative. Upon returning from the New World, Columbus shows off his parrots and Indians (again
no question of the propriety of the unequal relationship between "natives" and
colonizers), and immediately following the show, "the king and queen lead the
way to a near-by church. There a song of praise and thanksgiving is sung."[7]
Intended or not, the function of linking church and Columbus is to remove him
and his actions still further from question and critique. My job, on the other hand,
is to encourage students to pry beneath every phrase and illustration, to begin to
train readers who can both understand the word and challenge it.

I give students a week before I ask them to bring in their written critiques. In
small groups, they share their papers with one another. I ask them to take notes
toward what my co-teacher Linda Christensen and I call the "collective text":
What themes seem to recur in the papers and what important differences emerge?

Here are some excerpts from papers written this year by students in the Literature and U.S. History course that Linda and I co-teach.

Maryanne wrote:

"In 1492 Columbus sailed the ocean blue." He ran into a land mass claiming it in the
name of Spain. The next day Columbus went ashore. "Indians," almost naked, greeted
Columbus who found them a simple folk who "invite you to share anything they possess." Columbus observed that "fifty Spaniards could subjugate this entire people."
Then we are told, "By 1548 the Indians were almost all wiped out."—from a passage
in *The Impact of Our Past*.

That story is about as complete as Swiss cheese. Columbus and the Spaniards
killed off the "Indians," they didn't mystically disappear or die of diphtheria.

Trey wrote his critique as a letter to Allyn and Bacon, publishers of *The
American Spirit*:

. . . I'll just pick one topic to keep it simple. How about Columbus. No, you didn't
lie, but saying, "Though they had a keen interest in the peoples of the Caribbean,
Columbus and his crews were never able to live peacefully among them," makes it
seem as if Columbus did no wrong. The reason for not being able to live peacefully
is that he and his crew took slaves, and killed thousands of Indians for not bringing
enough gold. . . .

If I were to only know the information given in this book, I would have such a
sheltered viewpoint that many of my friends would think I was stupid. Later in life
people could capitalize on my ignorance by comparing Columbus's voyage with
something similar, but in our time. I wouldn't believe the ugly truths brought up by

the opposition because it is just like Columbus, and he did no harm, I've known that since the eighth grade.

Keely chose the same book, which happens to be the text adopted by Portland Public Schools, where I teach:

> . . . I found that the facts left in were, in fact, facts. There was nothing made up. Only things left out. There was one sentence in the whole section where Indians were mentioned. And this was only to say why Columbus called them "Indians." Absolutely nothing was said about slaves or gold. . . .
>
> The book, as I said, doesn't mention the Indians really, so of course you're on Christopher's side. They say how he falls to his knees and thanks God for saving him and his crew and for making their voyage successful.

After students have read and discussed their papers in small groups, we ask them to reflect on the papers as a whole and write about our collective text: What did they discover about textbook treatments of Columbus? Here are some excerpts.

Matthew wrote:

> As people read their evaluations the same situations in these textbooks came out. Things were conveniently left out so that you sided with Columbus's quest to "boldly go where no man has gone before." . . . None of the harsh violent reality is confronted in these so-called true accounts.

Gina tried to account for why the books were so consistently rosy:

> It seemed to me as if the publishers had just printed up some "glory story" that was supposed to make us feel more patriotic about our country. In our group, we talked about the possibility of the government trying to protect young students from such violence. We soon decided that was probably one of the farthest things from their minds. They want us to look at our country as great, and powerful, and forever right. They want us to believe Columbus was a real hero. We're being fed lies. We don't question the facts, we just absorb information that is handed to us because we trust the role models that are handing it out.

Rebecca's collective text reflected the general tone of disillusion with the official story of textbooks:

> Of course, the writers of the books probably think it's harmless enough—what does it matter who discovered America, really, and besides it makes them feel good about America. But the thought that I have been lied to all my life about this, and who knows what else, really makes me angry.

The reflections on the collective text became the basis for a class discussion of these and other issues. Again and again, students blasted their textbooks for consistently making choices that left readers with inadequate, and ultimately untruthful, understandings. And while we didn't press to arrive at definitive explanations for the omissions and distortions, we did seek to underscore the contemporary abuses of historical ignorance. If the books wax romantic about Columbus planting the flag on island beaches and taking possession of land occupied by naked red-skinned Indians, what do young readers learn from this about today's world? That white people have a right to dominate peoples of color? That might or wealth makes right? That it's justified to take people's land if you are more "civilized" or have a "better" religion? Whatever the answers, the textbooks condition students to accept some form of inequality; nowhere do the books suggest that the Indians were, or even should have been, sovereign peoples with a right to control their own lands. And if Columbus' motives for exploration are mystified or ignored, then students are less apt to look beyond today's pious explanations for U.S. involvements in, say, Central America or the Middle East. As Bobby, approaching his registration day for the military draft, pointed out in class: "If people thought they were going off to war to fight for profits, maybe they wouldn't fight as well, or maybe they wouldn't go."

It's important to note that some students are left troubled from these myth-popping discussions. One student wrote that she was "left not knowing who to believe." Josh was the most articulate in his skepticism. He had begun to "read" our class from the same critical distance from which we hoped students would approach textbooks:

> I still wonder. . . If we can't believe what our first grade teachers told us, why should we believe you? If they lied to us, why wouldn't you? If one book is wrong, why isn't another? What is your purpose in telling us about how awful Chris was? What interest do you have in telling us the truth? What is it you want from us?

What indeed? It was a wonderfully probing series of questions and Linda and I responded by reading them (anonymously) to the entire class. We asked students to take a few minutes to write additional questions and comments on the Columbus activities or to try to imagine our response as teachers—what was the point of our lessons?

We hoped students would see that the intent of the unit was to present a whole new way of reading, and ultimately of experiencing, the world. Textbooks fill students with information masquerading as final truth and then ask students to parrot back the information in end-of-the-chapter "checkups."

The Brazilian educator Paulo Freire calls it the "banking method": Students are treated as empty vessels waiting for deposits of wisdom from textbooks and teachers.[8] We wanted to assert to students that they shouldn't necessarily trust the "authorities," but instead need to be active participants in their own learning, peering between lines for unstated assumptions and unasked questions. Meaning is something they need to create, individually and collectively.

Josh asked what our "interest" was in this kind of education and it's a fair, even vital, question. Linda and I see teaching as political action: We want to equip students to build a truly democratic society. As Freire writes, to be an actor for social change one must "read the word and the world."[9] We hope that if a student is able to maintain a critical distance from the written word, then it's possible to maintain that same distance from one's society: to stand back, look hard, and ask, "Why is it like this, how can I make it better?"

POSTSCRIPT

As the final assignment in our unit on Native American history, Linda and I asked students to create a project that would reach beyond the walls of the classroom to educate others in the school or larger community. As a class we had multiple layers of a twisted and biased history. We worried that unless we offered students a chance to act on these new understandings, the unintended subtext or "hidden curriculum" embedded in our teaching was a cynical one: Your role as students is to uncover injustice, not to do anything about it.

We told students the form their projects took didn't matter; the only requirement was that each of them would make some kind of presentation to others outside the classroom. And they took us at our word. One group of aspiring musicians produced a raucous rock video about the damming of the Columbia River, which drowned the ancient fishing grounds of the Celilo Indians. Another group choreographed and performed for other classes a dance, at the same time bitter and humorous, on Columbus's "discovery" and search for gold. Several students interviewed local Northwest Indian tribal leaders about their struggle over fishing rights on the Columbia River. The group produced a video tape subsequently broadcast over the school's closed-circuit TV news show.

One young woman, Nicole Smith, wrote and illustrated a children's book, *Chris*. In the story, a young boy named Christopher moves from his old Spain Street neighborhood to a new house on Salvadora Street. He's miserable and misses his old friends, Ferdie and Isle. While wandering the new neighborhood he spots a colorful playhouse and declares, "I claim this clubhouse in the name of me, and my best friends Ferdie and Isle." The rightful owners of the clubhouse soon return and confront Christopher, who insists that the structure is now *his* because he "discovered" it. "How can you come here and discover something that we built and really care about?" the boys demand. The story ends happily when they agree to let Christopher share the clubhouse if he helps with the upkeep—a metaphorical twist that would have been nice five hundred years earlier.

Linda arranged for Nicole to read her story to a number of classes in a local elementary school. She opened each session by asking if anyone had something with which to write. When an unsuspecting youngster volunteered a pencil, Nicole thanked the student, then pocketed it. This elementary school version of purse-stealing gave Nicole a handy introduction to the theft-posing-as-discovery lesson in her short story.

A Reader

Like Rebecca and many other students, Nicole was angry she had been lied to about Columbus and the genocide of indigenous people in the Caribbean. However, the final project assignment encouraged her to channel that anger in an activist direction. She became a teacher, offering the youngsters a framework in which to locate and question the romanticized textbook patter about "exploration" and "discovery," providing a hoped-for inoculation against the lies and omissions they will be sure to encounter in their schooling. Nicole's story and lesson were a kind of revenge: getting back at those who miseducated her so many years before. But as she was teaching she was also learning that the best way to address injustice is to work for change.

NOTES

1. *The Annals of America, Volume 1:1493–1754, Discovering a New World* (Chicago: Encyclopaedia Britannica, 1968), pp. 2, 4.

2. Quoted in Hans Koning, *Columbus: His Enterprise*, p. 53. As Koning points out, none of the information included in his book is new. It is available in Columbus's own journals and letters and the writings of the Spanish priest Bartolomé de las Casas. Even Columbus's adoring biographers admit the admiral's outrages. For example, Pulitzer Prize winner Samuel Eliot Morison acknowledges that Columbus unleashed savage dogs on Indians, kidnapped Indian leaders, and encouraged his sailors to rape Indian women. At one point Morison writes, "The cruel policy initiated by Columbus and pursued by his successors resulted in complete genocide." See Samuel Eliot Morison, *Christopher Columbus, Mariner* (New York: New American Library, 1942), p. 99. But the sharpness of this judgment is buried in Morison's syrupy admiration for Columbus's courage and navigational skills.

3. Koning, *Columbus*, p. 83; emphasis in original.

4. Ibid., pp. 83–84.

5. It's useful to keep in mind the distinction between cynicism and skepticism. As Norman Diamond writes, "In an important respect, the two are not even commensurable. Skepticism says, 'You'll have to show me, otherwise I'm dubious'; it is open to engagement and persuasion. . . . Cynicism is a removed perspective, a renunciation of any responsibility." See Norman Diamond, "Against Cynicism in Politics and Culture," *Monthly Review*, vol. 28, no. 2 (June 1976): 40.

6. Edna McGuire, *The Story of American Freedom* (New York: The Macmillan Company, 1964), p. 24.

7. Ibid., p. 26.

8. See Paulo Freire, *Pedagogy of the Oppressed* (New York: Continuum, 1970). This banking method of education, Freire writes (p. 58), "turns [students] into 'receptacles' to be 'filled' by the teacher. . . . Education thus becomes an act of depositing, in which the students are depositories and the teacher is the depositor. Instead of communicating, the teacher issues communiques and makes deposits which the students patiently receive, memorize, and repeat. This is the 'banking' concept of education, in which the scope of action allowed to the students extends only as far as receiving, filing, and storing the deposits. They do, it is true, have the opportunity to become collectors or cataloguers of the

things they store. But in the last analysis, it is men [people] themselves who are filed away through the lack of creativity, transformation, and knowledge in this (at best) misguided system."

9. Paulo Freire and Donaldo Macedo, *Literacy: Reading the Word and the World* (South Hadley, MA: Bergin and Garvey, 1987).

The Thanksgiving Epidemic

Kathy Kerner

A first-grade teacher is presenting a Thanksgiving unit to her class of six year olds. The class learns about "The First Thanksgiving" during which, she says, the Pilgrims and Indians shared a feast celebrating the Pilgrims' survival in America. To underscore the lesson, the teacher divides the children into two groups. The "Pilgrims" make hats, the "Indians" make construction paper feather headbands and cardboard tomahawks. Later, there will be a pageant presented for parents in which "The First Thanksgiving" is reenacted.

This scene is epidemic—repeated every November in thousands of elementary schools across the country, and we probably all grew up with it. I see it replicated every year in the schools I serve, and I am ashamed. Why? What's wrong with this picture?

The history in this simple scenario is questionable, the context is missing, and the events surrounding the arrival of Europeans on these shores are usually presented from an exclusively Eurocentric viewpoint. The point of view of the Native peoples impacted by the arrival of the invaders is virtually ignored.[1]

The historical gaps and inaccuracies are not the biggest problem with the typical school portrayal of "The First Thanksgiving," however. The demeaning, inaccurate, and stereotypical portrayal of Native people that accompanies the typical Thanksgiving tableau is a national disgrace.

Stereotypes begin with images. They in turn foster or reinforce misconceptions and rigid ideas. Misconceptions about Native people depend on stereotypes that are pervasive in popular culture. Many, like those in the Thanksgiving unit, are transmitted through the "educational" content presented to children at the earliest levels of schooling. These fixed images then become part of the cultural air we breathe—accepted by mainstream society without question, and exist without our even being aware of them.

The following are just a few of the misconceptions perpetuated by the way we teach "Thanksgiving" in the public schools:

1. The yearly ritual cements the notion that Indians are relics of the past, like pirates (or dinosaurs) rather than the resilient, adaptable peoples that they are. Very seldom is their continued existence, let alone the diversity and vitality of the

500-plus nations of Native peoples, taught in school. The "buckskin and feathers" outfits convey an anachronistic, monolithic image of a generic "Indian" that doesn't, and never has, existed.

2. The "dressing-up-as" imitation of the popular conception of "Indians" is a form of racism we would not tolerate toward any other group. We would never allow children to put on blackface and sing "Mammy" for African-American Heritage Month. Yet most people think nothing of encouraging children to don fake feathers and sing "Ten Little Indians," the equivalent of the blackface scenario.

3. We transmit ignorance and disrespect of traditional spiritual practices, which are still very much in existence among many Native nations. The spiritual meaning of eagle and other feathers for Native peoples makes their imitation and use a sacrilege. Can you imagine facilitating a "fun" activity in which a kindergarten class imitates a communion service or makes construction paper crucifixes for Easter?

4. Most non-Indians don't know that many Native people observe Thanksgiving as a day of mourning because of the genocide, land loss, and cultural decimation that resulted from their people's early generosity toward the new arrivals. In fact, the history of "The First Thanksgiving" is shrouded in historical controversy and is far from clear. There is very little hard evidence that the image-myth we celebrate—Indians and Europeans sitting down to give thanks to God for a bountiful harvest—ever happened at all.

William Bradford, whose journal is considered the most complete account of the early settlement, never mentions such an event. The source of the story seems to have originated from a letter by Edward Winslow written December 11, 1621, and published in *Mourt's Relation*. In it, he describes a feast held in the fall of 1621. The Pilgrims had survived their first winter, and were now reaping their first harvest with extensive assistance from the Wampanoags. Winslow describes the presence of Massasoit and 90 other Wampanoag men at a three-day feast at which the Pilgrims displayed their military firepower. There is no mention of the Pilgrims' giving thanks to either the Creator or the Wampanoags, without whom they would have surely starved.[2]

Although not associated with that early feast, there is another thanksgiving that took place following the war against the Pequots in 1637. The most dramatic incident in that war was the slaughter of 700 Pequot men, women, and children at Fort Mystic, most of whom were burned alive.[3] In his *Brief History of the Pequot War*, John Mason, who was a participant and was asked by the General Court of Connecticut to write an eyewitness account, wrote:

> Thus we may see how the face of God is set against them that do evil, to cut off the remembrance of them from the Earth. . . . Let the whole earth be filled with [God's] Glory! Thus the Lord was pleased to smite our enemies in the hinder parts, and to give us their land for an inheritance.[4]

Historian Alfred Cave notes that John Underhill "rejoiced that through God's will 'their country is fully subdued and fallen into the hands of the English,' and called on readers to 'magnify his honor for his great goodness.'"[5]

Finally, the late Professor William Newell (Mohawk), former chairman of the anthropology department at the University of Connecticut, found documentation indicating that the first *official* "Day of Thanksgiving" was declared in 1637 by the Governor of the Massachusetts Bay Colony in gratitude for that slaughter at Fort Mystic and observed for the next 100 years.[6]

5. Virtually all Native nations have given primary importance to giving thanks to the Creator and to all of creation. To label a European-American event "The First Thanksgiving" is grossly inaccurate. The Lenape people, now called Delaware, for example, celebrated "Gam'wing" an autumn ceremony of thanksgiving lasting for almost two weeks. It is an intense celebration in which the feasting and reunions are secondary to ceremonies, which take place in a massive high-ceiling Big House. The Big House represents the entire universe, and all of Creation is thanked through dance, song, and story for providing for the people.

In the Native American newsletter *Oyaka,* Roger Buffalohead writes about giving talks to schools about seasonal feasts, especially Indian harvest celebrations:

> We told about offering the first fruits in thanks to the provider. We talked about harmony among the creatures of the earth—the two-legged and the four-legged, the winged in the air and those rooted in the fields and forest. We spoke of mutual need and respect for the other.[7]

In a report to the *Navajo Times,* Interim Tribal Chairman Leonard Haskie also spoke of how important the harvest time was to all tribal cultures in North America, but that the spirit of cooperation that supposedly infused the Pilgrims–Indian first Thanksgiving is harder to find in our society.[8] In an interview with Bill Moyers, Onondaga Chief Oren Lyons also discussed the ceremonial practice of giving thanks among all tribal people:

> This was our first instruction, the ceremonies. And the ceremonies, which are as ancient as we are, were our 'thanksgivings,' every one of them. So we have these extraordinary rounds of thanksgivings every year at certain times. . . . If you go down and watch the Pueblos as they do their bean dance, their deer dance, if you watch the Hopi as they do their snake dance, these are old, ancient ceremonies. . . . And you continue because they are what you are instructed to do, which is to give thanks for what is given to you here. The Pilgrims got hold of it and called it Thanksgiving, but that's only the harvest part. They don't go all the way around the whole clock.[9]

Joseph Bruchac (Abenaki) has written a book for children called *The Maple Thanksgiving,* which depicts the Iroquois practice of giving thanks to the maples at the end of winter. This also illustrates the point that Native 'thanksgiving' ceremonies were and are year-round occurrences. The Wampanoag people, who were involved in that questionable "first Thanksgiving," traditionally did and still do celebrate the harvest on "Cranberry Day" in the autumn.[10]

In elementary school classrooms, the month of November is a fertile breeding ground for stereotypes about Native people and "Thanksgiving." It is also a perfect time and place for corrective action. What can the culturally sensitive teacher do to counteract the onslaught of fake feathers and cardboard tomahawks?

Patricia Ramsey, assistant professor of early childhood education at Indiana University, details a number of ideas that can be incorporated into the late fall curriculum. Among them are the ideas and practices of community feasts and harvest celebrations, which are typically practiced by cultures all over the world.

Thanksgiving celebrations in cultures around the world occur at various times of year depending on the location and time of harvest. Among them are the Harvest Home Festival in England and Canada (October), the Harvest Moon Festival in China and elsewhere in Asia (August), and Sukkot (September/October), a Jewish holiday celebrating the harvest and the forty-year period after the Exodus from Egypt. Ashura (February) are holidays of thanksgiving celebrated by Moslems, and Kwanza (December), meaning "first fruits," is celebrated by some African-American families.

Teaching about the hunting practices of various cultures can take the focus off the ubiquitous turkey and convey some real knowledge about how real societies operate in our world. Such an approach can incorporate ceremonies, skills, celebrations, and artifacts. Indigenous cultures all over the world have a deep knowledge and respect for the natural world they depend on for survival and an ethic of taking only what they need. Those concepts can also be conveyed.

Because interest in Indians seems to peak at this time of year, there are several things teachers who teach about Native people should do to make what they convey as concrete and relevant as possible. They should:

- Provide accurate information.
- Emphasize the diversity among the 500+ nations of indigenous peoples of North America and the differences between historical and contemporary life.
- Convey the vast diversity among individual Native people, their life circumstances, and their views.
- Include Native guest speakers and/or visits to a nearby reservation or other Indian community whenever possible.

Thanksgiving is also a perfect time to teach social and political issues. Even very young children can participate in exercises designed to foster empathy for the viewpoints and reactions of groups who have conflicting goals. As Ramsey says:

> For children to come home saying, 'All white people are bad because they hurt Indians' is not much better than the original stereotype. Efforts can be more productively directed toward helping children understand that when two or more groups of people want the same resources . . . there are many opposing points of view.[11]

Finally, Vicki Patterson in *News from Native California* suggests that an incentive such as a cash reward or day off be offered to "the first teacher in a school to use his or her training in research skills to discover the answer to the question, 'Who were the Indians who helped the Pilgrims survive their first winter in the American continent?' and present it to the rest of the staff . . . would you win?"[12]

Michael Dorris (Modoc) asks, "Considering that virtually none of the standard fare surrounding . . . Thanksgiving contains an ounce of authenticity, historical accuracy, or cross cultural perception, why is it so apparently ingrained?"[13] James Loewen offers an answer: "More than any other celebration, more even than such overtly patriotic holidays as Independence Day and Memorial Day, Thanksgiving celebrates our ethnocentrism."[14] The resistance to change in the way this national origin myth is presented to young children is, therefore, intense.

Yet change is essential for at least three reasons:

1. The stereotyping of Native people is devastating to the self-esteem of Indian children.
2. Non-Indian children (and adults) will continue to be deprived of accurate information, let alone an empathic understanding, of the richness of Native history and culture and their against-the-odds survival into the present.
3. As long as Native people are marginalized and stereotyped, it will be difficult for adults raised with these images to take seriously the social and political life-and-death struggles waged by Native peoples every day of their lives.

NOTES

1. James W. Loewen, "The Truth About Thanksgiving," in *Lies My Teacher Told Me* (New York: The New Press, 1995), pp. 67–69; Doris Seale, Beverly Slapin, and Carolyn Silverman, *Thanksgiving: A Native Perspective* (Berkeley: Oyate).

2. George Mourt, *A Journal of the Pilgrims at Plymouth: Mourt's Relation* (1622; reprint, New York: Corinth Books, 1963).

3. Alfred A. Cave, *The Pequot War* (Amherst: University of Massachusetts, 1996), p. 151.

4. John Mason, *A Brief History of the Pequot War* (1656; reprint, Ann Arbor, MI: University Microfilms, Inc., 1966), pp. 20–21.

5. Cave, *Pequot*, p. 169.

6. Seale, *Thanksgiving*, pp. 71–72. *Documents of Holland*, 13 volumes of colonial documentary history including letters and reports from colonial officials to their superiors and the King of England and the private papers of Sir William Johnson, British Indian Agent for the New York Colony.

7. Roger Buffalohead, "The Time of Survival," *Oyaka Native American Newsletter*, vol. 13, no. 6 (December 2, 1988).

8. Leonard Haskie, "Thanksgiving Has Cultural Roots," *Navajo Times*, vol. 27, no. 47 (November 22, 1989).

9. Oren Lyons and Bill Moyers, "The Faithkeeper: Oren Lyons with Bill Moyers." New York: Mystic Fire Video, 1991.

10. Joan Lester and Judy McCann, *Indians Who Met the Pilgrims, A Unit of Social Studies Materials and Activities for the Intermediate Grades.* (Boston: American Science and Engineering Assn., 1974), p. 39.

11. Patricia Ramsey, "Beyond 'Ten Little Indians' and Turkeys," *Young Children,* vol. 34, no. 6 (September 1979): 2851.

12. Vicki Patterson, "Thanksgiving Thoughts," *News from Native California,* vol. 1, no. 5 (November/December 1987), p. 20.

13. Michael A. Dorris, "Why I'm Not Thankful for Thanksgiving," *Through Indian Eyes: The Native Experience in Books for Children,* eds. Beverly Slapin and Doris Seale (Philadelphia: New Society Publishers, 1987), 1987.

14. Loewen, "The Truth," p. 85.

REFERENCES

Bradford, William. *Of Plymouth Plantation, 1620–1647.* Ed. Samuel Eliot Morison. New York: 1976.

Brasser, T. J. "Early Indian-European Contacts" in *Handbook of North American Indians: Northeast,* vol. 15. Washington, D.C.: Smithsonian Institution, 1978. pp. 82–83.

Bruchac, Joseph. *The Maple Thanksgiving.* Glenview, IL: Celebration Press, 1996.

Buffalohead, Roger, "The Time of Survival," *O'Yaka Native American Newsletter* vol. 13, no. 6 (December 2, 1988).

Bushnell, A. P. "Bloody Tinge to First Thanksgiving?" *Boston Globe,* Nov. 23, 1978.

Carney, Leo H. "How the Lenapes Celebrated," *New York Times,* 22 November 1981.

Cave, Alfred A. *The Pequot War.* Amherst, MA: University of Massachusetts Press, 1996.

Council on Interracial Books for Children. *Unlearning Indian Stereotypes.* New York: Council on Interracial Books for Children, 1977.

Davids, D. W., and R. A. Gudinas. "Packet of Teacher Materials." Center for Community Leadership Development, University of Wisconsin—Extension, 1976.

Deetz, James, and Jay Anderson. "Partakers of Plenty: A Study of the First Thanksgiving." First published as "The Ethnogastronomy of Thanksgiving" in *Saturday Review of Science,* 25 November 1972.

Dorris, Michael A. "Why I'm Not Thankful for Thanksgiving," in *Through Indian Eyes: The Native Experience in Books for Children,* eds. Beverly Slapin and Doris Seale. Philadelphia: New Society Publishers, 1987.

Flemming, B. M., D. S. Hamilton, and J. D. Hicks. *Resources for Creative Teaching in Early Childhood Education.* New York: Harcourt Brace Jovanovich, 1997.

Haskie, Leonard. "Thanksgiving Has Cultural Roots," *Navajo Times,* vol. 27, no. 47, Nov. 22, 1989.

Hirschfelder, Arlene, and Jane Califf. "Celebration or Mourning? It's All in the Point of View." New York: Council on Interracial Books for Children, Bulletin 10, no. 6, 1979.

James, Frank. "Frank James' Speech." New York: Council on Interracial Books for Children, Bulletin 10, no. 6, 1979.

Jennings, Francis. *The Invasion of America: Indians, Colonialism and the Cant of Conquest.* Chapel Hill: University of North Carolina Press, 1975.

Lester, Joan, and Judy McCann. *Indians Who Met the Pilgrims, A Unit of Social Studies Materials and Activities for the Intermediate Grades.* Boston: American Science and Engineering, 1974.

Loewen, James W. "The Truth About the First Thanksgiving." In *Lies My Teacher Told Me.* New York: The New Press, 1995. pp. 67–89.

Marten, Catherine. *The Wampanoags in the 17th Century: An Ethnohistorical Survey.* Occasional Papers in Old Colony Studies #2. Plymouth, Massachusetts: Plimoth Plantation, Inc., 1970.

Mason, John. *A Brief History of the Pequot War.* 1656. Reprint, Ann Arbor: University Microfilms, Inc. 1966.

Museum of the American Indian. "Diplomacy in New England: The First Thanksgiving." Museum of the American Indian-Heye Foundation, 1987.

Mourt, George. *A Journal of the Pilgrims at Plymouth: Mourt's Relation.* 1622. Reprint, New York: Corinth Books, 1963.

Patterson, Victoria. "Thanksgiving Thoughts," *News from Native California,* vol. 1, no. 5, November/December 1987.

Ramsey, Patricia G. "Beyond 'Ten Little Indians' and Turkeys: Alternative Approaches to Thanksgiving." *Young Children,* vol. 34, no. 6 (September 1979): pp. 28–51.

Salisbury, Neal. *Manitou and Providence.* New York: Oxford University Press, 1982.

Salwin, Bert. "Southern New England and Long Island Indians: The Early Years." In *Handbook of North American Indians: Northeast,* vol. 15. Washington, DC: Smithsonian Institution, 1978. pp. 160–176.

Seale, Doris, Beverly Slapin, and Carolyn Silverman. *Thanksgiving: A Native Perspective.* Berkeley, CA: Oyate, nd.

Segal, Charles M., and David C. Steinback. *Puritans, Indians and Manifest Destiny.* New York: Putnams, 1977.

Simmons, William S. *Spirit of the New England Tribes: Indian History and Folklore, 1620–1984.* Hanover, MA: University Press of New England, 1986.

Skinner, Linda, and Gregory Schaaf. "Thanksgiving: Beyond Pilgrims and Indians." Tulsa, OK: Traditions for Teaching, Resource and Evaluation Center Five, 1987.

Stoddard, Francis R. *The Truth About the Pilgrims.* New York: Society of Mayflower Descendants, 1952.

Washburn, Wilcomb E. "Seventeenth-Century Indian Wars." In *Handbook of North American Indians: Northeast,* vol. 14. Washington, DC: Smithsonian Institution, 1978. pp. 89–100.

Winthrop, John. *Winthrop's Journal, History of New England, 1630–1639.* Ed. James K. Hosmer. New York, 1908.

Wright, J. Leitch. *The Only Land They Knew.* New York: Free Press, 1981.

Zinn, Howard. *A People's History of the United States.* New York: Harper Perennial, 1995.

Chapter 8

Art for Truth's Sake

Indian Artists Rescue the Truth

Paulette Fairbanks Molin

Native artists, working in many mediums, are creatively addressing the issue of stereotyping in both their visual and written expressions. Among many fine examples are the selections here by Dorothy Grandbois and Charlene Teters, who unmask and counteract the pervasive, mass-produced images associated with stereotypes.

Like countless other children, Grandbois used Big Chief writing tablets during her childhood. Her work illustrates the stark contrast between the stereotypical image of the figure used to sell writing paper and the one she has humanized and dignified through her artistry. Teters, who is nationally known for her work against mascots, vividly demonstrates how stereotypical images block people from seeing actual American Indians, including children.

Artists who resist stereotyping are subject to a range of outcomes, among them controversy. An example is a work by Edgar Heap of Birds, Cheyenne and Arapaho, who was commissioned by the Cleveland Institute of Arts to create a public art piece as part of the Institute's exhibition that opened in December of 1996.

Heap of Birds designed a 25 × 12-foot billboard in which he used the mascot image of Chief Wahoo of the Cleveland Indians juxtaposed with the words "Smile for Racism." The resulting furor nearly resulted in the work being banned by the commissioning agency, which was fearful of offending members of the larger community. Works by artists such as these counteract stereotypes in creative ways, while exposing harsh truths about our society. They also mirror Native life in all the beauty, richness, and complexity of its humanity.

"BIG CHIEF" (6"×9" PHOTO ETCHING), BY DOROTHY GRANDBOIS

The "Big Chief" tablet is an icon that we have all grown up with and accept as a representation of how Indian leaders and Indian men are portrayed. Although it is not considered terribly demeaning or offensive, it does create the misconception that Indians wear feathers and headdresses and perpetuates this stereotypical simplistic image of a leader or of Indian men overall. Because the image is on a school tablet and used where education is taking place makes it that much more offensive, especially in this day and age when these simplistic representations are so inaccurate and misguiding.

The image further shows how our ancestors and great tribal and religious leaders are downplayed and simplified in the minds of children. Could you imagine the response if the Pope or another religious icon appeared on a school tablet? People would be outraged.

"SLUM-TA," FROM THE INSTALLATION
"WHAT WE KNOW ABOUT INDIANS," BY CHARLENE TETERS

Images of noble savages, warriors, braves, and Indian princesses are non-Indians' perceptions of what is Indian, created by authors and writers and encouraged by the white establishment. These manufactured images are used to sell everything from butter to cars, and are powerful in their impact on non-Indian people. But this is not the American Indians' perceptions of themselves. (1994)

Indian Film and Video Makers Rescue the Truth

Beverly Singer

Before the 1960s, independent film and video-making by Aboriginal/American Indians or Alaska Natives was absent in America. Early films made by Native people in Canada and the United States were usually experiments that received little or no national exposure. The historical weight of Hollywood movies and their pervasive stereotypes of "Indians" actually prevented opportunities for Native Americans to be documentarians themselves. The result today is that far fewer opportunities exist for people to witness films and videos directed, produced, and written by Native people. The benefit to viewers who watch films made by Native people is not simply educational but rather a whole new introduction to our history and cultural legacy.

A strong spirit of perseverance and determination to locate the works of those making Native film and video is required, as well as the resources to purchase or rent copies of Native-made films. One option is to search the Internet for Aboriginal/American Indian/Alaska Native films and videos. Another option is to contact Native media organizations such as the Native American Public Telecommunications (NAPT) in Lincoln, Nebraska. NAPT produces programs for public television and radio. Native media publications such as *Aboriginal Voices*, published in Toronto, Canada, and *Native Peoples*, published in Phoenix, Arizona, review Native film and video. In addition, the Smithsonian Institution, National Museum of the American Indian Film and Video Center, has a large data bank about films and videos produced and directed by Native people in the Western Hemisphere.

In June 1998, modern film history was made with the national theatrical release of *Smoke Signals,* a fictional drama written and coproduced by writer Sherman Alexie, Spokane/Coeur d'Alene, and directed by Chris Eyre, Cheyenne/Arapaho. Native actors have the key roles. The film is about relationships that center on two young men, Victor and Thomas, who grow up in the shadow of a family tragedy that becomes the undercurrent of their relationship. The plot focuses on Victor, a young frustrated soul who makes a journey with Thomas, a sweet and meek fellow, to put closure on the recent death of Victor's father. The film captures vi-

251

gnettes of the community and, rather than giving an overview of the community where the young men live, the filmmaker's focus is on the relationships, most of which are positive or humorous. The isolation characterized by Victor, the protagonist, is juxtaposed with the charitable heart of Thomas. You can guess which energy prevails by the film's conclusion.

The film is not recommended for very young children due largely to the complex human interactions that are worked out in the film. Given this description of *Smoke Signals,* many familiar with formulaic "Indian movies" might ask, "What makes this film different from any other film about human relationships?" A follow-up question might be, "What makes it Indian?" Simply, the events and themes that permeate the Native community in *Smoke Signals* are experiences found in any community of people who share like values and traditions. The film itself is not an exhibition of Native culture, but rather it renders the feelings in Native life today, thereby suggesting to viewers that Indians, too, have family issues and life situations that have personal consequences. Leather and feathers are absent, thereby giving viewers an opportunity to watch this film about Native people with imperfect lives while they affirm their ties to a cultural inheritance illustrated in the last scene of the film.

The gifted writing of Alexie and the skilled directorial eye of Eyre, who both grew up in the Northwest, in collaboration with ShadowCatcher, an independent film company that initiated the purchase of *Smoke Signals* by Miramax, marks a beginning of a new collaboration between Native people and filmmaking. The film, originally titled *This Is What It Means to Say Phoenix, Arizona,* was renamed by Miramax. Its commercial title, *Smoke Signals,* is an ironically appropriate title for the film. The film received the Filmmakers' Trophy and Audience Award at the 1998 Sundance Film Festival and was released to video rental distribution in mid-January 1999.

The success of *Smoke Signals* as a groundbreaking film is encouraging other Native filmmakers, whose creative productions are less known but no less important. Of the thousand or so independent films and videos produced by Native people in recent years, only a select few are broadcast on cable and national public television. Six more unique programs that deserve wider exposure are suggested for viewing by young people. The selected list includes four nonfiction films and videos, a multimedia video installation, and one fiction piece:

Picturing a People: George Johnston, Tlingit Photographer, **by Carol Geddes.** Carol Geddes (Tlingit) has been producing and promoting filmmaking by Aboriginal people in Canada since the 1970s. This is her most recent film achievement (1997, 52 minutes), a historical record of change in the lifeways of the inland Tlingit of Canada documented in the photographs of George Johnston. In a narrative written by Geddes, she retells the history of the inland Tlingit struggle to survive especially during World War II, which marks the end of the people's traditional livelihood derived from a direct relationship with the land for food, shelter, and clothing. Geddes' film provides a unique perspective about the impact of global development among Aboriginal people in Canada, an experience familiar to Native people everywhere. The film is available from the National Film Board of Canada, U.S. Division in New York, NY.

Eyes of the Spirit, by **Alexie Isaac.** Alexie Isaac (Yup'ik) began working with KYUK-TV in Bethel, Alaska, a station that broadcasts in the Yup'ik language for the Alaska Yukon-Delta region. Isaac began using the video camera to document the restoration of Inuit cultural traditions such as mask making and mask dancing, which at the time was being rekindled in many villages. *Eyes of the Spirit* (1984, 28 minutes, KYUK-TV) is one of the films directed by Isaac, depicting the carving of dance masks and the apprenticeship of youngsters to older Inuit mask makers who learn the (sleeping) art of Yup'ik mask carving and dancing. Alaska Native culture, dance traditions, and stories linked with carved masks are poignantly represented in the video distributed by KYUK Video productions, Pouch 468, Bethel, AK 99559.

Siskyavi: The Place of Chasms, by **Victor Masayesva.** The filmmaking artistry of Victor Masayesva (Hopi) usually prompts audiences to rethink their images of Native people especially those about the Hopi, his people. In this video (1989, 28 minutes, IS Productions), Masayesva compares and contrasts pottery making with scientific inquiry and Hopi tradition and education. Drawing parallels in a story about a Hopi student who must remain at home while her classmates travel to learn about the pottery collection at the Smithsonian Institution in Washington, D.C., he uses an approach that navigates and contemplates both experiences by demonstration rather than explanation. The experimental process Masayesva uses in filmmaking breaks with traditional methods used in film documentation of Native people. The video is distributed by Electronic Arts Intermix in New York, NY.

Prayer of Thanksgiving, by **Melanie Printup Hope.** Melanie Printup Hope, Tuscarora, is an accomplished multimedia artist whose *Prayer of Thanksgiving* (1997, CD-ROM) shares the gift of life fortified by the Haudenosaunee (also known as the Iroquois) honoring the Creation. It combines beadwork created by Printup Hope, which is the physical manifestation of animals and plants, and other intricate designs evoked in the prayer, which are simulated in computer graphics and accompanied by an audio track that recounts the Prayer of Thanksgiving. To complement her visual production, Printup Hope constructed a shrine-like environment, creating a space for audiences to get the full benefit of interacting with the *Prayer of Thanksgiving.* This multimedia installation is a technological homage to her people, the Tuscarora, and to all Native people, imparting ancestral lessons to the public in a sanctified manner. Information about the *Prayer of Thanksgiving* is available from http://www.albany.net/~printup/index.html.

Pepper's Pow Wow, by **Sandra Osawa.** Sandra Osawa (Makah) pays tribute to Jim Pepper, an internationally renowned jazz composer and musician of Kaw/Creek ancestry. Osawa's portrait of Pepper (1996, 53 min.) makes a direct link between the Native ceremonial music tradition, which inspired Pepper in his youth, and the translation or "fusion" of that cultural experience with jazz music. Osawa provides a framework for helping audiences understand Pepper's personal motivation and family's encouragement to pursue his dream despite the many obstacles he faced in the music industry, including his Native heritage. Once viewed as a jazz musician anomaly, Pepper's contribution to the music world was notably realized after his untimely death. However, his music will live on because, as Osawa points out, it is original and spiritually reviving. Upstream Productions, Osawa's production company located in Seattle, Washington, distributes *Pepper's Pow Wow*.

Haircuts Hurt, **by Randy Redroad.** This film by Randy Redroad (Cherokee) (1991, 10 minutes), is a classic story about a Native boy's first haircut at a "redneck" barber shop. The film reflects the child's fear through his mother's childhood memories that intensify her decision to have her son's hair cut. Native identity is often confused with and determined by physical appearance. Redroad evokes a passionate response to a simple act like a haircut and reconstructs a different sensibility about Native identity. Redroad's fictional film narrative is further enhanced by his compelling skill for visual insight. *Haircuts Hurt* is distributed by Third World Newsreel located in New York, NY.

Bibliography

Yvonne Wakim

STEREOTYPING OF NATIVE AMERICANS

Abel, Midge B. "American Indian Life As Portrayed in Children's Literature." *Elementary English*, vol. 50, no. 2 (February 1973): 202–8. Bibliography.
Although Abel begins with an overview of the evolution of children's books about tribal life from 1900–1960, her focus is on analyzing materials published since 1960 for grades 1–3. She briefly reviews picture books, Indian biographies, informational books, fiction, folktales, and legends suggesting that there is not enough material for this age group. However, many of the books she gives a high rating are not recommended.

Agent, Dan and Tenequer, Bob. "Indian Images in Advertising." *The Eagle*, vol. 10, no. 4: 11. Also in *Smithsonian Runner* (March-April 1992).
The writers give several examples of Indian culture being exploited in business for a wide variety of products, logos, sports teams, and so forth. They point out that non-Indians have been helped greatly by the Native Americans' extensive knowledge of pharmacopeia and that the helpful image has been turned into a stereotype and is still being capitalized on at great concern to contemporary American Indians.

Aleiss, Angela. "In the Land of Hollywood Make-Believe 'Anyone Can Say They're Indian.'" *ICE: Indian Cinema Entertainment*, vol. 4, no. 1 (Winter 1995): 7, 9.
The writer discusses how more non-Indians are pretending to be Indians in order to land acting roles in Hollywood and cites several examples of Indian wannabes in the movies. In *ICE*, vol. 3, no. 2 (Spring 1995): 11, Tailinh Prado responds to the "In the Land of Hollywood Make-Believe . . ." piece and argues that Aleiss mistakenly refers to Jesse Borrego as a *Mexican actor*. Prado also deals with the internal racism in the Indian community against Indians who are of mixed heritage other than English or French and with the way Hollywood pigeonholes Native actors.

———. "Moving in Images." *European Review of Native American Studies*, vol. 7, no. 2 (1993): 49–54.
The archives of the Library of Congress contain over 200 movies with Indian content dating back to the first western, "The Redman and the Child," made by D. W. Griffith in 1908. By appointment, viewers may watch films by the first Indian director, James Young Deer, or see films with Native actors like Mona Darkfeather, Chief Yowlachie, or Canadian tribal actors in a 1930 film "The Silent Enemy."

———. "A Race Divided: The Indian Westerns of John Ford." *American Indian Culture and Research Journal*, vol. 18, no. 3 (1994): 167–86.
The writer argues that regardless of studios, writers, or national policies, John Ford's Indian-themed westerns show Indian characters holding firmly to a distinct identity and culture (although restricted to stereotypes of either the hostile warrior or the noble savage) and never fully embracing white society. After analyzing twelve Indian-themed features beginning with *The Iron Horse* in 1924 and ending forty years later with *Cheyenne Autumn* in 1964, she states "the dominant theme in Ford's dozen Indian-themed Westerns . . . is cultural and political autonomy." Notes list other studies about Ford and his Indian themes.

American Heritage Editors. "The Image Makers." In *The American Heritage Book of Indians*. New York: American Heritage Publishing Co., Inc., 1961. pp. 237–252. Illustrations.
The editors describe the distorted ideas held by Europeans about Native peoples as early as 1493 when people were influenced by letters written by Columbus. The editors look at ways the Indian image (romanticized, demonized, and vanishing, but not taken seri-

ously) influenced the new countries and peoples that came into being in the Americas through the mid-nineteenth century when "jumbled Indian images occupied the popular fancy."

American Indian Historical Society. *Textbooks and the American Indian*. San Francisco: The Indian Historian Press, 1970. Bibliography.

Thirty-two Native American scholars and students evaluated more than 300 books currently being used in elementary and high schools. They concluded that not one book could be approved as a dependable source of knowledge about the history and culture of Native people. The nine general criteria used for evaluation are listed and discussed. Categories include American History and Geography, State and Regional History, Government and Citizenship, general American Indian books, and World History and Geography.

American Indian Media Task Force, National Conference of Christians and Jews. *American Indian and the Media*. National Conference of Christians and Jews, 1991. Illustrations. Bibliography.

This handbook for journalists is intended to encourage truthful and fair journalism. A Resource Directory is included that contains lists and addresses of national tribal councils, offices for the Bureau of Indian Affairs, State Indian Commissions, and urban Indian centers.

Ames, Michael M. "Free Indians from Their Ethnological Fate: The Emergence of the Indian Point of View in Exhibitions of Indians." *Muse* (Canadian Museum Association), vol. 5, no. 2 (Summer/July 1987): 14–19.

The author reviews changes in Canada in the relations between Indians and museums and the emergence on the museum scene of the "Indian point of view" and Indians' efforts to take charge of their own cultural identities. He refutes the common notion that Indians have either disappeared or been assimilated.

Anderson, Terry L. *Sovereign Nations or Reservations: An Economic History of American Indians*. San Francisco: Pacific Research Institute, 1995. Bibliography.

The author debunks much of the romanticism surrounding American Indian culture and demonstrates that Indians developed forms of property rights, contracts, and market exchanges resembling those used by modern western cultures. He argues that poverty among Indian tribes living on reservations today is due to U.S. government policies borne of a romantic image of Indian life that does not square with the historical record.

Arnold, Ellen L. "Reframing the Hollywood Indian: A Feminist Highway and Thunderheart." In *American Indian Studies: An Interdisciplinary Approach to Contemporary Studies*. Ed. Dane Morrison, pp. 347–62. New York: Peter Lang, 1997. Notes and Bibliography.

After summarizing how revisionist Indian films released in the early 1990s are really about white men and define Indians in terms of interactions with European-Americans, the author deals with two mainstream movies, "Powwow Highway" and "Thunderheart" that make genuine attempts to raise the consciousness of audiences. She points out, however, that the two films, both within the context of the conventional Hollywood western, can be interpreted as attempts to reassert masculine values and power in the face of social and political challenges and they reinscribe women as objects and obstacles to male bonding and adventure.

Ashliman, D. L. "The American Indian in German Travel Narratives and Literature." *Journal of Popular Culture*, vol. 10, no. 4 (Spring 1977): 833–39.

The author examines two groups of German writers: German visitors and immigrants in North America who had firsthand experiences among Indians and published hundreds of travel-adventure narratives for Germans and those observers who provided both authentic and fictitious accounts. Beginning with Seume's firsthand account of Canadian Huron life in the late 1700s and Chamisso's poems about Indians, he argues that the two illustrate romantic tendencies toward noble savagery evidenced in virtually all German language fiction about Indians. He also suggests that the Indians of the travel narratives were much less idealized than those found in the fictional accounts. Based on German secondary writings, he concludes by discussing Karl May, a popular adventure novelist, who did not have a store of personal experiences, but who created stories still read today.

Baird, W. David. "The Quest for a Red-faced White Man: Reservation Whites View Their Indian Wards." In *Red Men and Hat Wearers: Viewpoints in Indian History.* Ed. Daniel Tyler, pp. 113–31. Fort Collins, CO: Colorado State University, 1976. Footnoted.
Baird analyzes four classes of white observers: military personnel "disgusted" by Native appearance and customs but who had "grudging" respect for Indians as warriors and had some ability to see the "admirable" side of Indian character; Westerners who appreciated the Indians' reluctance to part with his land; government officials who felt Indians deficient in key attributes of civilization; and reformers who had more sympathy for Indians but felt they needed to make a transition from "barbarism" to civilization. The writer looks at policies emanating from the varied viewpoints.

Bales, Fred. "Hantavirus and the Media: Double Jeopardy for Native Americans." *American Indian Culture and Research Journal*, vol. 18, no. 3 (1994): 251–63.
Bales criticizes the media in its handling of the Hantavirus illness, which had an outbreak in 1993 bringing more than death to the Navajo people. The media tagged the illness as "Navajo Flu" or "Four Corners Illness" despite the Center for Disease Control's public statements that the disease had little to do with the Navajo or was in any way confined to Navajo people. Because of the press's unrelenting coverage of Navajo communities, the Navajo people had their privacy (even their funerals) invaded and their culture was once again misrepresented. The author contends that no other viral outbreaks have been given a racist perspective and the media should be more responsible in reporting.

Banks, Marge. "Real Indians War on Our Tribe, Call Chief Wahoo Degrading." *The Cleveland Press*, 17 March 1970.
Banks describes how an organization of American Indians, CLAIM (Cleveland American Indian Movement), protested the name of the city's baseball team, the Cleveland Indians. CLAIM argued that the mascot, Chief Wahoo, was a degrading and insulting caricature that stereotyped Native Americans and should be eliminated.

Barnett, Louise K. *The Ignoble Savage: American Literary Racism 1790–1890.* Contributions in American Studies, no. 18. Westport, CT: Greenwood Press, 1975. Bibliography.
The author examines frontier romances, a genre predominantly concerned with white-Indian confrontations along the frontier as a background for the development of conventional love stories. Beginning in the 1790s and gathering momentum during the early decades of the nineteenth century, the stories declined during the decade preceding the Civil War. Barnett argues that the romances provided a more complex attitude about white-Indian relations than captivity narratives, which she places within the larger context of the struggle for possession of the continent. Describing three Indian stereotypes of pre–Civil War frontier romances: the bad Indian, the noble savage, and the

good Indian, she notes that all three images share traits such as a superb physique, proficient wilderness skills, stoicism, and figurative speech. Arguing that a subgenre of Indian-hater fiction like Hawthorne's and Melville's created Indian characters that are paradigms for racism, she concludes by discussing the failure of frontier romance as art and briefly looks at fiction written later in the century. A chronology of frontier romances and an unannotated bibliography are included.

Barry, Roxana. "Rousseau, Buffalo Bill, and the European Image of the American Indian." *Art News*, vol. 74, no. 10 (December 1975): 58–61. Illustrations.
The author discusses how American Indians were the logical choice as subject matter for European sculptors out of the French Romantic school. She compares work of Edouard Drouot, French sculptor, done around 1880 to work of French sculptors Isidore Bonheur and Alfred Barye done after 1889, the time William Cody toured Europe with his "Wild West" shows. Barry discusses the work of Carl Kauba, whose realistic works she compared with Frederic Remington and Charles Russell. She concludes by suggesting Indians were finally "too coarse" for "refined" European sculptors who abandoned the Indian at the start of the twentieth century.

Bataille, Gretchen, ed. *Asail Newsletter (Studies in American Indian Literatures)*, vol. 4, no. 1 (Winter 1980): 1–10. Bibliography.
A special issue on American Indians in film, an interview with N. Scott Momaday is included. Momaday discusses Hollywood "Indians" and his reaction to and participation in the preparation of his novel, *House Made of Dawn*, as a film. An overview of multidisciplinary courses dealing with American Indian film studies and an annotated list of articles on "Indians in the Movies" are also presented.

———. "Education and the Images of the American Indian." *Explorations in Ethnic Studies*, vol. 1, no. 1 (January 1978): 37–49.
The writer argues that curricula include American Indian history, literature, and values to provide students with concepts of pluralistic society. She argues that the misrepresentations of Indians (ignoble savages or romantic nomads of the forest) have resulted in obstacles for teachers and students who must reconcile two divergent views—those perpetuated by the media and outdated texts and materials presenting a picture closer to reality.

Bataille, Gretchen and Silet, Charles L. P. "The Entertaining Anachronism: Indians in American Film." In *The Kaleidoscope Lens: How Hollywood Views Ethnic Groups*. Ed. Randall M. Miller, pp. 36–53. Englewood, NJ: Jerome S. Ozer, Publishers, 1980. Illustrations. Notes.
The authors briefly summarize how early historical accounts about Indians that solidified Indian stereotypes by the end of the nineteenth century were transferred to the screen beginning with Edison's films in the 1890s through 1980. Of films seen during the 1960s and 1970s, they see that contemporary reviewers demonstrated a heightened awareness and questioned stereotypes appearing on the screen. Besides pointing out that more balanced views of Native people in film are not received as films about Indians, they argue that pro-Indian films of the 1970s did little to correct popular stereotypes but did provide a study of white America trying to come to grips with itself.

Bataille, Gretchen and Silet, Charles P., eds. *Images of American Indians on Film: An Annotated Bibliography*. New York: Garland Publishing, 1985.
After an historical introduction, the bibliography is divided into four sections: (1) general approaches to Indians as seen by whites, (2) general film studies of Indians, (3) re-

views and essays on single films, and (4) selected sound films including Indians as subjects. The second section contains references to comprehensive listings. The index lists titles, directors, and actors.

―――――. *The Pretend Indians: Images of Native Americans in the Movies.* Ames: Iowa State University Press, 1980. Illustrated. Bibliography.

This volume contains a collection of essays that discuss the myths, stereotypes, and absurdities perpetuated through the visual media about Native Americans from the earliest movies to contemporary times. Several Indian voices are included as well as reasons why white Americans have demanded distortions of Indian cultures. Film reviews, a chronological photographic essay, and an annotated checklist of articles and books on the popular images of Indians in American film are all presented.

Bean, Lowell John. "The Language of Stereotype, Distortion and Inaccuracy." *The Indian Historian,* vol. 2, no. 3 (Fall 1969): 6–11. Illustrated. Bibliography.

The writer provides a detailed exposition of a book entitled *California Indian Days* by Helen Bauer (Doubleday & Co., 1958; revised, 1968) as an example of the means by which distorted and factually incorrect images of the California Indians persist. This book was selected because it was widely used in California for fourth grade students and because of its distorted/stereotypical and incomplete information.

Becenti, Deenise. "Native Images Remain Out of Focus." *ICE: Indian Cinema Entertainment,* vol. 2, no. 3 (Summer 1994): 11.

The writer summarizes concerns of Native actors, producers, writers, and directors who gathered at the June "Imagining Indians: Native American Film & Video Festival" in Scottsdale, Arizona. She quotes (and discusses the belief expressed by) Sandy Johnson Osawa, Makah filmmaker, who says: "Somebody else has been telling the world who we are and what we are all about. . . ."

Beider, Peter. "Scientific Attitudes toward Indian Mixed Bloods in Early 19th Century America." *Journal of Ethnic Studies,* vol. 8, no. 2 (Summer 1980): 17–30. Bibliography.

The writer delineates a shift in attitude of monogenists (who saw mankind as one species derived from a single pair) from a positive belief in capabilities of Indian mixed-bloods (descended from Indians and Europeans) to discouragement over their lack of "progress." Beider explores the ascendancy after 1830 of the polygenists (who saw various races as separate acts of creation) who attacked the potential of mixed-bloods to adjust into American society. By the 1850s, they feel mixed-bloods, who identified with Indian tribes rather than American society, were no different from Indians and were headed for extinction.

Berkhofer, Robert F. Jr. "White Conceptions of Indians." In *Handbook of North American Indians,* vol. 4. Ed. Wilcomb E. Washborn, pp. 522–47. Washington, D.C.: Smithsonian Institution, 1988.

The author looks at early European nomenclature and imagery and persisting white presuppositions about Indians including the "good" and "bad" Indian in literature and ideology. He touches on explanations from anthropologists to environmentalists to scientific racists concluding with imagery being used to justify white policy.

―――――. *The White Man's Indian: Images of the American Indian from Columbus to the Present.* New York: Alfred A. Knopf, Inc., 1978. Illustrated.

The author examines how the white image of the Indian developed over time in order to understand the present perception of Indians. He argues that this examination tells more about white societies and intellectual premises over five centuries of contact than it does about the diversities of Native Americans. Science, the arts, and government policies are all touched on. Lengthy notes provide a comprehensive bibliography.

Berkman, Brenda. "The Vanishing Race: Conflicting Images of the American Indian in Children's Literature, 1880–1930." *North Dakota Quarterly*, vol. 44, no. 2 (Spring 1976): 31–50.

The writer analyzes two different images of American Indians presented in children's literature between 1880 and 1930: the "savage Indian" and the "noble Indian." She delineates both adult attitudes of the period and the kinds of predispositions about Native Americans that were being passed on to children. Focusing on five writers of popular fiction (Stoddard, Brooks, Altsheler, Grinnell, and Schultz), Berkman includes footnotes based on their works.

Berry, Brewton. "The Myth of the Vanishing Indian." *Phylon*, vol. 2, no. 1 (Spring 1960): 51–57.

The author counters centuries of myths that Indians were doomed and disappearing and looks at statements of politicians either rejoicing or lamenting the inevitable extinction of Indians. Besides looking at reasons for doubting the dire predictions, he discusses the routing of the KKK by Lumbee Indians in Robeson County, North Carolina, on January 18, 1958. He explains why census figures do not tell the whole story about Indian populations.

Berson, Misha. "Native American Images: Stage and Screen Reflect More Indians, But Has Picture Really Changed?" *ICE: Indian Cinema Entertainment*, vol. 2, no. 2 (Spring 1994): 6–7.

The writer reviews movie and television productions underway marking a new chapter in increased Indian participation, points out some success stories in theater and movies, but observes that Hollywood still favors stories about the bloody, action-packed Indian wars over human-interest stories about Native life today.

Beuf, Ann H. *Red Children in White America*. Philadelphia: University of Pennsylvania Press, 1977. Bibliography.

Discussing a study of 117 Native American children from 3 different unnamed communities, ages 3 to 5, this author shares how racism even affects children who have little interaction with whites. There is a statement of the research problem and a description of the study's sample, methodology, and results. Also, an analysis of the implications of the experiment and an extensive bibliography of sources on psychology, sociology, ethnology, and history are provided.

Bidney, Donald. "The Idea of the Savage in North America Ethnohistory." *Journal of History of Ideas*, vol. 15, no. 2 (April 1954): 322–27.

In a review of J. H. Kennedy's *Jesuit and Savage in New France* and Roy H. Pearce's *The Savages of America*, the writer shows how each writer dealt with the concept of savage. Kennedy showed how Jesuits, who took a scholarly interest in Indians, their languages, and cultures, wrote reports from 1632 to 1674 that formed the European concept of the noble savage who required Christian gospel to humanize his conduct. The writer argues against the theory of savagism determining colonial attitudes and critiques Pearce for not dealing with historical and sociological conditions prevailing in late-eighteenth-century America. Land hunger, a growing population, and economic development led colonists to view Indians as obstacles to expansion, the writer concludes.

Billington, Ray Allen. *Land of Savagery, Land of Promise: The European Image of the American Frontier in the Nineteenth Century*. New York: W. W. Norton & Co., 1981. Illustrated. Bibliography.

This work deals with European literature of the eighteenth and nineteenth centuries and the way in which Indians were portrayed. The "hostile" Indian, "barbaric" Indian, "noble" Indian, and "disappearing" Indian are images that are addressed. The bibliography is divided topically and deals with the frontier image before and after the nineteenth century, novelists and travelers as imagemakers, the frontier image and immigrations, the image in promotional literature, the impact of the image on Europe, and the persisting image.

———. "The Wild West in Norway, 1877." *Western Historical Quarterly*, vol. 7, no. 3 (July 1976): 271–78.
The writer discusses the impact of James Fenimore Cooper and his Leatherstocking Tales on European writers who turned out westerns "at a furious pace." He gives extracts from a play entitled *The Frontiersman's Daughter: A Play in Three Acts* written by P. M. Peterson, a Norwegian, which reveals the image of Indians in Norway and the rest of Europe in the nineteenth century.

Bird, S. Elizabeth. *Dressing in Feathers: The Construction of the Indian in American Popular Culture.* Boulder, CO: Westview Press, 1996. Illustrations. Bibliography.
The author has collected historical and sociological studies by academic contributors that show how whites have portrayed Native Americans in a wide range of media for the last two centuries. Essays deal with photographic images taken of Sitting Bull following his surrender, nineteenth-century advertising, Native images in early cinema up to "Dances with Wolves," representations of Indians in southern history, Florida Seminoles on display for tourists, the national monument at the Battlefield of the Little Bighorn, how news frames Native conflicts, sexual images of the Native male, cultural heritage in "Northern Exposure," and Indian imagery in "Dr. Quinn, Medicine Woman."

Bissel, Benjamin. *The American Indian in English Literature of the Eighteenth Century.* Yale Studies in English, vol. 68. New Haven: Yale University Press, 1925. Illustrated.
The writer gives a brief survey of some of the early sixteenth-century histories, descriptions of voyages and travels, and various miscellaneous writings in which Indians are described, and he analyzes which aspects of their character were admired and why. He addresses the movement to romanticize American Indian cultures. There are several illustrations that indicate the aesthetic concepts of Indians. Footnotes and an appendix that contains "The Four Indian Kings" are included.

Black, Nancy B. and Weidman, Bette S. *White on Red: Images of the American Indian.* Port Washington, NY: Kennikat Press, 1976.
The authors draw together literary treatments of North American Indians by whites and arrange them chronologically roughly from the settlement of Virginia in 1607 to the 1890 Battle of Wounded Knee. Throughout, headnotes place the excerpts in the context of the whole works from which they are taken.

Blanche, Jerry D. "Ignoring It Won't Make It Go Away." *Journal of American Indian Education,* vol. 12, no. 1 (October 1972): 1–4.
Blanche, a Choctaw, discusses how American Indians have been misrepresented or ignored in history books and courses and suggests ample material is available to rescind the discriminatory practice.

Bolz, Peter. "More Questions Than Answers: Frank Rinehart's Photographs of American Indians." *European Review of Native American Studies,* vol. 8, no. 2 (1994): 35–43. Illustrations.
Rinehart photographed hundreds of Indian delegates representing dozens of tribes who attended the Omaha Exposition in 1898. Illustrations in the article show staged and in-

authentic portraits: Indians wearing the same war shirt, using the same bandolier bag over their shoulder and quiver of arrows hanging on their back, and holding the same bow in their hands. These contrived identical outfits blurred tribal identification and resulted in exotic images that satisfied the demands of the marketplace.

Bosmajian, Haig. "The Language of Indian Derision." In *The Language of Oppression.* Washington, D.C.: Public Affairs Press, 1974. pp. 62–89.

The author discusses how linguistic racism categorized Indians into "beasts," "savages," and "uncivilized" for the past 500 years. Covering everything from boarding school practices to judicial language, he contends that linguistic racism has dehumanized Native peoples.

Bowker, Ardy. "Racism and Stereotyping in Native America." In *Sisters in the Blood: The Education of Women in Native America.* Bozeman: Center for Bilingual/Multicultural Education, Montana State University and Newton, MA: WEEA Publishing Center, 1993. pp. 29–42.

Bowker examines various stereotypes and their origins, including the "vanishing" race; American Indians as artists and athletes, and as welfare wards of the government; the "drunken" Indian, the "princess," or the "squaw"; and the Indian of the media. He addresses the Indians' image of themselves closely linked to white stereotypes of Indians, the way past negative stereotypes continue to promote current ones, and stereotypical views of teachers and others who worked with Indian populations in schools.

Bowker, Lee H. "Red and Black in Contemporary American History Texts: A Content Analysis." In *Native Americans Today Sociological Perspectives.* Eds. Howard M. Bahr, Bruce A. Chadwick, and Robert C. Day, pp. 1–110. New York: Harper and Row, 1972.

This study systematically examines the treatment of American Indians and Blacks in sixty-seven contemporary American history texts published in the 1960s to determine the nature and extent of the coverage of American Indians and Blacks. There are seven tables of data and notes.

Braroe, Niels Winther. *Indian and White: Self-Image and Interaction in a Canadian Plains Community.* Stanford: Stanford University Press, 1975. Illustrations. Bibliography.

Although a major part of this study is how Short Grass Indians (a small Canadian Prairie community) maintain positive self-images, the author addresses their adjustment to the fact that their moral worth is denied by whites. He explains why Indians hide their traditional culture and allow themselves to be seen in stereotypical roles.

Brascoupe, Simon. "What Is an Indian? What Is a Stereotype?" *Turtle* (Native American Center for the Living Arts, Niagara Falls, NY), vol. 3, no. 2 (Summer 1981): 2–3.

The author briefly looks at the popular image of North American Indians in movies, art, and literature. He also looks at the past and present terms used to designate "Indian" in the United States and Canada.

Brauer, Ralph and Brauer, Donna. "Indians, Blacks, Mexicans, Old People, Long Hairs and Other Assorted Deviants." In *The Horse, the Gun, and the Piece of Property. Changing Images of the TV Western.* Bowling Green, Ohio: Bowling Green University Popular Press, 1975. pp. 171–94.

In a portion of this chapter, the writers discuss Indians of TV westerns and argue that they are deviants who represent a threat to certain values and themes and that they are so different that we cannot possibly understand them. Several examples of shows are cited.

Briggs, Harold. "Indians!: Native Opera Romanticized the American Savage." *Opera News,* vol. 40, no. 23 (June 1976): 22–24, 51.

The writer describes the 1910 premiere of Arthur Nevin's opera "Poia," at the Royal Opera, Berlin—one of many operas written in the early twentieth century on American Indian topics. Nevin spent two summers (1903–1904) at Montana's Blackfeet Reservation collecting melodies, six of which he incorporated into his "all-Indian" opera. The writer gives background information on "Natoma" (premiered February 25, 1911, in Philadelphia), "Shanewis" (premiered March 23, 1918), and "Oglala: A Romance of the Mesa," (1924) and summarizes stage works that appeared from 1900 to 1930.

Brownlow, Kevin. *The War, the West and the Wilderness.* New York: Alfred A. Knopf, 1979. pp. 327–38.
The author contends that early filmmakers cared a lot more for Indians than people gave them credit for and supports his stand with several film critiques and history, most filmed before 1917. He tells of some early Indian actors and there are photographs.

Buffalohead, Priscilla. "The Minnesota State Seal." *Osseo American Indian Education News*, Spring 1997: 14–15.
The author discusses how the Minnesota State seal misrepresents the true history of the Native experience in the state as well as the history of the origins of agriculture in Minnesota.

Butterfield, Nancy. "Squaw Image Stereotyping." In *Words of Today's American Indian Women: Ohoyo Makachi: A First Collection of Oratory by American Indian/Alaska Native Women.* Comp. by Ohoyo Resource Center Staff, pp. 20–24. Wichita Falls, TX: Ohoyo Resource Center, 1981.
The author briefly describes media images of Indian women and counters with a discussion of the roles of Indian women in the past.

Calder, Jenni. "Taming the Natives." In *There Must Be A Lone Ranger.* London: Hamish Hamilton, 1974. pp. 38–57. Illustrated. Bibliography.
The author examines the myth of the American West from the end of the Civil War to the end of the nineteenth century and looks at the ways in which Indians have become imaginary figures in films. There is a bibliography of contemporary accounts and memories, nonfiction, and fiction about the nineteenth-century West.

Caweti, John G. "Cowboys, Indians, and Outlaws: The West in Myth and Fantasy." *American West*, vol. 1, no. 2 (Spring 1964): 28–35, 77–79. Illustrated.
The writer discusses the "western" as it is known in novels, movies and television and the elaboration of the image of the West created by the Wild West show of Buffalo Bill and the dime novels of the late nineteenth century. There are photographs of Wild West Shows, dime novels, and TV programs. There is a selected, annotated bibliography on westerns and popular culture, the myth, westerns and the media, western heroes, and humor and western "classics" and their authors.

Cembalest, Robin. "Pride and Prejudice." *Art News* (February 1992): 86–90.
The author gives a brief overview of the contemporary Indian art world. She discusses the pejorative images in American art of the nineteenth century and explains the problems facing contemporary Native American artists.

Charles, Jim. "For the Sake of a Fad: The Misrepresentation of American Indians and Their Literature in High School Literature Anthologies." *Journal of Ethnic Studies*, vol. 15, no. 2 (Summer 1987): 131–40.
Charles analyzed the content of American Indian literary selections in North Carolina's high school anthologies and argues that when considered collectively, they do not represent tribal diversity or the literary genre Indian people produce. He contends that "textbook bias against American Indians is alive and well today."

Churchill, Ward. "Fantasies of the Master Race: Categories of Stereotyping of American Indians in Film." In *Fantasies of the Master Race.* Ed. Annette Jaimes, pp. 231–41. Monroe, ME: Common Courage Press, 1992.

The author deconstructs and analyzes the various ways in which movies distort and protract already distorted images of Native Americans. He cites three main problems: movies do not show Indians in their historical experience; European values are the only ones in which Indians are understood, and they are therefore misrepresented; and cinematic representations, even when they attempt to be accurate and sympathetic, are too often mixtures of many different and separate Indian cultures.

———. *Fantasies of the Master Race: Literature, Cinema, and the Colonization of American Indians.* Revised ed. San Francisco: City Lights, 1998.

The author exposes some of the subtler manipulations of Native American culture in this revised edition of his 1992 collection.

———. "Hi Ho, Hillerman . . . (Away): Unmasking the Role of Detective Fiction in Indian Country." In *Fantasies of the Master Race.* Ed. Annette Jaimes, pp. 249–88. Monroe, ME: Common Courage Press, 1992.

The author criticizes detective writer Tony Hillerman for his novels set in Navajo and Hopi country and his two Indian policeman (both heroes), Leaphorn and Chee. Churchill contends that Hillerman created Indian characters that are based on white values rather than Indian ones and that many problems on the reservations are completely ignored.

———. *Indians Are Us? Culture and Genocide in Native North America.* Monroe, ME: Common Courage Press, 1994.

The writer examines the nature of genocide and discusses the covert genocide, both political and cultural, that has been occurring in the United States throughout its history. He covers U.S. reticence in ratifying the Genocide Convention of 1948 and its continuing wavering stance on genocide and gives a history of atrocities committed against Native North Americans for the last 500 years. The mascot issue, the American Indian Movement, the Men's Movement, and the "New Age" exploitation of Indian culture are all addressed.

Churchill, Ward; Hill, Norbert; and Hill, Mary Ann. "Media, Stereotyping and Native Response: An Historical Overview." *Indian Historian,* vol. 11, no. 4 (December 1978): 45–56, 63. Bibliography. Reprinted in Bataille, Gretchen and Silet, Charles L. P., eds., 35–48.

The authors review and discuss the functions of stereotypical misrepresentations in the U.S. media of Native American peoples who participated in spectacles such as Buffalo Bill Cody's Wild West Show and who left a legacy of Indians as objects and entertainment rather than as entertainers. They address three areas of stereotyping: "The Native as a creature of a particular time," "Native cultures interpreted through white values," and "Seen one Indian seen 'em all." A bibliography of sources regarding the media is included.

Coen, Rena Neumann. *The Indian as the Noble Savage in Nineteenth Century American Art.* 2 vols. Ph.D. dissertation, University of Minnesota, 1969; Ann Arbor MI: University Microfilms, Inc., 1970. Bibliography.

The purpose of this work is to demonstrate that the romantic concept of the noble savage was an essential part of the cultural background of American artists of the nineteenth century, that it had European antecedents, and that it affected their attitudes and paintings and sculptures of Indians. Volume two contains plates of 115 illustrations drawn from the works of painters and sculptors discussed. There is a bibliography of books, exhibition catalogs, and manuscript materials.

Cohen, Jeff and Solomon, Norman. "Glimmers of History: Improve Coverage of Native Americans." *EXTRA!* (January/February 1995): 15.

The writers commend CNN for its series, "The Invisible People," a program dealing with a variety of subjects about Native Americans. Some of the programs include treaty rights, hunting and fishing rights, and religious freedom. The authors hope that this will be a trend and not just a passing fad.

Cooper, Karen C. "I is for Indian: Basic Reference Materials—Where It All Begins." *The Eagle Wing Press,* vol. 7, no. 3 (June–July 1988): 2.

This western Cherokee author argues that widespread ignorance about Indians is due in part to "Sources of information such as reference books [that] lie and misrepresent details about us." She looks at several dictionaries and one reference encyclopedia to document her case.

———. "The Supermarket Wars." *Eagle Wing Press,* vol. 6, no. 2 (Early Summer 1986): 2, 20. Illustrations.

Cooper criticizes business for exploiting Indian images and perpetuating stereotypes. She writes, "Stereotypes carry extensive meanings. If a picture is worth a thousand words, a stereotyped picture is worth ten-thousand words." She contends that although these offensive pictures sell products, "Do Indians, who pay dearly for all this stereotyped information, get a cut of the net profits? No."

———. "When 'One Little' Is Too Much." *The Eagle,* vol. 9, no. 1 (January–February 1991): 3.

Cooper points out that Native American people have been objectified in everything from advertising to children's songs to sports teams and it is unsurpassed by objectification of any other ethnic group. She argues that the brainwashing against the true culture of Indians is so endemic that sometimes Native American people are not even able to recognize the harm it has done them.

Cornstock, W. Richard. "On Seeing With the Eye of the Native European." In *Seeing With a Native Eye: Essays on Native American Religion.* Ed. Walter Holden Capps, pp. 58–78. New York: Harper and Row, 1976.

The author discusses the refusal of Europeans to see Native Americans in factual terms, but rather their insistence on seeing them through the eyes of myth and legend. He recounts the number of significant portrayals of Native Americans by "native Europeans." Using the cinema, he chronicles the recent shift in imagery.

Costo, Rupert. "Errors Multiply in Smithsonian Handbook." *Indian Historian,* vol. 12, no. 3 (1979): 2–5.

The writer explains, with examples drawn from the text, why the *Handbook of North American Indians, California,* volume 8 in the Smithsonian Institution project of twenty volumes, has a "hodgepodge of old and new material."

———. "Fact from Fiction." *Indian Historian,* vol. 10, no. 1 (Winter 1977): 31–36.

The writer discusses instructional materials of publishing houses that contain sheer falsifications of Indian history, either intentionally or through ignorance.

Cracroft, Richard H. "The American West of Karl May." *American Quarterly,* vol. 19, no. 2, part 1 (Summer 1967): 249–58.

The author discusses May's image of the American West, which the German really never saw, tells of May's life, and analyzes May's treatment of Indians and his use of authentic anthropological fact blended with imaginative detail into tales that lacked literary realism. Cracroft compares James Fenimore Cooper with May.

Crum, Steven. "Making Indians Disappear." *Tribal College*, vol. 4, no. 3 (Winter 1993): 28–31.

Crum criticizes two noted American historians, Frederick Jackson Turner and Arthur M. Schlesinger Jr., on their treatment of Native issues. The Turner thesis of 1893, celebrating the settlement of the free and unused West as of 1890 as a symbol of democracy and individualism, is obviously rejected by the author, an Indian historian. The author debates Schlesinger's opposition to multicultural approaches to American History.

"Dartmouth Loses Its Indian Mascot." *New York Times*, 12 October 1969, sec. 1, 78.

The article discusses how a few Native American undergraduates at Dartmouth College successfully challenged the concept of an Indian as the college's cheerleader mascot. See entry under Kleiman, Dena.

Deloria, Philip J. "Mascots and Other Public Appropriations of Indians and Indian Culture by Whites." In *Encyclopedia of North American Indians*. Ed. Frederick E. Hoxie, pp. 359–61. New York: Houghton Mifflin, 1996.

The author argues that Indian chiefs and braves represented the aggressiveness and fighting spirit that was supposed to characterize good athletic teams. The performative aspects of mascot ritual of the Florida State Seminole and other professional sports clubs bring the American narrative of peaceful cowboys and settlers defending themselves against aggressive Indians to life. The author traces the history of Native reaction to the use of Indian mascots from the 1950s to the 1990s and also describes how environmentalists and communitarians appropriated new meanings for Indians. He concludes that the continual use of Indians as an American symbol has raised serious questions and dilemmas for Native people.

———. *Playing Indian*. New Haven: Yale University Press, 1998. Illustrations.

There have been thousands of books, essays, articles and ethnographies written about Indians and "Indianness." In this book, the author introduces ideas about how "Indianness" has profoundly directed the American experience and influenced it at almost every turn. He examines the Boston Tea Party, the Order of Red Men, Camp Fire Girls, Boy Scouts, Grateful Dead concerts, and other examples of the American tendency to appropriate Indian dress and act out Indian roles. He explores how white Americans have used their ideas about Indians to shape national identity in different eras and how Indian people have reacted to these imitations of their Native dress, language, and ritual. He also points out that throughout American history the creative uses of Indianness have been interwoven with conquest and dispossession of the Indians.

Deloria, Vine, Jr. "The American Indian Image in North America." In *Encyclopedia of Indians of the Americas*, vol. 1. St. Clair Shores, MI: Scholarly Press, 1974. pp. 40–44. Reprinted in Bataille, Gretchen M. and Silet, Charles L. P., eds., 49–54.

The author discusses the image of the Indian as held by white people and the image that the Indians hold of themselves. He gives some opinions on the problems that stereotyping by whites and the Indians' image of themselves cause.

DesJarlait, Robert. *Rethinking Stereotypes: Native American Imagery in Non-Native Visual Art and Illustrations*. Coon Rapids, MN: Anoka-Hennepin Indian Education Program, 1993.

A powerful introduction of the author's experiences with names hurled at him as a child and adult is followed by a discussion of 500 years of invented visual images of Native

Americans. He gives special attention to how photography and picture postcards in the 1920s transformed whole tribes (notably the Minnesota Chippewa) into "bastardized Plains-styled cultures" and how postcards gave the "impetus for the development of an invented Ojibway present." He focuses attention on two practitioners of western art—Chuck Ren and Michael Gentry—who paint historic Indians in fictional clothing. He also tells how Brenda K. Grummer, a "Native artist," incorrectly uses contemporary clothing in historical Indian paintings. He concludes with a protest against use of team mascots, logos, and names. One section deals with stereotypes in children's illustrations.

Dickason, Olive Patricia. "Part 1: American Discoverers and European Images." In *The Myth of the Savage: And the Beginnings of French Colonialism in the Americas.* Edmonton, Alberta: University of Alberta Press, 1984. pp. 3–84.

The author looks at the processes of identifying American Indians with savages on the level of ideology as well as that of popular mythology. Part 1 deals with the development of European beliefs about and attitudes toward American Indians.

Dixon, Susan. "Images of Indians: Controlling the Camera." *Northwest Indian Quarterly* (Cornell University), vol. 4, nos. 1–2 (Spring/Summer 1987): 23–27.

The author discusses the stereotypical images of European artists, chroniclers, colonists, and "images today from the cameras of the white world [that] still betray ambivalence and anxiety." She tells how Native photographers have begun to use the medium their own way. She refers to exhibitions of Native photographs that communicate "motion, action, and relationships."

Dixon, Susan R. "Indians, Cowboys, and the Language of Museums." *Akwe:kon Journal,* vol. 9, no. 1 (Spring 1992).

The author discusses the immense controversy surrounding the 1991 exhibit, "West as America," at the National Museum of American Art. The exhibit comprised nineteenth-century paintings of the frontier, many of them romanticizing the spirit of westward expansion, but the focus was to point out the fallacies of these images and to challenge the prevailing view that the Old West was all glory and adventure. The exhibit's creators were severely criticized. Dixon stresses the need to present revisionist views to the public in a responsible fashion so as not to undermine their intended effectiveness.

Dockstader, Frederick J., comp. *The American Indian in Graduate Schools: A Bibliography of Theses and Dissertations.* Contributions from the Museum of the American Indian, Heye Foundation, vol. 15. New York: Museum of the American Indian, Heye Foundation, 1957; supplement, 1973.

This uncritical bibliography lists over 3,500 theses and dissertations that deal in any way with North, Central, and South American Indians and Inuits as presented for graduate degree requirements at 203 colleges and universities in the United States, Canada, and Mexico from 1890 to 1973. Image studies are listed under "Fiction," "Literature," and "Literature in Spanish, French and German." There is a topical index.

Dorris, Michael. "Indians on the Shelf." In *The American Indian and the Problem of History.* Ed. Calvin Martin, pp. 98–105. New York: Oxford University Press, 1987.

The author, a Modoc Indian, discusses worldwide mythic perceptions of Indians and suggests that for most people, "the myth has become real and a preferred substitute for ethnographic reality." He argues that people must begin the "quest of regarding them [Indians] as human beings."

———. "Why I'm NOT Thankful for Thanksgiving." *Interracial Books for Children Bulletin,* vol. 9, no. 7 (1978): 6–9. Illustrated.

In an essay, this Native American parent explains why he is not thankful about the American version of Thanksgiving because he feels it is one of the peak periods for displays of Native American stereotypes. He suggests children must be protected from racism, which "is every bit as important as insuring that they avoid playing with electrical sockets." There is a selection of Indian imagery, mostly of greeting cards.

Dorsey, Valerie Lynn. "Indian Mascots Still Sensitive Debate: What's in a Nickname?" *USA Today*, 23 October 1991. pp. 6A, 6C.
Dorsey gives a brief history of the conflict around naming mascots and teams after ethnic groups, especially American Indian groups. She lists state-by-state high school team nicknames that could be considered offensive.

Doxtator, Deborah. *Fluffs and Feathers: An Exhibit on the Symbols of Indianness: A Resource Guide*. Brantford, Ont.: Woodland Cultural Center, 1988. Illustrations. Bibliography.
This exhibition catalog contains articles that discuss the range of Indian images in historical and contemporary Canadian society. The long history of the public's fascination with Indians is attributed to Wild West shows, museum exhibitions, and Indians captured and displayed in Europe. The articles look at Canadian cultural expressions of non-Indian "Indianness," Indians in books and film and in children's toys, the use of Indian symbols in advertisements, and the role of Indians in history in which Indians are placed in peripheral roles of savages and a vanquished disappearing race.

Durham, Jimmie. "Cowboys and . . . : Notes on Art, Literature, and American Indians in the Modern American Mind." In *The State of Native America*. Ed. Annette Jaimes, pp. 123–38. Boston: South End Press, 1992.
The author seeks to describe and account for the tendency of Westerners to overlook Indians and other indigenous groups as existing, living, contemporary people. He reviews products, films, and books that use Indian themes and stereotypes; outlines and contrasts similar treatments from Latin America; and concludes with an account of how Indian art is being appropriated by a larger, insensitive art market.

Edgerton, Gary. "A Breed Apart: Hollywood, Racial Stereotyping, and the Promise of Revisionism in *The Last of the Mohicans*." *Journal of American Culture*, vol. 17. no. 2 (Summer 1994): 1–17.
The writer looks at complex reasons why *The Last of the Mohicans* has endured as a popular adventure for more than a century and a half and has been a popular source of material for film producers since the beginnings of Hollywood. The American film industry has adapted *Mohicans* at least eleven times. He analyzes the absence of women, violence, implicit cynicism about the mixing of races, and lack of an in-depth portrayal of Indian life and culture in the film. He argues the film replaces "the pernicious distortion of the old Hollywood Indians" with a "fading Native American presence altogether" and "opts for romance and nostalgia." Illustrated with photographs. Bibliography.

Ellison, Harlan. "15 January '71—The Red Man's Burden: Part One" and "29 January '71—The Red Man's Burden: Part Two." In *The Other Glass Teat: Further Essays of Opinion*. New York: Pyramid Books, 1975. pp. 335–45.
The writer discusses how TV portrays Indians and TV's responsibility in presenting little of the more involved aspects of the American Indian history or struggles for survival. He discusses what infuriates Indians the most—that Indians rarely play Indians. In the second essay, he considers the reality of Indian life in the late twentieth century and then discusses the beauty and accuracy of NET's "Trail of Tears." He also lists things that Indians find offensive about portrayals of themselves on TV.

Ewers, John, C. "An Anthropologist Looks at Early Pictures of North American Indians." *New York Historical Society Quarterly*, vol. 33, no. 4 (October 1949): 223–34. Illustrated. Ewers outlines briefly the most common differences in facial appearance between Indians and whites. He then looks at early pictures, from an anthropologist's viewpoint, created by those artists who had historically proven firsthand knowledge of Indians: Jacques Le Moyne de Morgues, John White, and A. De Batz and examines their degree of success in recreating the faces.

———. "Fact and Fiction in the Documentary Art of the American West." In *The Frontier Re-examined*. Ed. John McDermott, pp. 79–95. Urbana: University of Illinois Press, 1968. Illustrated.
The author discusses how the drawings and paintings that portray the American West as it was before the disappearance of the frontier are documents worthy of critical study. He argues that many of the works by the artists have value as pictorial documents. He briefly but critically considers how different artists represented a few themes that appear repeatedly in the art of the Old West from the buffalo chase to Indian attacks on wagon trains to the Indian portrait. He offers five criteria for selecting pictures of the past.

———. "The Static Images." In *Look to the Mountaintop*. Ed. Robert Iocopi, pp. 107–9. San Jose: Gousha Publications, 1972. Reprinted in Bataille, Gretchen M. and Silet, Charles L. P., eds., 16–21.
The writer discusses several elements in the most common stereotypes of Native Americans including clothing, housing, pottery, and jewelry. He contends that the white culture has accepted Plains Indians as the symbol of Indianness and that this kind of thinking is static and prevents people from realizing the richness and variety of Indian life in North America.

Fairchild, Hoxie Neal. *The Noble Savage: A Study in Romantic Naturalism*. New York: Columbia University Press, 1928. Bibliography.
The author examines the attitudes of and use by French and British writers of romantic naturalism from 1730 to 1830 of the Noble Savage (Indians, "Negroes," and South Sea Islanders), defining Noble Savage as "any free and wild being who draws directly from nature virtues which raise doubts as to the value of civilization." He covers how the Noble Savage idea results from the fusion of three elements: explorers' observations, classical and medieval conventions, and philosophers' deductions. He examines the Early Romantic period and also touches on Rousseau, Jacobinism, Wordsworth, Coleridge, Southey, Johnson, Campbell, and Moore. There is a list of sources drawn on for the study.

Feest, Christian F. "The Indian in Non-English Literature." In *Handbook of North American Indians*, vol. 4, ed. Wilcomb E. Washburn, pp. 582–86. Washington, D.C.: Smithsonian Institution, 1988.
The author looks at the "small but at times influential role" of North American Indians and Eskimos in French, German, and other non-English literature.

Ferguson, Maxel J. "Native Americans in Elementary School Social Studies Textbooks." *Journal of American Indian Education*, vol. 23, no. 2 (January 1984): 10–15.
A quantitative study of the treatment of Native Americans in thirty-four elementary textbooks, grades K-7, shows that key concepts were badly neglected, especially contemporary Indians and issues in their lives; that the use of biased language was minimal; and that illustrations of Native Americans in selected texts concentrated on the past.

Fiedler, Leslie A. "The Indian in Literature in English." In *Handbook of North American Indians,* vol. 4, ed. Wilcomb E. Washburn, pp. 573–81. Washington, D.C.: Smithsonian Institution, 1988.
The author looks at literary works in English by "white American authors that attempt to describe Indian life from an Indian point of view." He looks at the Pocahontas myth in literature, at eighteenth- and nineteenth-century American fiction and at twentieth-century writers of Indian and non-Indian heritage.

———. *The Return of the Vanishing American.* New York: Stein and Day, 1968.
The author covers the classic and new westerns that have been written, analyzing the myths that the older forms contain about Indian-white confrontations, Pocahontas images, and so forth, and the alterations of these myths in the new westerns. He also considers the portrayals of Pocahontas by American writers from Mark Twain to Arthur Miller.

Fienup-Riordan, Ann. *Freeze Frame: Alaska Eskimos in the Movies.* Seattle: University of Washington Press, 1995. Illustrations. Bibliography.
The author examines representations of Alaska Eskimos in nearly a century of film, from the pioneering documentaries of missionaries and Arctic explorers, and what these nonfiction films said and did not say about Alaska Eskimos, to Eskimo Pie commercials of the 1990s. She shows how Eskimos more often are represented as "pure primitives" in opposition to "savage Indians." She details the history of Hollywood representations of Eskimos, Alaska Eskimo participation in the construction of documentary and ethnographic film, and the media revolution in the last two decades and its impact on Alaska's first people. The author reviews the half-dozen feature films made in Alaska in the early 1990s as well as current Yup'ik and Iñupiat involvement in film and video production.

———. "Yup'ik Warfare and the Myth of the Peaceful Eskimo." In *Eskimo Essays.* New Brunswick, NY: Rutgers University Press, 1990. pp. 146–66.
The author contrasts the traditional notion of the peaceful Eskimo with an overview of Yup'ik aggression. She explains the origin of the stereotype and provides a description of Yup'ik warfare. In conclusion, the author evaluates the harm of this singular stereotype.

———. "The Yupiit Nation: Eskimo Law and Order." In *Eskimo Essays.* New Brunswick, NJ: Rutgers University Press, 1990. pp. 192–220.
The author traces the origins of the Yupiit Nation against the backdrop of traditional stereotypes and presents an overview of traditional law and order based on the testimony of Yupiit Nation Elders.

Fiorentino, Daniele. "'Those Red-Brick Faces': European Press Reaction to the Indians of Buffalo Bill's Wild West Show." In *Indians and Europe: An Interdisciplinary Collection of Essays.* Ed. Christian F. Feest. Aachen, Germany: Edition Herodot, 1987.
The writer examines the mixture of scientific interpretation of Indian culture used by the press to edify the public and the repetition of popular stereotypes that confirmed prevailing popular attitudes toward Indians. The depth of European sympathy for the Indians was reflected in some press accounts about the mistreatment of the Indians on the tour. Ultimately, however, condescension toward the Indians superseded empathy. The press portrayed Indians as both bestial and immature, reinforcing European views of their own cultural superiority.

Fisher, Frank L. "Influences of Reading and Discussion on the Attitudes of Fifth Graders Toward American Indians."*Journal of Education Research*, vol. 62, no. 3 (November 1969): 130–34. Bibliography.

The writer describes the results of a study that reading literature changes children's attitudes and that discussion following reading increases the attitude change. Done with eighteen fifth grade classes representing three different socioeconomic areas of Berkeley, California, the study found that attitudes in the reading groups were changed more than the attitudes in the control groups and reading and discussion changed attitudes more than reading alone. There are secondary sources cited as well as test procedures and analysis.

Fisher, Laura. "All Chiefs, No Indians: What Children's Books Say About American Indians." *Elementary English*, vol. 51 (February 1974): 185–89. Bibliography.

The writer summarizes how the mass of literature for children about American Indians conveys false impressions and reinforces stereotyped images and misconceptions about Indians such as their living only in the past, having no sense of humor, and routinely murdering people. There is a bibliography of children's books about Indians.

FitzGerald, Frances. *America Revised: History Schoolbooks in the Twentieth Century.* Boston: Atlantic/Little, Brown and Co., 1979. pp. 89–93. Bibliography.

The author briefly describes the treatment of North American Indians in the texts of the 1830s-1840s, the Civil War era, the 1890s, the 1930s, and 1960s. She feels that the earlier texts have more enlightened attitudes than the later ones. A bibliography of nineteenth- and twentieth-century U.S. textbooks and secondary sources is included.

Fontana, Bernard L. "Savage Anthropologists and Unvanishing Indians of the American Southwest." *Indian Historian*, vol. 6, no. 1 (Winter 1973): 5–8, 32.

The writer points out how anthropologists have from the beginning somewhat arbitrarily selected from the total range of Indian cultural behavior only those things that seemed to make them "aboriginal" or "native" while ignoring all other facets of Indian life. In so doing, these anthropologists promoted limited, static views of what Indians' lives should be. He suggests that if Indians do things non-Indians do, they have been written off as "non-Indian" or as "assimilated." He also suggests it's time anthropologists stop their preconceived notions of what's "Indian" and take into account Indians who use whatever elements in their environment they see fit.

Forbes, Jack D. "The Historian and the Indian: Radical Bias in American History." *The Americas*, vol. 19, no. 4 (April 1963): 349–62.

Forbes (Powhatan) questions why American historians dismiss the first 30,000 years of American Indian history and concentrate on 500 years of Europeans wresting the continent from Indians, almost completely ignoring Native Americans in the period from 1513 to1890. He argues Indians were significant in American history and any treatment of the post-1513 period should deal with Indian reactions to European and Hispanic advances into the southwest.

Forst, Dietmar. "We Germans Love Indians. . . ." *The Bulletin.* University of South Dakota, August 1992. pp. 35–37.

Germans, the author claims, are fascinated with American Indians. He cites some very familiar reasons for this interest, mainly that Indians represent a group of people who have preserved an old culture and as part of this have remained attached to their land despite all adversity.

Fowler, Don D. "Images of American Indians, 1492–1892." In *Halcyon/1990: A Journal of the Humanities,* vol. 12. Reno: Nevada Humanities Committee, 1990. pp. 75–100.

The author examines European and U.S. images and stereotypes and how they grew, between 1492 and 1892 and on into the twentieth century. He explains how these images of "primitive others" found in travel descriptions, official reports, literature, paintings, drawings, and photographs made statements about European political systems and social practices. He also tells how images of Indians in the United States are principally pejorative.

Frances, Daniel. *The Imaginary Indian: The Image of the Indian in Canadian Culture.* Vancouver, B.C.: Arsenal Publishers, 1992. Illustrations. Bibliography.
The writer describes images of imaginary Indians in Canada since the mid-nineteenth century manufactured by white Canadians—some derogatory, some not. He concerns himself with the origins of the images, how Indian images affected public policy in Canada, and how the images shaped the myths non-Natives tell themselves about being Canadians. He focuses on the vanishing image perpetuated by artists, travelers, and missionaries as well as the bad-guy image of Indians in the literature of the Mounted Police produced between 1885 and World War II. He deals with the impact of Buffalo Bill's Wild West shows on creating imaginary Indians, the popularity of celebrity Indians like Pauline Johnson, and nature-loving Indians presented by Ernest Thompson Seton who expressed aspects of the imaginary Indian. He deals with the appropriation by non-Indians of Indian images to sell products. Finally he deals with Canadian Indian policy premised on an image of Indians as inferior and aimed, in the early twentieth century, at assimilating Native people into Canada.

Frazier, Jane. "Tomahawkin' the Redskins: 'Indian' Images in Sports and Commerce." In *American Indian Studies: An Interdisciplinary Approach to Contemporary Issues.* Ed. Dane Morrison, pp. 337–45. New York: Peter Lang, 1997. Notes.
The author reviews a small sample of the "staggering" number of Native American names, terms, and images on consumer goods and services; sports teams that have latched onto popular images of Indians; and Hollywood films. She contends that the use of "Indian" images—as distinct from authentic representations of Native American people—in sports and business shapes our views of Native people. By reducing Native Americans to the status of mascots and shills to sell products, people are lulled into believing that they truly depict Native Americans. The "tomahawk chop" and war dances at sporting events and the use of Native names and icons perpetuate simplistic "cowboy and Indian" images of Native Americans.

French, Philip. "The Indian in the Western Movie." *Art in America,* vol. 60, no. 4 (July–August 1972): 32–39. Illustrations.
French looks at Indians in western movies since 1950, supposedly a watershed year in the way movies treated Indians, and concludes Indians remained a pawn in the western game, to be cast in whatever role the filmmaker chose. He identifies two dominant traits during the 1950s and early 1960s—the role of the Indians as an external force in uniting Americans and the cultural clash between pioneer and Indian. He also sees a gradual move in the direction of presenting Indian life as a valid counterculture and describes movies like "Soldier Blue" and "Little Big Man" with their fashionable attacks on white "civilization."

———. "Indians and Blacks." In *Westerns: Aspects of a Movie Genre.* London: Secker and Warburg, Ltd., 1973. pp. 76–99. Illustrated. Bibliography.
The writer describes the treatment of Indians in western movies during the 1950s and 1960s.

Friar, Ralph E. and Friar, Natasha A. *The Only Good Indian: The Hollywood Gospel.* New York: Drama Book Specialists, 1972. Illustrated.

The authors investigate the misrepresentation of Native Americans in all media but emphasize the filmic creature called "Indian." There are eighty illustrations, a list of "Actors in Redskin," and a selective list of some of the several thousand films made prior to the publication of this book.

Friedrichs, Michal. "Tecumseh's 41 Names in the English Language: Some Remarks on Their Genesis." *European Review of Native American Studies,* vol. 8, no. 2 (1994): 6–10. Friedrichs shows how the various forms of Tecumseh's name exemplify racist oppression. Imposing names that Europeans could pronounce is one way to obliterate indigenous identity. The writer argues Tecumseh's true name can never be restored because Indian orthography is now so unfamiliar it can no longer be recovered.

Ganje, Lucy A. "Native American Stereotypes." In *Images That Injure: Pictorial Stereotypes in the Media.* Ed. Paul M. Lester, pp. 41–46. New York: Praeger, 1996. Illustrated. A collection of essays that discuss the visual messages that harm and perpetuate misleading myths about members of various cultural groups. Experts in communication and graphics analyze images that present various stereotypes (ethnic, gender, age, physical disabilities, sexual orientation, and miscellaneous), looking at the impact of such images on individuals and society and the motivations of those who made the images. Ganje deals with the subtle ways media organizations stereotype contemporary Native people including "bloodthirsty savages" on covers of romance novels, images that sell sports teams (the Cleveland Indians and the Atlanta Braves), noble savages in advertising, Indians as spirit guides, and Indians as protestors. The author argues that the constant visual diet of Native people in traditional regalia, as names for sports teams and mascots, plus the lack of identifying captions under photos are subtle forms of racism. Ganje concludes that the Native American Journalists Association and other Native organizations must take steps to address the imbalance in the media.

Garcia, Jesus. "Native Americans in U.S. History Textbooks: From Bloody Savages to Heroic Chiefs." *Journal of American Indian Education,* vol. 17, no. 2 (January 1978): 15–19. The writer examines the changes in the treatment of Native Americans in five California-adopted eighth grade U.S. history textbooks from 1956 to 1976. He concludes that the portrayal of Indians has not changed significantly and includes three phases used in evaluating the textbooks. The article is based on the writer's teaching and research experience and materials on analyzing texts.

Gerbi, Antonello. *The Dispute of the New World: The History of a Polemic, 1750–1900.* Rev. ed. Trans. Jeremy Moyle. Pittsburgh: University of Pittsburgh Press, 1973. Bibliography. (Originally published in Italy in 1955 as *La disputa del nuovo mondo: Storia di una polemica, 1750–1900* by Riccardo Ricciardi Editore.) The author discusses the basic theme, expressed in various manifestations by diverse authors, of the presumed inferiority of America, particularly its people and fauna, in comparison to the "Old World." There is an extensive bibliography of works cited and an extensive bibliography of works the author did not see which promise to contain material that would serve to enrich and develop some area of the history of the polemic.

Gerdts, William H. "The Marble Savage." *Art in America,* vol. 62, no. 4 (July–August 1974): 64–70. This article deals with the depictions of Indian men and women by nineteenth-century American neo-classical sculptors whose style was related to European forms but whose subject matter was specifically American in theme. He discusses how the sculptors reflect the ideology of the good and bad Indian; characterize the politics, combative and legal, violent and peaceful, of Indian-white relations; and represent the country's ambivalence toward the subject during the expansionist course of the nineteenth century. There are twelve photographs of sculptures that illustrate the narrative.

Gerogakas, Dan. "They Have NOT Spoken: American Indians in Film." *Film Quarterly,* vol. 25, no. 3 (Spring 1972): 26–32.

The writer reviews *A Man Called Horse* ("parades the standard myth that white people can do everything better than Indians"), *Soldier Blue* ("director relies totally on explicit scenes of carnage for his argument and effect"), *Little Big Man* ("massacres are once more reduced to racial mania unconnected with social or economic considerations"), and *Tell Them Willie Boy Is Here.* There is a bibliography of suggested readings.

Gibbs, William T. "American Indians on Coins." *Whispering Wind.* vol. 26, no. 5 (1994): 16–23. Bibliography.

An interesting and fluid account of the history of Native American imagery on U.S. coins. The author traces Anglo-Indian relations, westward expansion, and artistic and currency development from Columbus to the present. He shows how images on coins, like other artistic, musical and literary developments, reflect the "zeitgeist" or worldview of the time and place in which they develop.

Gillespie, Phyllis. "The Wild West Thrives." *Arizona Highways*, vol. 70, no. 10 (October 1994): 12–17. Illustrations.

The author tells of the European, and most notably the German, fascination for Indian culture. The trend started with Karl May, an author and convicted felon, who wrote over 70 romanticized novels about the American West, Asia, and the Middle East in the late 1800s and early 1900s without ever having traveled to any of those places until long after his books had created a national fervor. For the last century, the Germans have participated in "cowboy and Indian" clubs, put lots of time and energy into learning how to make Indian outfits and crafts, and even put on powwows complete with tipis—their own interpretations of Indian cultures. "No Name City," a tourist attraction named after the town in "Paint Your Wagon," even sports an Indian elder who retired from the service in Germany and draws a crowd as he demonstrates beadwork.

Goldie, Terry. *Fear and Temptation: The Image of the Indigene in Canadian, Australian, and New Zealand Literature.* Montreal: McGill-Queen's University Press, 1989.

The author identifies strong similarities in the depiction of indigenous peoples in works by white writers from Canada, New Zealand, and Australia. He demonstrates the major elements involved in representing indigenous peoples: The Natural, Form, Sexuality, Violence, Orality, Mysticism, Historicity, Theater. The author agrees that such stereotypes as the "treacherous redskin" and the "Indian maiden" embody the whites' dual feelings of repulsion from and attraction to the Indigene and the land.

Gonzales, Paul. "Appropriation of Culture." *Indian Art*, (Summer 1996): 38.

The writer gives examples of the offensive use of Indian images and names by sports teams and lauds the efforts of Charlene Teters, the Spokane graduate student and mother who confronted the use of an Indian mascot at the University of Illinois.

Green, Rayna. "The Indian in Popular American Culture." In *Handbook of North American Indians,* vol. 4. Ed. Wilcomb E. Washburn, pp. 587–606. Washington, D.C.: Smithsonian Institution, 1988.

The author, a Western Cherokee, examines the Indian as a "central figure in the New World iconography," in the expressive forms of American vernacular culture. She describes oral expressions—songs, jokes, legends, anecdotes, proverbs, and ethnic slurs;

visual representations—medals, coins, stamps, ceramics, and so forth; and dramatic expressions— entertainment, medicine shows, games, sports, and so on.

———. "The Pocahontas Perplex: The Image of Indian Women in American Culture." *Massachusetts Review*, vol. 16 (Autumn 1975): 698–714.

The author discusses the impact of the Pocahontas story on American culture and as a model for the national understanding of Indian women. Describing symbols like the "princess", "squaw," and "mother-goddess" figure, she also looks at the relationship of these to white male figures.

———. "The Tribe Called Wannabee: Playing Indian in America and Europe." *Folklore* (London), vol. 99 (1988): 30–55. Notes.

Green gives a history of the obsession of Europeans and American Whites and Blacks of "playing Indian." She cites examples of many claiming Indian heritage and particularly Cherokee ancestry and then inventing their idea of what an Indian is and how an Indian behaves. All of this "playing" has resulted in the rejection of bona fide Indian cultures and the unacceptance of Indian people dressing in other than traditional dress or doing anything other than what "Indians historically did."

Green, Richard G. "Buffalo Bill's History Lesson or The Indian Image in Hollywood Films." In *Turtle Quarterly* (Native American Center of the Living Arts, Niagara Falls, NY), vol. 2, no. 3 (Summer 1988): 32–35.

The author discusses Hollywood's mistreatment and misrepresentations of Indians. He looks at the roles of Chief Dan George, Will Sampson, and other Indian actors. Included are short biographies on Preston Smith (Jay Silver Heels) and Gary Farmer.

Greenway, John. "Will The Indians Get Whitey?" *National Review*, vol. 21 (March 11, 1969): 223–28, 245.

The writer indicates several books indicting U.S. federal Indian policy and then suggests they are full of illusions, not reality, about Indians whom he calls ferocious, cruel, and so on. He takes on Dale Van Every's *Disinherited* ("When Van Every's heart is not weeping for the Cherokee, it is hemorrhaging for the Seminole") plus other books.

Greer, Sandy. "Fluffs and Feathers." *Turtle Quarterly* (Native American Center of the Living Arts, Niagara Falls, NY), vol. 3, no. 2. (Spring-Summer 1989): 31–33.

The author discusses the 1988 conference about Indian stereotyping she attended at the Woodland Cultural Center in Brantford, Ontario. She recalls some of the remarks made by conference speakers and tells of her observations while walking through the exhibition hall. See Deborah Doxtator.

———. "Media Education and Native Peoples." *Winds of Change*, vol. 6, no. 4 (Fall 1991) and vol. 7, no. 1 (Winter 1992).

The author discusses the central importance that the media plays in contemporary perceptions about society and how "media literacy," our ability to "demystify" media and view it critically, can assist in the deconstruction of stereotypes and the clarification of authenticity. She cites advertising as the essential force propagating the values that often betray the truths about Native Americans.

———. "Native People on Television." *Kainai News* (Stand Off, Alberta, Canada), vol. 23, no. 21 (June 14, 1990): 17–18.

Greer looks at positive changes in television programming about Native Americans in the United States and Canada and briefly covers characters in shows like "The Young Riders," and "Paradise." She mentions the work of Carol Geddes, Tlingit filmmaker.

————. "The Noble Savage." *Winds of Change,"* vol. 8, no. 2 (Spring 1993): 89–92.
   The writer investigates the origins and meanings of the term "noble savage," and how
   its continued use affects Native people today.
Hagan, William T. "Reformers' Images of the Native Americans: The Late Nineteenth
   Century." In *The American Indian Experience: A Profile: 1524–the Present.* Ed. Philip
   Weeks. Arlington Heights, IL: Forum Press, Inc., 1988. Bibliography.
   Hagan discusses how reformers and reform organizations between 1865 and 1900 were
   in general agreement that Indian civilization was at a lower evolutionary stage, generations behind white civilization. He briefly focuses on Alice Fletcher, an ethnologist and
   reformer, who defended the Native way of life but concluded Indians had to abandon
   their lifestyle because the "peculiar environment" that had shaped them no longer existed. The writer tells how reformers disagreed with each other about civilization policies, but nevertheless believed Indians were human beings who deserved to be full-
   fledged citizens.
Hamilton, Wynette. "The Correlation between Societal Attitudes and Those of American
   Authors in the Depiction of American Indians, 1607–1860." *American Indian Quarterly*,
   vol. 1, no. 2. (Spring 1974): 1–26.
   Hamilton traces the early representation of Indians in colonial America and touches on
   writers like James Fenimore Cooper, Henry Wadsworth Longfellow, Philip Freneau,
   and Charles Brockden Brown among others. She points out that the image of Indians in
   literature of any time was consistently a projection of the Anglo-American mind and
   that the image was used to further White needs, not explore the Indian reality.
Hansen, Klaus J. "The Millennium, the West, and Race in the Antebellum American Mind."
   Western Historical Quarterly, vol. 3, no. 4 (October 1972): 373–90.
   Hansen shows how the pursuit of the American millennium led to images of Indians as
   savages to be annihilated or assimilated and to earlier images of Indians as prodigal
   members of the House of Israel, a belief that impelled Puritan millennialists to engage
   in attempts to convert Indians in order to include them in the millennial kingdom.
Harjo, Susan Shown. "Sportsfans." *Winds of Change,* vol. 4, no. 4 (Autumn 1989): 31–32.
   This Cheyenne writer decries the use of Indian names and mascots by professional and
   college sports teams and argues that "It is well past time to rid the sports world of these
   nasty symbols. . . ."
Harrington, John. "Understanding Hollywood's Indian Rhetoric." *Canadian Review of
   American Studies,* vol. 8, no. 1 (Spring 1977): 77–88.
   The author argues that "most North Americans learn about Native Americans from the
   movies." He discusses the Indian culture, rather than Native American culture, created
   by Hollywood. He gives several examples of Hollywood's treatment of American
   Indians and states that although that treatment is fictitious, it causes real damage to real
   people even though the intentions of the creators are purely to fictionalize.
Hartman, Hedy. "A Brief Review of the Native American in American Cinema." *Indian
   Historian,* vol. 9, no. 3 (Summer 1973): 27–29. Bibliography.
   The writer briefly reviews stereotypes and inaccuracies of Native peoples in films. She
   lists eleven complaints of the American Indian Movement about films. There is a bibli-
   ography of articles and books about the subject.
Haskins, Bette. "Breaking Out." *Turtle Quarterly,* vol. 3, no. 3 (Summer 1990): 47–49.
   The writer reviews the inhumane treatment of Indians by Europeans before examining
   the many Native American contributions to the world.

Hauptman, Laurence M. "Mythologizing Westward Expansion: Schoolbooks and the Image of the American Frontier by Turner." *Western Historical Quarterly,* vol. 8, no. 3 (July 1977): 270–82.

In this essay, the writer points out that the most extensive treatment accorded the frontier experience in more than two-thirds of the schoolbooks before 1886 was in the realm of Indian life and Indian-White relations. He studies the constant interchanging of the nouns "Indians" and "savages" and language describing Indians as lacking intelligence as well as the universal praise for the conquest of the wilderness and Indian populations.

———. *Tribes & Tribulations: Misconceptions About American Indians and Their Histories.* Albuquerque: University of New Mexico Press, 1995. Notes.

In nine essays, the author selects topics from the seventeenth century to the present as examples of some commonly held but erroneous views about Native Americans and their histories. He shows how scholars have misunderstood genocide in American Indian history, how they have created the myth of the frontier hero rationalizing violence against Indians; how they have propagated myths that the U.S. Constitution derived some of its concepts from the Iroquois, how they have failed to understand Indian removal policies and have been misled by the paternalistic rhetoric of Washington officials about Indian policies, how Indians served in the Union as well as Confederate war machines, how many Americans assume all Native people live west of the Mississippi River, and how major league sports franchises and Hollywood have perpetuated false assumptions about Natives and still do.

———. "Westward the Course of Empire: Geography Schoolbooks and Manifest Destiny, 1783–1893." *The Historian: A Journal of History,* vol. 40, no. 3 (May 1978): 423–40.

The writer analyzed over 1,000 schoolbooks for first grade through college, published between 1783 and 1893, for the treatment of the frontier and the widespread belief in the inevitability of America's westward destiny. He explains that most geography books present one attitude–"the superiority of the white race." The author concludes that these geography texts would imbue children with the ideas that Indians were few in number, savage, and vanishing. There is an appendix of the twenty leading authors of geography books from 1783 to1893.

Haycock, Ronald G. *The Image of the Indian: The Canadian Indian as a Subject and a Concept in a Sampling of the Popular Magazines in Canada, 1900–1970.* Waterloo, Ontario: Waterloo Lutheran University, 1971.

The author deals with the image of Canadian Indians in popular magazines in three parts: the first deals with Indian as a poor doomed savage in the period 1900–1930; the second deals with the Indian in the period of humanitarian awareness and guilt, 1930–1960; and the third part deals with the Indians' struggle for equality and civil rights from 1960 to 1970.

Healy, George R. "The French Jesuits and the Idea of the Noble Savage." *William and Mary Quarterly,* vol. 15, no. 2 (April 1958): 143–67.

The writer discusses how the Jesuits in New France during the seventeenth and eighteenth centuries described Indians as finer beings than they were usually judged elsewhere. He looks at the basic philosophy and theology of the Society of Jesus that underlay the entire course of Jesuit education and explains how much of the missionaries' attitudes affected the Jesuit understanding of Indians. The writer discusses how the philosophers employed Jesuit sources, usually out of context, for anti-Catholic purposes.

Henderson, Rob. "The Indians are Changing but the Movies Aren't." *The Northian: Journal of the Society for Indians and Northern Education*, vol. 9, no. 1 (Fall 1972): 1–3. The writer argues that although new Indian movies in the late 1960s and early 1970s are not necessarily aesthetic improvements, the attitudes they express have changed. Indians, no longer presented as subhumans, are now presented as an oppressed minority. The writer also argues the movies suggest being Indian is desirable, as in "Little Big Man" and "A Man Called Horse" where the plots hinge on white men becoming Indians. He also mentions "Billy Jack," which he calls a pro-Indian, but bad, movie.

Henry, Jeannette. "Native Americans in the Textbook Literature." In *Indian Voices: The First Convocation of American Indian Scholars*. Ed. American Indian Historical Society, pp. 365–76. San Francisco: Indian Historian Press, 1970. This is one of the papers given at a session of the First Convocation at which fourteen representatives of seven publishing houses were present. The author argues that publishers don't think the truth about Native Americans will be profitable and that the publishing industry should be subjected to examination.

———. "Our Inaccurate Textbooks." *Indian Historian*, vol. 1, no. 1 (1967): 21–24. In this article, the author reports on conclusions reached by a group of Indian scholars after evaluating forty-three social science textbooks used in California's grades four, five, and eight. She describes all the textbooks as containing inaccurate information on Native–White relations and supplies some of the criticisms made of certain textbooks. See this article in *Civil Rights Digest* 1 (Summer 1968): 4–8, where it is titled "Textbook Distortion of the Indian."

Herbst, Laura. "That's One Good Indian: Unacceptable Images in Children's Novels." *Top of the News* (January 1975): 192–98. Bibliography. The author discusses three objectionable book treatments of both Indian individuals and Indian cultures. The latter are most often portrayed as so inferior to white culture that they should be abandoned, or savage and only worth annihilating and quaint or superficial. There is a bibliography of books with objectionable images.

Hilger, Michael. *The American Indian in Film*. Metuchen, NJ: Scarecrow Press, Inc., 1986. Bibliography. Hilger focuses on narrative films that have used images of bloodthirsty savages and noble-but-doomed savages to emphasize superiority of white heroes, to comment on contemporary political issues, or to serve the needs of the western genre. He notes that images of Indians as always too good or too bad and never real are repeated through four historical periods (the silent films, early sound films, films of the 1950s and 1960s, and films of the 1970s and 1980s). He arranges 830 films chronologically from each period to illustrate the development and the sometimes strange mixture of images and themes in each period. He summarizes various films focusing on actions of and actors who play the Indian roles and cites complete information (director, company, etc.).

———. *From Savage to Nobleman: Images of Native Americans in Film*. Lanham, MD: Scarecrow Press, 1995. The author traces the portrayal of Native Americans from the silents and early sound films of each decade, covering over 800 films. An introduction discusses the traditional images of the Noble Red Man and the Savage. The final chapter discusses new images based on tribal identities in recent films such as "Powwow Highway."

Hill, Richard. "Sex, Lies and Stereotypes." *Turtle Quarterly*, vol. 4, no. 1 (Spring–Summer 1991): 14–23.

The writer discusses the union of sexual and savage characteristics in the European picture of Native Americans. He attributes these images to the original reports of early encounters with Indians, when their relative nakedness was a most prominent and talked about characteristic. He gives an overview of the diffusion of Indian stereotypes, from early literature, art, film, and toys.

Hinkle, Jeff. "Proud Heritage or Institutional Racism?" *American Indian Report,* April 1998: 24–25.

The writer discusses the lawsuit by Jim Pitillo, an alumni of Birmingham High School, against the Los Angeles School District, an attempt by him to halt the district's decision to ban the Indian team mascot. After a task force of the Los Angles Board of Education recommended resurrecting an eighteen-year-old ruling banning Indian logos, Pitillo sued on the grounds that the ban restricts his right to free speech.

Hirschfelder, Arlene. "Headdresses, Drums, and Bows and Arrows: Indian Imagery in Children's Toys." In *Ethnic Images in Toys and Games,* ed. Pamela B. Nelson, pp. 40–47. Philadelphia: Balch Institute, 1990.

The author discusses the toy industry's part in stereotyping Indian cultures and belittling spiritual traditions. She focuses on headdresses, drums, masks, and other paraphernalia for "playing Indian," or violent-looking Indian toys, and on the way toymakers belittle Indian names.

———. "Unlearning Indian Stereotypes." In *Halcyon/1990: A Journal of the Humanities,* vol. 12. Reno: Nevada Humanities Committee, 1990. pp. 49–61.

The writer discusses problems in children's books published over the last thirty years and tells of children's books about Indians written with care and respect.

Honour, Hugh. *The New Golden Land: European Images of America from the Discoveries to the Present Time.* New York: Pantheon Books, 1975. Illustrated.

The author explores the changing image of America as it has evolved in the European mind over the last four centuries. He draws upon a vast variety of material to show how the landscapes of the New World, its flora and fauna, and its peoples and their customs, have been seen by European artists from early explorers to this century. Notes include discussions and bibliographical information on European attitudes toward American Indians.

Horsman, Reginald. "Scientific Racism and the American Indian in the Mid-Nineteenth Century." *American Quarterly,* vol. 27, no. 2 (May 1975): 152–68.

The writer deals with the development of the concept of Native racial inferiority in pre–Civil War America. He feels that by the middle of the nineteenth century, science had endorsed earlier popular feelings that Indians were not worth saving and "envisaged a world bettered as the all-conquering Anglo-Saxon branch of the Caucasian race superseded inferior peoples." He summarizes the arguments of the "American school" of ethnologists from Morton to Combe to Gliddon whose works presented the "scientific" proofs of Indian inferiority and permeated political and diplomatic arguments of the late 1840s. There are footnotes.

Houts, Kathleen C. and Bahr, Rosemary S. "Stereotyping of Indians and Blacks in Magazine Cartoons." In *Native Americans Today: Sociological Perspectives.* Eds. Howard M. Bahr, Bruce A. Chadwick, and Robert C. Day, pp. 110–14. New York: Harper and Row, 1972.

The authors illustrated the nature and extent of negative stereotyping of Blacks and Indians, which occurred in cartoons appearing in the *Saturday Evening Post* from the

1920s to the 1960s, in order to identify changes in the content and frequency of that stereotyping over time. They conclude, based on data collected and analyzed via techniques of content analysis, that the American Black had virtually disappeared as a cartoon character during that time and that the stability of the Indian warrior as a stock character suggests that the Indian in American life is important only as a primitive, historical bow-and-arrow type who has no place in modern society. There are two tables of data and footnotes. See White, John R.

Hoxie, Frederick E. "Red Man's Burden." *Antioch Review,* vol. 37, no. 3 (Summer 1979): 326–42.

The writer looks at four world fairs staged between the Civil War and World War I and argues that they reflected how Americans viewed Indians. He describes three fairs that rejected the idea Indians could be both Indian and American: Philadelphia Centennial in 1876; the Chicago Columbian Exposition of 1893 where "living specimens" were put on display along with a government schoolhouse stressing "progress"; and the St. Louis exhibits of 1904 where Indians were viewed as members of "backward races." The fourth fair, the 1915 Panama-Pacific International Exposition in San Francisco, devoid of elaborate anthropological displays, marginalized Native people altogether.

Hoy, James F. "The Indian Through the Eyes of *The Cattleman.*" *Indian Historian*, vol. 12 (Summer 1979): 41–46, 62.

The Cattleman is the official voice of the Texas and Southwestern Cattle Raisers Association, published monthly since 1914. Though the publication is primarily a trade journal, this article traces the representations of Indians and rancher-Indian relations in an effort to find editorial patterns. Though the author concludes there is not distinct anti-Indian policy, the examples he provides show the bigotry and bias.

Hughes, J. Donald. "The De-racialization of Historical Atlases: A Modest Proposal." *Indian Historian,* vol. 7, no. 3 (Summer 1974): 55–56.

This brief article demonstrates how historical maps, teaching aids in every American history classroom, and maps in an atlas of American history almost completely ignore Indian possession of land. He argues that American historical maps are racially and historically inaccurate, drawn from a white narrow ethnocentric point of view, and educate students with its implicit message that Indians have no real claim to land ownership.

Jaimes, M. Annette. "Hollywood's Native American Woman." *Turtle Quarterly*, vol. 5, no. 2 (Spring-Summer 1993): 40–45.

The author points out that racist and sexist tendencies in Hollywood have doubly degraded the Native American woman.

Johansen, Albert. *The House of Beadle and Adams and Its Dime and Nickel Novels: The Story of a Vanished Literature.* 2 vols. Norman: University of Oklahoma Press, 1950. Illustrated.

Part three of the first volume lists the various series of novels published by the House of Beadle and Adams in the order of appearance of their first numbers with brief synopses of most of the novels from 1860 to the early 1900s. There are hundreds of facsimiles of the covers of the publications. Many of the novels have to do with Indians.

Jones, Eugene H. *Native Americans as Shown on the Stage, 1753–1916.* Metuchen, NJ: Scarecrow Press, Inc., 1988. Bibliography.

Jones examined attitudes toward Native Americans in the way they were characterized by playwrights in nearly 300 theater works written for American audiences between 1753 and 1916. He shows that Native Americans were stereotyped by the playwrights who "apparently masked white people's fear of Indians as obstacles to the fulfillment of their desire to settle in the New World." An appendix contains a chronological checklist of plays and other theater works featuring Native characters from 1658 to 1982.

Kaufman, Donald L. "The Indian as Media Hand-Me-Down." *The Colorado Quarterly,* vol. 23 (Spring 1975): 489–504. Reprinted in Bataille, Gretchen M. and Silet, Charles L. P., eds., 22–34.

The author traces the image of Native Americans as it has been "handed down" from the early American novelists and poets to the American state, to the Wild West Shows, to dime novels (the last of which appeared in 1912), to "minor writers," and to movies, radio, and television. Throughout, the author compares the treatment of Blacks and Indians in these various media. The writer concludes that since the mid-1960s there have been signs that the media might "clean up the image of the Indian" and that Indians may be "inching toward a future in media where their presence will be as powerful as that of Blacks today."

Keizer, Albert. *The Indian in American Literature.* New York: Oxford University Press, 1933. Bibliography. Reprint ed.: New York: Octagon Books, 1970.

This book examines and analyzes Indian portraits drawn by major American writers of fiction from the early 1600s until the early twentieth century. He begins with the treatment of Pocahontas and Captain John Smith, briefly examines captivity narratives, and touches on James Fenimore Cooper and William Gilmore Simms. He presents many other authors including Helen Hunt Jackson, Hamlin Garland, Henry Wadsworth Longfellow, and John G. Niehardt. The bibliography lists writings quoted from or used in the study.

Kellerman, Barbara L. "Even in a Museum Depicting His History, the Indian Is Cheated." *New York Times*, 27 November 1980, A27.

The writer discusses how the exhibits of Native Americans in the Museum of the Plains Indian in Browning, Montana, administered by the federal government, mislead its visitors. She cites labels accompanying historic exhibits that deceive visitors into thinking that white people helped Indians achieve their greatest glory while completely ignoring the cultures of the Plains peoples before contact.

Kelly, Inga K. and Falkenhagen, Maria. "The Native American in Juvenile Fiction." *Journal of American Indian Education,* vol. 13, no. 2 (January 1974): 9–23.

The authors give results of a survey administered to thirty elementary teachers who were asked to identify stereotypes of Native Americans that appear in juvenile literature, and then identify important criteria in selecting juvenile literature about Native Americans. They found that the teachers' stereotypes fell into three categories: dress, living conditions, and customs. Investigators were more concerned with subtle stereotypes than the traditional explicit ones with which the teachers were most concerned. The investigators feel there is a need to build more accurate awareness of types of stereotypes likely to appear in contemporary Native American literature for children. They include criteria to assist educators in evaluation of juvenile literature.

Kerber, Linda. "The Abolitionist Perception of the Indian." *Journal of American History,* vol. 62, no. 2 (September 1975): 271–95.

The writer, who looked at the abolitionist work of the 1830s, 1840s, and 1850s, describes how liberal abolitionists attempted to treat the problems of freedmen and

Indians in the same way. They perceived that both Blacks and Indians required the "civ-ilizing" influence of white society and perceived the tribe as an institutional artifact standing between the individual and his freedom. Kerber also focuses on Hampton Institute's addition of Indians to its student body and how the education was designed to free Indian students from identifying with their tribes just as it was intended to en-able freedmen to participate as individuals in non-Black communities.

Keshena, Rita. "The Role of American Indians in Motion Pictures." *American Indian Cul-ture and Research Journal*, vol. 1, no. 2 (1974): 25–28. Reprinted in Bataille, Gretchen M. and Silet, Charles L. P., eds., 106–11.

The author presents a history of Indian people in film, which she describes as a "long chronicle of exploitation, distortion, denigration, debasement, denial and deceit." She encourages Indians to learn film production to counter constant stereotyping.

King, J. C. H. "A Century of Indian Shows: Canadian and U.S. Exhibitions in London, 1825–1925." *European Review of Native American Studies,* vol. 5, no. 1 (1991): 35–38. Illustrated. Bibliography.

King looks at ways exhibitions of feather-bonneted chiefs, Inuit, and other people dressed as marauding warriors plus dime novels and movies of the 1920s misrepre-sented the Native peoples of North America.

———. "Family of Botocudos Exhibited on Bond Street in 1822." In *Indians and Europe: An Interdisciplinary Collection of Essays*. Ed. Christian F. Feest. Aachen, Germany: Edition Herodot, 1987.

King illustrates how Indians were used as circus freak shows. Though billed as a way of educating Europeans about Indian culture, these shows were also designed to titillate the European imagination by exposing such practices as polygamy, adultery, and slav-ery within Indian culture.

King, Thomas; Calver, Cheryl; and Hoy, Helen. *The Native in Literature: Canadian and Comparative Perspectives*. Oakville: ECW Press, 1987.

Papers from a conference in Lethbridge (1985) examine the Native Americans in liter-ature from many perspectives. The papers fall into three categories : general surveys that consider the effects of the presence of Indians as romantic and primitive figures on non-Native writing and thinking; writings about Indians by non-Indian early explorers and religious images by Charles Gordon and Rudy Wiebe; and pieces about Native litera-ture including Metis, Native women's, and Inuit traditional narratives, contemporary Native use of humor, and the assimilation of European folktales in Native societies.

Kleiman, Dena. "Dartmouth Alumni Trying to 'Bring Back the Indian.'" *New York Times,* 3 August 1980, sec. 1, 16.

Kleiman discusses how the Dartmouth Alumni have elected a nonofficial candidate for trustee in a revolt to "bring back the Indian: as the symbol of the college." See entry under "Dartmouth Loses Its Indian Mascot."

Koster, John. "American Indians and the Media." *Cross Currents*, vol. 26, no. 2 (Summer 1976): 164–71.

The writer argues the news media is reluctant to deal with American Indian issues in a serious way. He focuses on the "sad case" of Wounded Knee in 1890 and how in 1975 the massacre got reinvented as a battle so the U.S. Department of Defense could elude paying reparations to the Sioux. He deals with the U.S. press response (some printing the Army's version of story almost verbatim). He suggests the press failed again in its coverage of Wounded Knee in 1973 and ascribes three causes of the shoddy news cov-

erage: ignorance, prejudice, and laziness, concluding that the mass media cannot be re-
lied on for stories about thefts of Indian land in this century.

Krees, Karl Markus. "'Indians' on Old Picture Postcards." *European Review of Native
American Studies*, vol. 6, no. 1 (1992): 39–48.
Krees looks at three groups of Native images appearing on industrially mass-produced
postcards. (In 1905, importers and wholesalers sold one billion postcards in the United
States alone). The three categories of images included known named persons realistically depicted by painters like Frederic Remington, stylized images staged for ethnographic purposes, and popular legends. Nineteen illustrations are included.

Lanouette, JoAnne. "Teacher's Corner: Erasing Native American Stereotypes." *Anthro
Notes*, vol. 12, no. 3 (Fall 1990): 7–9. Illustrations. Bibliography.
The writer combines work by June Sark, director of a Chicago alternative school for
Native American students, and The D'Arcy McNickle Center for the History of the
American Indian, the Newberry Library in Chicago, into a list of questions to help
teachers evaluate their own materials and teaching about Native Americans.

LaRoque, Emma. *Defeathering the Indian*. Agincourt, Ont., Canada: The Book Society of
Canada, Ltd., 1975. Illustrated.
This handbook, written by a Cree-Metis woman, was designed to raise questions and issues for those educators in the process of teaching about Native studies and to expose
stereotypes and myths concerning Indians. She covers a wide range of topics such as
relegating Indian culture to the past, analyzing stereotypes like the noble savage and
Indian ecologist, and analyzing ethnocentricity and anachronisms in books, and so forth.
Concluding with a personal reflection on dwelling on differences or universalities, she
also includes footnotes and recommended readings.

League of Women Voters. *Young People's Concepts of Native Americans: A Survey of Suburban Ninth and Twelfth Grade Students*. New Brighton, MN: League, 1976. Bibliography.
This publication contains results of a survey assessing ninth and twelfth graders on their
knowledge and attitudes regarding American Indians, which tended to be positive.
Graphs, methodology, and a bibliography are included.

Leechman, Douglas. "The Indian in Literature." *Queen's Quarterly*, vol. 50 (Summer
1943): 155–63.
The author explores eight stages in the growth of the modern popular conception of
North American Indians beginning with writers who created the pictures of Indians of
early days and ending with the Indian of today, a blend of many ideas.

Lester, Joan. "A Museum's Eye View." *Indian Historian*, vol. 5, no. 2 (1972): 25–31.
The writer looks at the exhibitions of American Indian artifacts as they were presented
to the public in the early years of museum going and then in a selected sample of
American museums from the late nineteenth century to the present time. She points out
that the public largely regarded representations of Indians in exhibits as "curiosities."

Levchuk, John. "Racism in Postage Stamps." *Akwesasne Notes*, vol. 3, no. 2.
The writer responds to a letter to the editor expressing a desire for a postage stamp honoring American Indians. Levchuk, a stamp collector, gives a chronological history of the
numerous times an Indian image has been used on stamps and not once has it been an
accurate or honoring portrayal.

Lewis, James A. "The Natives as Seen by the Missionaries: Preconception and Reality." In
The Missions in California: A Legacy of Genocide. Eds. Rupert Costo and Jeannette
Henry Costo. San Francisco: Indian Historian Press, 1987. pp. 81–89.

The author uses excerpts from writings of Franciscan missionaries in early California to illustrate the erroneous accounts of singular events or observations that served to justify the treatment of Indians by the missionaries. He argues that past distortions influence the present.

Little Eagle, Avis. "Braves Fans Assault Protesters." *Lakota Times.* 30 October 1991. Vol. 11, issue 18. pp. A1–A2.

This article tells of the seven American Indians who were arrested for protesting against the Atlanta Braves during the World Series. The controversy over racist symbolism throughout the sports world is addressed.

———. "Chief Miami, a Mascot with a Tribal Blessing." *Lakota Times.* 19 February 1992. vol. 11, issue 34. pp. A1–A2.

This article covers the Miami tribe's endorsement of the Miami University mascot, Chief Miami and their close relationship with the University to ensure that the mascot be a "tasteful" one. A speech by The National Coalition of Concerned Parents against Racism in Sports and their objection is included.

———. "Protesters Challenge Racist Mascot Names." *Indian Country Today,* vol. 12, issue 21. pp. A1, A7.

This article gives details of the November 15, 1992, protest that occurred outside a Washington Redskins and Kansas City Chiefs gym. Quotations from both protestors and fans are included.

———. "Time for High Schools to Take a Look at Their Mascots." *Indian Country Today.* 10 December 1992. pp. 3–5.

The writer covers the use of Indian nicknames and symbols by high school teams in South Dakota, where there are several Native Americans and Indian team logos and how one school opted to change to a non-Indian name and the protests that it sparked.

Livingston, Richard O. Jr. "Carol Burnett TV Show Degrades the American Indian." *Indian Historian,* vol. 6, no. 2 (Spring 1973): 23.

This page contains a copy of a letter to the general manager of CBS TV from Richard O. Livingston, Jr., Instructor of Native American Studies, protesting the disgraceful and degrading portrayal of Native American people and culture on the December 30, 1972, Carol Burnett Show. He explains some of the abuses of this "comedy show" and concludes that the show was shameful and compensation for damages should be in order.

Loewen, James W. "Red Eyes." In *Lies My Teacher Told Me: Everything Your American History Textbook Got Wrong.* New York: The New Press, 1995. pp. 91–129. Illustrations. Notes.

The writer argues that American Indians have been "the most lied-about subset of U.S. population" in textbooks. He examines twelve texts and concludes that current ones do "confer civilization on some Natives." He deals with the cultural transformation of Indian societies after contact with Europeans and Americans (and the ways Europeans changed as well), the incorporation of Native societies into global economy, the ways contact worked to "deskill" Indians, and increased Indian warfare and slave trade. He tells how history texts obliterate the interracial, multicultural nature of frontier life; how they omit the attraction of Native societies to European and African Americans; and how they stop short of suggesting society might benefit from Indian ideas.

———. "The Truth About The First Thanksgiving." In *Lies My Teacher Told Me: Everything Your American History Textbook Got Wrong.* New York: The New Press, 1995. pp. 67–89.

The author deals with the treatment of the "First Thanksgiving" in American history texts (a story now elevated to a national origin myth) that marginalizes Indians and omits Spanish settlement in one-third of the United States in the sixteenth century as well as the Dutch in New York by 1614. To counter the ethnocentric version, the writer tells how the Pilgrims robbed Indian graves, how the British raiders enslaved Squanto in 1614, and how a plague wiped out Patuxet, Squanto's home village. He points out that King James gave thanks to "Almighty God for sending this wonderful plague among the salvages[sic]" and describes the history of other epidemics that killed Native peoples. He argues that students should learn "good" and "bad" sides of the Pilgrim tale and decries the fact Frank James was denied the right to speak about Indian grave robbing by Pilgrims at the 350th anniversary of the Pilgrim's landing.

Lombard, Charles M. "Introduction" to *The Romantic Indian: Sentimental Views From Nineteenth Century American Literature.* Scholar's Facsimiles & Reprints, 1981.

Lombard's Introduction deals with a representative collection of nine novels and poetry by J. H. Ingraham, J. N. Barker, Robert Dale Owen, Elbert Smith, Nathaniel Deering, Henry Rowe Schoolcraft, and Henry Whiting, dating from the early 1800s. Each work illustrates an American writers' treatment of the "noble savage" idea.

Lopez, Andra. *Pagans in Our Midst.* Rooseveltown, NY: *Akwesasne Notes,* n.d. Illustrations. Covering the years 1885 to 1910, the author examines newspaper, magazine, and official reports dealing with the Iroquois Indians of New York State, drawing on materials from local newspapers. Presented in chronological order and with photographs and cartoons, ads, and so forth, the material reveals the "pattern of racism established by the press in the coverage of Indian affairs throughout the state. The materials offer a first-hand, in-their-own-words evidence of the . . . stereotyping that was manifest" in America.

Lucas, Phil. "Images of Indians." *Videoforum: A Videography for Libraries* (Native American Issue), vol. 1 (Winter 1993).

A Choctaw independent film/video producer for more than two decades and the producer of a five-part PBS series "Images of Indians" explains that since films produced by Indian filmmakers are diametrically opposed to American myths about Indians, mainstream audiences reject them. He suggests "Dances with Wolves" had a major impact on non-Indian audiences, opening a window of opportunity for Indians to tell their own stories. He lists some films that give Indians a voice and some Native films successful in communicating to the non-Indian world.

Lutz, Hartnut. "Indians' Through German vs. U.S. Eyes." *Interracial Books for Children Bulletin,* vol. 12, no. 1 (1981): pp. 3–8. Illustrated.

The author, a West German, cites, analyzes, and compares the results of a questionnaire given to sixth grade West German and California students assessing their attitudes and what they know about Native Americans. He concludes that West German students know the names of more Native nations than their U.S. peers, that West German students know more fictitious characters than real people, and that the U.S. image of Native Americans is determined less by fictitious sources and more by history textbooks and other sources that name several "good" and "bad" Indians. He gives brief histories that explain in part some of the functions that stereotypes about Native Americans have served in the United States and Germany.

Lybarger, Dan. "Hollywood Changes Attitude." *American Native Press,* no. 10 (Spring 1991).

The author critiques two westerns, "Dances with Wolves" and "Son of the Morning Star," to show that "Native Americans are finally being portrayed in a more dignified manner."

Lyman, Christopher M. *The Vanishing Race and Other Illusions: Photography of Indians by Edward S. Curtis.* New York: Pantheon Books, 1982. Bibliography.

In Curtis's twenty-volume project containing over 40,000 pictures, *The North American Indian,* that took him thirty years (1900–1930) to complete, the author argues the photographer perpetuated the myth of the noble Indian, romanticizing and immortalizing an image of "the Indian" that many still accept. Using over 120 of Curtis' photos, the writer documents numerous ways Curtis imposed his own views on all his Indian subjects by manipulating them (prohibiting signs of acculturation) and the photo darkroom process (adding highlights, blurring backgrounds) thus presenting a seriously distorted picture of Indian life. Lyman also tells how Curtis staged reenactments of activities no longer practiced.

MacCann, Donnarae and Richard, Olga. "Picture Books and Native Americans: An Interview with Naomi Caldwell-Wood." *Wilson Library Bulletin,* February 1993: 30–34, 112.

In Q-and-A format, Caldwell-Wood, a Ramapough woman, president of the American Indian Library Association, points out inaccuracies in text and illustrations in picture books as well as problems of authenticity in retellings of "legends" and "folktales."

MacGregor, Alan Leander. "Tammany: The Indian as Rhetorical Surrogate." *American Quarterly,* vol. 35, no. 4 (Fall 1983): 391–407.

In this article, the author discusses the "canonization" of Lenni-Lenape Chief Tammany of Pennsylvania, first by the Schuylkill Fishing Company, then by rebel forces during the Revolution, and then as an innocuous hero in works such as those by James Fenimore Cooper. The author shows that the use of Indians as images of conformity to the democratic rules of nationhood in America actually served the parallel purpose of deleting real Indians in the sociopolitical world.

Mallam, R. Clark. "Academic Treatment of the Indian in Public School Texts and Literature." *Journal of American Indian Education,* vol. 13 (October 1973): 14–19.

The author conducted an evaluation of texts and library materials at an elementary school in Lawrence, Kansas. He explains why he concludes that the educational materials in this school are in large part ethnocentric, inaccurate, distorted, and defamatory. There is a bibliography of sources cited in the evaluation.

Manitoba Indian Brotherhood. *The Shocking Truth About Indians in Textbooks.* Winnipeg, Manitoba: Manitoba Indian Cultural Education Centre, 1977.

This report deals with social studies textbooks approved for sixth grade classes in Manitoba. Native people analyzed text, pictures, and terminology and concluded that people of Native ancestry are given a "biased and inadequate treatment . . . in grade six social studies textual materials." They found that the main failure of the textbooks is "their tendency to treat the Native as an impediment to be removed so that the goals of European 'progress' can be realized" as well as to ignore the later history of Native people after dealing with the conflicts.

Mantell, Harold. "Counteracting the Stereotype: A Report on the Association's National Film Committee." *The American Indian,* vol. 5, no. 4 (Fall 1950): 16–20.

Screenwriter Mantell discusses the origins of the film committee ("most Americans continue to get their ideas about Indians from the movies"), describes some of its work with Hollywood studios as "constructive consultants to bring the truth about the Indian to the motion picture industry," and notes that the committee is not about censorship, but rather about making sure history is not twisted toward group defamation of Indians.

Maracle, Brian. *Crazywater: Native Voices on Addiction and Recovery*. Toronto: Penguin Books Canada, 1993.

Maracle, a member of the Mohawk Nation in Canada, did 200 interviews with Indians and Inuits—men, women, young, old, drinkers and nondrinkers, reserve residents and city dwellers, professionals and welfare recipients—over a three-year period. He asked them to tell anything and everything about Native people and alcohol.

Marsden, Michael T. and Nachbar, Jack. "The Indian in the Movies." In *Handbook of North American Indians*, vol. 4. Ed. Wilcomb E. Washburn, pp. 607–16. Washington, D.C.: Smithsonian Institution, 1988.

The author looks at the many Hollywood versions of Indians, some racist, some respectful. He looks at three primary Indian stereotypes—Pocahontas, Noble Anachronism, and the Savage Reactionary.

Marshall, Joseph. "Not All Indians Dance." In *On Behalf of the Wolf and the First Peoples*. Santa Fe, NM: Red Crane Books, 1995. pp. 27–41. Notes.

The author (Lakota) gives a down-to-earth account of his personal experiences with stereotyping. The title comes from an experience he had with non-Indians who expected him to dance at a powwow and were disappointed and bewildered that "all Indians don't dance and sing." Marshall says that "on one hand Indians were considered the 'children of nature,' and on the other hand, they were seen as the 'vilest miscreants of the savage race.'" In contemporary times, non-Indians still form their misconceptions of Indians from authors like Cooper and Parkman, images that Indians steadfastly resist. "This is the reality that non-Indians still have difficulty discovering and it is this difficulty, I believe, that prevents other Americans from perceiving us and interacting with us as who we are: human beings no better or worse than any other group of human beings." There is a list of Indian contributions and facts. This book contains many other valuable essays by the author.

Martin, Joel. "Indian Sightings in Lancaster County: The Mythic, Religious Significance of 'Indians' for Non-Indians." *American Indian Religions: An Interdisciplinary Journal*, vol. 1, no. 2 (Spring 1994): 151–72.

A Franklin and Marshall College teacher asked students to keep an "Indian diary" documenting Indian stereotypes ("sightings") in American culture. He discusses class findings concluding that Indians have unparalleled symbolic value in the United States (echoing the conclusion of other scholars) and argues no other "ethnic" group is represented symbolically as frequently as American Indians. He also states that because non-Indians spiritualize Indians and associate them with wilderness, land, and nature, they serve, on the symbolic level, as intermediate spirits connecting non-Indians to these things.

Martin, Lee-Ann. "Opinion: Reflections on a Trip to Florida." *Atlatl: Native Arts Update*, vol. 5, no. 4 (Winter 1990): 6.

In a brief essay, the writer discusses the perpetuation of inaccurate and stereotypical images of Indian people by tourist attractions in Florida (Disney World and Sea World).

McNickle, D'Arcy. "American Indians Who Never Were." *Indian Historian*, vol. 3, no. 3 (Summer 1970): 4–7. Bibliography.

The author discusses the consequences of anthropologists, sometimes misinformed, interpreting Indian history and Indian society to the world. He argues they have obscured the realities of Indian life in advancing their theories of societies. He suggests Indians be seen in the perspectives of their own time-space experiences. References are cited.

Medicine, Bea. "The Anthropologist as the Indians' Image-Maker." *Indian Historian*, vol. 4, no. 3 (Fall 1971): 27–29.

This Dakota anthropologist argues that "it is the casting of American Indian lifestyles into the printed word which has allowed a certain unchallenged expertise and validity to the anthropologist as the Indians' image-makers. The printed word . . . has resulted in the corrupting concept of the ethnographic present which has poled the Native American in a stilted, static stance which has had great repercussions in the image-molding perspective of American anthropology."

Meek, Ronald L. *Social Science and the Ignoble Savage*. Cambridge: Cambridge University Press, 1976.

The author argues that contemporary literature about American Indians played an important part in determining some of the leading emphases of the four-stages theory—a theory of socioeconomic development espoused from 1750 to 1800, which stated that the key factor in the process was the mode of subsistence. He investigates the origins and early development of the four stages and traces the gradual emergence of the notion that a study of the way of life of American Indians could help illuminate certain aspects of the problem of the development of people and society. In the afterword, he briefly discusses the elements of truth and falsity in a number of modern assessments of the socioeconomic thought of the Enlightenment. There are footnotes.

Merritt, Judy. "Indians Imaging Indians." *Winds of Change*, vol. 8, no. 2 (Spring 1993): 82–86.

This article covers the Deadwood film festival, the first festival dedicated to films made by Native Americans. Merritt points out the importance of Indian images projected by Indians rather than Whites; this alternative view could counter the stereotypes perpetuated by Hollywood. A summary of the films is included.

Mickinock, Ray. "The Plight of the Native American." *Library Journal*, vol. 96, no. 16 (September 15, 1971): 2848–51.

The author, a member of the Ojibway Nation, reviews misconceptions spread by various children's books such as Pine's *The Indians Knew* (McGraw 1957) whose illustrator Ezra Jack Keats "spoils a reasonably well done work by mixing hair styles of Eastern tribes with the tipis of the West, the pottery of the Southwestern tribes with the travois of the North." He evaluates misconceptions about Custer and suggests certain books to read of "verified accuracy and intelligent perspective."

Mihesuah, Devon A. *American Indians: Stereotypes and Realities*. Atlanta, GA: Clarity Press, Inc., 1996. Bibliography.

A sourcebook intended for educators and the public at large, the author refutes some of the most common myths about Indian peoples. In twenty-four topical sections, she corrects misconceptions ("Indians are all alike," "Indians have no religion") and offers titles for further readings. An afterword discusses the effects of stereotyping and there are several appendices: do's and don'ts for teachers and parents, guidelines for research on American Indians, and sample survey courses.

Miller, David Harry and Savage, William W. Jr. "Ethnic Stereotypes and the Frontier: A Comparative Study of Roman and American Experience." In *The Frontier: Comparative Studies*. Ed. David Harry Miller and Jerome O. Steffen, pp. 109–37. Norman: University of Oklahoma Press, 1977.

The authors explore the role of the frontier in developing politically useful stereotypes and offer a comparative model based on the Roman and Anglo-American experiences that may be useful in analyzing the development of stereotypes in other frontier situations. They conclude with a model that may be applicable to other instances of culture contact in frontier zones. There are seven parts to this model, such as "Frontier stereotypes make atrocities possible and, indeed, even encourage them."

Miller, Mary Rita. "Attestations of American Indian Pidgin English in Fiction and Nonfiction." *American Speech*, vol. 42, no. 2 (May 1967): 142–47.

The author argues the existence of an American Indian pidgin English and discusses its characteristics as found in fiction. There are footnotes.

Money, Mary Alice. "Broken Arrows: Images of Native Americans in the Popular Western." In *American Indian Studies: An Interdisciplinary Approach to Contemporary Studies.* Ed. Dane Morrison, pp. 363–88. New York: Peter Lang, 1997. Notes and Bibliography.

The author identifies seven types of images of Native Americans in popular westerns coexisting in fiction, film, and television. She briefly looks at the Indians in works of James F. Cooper, Helen Hunt Jackson, Owen Wister, and John Ford. She looks at Delmar Daves's 1950 film "Broken Arrow," a work that transformed the depiction of Native Americans and inspired a cycle of films sympathetic to them. She also discusses how television westerns reevaluated images of Native Americans in the 1950s and 1960s and how Indian heroes began to appear in popular paperback westerns during the 1960s and 1970s. She concludes with a discussion of "Dances with Wolves," in which Native actors have major and minor roles, and recent fiction and television that have further expanded Native American roles.

Monkman, Leslie. *A Native Heritage: Images of the Indian in English-Canadian Literature.* Toronto: University of Toronto Press, 1981.

The author supports a conclusion reached by novelist Norman Newton that white Canadians "have never really come to terms with their intellectual history of [their] country which is preponderantly the intellectual history of the Indians. Instead [they] have invented the idea of 'wilderness,' simply to avoid facing it." The author analyzes treatment of Indians by English-Canadian writers from the eighteenth to the twentieth centuries, focusing on nineteenth-century writers concerned with presenting historical Indians as heros and contemporary authors locating in past Indian heroes a source of visions and values denied them by North American white culture.

Moore, Robert. *Stereotypes, Distortions, and Omissions in U.S. History Textbooks.* New York: Council on Interracial Books for Children, 1977.

The section of the book on Native Americans quotes more than forty typical textbook passages, comments on the biases that they convey, and cites a number of references that refute them. Though the study reviews only a handful of texts, it includes a checklist for each group to help students and teachers scrutinize the language and meaning, apparent or hidden, in any textbook.

Morris, Joann Sebastian. "Television Portrayal and the Socialization of the American Indian Child." In *Television and the Socialization of the Minority Child.* New York: New York Academic Press, 1982. pp. 187–202. Bibliography.

The writer argues television, with its underrepresented and stereotyped Indian characters, harms American Indian children by espousing values of the dominant society that contradict traditional Indian values. Morris also contends that since teachers are raised on the same negative television programs, they make erroneous assumptions about

Indian children. So, too, do non-Indian children who tease their Indian peers. Finally, she argues that television affects the mental health of Indian children because the primary message conveyed is that "to be an Indian is neither good nor valued."

Moses, Lester George. *Wild West Shows and the Images of American Indians, 1883–1933*. Albuquerque: University of New Mexico Press, 1996. Illustrations. Notes and Bibliography.

The author examines the lives and experiences of Wild West Show Indians who between the 1880s and 1930s depicted their warfare with whites and portrayed scenes from their cultures in productions that traveled throughout the United States and Europe and drew huge audiences. Through firsthand narratives, he argues that as Indians traveled the world reenacting dances, battles, and village encampments, they preserved their heritage through decades of forced assimilation and had a good time doing it. The author also looks at Wild West shows as ventures in the entertainment business and reveals the complexity of the enterprise and the often contradictory meanings the shows had for Indians.

Murphey, James E. and Murphey, Sharon M. "American Indians and the Media: Neglect and Stereotype." In *Let My People Know: American Indian Journalism, 1828–1978*. Norman, OK: University of Oklahoma Press, 1981. pp. 3–15.

The authors trace nearly two centuries of neglect of this country's Native peoples and their portrayals as stereotypes that serve the needs of the majority.

Napier, Rita G. "Across the Big Water: Americans Indians' Perspectives of Europe and Europeans, 1887–1906." In *Indians and Europe: An Interdisciplinary Collection of Essays*. Ed. Christian Feest. Aachen, Germany: Edition Herodot, 1987.

In the only essay in this collection to examine the Indians' attitudes and experiences in Europe, the author details Indians' activities as tourists as well as performers in Buffalo Bill's Wild West Show. Attracted by high wages and an opportunity to leave the degradation and confinement of reservation life, many Lakota joined the European tour. They were not awed by heads of state, reflecting their own culture's more egalitarian distribution of power, and they often laughed at aspects of European culture that seemed ridiculous to them.

Nash, Gary B. "The Image of the Indian in the Southern Colonial Mind." *William and Mary Quarterly*, vol. 29, no. 2 (April 1972): 197–230.

The author discusses the southern colonial English image of the Indian that reveals the conscious and unconscious workings of Anglo-American minds and gives meaning to English relations with Indians and to English policies directed at controlling, "civilizing," and exterminating them. He argues that the images of Indians were indicators of attitudes toward them. Beginning with the early 1580s, he touches on Indian images created by the English to the 1600s. Continuing to the 1700s, he chronicles the changed social context in which Indians were seen. There are footnotes. See Jacobs, Wilbur R. "The Noble Savage Theme: Attitudes and Policies Toward the Indian in the British Colonies." In *Dispossessing the American Indian: Indians and Whites on the Colonial Frontier.* New York: Charles Scribner's Sons, 1972. pp. 107–25.

"NCAI Wages War on Indian Images." *NCAI Sentinel*, vol. 14, no. 1 (Winter–Spring 1969): 5–7.

The NCAI discusses its nationwide public awareness campaign aimed at improving the image of American Indians in the past and the present. The article not only highlights steps taken by the National Congress of American Indians to remedy stereotypical and inaccurate portrayal of Indians, but also gives details of their successes.

Nemerov, Alexander. "Projecting the Future: Film and Race in the Art of Charles Russell." *American Art*, vol. 8, no. 1 (Winter 1994): 70–89. Illustrations. Notes.

The writer discusses how Indian images painted by Russell (1864–1926), who lived in Great Falls, Montana, much of his career, are symbols for an earlier America. He analyzes Russell's painting "When Shadows Hint Death," remarking on its "remarkably cinematic" quality as well as how its "shadows depict a generic death" and that of a preindustrial past for which Indians have been a metaphor. Another painting, "Buffalo Bill's Duel with Yellowhand," that borrows images from photos of Wounded Knee, is discussed in detail as a "picture about the politics of representation."

O'Barr, William M. "Native Americans." In *Culture and the Ad.* Boulder: Westview Press, 1994. pp. 49–53. Illustrations.

The author examines images of Indian "otherness" in travel advertisements that appeared in 1929 issues of the *National Geographic.* He argues that while the ads suggest recent Indian cultures may have been fierce and unfriendly, their ancient civilizations are mysterious and worthy of attention. Footnotes are included.

O'Conner, John E. *The Hollywood Indian: Stereotypes of Native Americans in Film.* Trenton: New Jersey State Museum, 1980. 79 pp. Illustrations.

This exhibition catalog, illustrated with photographs, explores society's perceptions of Native Americans as influenced by movies and suggests some reasons why stereotypical images have prevailed. The author examines production considerations—dramatic, commercial, and political—and how these factors influenced ten films dealing with Native Americans.

O'Donnell, Thomas F. "More Apologies: The Indians in New York Fiction." *New York Folklore Quarterly*, vol. 23, no. 4: 243–53.

This writer discusses New York novelists and storytellers who have clung to old themes and stereotypes, creating mediocre fiction about Indians. There are footnotes.

Orestano, Francesca. "Dickens on the Indians." In *Indians and Europe: An Interdisciplinary Collection of Essays.* Aaachen, Germany: Edition Herodot, 1987.

Orestano describes Charles Dicken's attitudes toward Indians from his experiences traveling in the American West. Initially captivated by the romantic rhetoric of the noble savage, Dickens wrote that the Indian was a "gentleman of nature." However, with the rising popularity of Darwin's theory of evolution, Dickens abandoned his earlier view in favor of a scientifically grounded defense of Indian extermination in the name of Progress.

Otis, Morgan. "Textbooks and the People Known As American Indians." *Indian Historian*, vol. 10, no. 4 (Fall 1977): 40–46.

The author gives examples of generalizations presented in social studies textbooks accompanied by facts and insights to aid people in developing, understanding, and appreciating peoples different from them. He concludes with suggestions to help identify authentic and reliable materials.

Pakes, Fraser J. "Seeing with the Stereotypic Eye: The Visual Image of the Plains Indian." *Native Studies Review*, vol.1, no. 2 (1985): 1–31. Illustrations. Notes.

The author discusses the "contributions made by the non-Indian world to the building of an image of the Plains Indian. The artists, sculptors, illustrators, photographers, film and television producers, as well as the world of advertising and business, have all made their impact upon this image." He argues that while at times this image has either been extremely positive or extremely negative, it has always remained a permanent stereotype.

Parry, Ellwood. *The Image of the Indian and the Black Man in American Art, 1590–1900.* New York: George Braziller, 1974. Illustrated. Bibliography.

The author illustrates and discusses the changing image in white people's minds of the two major races they encountered in America over a period of three centuries. He provides a "visual anthology" of image-making methods: etchings, lithographs, color lithographs, metal plate engravings, paintings, sculpture, and photographs that contain representations of Indians and Blacks. There are chapter notes and a selected bibliography divided into three categories: Indians, Blacks, and American Art and Artists.

Pearce, Roy Harvey. *Savagism and Civilization: A Study of the Indian and the American Mind.* Baltimore: Johns Hopkins Press, 1965.

The author records and critically appraises the facts of savagism and civilization as reflected in American writings on Indians that appeared in political pamphlets, missionaries' reports, drama, poetry, novels, and anthropological accounts from 1609 to 1851. He also deals with images after 1851 in the final chapters.

Peavy, Charles D. "The American Indian in the Drama of the United States." *The McNeese Review*, vol. 10 (Winter 1958): 68–86.

Twenty-four dramas (from 1766 to 1905) are included in a chronological "Tabulation of Nineteenth Century American Dramas Involving the Theme of the American Indian." The author traces the stage history of how Indians were relegated to be part of America's "romantic past."

Powell, Robin. "Recycling the Redskins." *Turtle Quarterly,* vol. 5, no. 1 (Winter 1993): 8–11.

The author examines the deleterious effects that the use of the name "Redskins" in sports has had on contemporary Indian people and gives a history of the derisive term's use and the conflict that surrounds it.

Powers, William K. "The Indian Hobbyist Movement in North America." In *Handbook of North American Indians*, vol. 4. Washington, D.C.: Smithsonian Institution, 1988. pp. 557–61.

The author looks at the origin and history of American Indian hobbyism, a pursuit of non-Indians with an interest in American Indian culture like arts, crafts, dancing and singing. He suggests that hobbyism has tended both to reinforce American Indian stereotypes and to dispel some of the myths.

Prado, Tailinh. "In Response. . . ." *ICE*, vol. 3, no. 2 (Spring 1995): 11.

Prado responds to the article, "In The Land of Hollywood Make-believe, Anybody Can Say They're Indian," which appeared in *ICE,* Winter of 1995. She contends that Indian people are more accepted if they are either all Indian or if they are "mixed" with White. Indians who have Spanish surnames or are mixed with anything other than White or do not come from the United States or Canada are not seen as being "real" Indians. She feels that people of color should support each other and not fight over the roles that are available to them. The real problem, Prado argues, is that Indians are only allowed to act in Indian roles; other performances are not even offered to them.

Price, John A. "Stereotyping by Indians." In *Native Studies: American and Canadian Indians.* Toronto: McGraw-Hill Ryerson Ltd., 1978. pp. 217–25.

The author discusses stereotypes about Whites within Indian society and gives examples of how white culture and its institutions have become the butt of jokes that circulate through Indian society. He concludes with examples of Indian ethnic jokes (about Whites).

————. "Stereotyping in Motion Pictures." In *Native Studies: American and Canadian Indians.* Toronto: McGraw-Hill Ryerson Ltd., 1978. pp. 200–16. A similar essay is reprinted in Bataille, Gretchen M. and Silet, Charles L. P., eds., 75–91.

Tracing basic stereotypes portrayed in the film industry since 1894, Price maintains that the American motion picture industry has created entertainment that has built a separate reality about Native cultures. He tells why Inuit cultures have largely escaped stereotyped portrayals and argues that quality documentaries like Nanook of the North should be produced.

Prucha, Francis Paul. "The Image of The Indian in Pre-Civil War America." Indiana Historical Society Lectures, 1970/71. pp. 2–19. Notes.

Prucha compares a few Americans who helped shape official government policy toward American Indians: President Thomas Jefferson; Secretary of War, Lewis Cass; President Andrew Jackson; newspaper editor, Horace Greeley; and historian, Francis Parkman. He argues that the image of the Indian held by men like Jefferson, Cass, and Jackson was that although the "red man" was barbaric, he was redeemable. Greeley did not like Indians, but felt they could be saved if they learned the work ethic, and Parkman felt that the Indian was too rigid to change. All agreed that Indian culture should be relegated to the past and set forth official policy to realize that goal.

Queenan, Joe. "Seeing Red." In *Movieline.* December, 1993. pp. 37–40, 82–83, 90.

The author takes on the American film industry in this strong critique of a whole genre of Indian movies. He argues that one of the worst things about the Indian movie genre is that not only does it perpetuate gross misrepresentations of Native American cultures, but also the films are usually very poorly made and embarrassing.

Rans, Geoffrey, "Inaudible Man: The Indian in the Theory and Practice of White Fiction." *Canadian Review of American Studies*, vol. 8, no. 2 (Fall 1977): 103–15.

The author discusses Indians in the works of James Fenimore Cooper, Washington Irving, Nathaniel West, William Faulkner, Thomas Berger, and Ken Kesey.

Redekop, Ernest. "The Redmen: Some Representations of Indians in American Literature Before the Civil War." *CAAS Bulletin*, vol. 3, no. 2 (Winter 1968): 1–44.

The author discusses how Indians are represented in nineteenth-century American literature almost entirely in counterpoint to White people and to help define white civilization. He touches on works of Cooper, William Gilmore Simms, Melville, Robert Montgomery Bird, Hugh Henry Brackenridge, and Charles Brockden Brown.

Remie, Cornelius H. W. "Changing Contexts, Persistent Relations: Inuit-White Encounters in Northern Canada 1576–1992." *European Review of Native American Studies*, vol. 7, no. 2 (1993): 5–11. Illustrations and Bibliography.

The story of the destruction of Inuit culture by the *Qablunaat* (white man) is told in four stages during which a stereotypical attitude of the Inuit as exploitable resources persisted and led to dehumanizing treatment. Inuits were taken to England to be displayed in the 1570s, exploited for two centuries by imperialistic explorers who depended on their map-making skills, hired by whalers in the 1800s and paid with scraps of food, and used as trappers by the Hudson Bay Company from 1911 until 1929 when fur prices dropped and the Inuit economy was destroyed.

Reynolds, Jerry. "Illini Mascot Roams South Dakota." *Lakota Times*, vol. 9, no. 48 (May 29, 1990): 1,3.

A long piece about mascot Chief Illiniwek, a fixture on the University of Illinois campus for more than sixty years, Reynolds discusses the controversy over the movement to "retire" Illiniwek despite the ardent support of the mascot and the racism that has surfaced against people who are antimascot. He also discusses the newest student to fill the role of Illiniwek for two years.

Rhonda, James P. "Singing Birds." In *The Lenape Indian: A Symposium.* Ed. Herbert C. Kraft, pp 11–18. South Orange, NJ: Archaeological Research Center, 1984.

The title of this article is meant to reflect the fictitious tales that the Dutch storytellers for the New Netherlands related about the Delaware Indians. The author offers a synopsis of numerous contemporary Dutch sources, which illustrate the widening gap between reality and the European perspective and how they influenced the Swedes and Quakers, causing the dehumanization of the Delaware. He concludes with a more sympathetic account by Moravian missionary, John Heckewelder, published in 1819.

Riley, Glenda. "Some European (Mis) Perceptions of American Indian Women." *New Mexico Historical Review,* vol. 59, no. 3 (July 1984): 237–66. Notes.

Riley analyzes early views of American Indian women that characterize them as savage, debased, and doomed for subjugation and extinction. She reviews and critiques a cross section of writings of eighteenth- and nineteenth-century European explorers and travelers who helped create the biased interpretations of Indian women, arguing that prejudiced images resulted from what the Europeans wished to see rather than what they saw, "a logical outcome of their pervasive belief that white people were destined to inherit the earth, and most immediately, the American frontier."

———. *Women and Indians on the Frontier, 1825–1915.* Albuquerque: University of New Mexico Press, 1984.

The author's study of white women's views of Indians in the trans-Mississippi West examines ways in which the frontier women reacted to their initial contact and subsequent relations with American Indians. Rather than "holding to the dark and dramatic picture presented them by myth and media, the women who went west frequently changed their minds to a more positive view of Indians." The author hypothesizes why the interplay between white women and American Indians developed a pattern that contradicted the accepted image.

Rollins, Peter C., ed. "The Hollywood Indian, Special Issue." *Film and History*, vol. XXXIII, nos. 1–4. Illustrations. Notes.

This issue is entirely devoted to American Indians in film. Contributors include Ted Jojola, John O'Connor, Hannu Salmi, Ken Nolley, Frank Manchel, Margo Kasdan, Jim Sandos, Robert Baird, and Jeffrey Walker. Articles cover a wide range of subjects like John Ford, stereotypes, and revisionism.

Rollins, Peter C. and O'Connor, John E., eds. *Hollywood's Indian: The Portrayal of Native Americans in Film.* Lexington: University of Kentucky Press, 1998. Illustrations.

A collection of essays offers in-depth analysis of specific films from the silent era all the way up to the present and overviews of Hollywood's depiction of Native Americans from the days of silent films to Disney's "Pocahontas." The writers explore the ways films reflect the attitudes toward the West, the conflict between the races, and the institutional pressures of Hollywood. Also examined are the use of the convention in Finland and "Spaghetti Westerns." Essays also explore the ways in which the differing portrayals—negative, sympathetic, or realistic—have reflected larger changes in American society and their impact on our collective cultural life.

Rose, Alan Henry. *Demonic Vision: Racial Fantasy and Southern Fiction.* Hamden, CT: Archon Book, 1976. Bibliography.

The author examines the humor of the Old South antebellum Southern fiction, and the work of G. W. Harris. He shows how the vision of "Negro" and Indian was first shaped by images of fire and power, then recast in terms of magus-like supernatural energy, and finally how it was repressed by a fearful South to emerge as an impotent stereotype that Whites could accept, reject or ignore. There is a bibliography of literary sources.

Rose, Wendy. "The Great Pretenders: Further Reflections on Whiteshamanism." In *The State of Native America.* Ed. M. Annette Jaimes, 403–21. Boston: South End Press, 1992.

The author takes a critical position against what Geary Hobson (Cherokee) has termed "whiteshamanism." This is the tendency of White, or non-Indian, writers to take on the role of shaman as a means to convey their thoughts. The author argues that these writers often present distortions and inaccuracies that are seen as being more correct than the actual truth from Native Americans. The practice also reduces Native American writing to the level of curiosity, not to be taken as seriously as non-Indian writing and may result in Indian writers misrepresenting themselves to compete with White writers who are seen as having a more genuine Indian point of view. Rose feels that although non-Native writers should make every attempt to be honest and responsible, Indians should view the existence of white shamans as a symptom of a foundering culture, and might contribute to the remedy by offering guidance and sympathy.

Rutland, Robert. "The American Indian Through English Spectacles, 1608–1791." *Chronicles of Oklahoma,* vol. 29, no. 2 (Summer 1951): 169–72.

The writer looks at published works of a number of English traders, soldiers, and adventurers who contributed to the growing shelves of Indian literature which retain "considerable historical interest" and merit reading because they show firsthand impressions, fears, and aspirations of men who pioneered this field of study.

Sando, Joe, S. "White-Created Myths About the Native American." *Indian Historian,* vol. 4, no. 4 (Winter 1970): 10–11.

Myths about American Indians are briefly cited and corrected.

Saum, Lewis O. *The Fur Trader and the Indian.* Seattle: University of Washington Press, 1965. Illustrated. Bibliography.

The author analyzes the attitudes fur traders held about American Indians that were recorded in their journals and letters. There is an extensive unannotated bibliography of fur trade accounts and other works.

Savage, William Jr., ed. *Indian Life: Transforming an American Myth.* Norman: University of Oklahoma Press, 1977. Illustrated.

The author discusses, in an introduction, white images of American Indians and the uses to which Whites put their images of Indians. There are thirteen selections, ranging from 1881 to 1914, that define stereotypes and over forty photographs that identify both how Indians were and what they were thought to be. Notes of secondary sources included.

———. "Monologues in Red and White: Contemporary Racial Attitudes in Two Southern Plains Communities." *Journal of Ethnic Studies,* vol. 2, no. 3 (Fall 1974): 24–31. Bibliography.

The writer looks at the racial attitudes of the white population in Norville and Victorio, Oklahoma, that vary in intensity in direct proportion to the amount of contact the informants have with Indians and concludes racial prejudice exists in both. He reports that Whites link Indians with "Negroes" as a potential "problem" and view Indians as clannish, and he points out other cultural stereotypical views they hold. He also reports how

Indians in the two communities (largely Kiowa and Kiowa-Apaches) are fully aware of White attitudes toward them.

Sayre, Robert F. *Thoreau and the American Indian*. Princeton, NJ: Princeton University Press, 1977.

Tracing Henry Thoreau's fascination with American Indians, the author details Thoreau's reflections on Indians and his idealization of them as solitary, self-reliant hunters, albeit doomed ones. Sayer studies Thoreau's use of savagism in his *A Week on the Concord and Merrimack Rivers* and *Walden* as well as other works. There is an appendix that discusses the name and number of the "Indian Books" and footnotes.

Scheick, William J. *The Half-Blood: A Cultural Symbol in 19th Century American Fiction*. Lexington: University Press of Kentucky, 1979. Notes.

The writer focuses on popular fiction of the nineteenth century (in southern, southwestern, northeastern, and Midwestern literature) because the "half-blood" (half-Indian/half-white) plays a significant role as a symbol in these works. He treats novelists who substituted the figurative half-blood for a literal mixed-blood, using Natty Bumppo, the protagonist in James Fenimore Cooper's *Leatherstocking Tales* and the prototypical half-blood, in countless imitations. He compares and contrasts mulatto and half-blood in terms of attractiveness to nineteenth-century writers, concluding the half-blood was a "safer" but "enigmatic" fictional protagonist.

Scholder, Fritz. *Indian Kitsch: The Use and Misuse of Indian Images*. Flagstaff, AZ: Northland Press, 1979. Illustrations.

Photographs from 1979 exhibition at Phoenix-based Heard Museum show the use and misuse of Indian images, sacred and secular. In his introduction, the renowned painter and printmaker who calls himself a "non-Indian Indian," writes: "In the beginning, it was the Indian who was exploited; later even the Indian would dilute the Indian."

Schuster, Helen. "Children's Drawings and Perceptions of Indianness." *Ethos*, vol. 6, no. 3 (Fall 1978): 159–74.

The author looks at a series of children's drawings collected in the Washington State rural public schools serving Native Americans, Mexican Americans, and European-Americans. The 1965 drawings by Indian and non-Indian students alike reflected largely a rural-white value orientation. The second set of drawings from 1975 in the same schools serving the same population showed a lower frequency of drawings with traditional Indian content. Schuster tries to account for the difference in the drawings.

Scotch, Norman A. "The Vanishing Villains of Television." *Phylon*, vol. 21, no. 1 (Spring 1960): 58–62.

Scotch argues that the pendulum has swung from one extreme to another in terms of Indian characterizations on television. Once savage villains, Indians are presented as strong, silent, and eminently virtuous while ranchers and cowpokes are characterized as Indian murderers. He argues the truth is more desirable, not a "new mythical conception of noble savage." He suggests the growing popularity of anthropology, a growing concern with a world picture of Americans as bigots, and genuine admiration for a "fantasy" group like Indians account for a "splurge of sentimentalizing the Indian."

Shaughnessy, Tim. "White Stereotypes of Indians." *Journal of American Indian Education*, vol. 17, no. 2 (January 1978): 20–24. Bibliography.

The author defines stereotypes and lists criteria that underlie them. He discusses the common stereotypes, and some of their origins, of Indians that are damaging to the contemporary Indian's self-image. The bibliography lists articles of research.

Sheehan, Bernard. "Images: The Problem of the Indian in the Revolution." In *The American Indian Experience: A Profile, 1524 to the Present*. Ed. Philip Weeks. Arlington Heights, IL: Forum Press, 1988. Bibliography.

The writer summarizes how during the American Revolution, Indians were an issue of "immense significance" both to the British and Americans. The Indian as a symbol proved indispensable in the making of American independence and in developing a revolutionary ideology. Americans distinguished themselves from Europeans by describing qualities of noble savagery. Although the noble savage functioned as an ideal that had been lost but might again be attained, its use as propaganda did not connote any particular affection for Native people.

Shively, JoEllen. "Cowboys and Indians: Perceptions of Western Films Among American Indians and Anglos." *American Sociological Review*, vol. 57 (December 1992): 725–34.

The author, who examines sociological models of how people use and interpret cultural materials, had matched groups of American Indian and Anglo males answer written questionnaires and participate in focus-group interviews after viewing *The Searchers*, a Western film with major conflict between cowboys and Indians. The author notes that both groups liked the film, but for different reasons implying that the meaning imputed to cultural works varies over social space.

Sholer, Bo. "Images and Counter-Images: Ohiyesa, Standing Bear, and American Literature." *American Indian Culture and Research Journal*, vol. 5, no. 2 (1981): 37–63.

The author gives an overview of literature written about Native Americans until 1925 and the development of stereotypical images by formula literature, serious literature, visual arts, and the Wild West Show. He analyzes six literary works by Siouan authors, Ohiyesa (Charles Eastman) and Standing Bear to establish a paradigm of Siouan counterimagery to correct the image of the Sioux.

Silet, Charles L. P. "The Image of the American Indians in Film." In *The Worlds Between Two Rivers: Perspectives on American Indians in Iowa*. Eds. Gretchen Bataille, David Gradwohl, and Charles L. P. Silet, pp. 10–15. Ames: Iowa State University Press, 1978.

The author traces the image of American Indians in film touching on the "noble savage" and a generic Indian "type" that existed only in the movies. He contends that more recent films proclaiming to be more authentic in their portrayal of Indians still ignore historical and contemporary realities of Indian culture and thus more stereotypes are created.

Slate, Joseph. "A Climate Favorable to Darwinian Theories of Race." In *Impact of Darwinian Thought in American Life and Culture*. Houston: American Studies Association of Texas, 1959. pp. 73–83.

The author argues that American culture assimilated Darwinian theories of racial evolution and survival of the fittest with earlier American views of the Indian because the frontier provided a continuity of experience that connected these differing perspectives. Early American attitudes toward Indians reflected a goal of "civilizing the savages," who were seen as morally and culturally inferior. Darwin's theory of natural laws of evolution and survival of the fittest were used to justify both public attitudes and government policies of extermination of the Indians as progress.

Slotkin, Richard. *Regeneration Through Violence: The Mythology of the American Frontier 1600–1860*. Middletown, CT: Wesleyan University Press, 1973. Bibliography.

The evolution of the American frontier myth and how it influenced and shaped the nation's literary outpourings between 1620 and 1860 is dealt with in this work. Puritan literature, the Boone narrative, Cooper, Melville, Thoreau, and other writers are all touched on. There is a lengthy bibliography.

Smart, George Gregory. "The Re-Creation of the American 'Indian' in Proceedings of Ephemera Symposium III." *The Ephemera Journal*, vol. 6 (1993): 12–20. Illustrations. After examining ephemera (travel brochures, souvenirs, playing cards, cigar labels, postcards, trade cards, and labels) in his own and in public and private collections throughout the country, the author argues that Indians were homogenized into cliches, stereotypes, and archetypes, romanticized to represent particular landscapes or products, used as a lone salesman, and objectified and separated from family, tribe, and human contexts.

Smith, James R. "Native American Images and the Broadcast Media." *American Indian Culture and Research Journal*, vol. 5, no. 1 (1981): 81–89. The author presents an overview of the images of Indians in broadcast programming, which, he argues, influence stereotypes. He suggests some intermedia differences with regard to Indian images.

Smith, Robert C. "The Noble Savage in Paintings and Prints." *Antiques*, vol. 74, no. 1 (July 1958): 57–59. Illustrated. This is a brief survey of European paintings of American Indians from the sixteenth through the nineteenth centuries that evoked the noble savage image. The article is condensed from the catalog of an exhibition "The Noble Savage" held at the University Museum, University of Pennsylvania, in 1958.

Smith, Sherry L. *The View from Officers' Row: Army Perceptions of Western Indians*. Tucson: University of Arizona Press, 1990. The author reveals American army officers' views about the Indians against whom they fought in the last half of the nineteenth century. She shows that officers and their wives did not share a monolithic negative view of their enemies, but instead often developed a great respect for Indians and their cultures. The author uses personal documents drawn from representative samples of the officer corps at all levels.

Sorber, Edna. "The Noble Eloquent Savage." *Ethnohistory*, vol. 19, no. 3 (Summer 1972): 227–36. Bibliography. Sorber contends that the myth of the "noble savage" has been related historically to the myth of the "eloquent savage." She discusses how people have unwittingly contributed to the perpetuation the idea of the "eloquent savage" even into this century. There is a bibliography of secondary research in speech journals.

Staniford, Edward F. "The California Indians: A Critique of Their Treatment by Historians." *Ethnohistory*, vol. 18, no. 2 (Spring 1971): 119–25. Bibliography. The author criticizes historians writing textbooks on California history for their misstatements, misconceptions, omissions, and disparaging remarks concerning California Indians. He cites cases and proposes the solution to the problem is a closer cooperation between historians and anthropologists. There is a brief bibliography of secondary sources.

Stedman, Raymond William. *Shadows of the Indian: Stereotypes in American Culture*. Norman: University of Oklahoma Press, 1982. 281 pp. Illustrations. Bibliography. The author studies racial and cultural stereotyping, documented with reproductions of historic paintings, engravings, and other drawings as well as examples of modern popular culture. He examines the emergence of mythic Indian people from their first contacts with white people, when Indians were viewed as a curiosity through various incarnations that ranged from "Noble Savage" to a satanic presence. He draws on literature, art and popular culture to describe themes and counterfeit images attached to Indians. Appended is a chronology of plays and printed works in American popular culture, 1493–1981.There is a lengthy bibliography of books, periodicals, and newspapers.

Strayer, Brian F. "Fur Trappers' Attitudes Toward the Upper Missouri Sioux, 1820–1860." *Indian Historian*, vol. 12, no. 4 (1979): 34–40.

The author explores relationships between the Sioux and trappers, who often competed with the Sioux and were considered "more savage" than the Indians by Whites. Although the trappers were hostile and showed great contempt for the Sioux, they sometimes intermarried with them only to later abandon their Sioux wives.

Strickland, Rennard. "Coyote Goes Hollywood." *Native Peoples: The Arts and Lifeways*, vol. 2, no. 3 (Spring 1989): 44–52, and "Coyote Goes Hollywood." *Native Peoples: The Arts and Lifeways*, vol. 4, no.1 (Fall 1989): 38–46.

Part 1 deals with sinister portrayals and historical distortions in film that date from the beginning of the motion picture industry. The author, of Osage/Cherokee heritage, also discusses Native Americans who are beginning to reshape their cinematic image. Part 2 addresses Native American cinemagraphic creations. Strickland discusses Bob Hick's (Creek) film, "Return of the Country," which satirizes every cliché of the Indian in film, and many other Native filmmakers including Chris Spotted Eagle and Victor Masayesva, Jr., as well as Native Americans who are remaking and replacing the old Hollywood Indians. Both articles are illustrated with old film photos and posters and photos of contemporary films starring Native people.

―――. "Tonto's Revenge, or, Who is That Seminole in the Sioux Warbonnet? The Cinematic Indian!" In *Tonto's Revenge: Reflections on American Indian Culture and Policy*. Albuquerque: University of New Mexico Press. pp. 17–45. Notes.

The author's premise for this chapter is that the media—radio, television, and film—is powerful and the media image of Indians equally powerful "because it is that image which looms large as non-Indians [in Congress] decide the fate of Indian people." He points out that if one's knowledge of Indians were limited to film viewing, there would appear to be few living twentieth-century Native peoples. After summarizing plots of historic films with their repetitive images of good or bad Indians, he describes with optimism film and video by Native producers and reviews with pessimism plots of contemporary films about Indians. He hopes that Tonto, arguably the most widely known Indian figure in film history, and old screen Tonto stereotypes he spawned vanish in the wake of Indian filmmakers who have converted the screen Indian into a real Indian.

Sturtevant, William C. "First Visual Images of Native America." In *First Images of America: The Impact of the New World on the Old*. Ed. Fred Chiappelli et al., pp. 417–54. 2 vols. Berkeley: University of California Press, 1976. Illustrated.

The author enumerates and describes 268 separate depictions representing about forty different artists from 1502 to 1588. He classifies twelve sources of the European iconography of Native Americans such as (1) "An artist may draw or paint directly from life either in America or in Europe" or (2) "Finally, European stylistic conventions inevitably affect New World scenes." There is a catalog of extant illustrations prior to DeBry, who served as the artist's source for at least two centuries, having some claim to ethnographic accuracy.

Swanson, Charles H. "The Treatment of the American Indian in High School History Texts." *Indian Historian*, vol. 10, no. 2 (Spring 1977): 28–37. Bibliography.

The author examines almost fifty history texts from the early 1960s and late 1960s to early 1970s to see if there have been any significant textual changes in the thematic depictions of historical Indian-White relations in contemporary times and to discuss how these depictions format and perpetuate unfavorable stereotypes about American Indians. There is a bibliography of references cited and six tables of data that show the number and percentage of texts that mention certain events and issues that are discussed in the text.

Tapia, John Reyna. *The Indian in the Spanish-American Novel.* Washington, D.C.: University Press of America, 1981.

Tapia discusses how at first the indigene in nineteenth-century Spanish American novels was used as a primordial theme and then, with the impact of Romanticism in Spanish America, was transformed into a romantic literary figure, and finally into a figure of social protest. The themes contained in the indigene novel include indigenous community property; development of Creole agrarian capitalism; present-day exploitation of Indians, not as a racial individual but as a worker in fields and mines; the centralist government and its political machinery, which destroys Indians; the church as a protector of the politician and land owner; and the role of intellectuals in the political and economic reform toward bettering Indian life.

Taylor, Colin F. "The Hobbyist Movement in Europe." In *Handbook of the North American Indians,* vol. 4. Ed. Wilcomb E. Washburn, pp. 562–69. Washington, D.C.: Smithsonian Institution, 1988.

The author discusses how, in European countries, there is a wide range of nonprofessional interests in Native North Americans manifested in regalia-making and powwows as well as dressing up like Indians, dancing and singing frequently in public. He looks at activities in the United Kingdom, Sweden, Germany, Holland, Belgium, France, Italy, Switzerland, Czechoslovakia, Finland, Poland, the Soviet Union, and Hungary. There are photos of the hobbyists.

Ten Kate, Herman, F. C. "The Indian in Literature." In *Annual Report of the Smithsonian Institution for 1921.* Washington, D.C.: Government Printing Office, 1922. pp. 509–14. Reprinted in *Indian Historian,* vol. 3, no. 3 (Summer 1970): 23–32.

Ten Kate covers literature from 1799 to 1916 that treats Indian figures as heroes. He assesses them from the ethnologist's and geographer's perspective rather than a literary one. Authors covered include Ferry, Miller, Mair, Humboldt, Wallace, and Nordenskiold among over thirty others. He contends that only ten of these authors have ethnologic and geographic value.

Todd, Ruthven. "The Imaginary Indian in Europe." *Art in America,* vol. 60, no. 4 (July–August 1972): 40–47. Illustrated.

The author examines how the British and French saw the American Indians in the eighteenth and nineteenth centuries and concludes that the Europeans were unable to perceive Indians by any other standards than European ones. There are illustrations of paintings, etchings, and tobacco labels. See Roxanna Barry, "Rousseau and Buffalo Bill and the European Image of the American Indian." *Art News,* vol. 74 (December 1975): 58–61.

Trafzer, Clifford E. "Indians and Textbooks." *News From Native California,* vol. 5, no. 1 (November–January, 1990/91): 40–41.

The author reviews the June 1990 meetings of California's Instructional Materials Evaluation Panel. He discusses the strengths and weaknesses of certain fourth, fifth, and eighth grade American and California history textbooks that the panel considered.

Trennert, Robert A. "Popular Imagery and the American Indian: A Centennial View." *New Mexico Historical Review*, vol. 51, no. 3 (July 1976): 215–32.

The author views popular imagery of American Indians in the centennial year and concludes that the vast majority of the public was treated to a one-sided view of Indians and that public attitudes exercised a strong effect on the course of Indian affairs. There are footnotes.

Tribal College: *Journal of American Indian Higher Education*, vol. 8, no. 4 (Spring 1997). Issue on Racism.

In nine articles, writers explore racism that affects Indian people on a daily basis and in the classroom as well as what is being done about it by both American Indians and non-Indians. The writers who look at how racism against Indian people differs from racism against other ethnic and racial groups also look at the role of tribal colleges as brokers between cultures.

Trigger, Bruce G. "Archaeology and the Image of the American Indian." *American Antiquity*, vol. 45, no. 4 (October 1980): 662–76. Bibliography.

The author argues that the most important single factor that has shaped the long-term development of American archaeology has been the traditional European-American stereotype, which portrayed America's Native peoples as being inherently unprogressive. He discusses how the idea that Indian cultures were static and primitive was reflected in the way archaeological data was interpreted prior to 1914 and that the stereotypes were unchallenged up until the 1960s. He concludes that the "new archaeology" continues to treat Native peoples as objects rather than subjects of research.

Trillin, Calvin. "US Journal: Hanover, NH: The Symbol as a Symbol." *The New Yorker*, May 7, 1979. pp.132–40.

The author discusses the battle over the Indian symbol at Dartmouth College (before the issue was resolved) against a backdrop of other Dartmouth issues involving fraternities, a controversial hockey game incident, and the Native American Program. He discusses the reaction of Indian students at Dartmouth who resented the Indian symbol and cheerleader in body paint and feathers and insisted they had to go. He also gives the history of the resistance of alumni to changing the symbol.

Troy, Anne. "The Indian in Adolescent Novels." *Indian Historian*, vol. 8, no. 4 (Winter 1975): 32–35.

In this article, the author attempts to determine what stereotypes of Indians exist in 1930 novels and where these same images can be found in 1960 novels. "In summary, the 1960 novels as well as the 1930 novels continued for the most part the traditional dual and contradictory image of the Indian: the dirty, drunken, cruel and warring savage as well as the glorified, noble but naive native. Both images are stereotyped: neither image describes real human-life characters." The writer makes four recommendations for potential writers of novels. This article summarizes Troy's Ph.D. dissertation entitled *The Indian in Adolescent Literature, 1930–1970* (The University of Iowa, 1972).

Utley, Robert M. "The Frontier Army: John Ford or Arthur Penn." In *Indian-White Relations: A Persistent Paradox*. Eds. Robert M. Kvasicka and Jane F. Smith, pp. 133–45. Washington, D.C.: Howard University Press, 1976. Illustrated.

Film directors, Ford and Penn, presented stereotypical interpretations of the character of the frontier army of the nineteenth century the author argues. Utley contends that the frontier army was a police force and confronted an unconventional military enemy in a conventional way. There is a map and footnotes. See William B. Skelton, "Army

Officers' Attitudes Toward Indians, 1830–1860." *Pacific Northwest Quarterly,* vol. 67, no. 3 (July 1976): 113–24. Illustrated.

Vagts, Alfred. "The Germans and the Red Man." *American-German Review,* vol. 24, no. 1 (October–November 1957): 13–17. Illustrated.

Vagts points out that German readers selected American Indians as the one group with which they could identify, although their only contact with Indians was through literature and not a colonial relationship like the French and English. He discusses the Indians' contribution to spoken and written German. There are sketches by Kurz and Slevogt and an illustration of the Indian Cafe at the 1873 Vienna World's Fair.

Van Hise, James. *Who Was That Masked Man? The Story of the Lone Ranger.* Las Vegas: Pioneer Books, Inc., 1990.

Although the author offers neither analysis of the Lone Ranger television series nor biographies, he does include plot summaries of which only twelve dealt with Indians. Tonto was at first depicted as equally daring and skilled in "Indian" ways, which enabled him to execute lifesaving rescues of the Lone Ranger, but then later relegated to just a sidekick. The author asserts that Tonto portrayed a defender of justice and equal treatment of the Indians, in part by defying a reservation existence.

Vaughan, Alden T. "From White Man to Redskin: Changing Anglo-American Perceptions of the American Indian." *The American Historical Review,* vol. 87, no. 4 (October 1982): 917–53.

The author discusses the use of colors to describe ethnicity and endeavors to understand its historical role. He proposes that the greater proximity of Indian skin color to European's than black skin color has influenced their respective treatment. The European goal was to assimilate the Indians and to enslave Blacks. Beginning with the European treatment of Africans, he argues that the linguistic implications of "black" in most European languages were enough to bias Europeans against Africans. The relative lightness of Native Americans gave rise to an altogether different type of treatment. Yet, the author continues, the question of nationality supplanted the question of racial differences in the nineteenth century, and as a result the isolation of Indians became more defined and negative images, as well as their identity as "redmen," grew prevalent. Skin color became the prime touchstone for scientific classification of humans in the eighteenth century and it became established in a good part of the scientific community that the Indians were of a distinct and inferior racial class. The author concludes with an explanation of how the ensuing disfavor of Indians among European-Americans, and the growing popularity of colorizing them, culminated in the hostilities that have existed ever since.

Vickers, Scott B. *Native American Identities: From Stereotype to Archtype in Art and Literature.* Albuquerque: University of New Mexico, 1998.

The author deals with the question "What is a Native American?" by juxtaposing stereotypes of Indians against Indian perceptions of themselves in art and literature. Vickers first outlines the religious, political, and media forces that shaped the images of America's indigenous peoples, and then he shows how non-Indian language and art manufactured the image of the Indian as a single homogenous entity. Finally, the author gives an overview of the ways noted Indian artists and writers have addressed questions of identity.

Vogel, Virgil J. *The Indian in American History.* Chicago: Integrated Education, 1968. Bibliography.

The author examines the maltreatment of Indians in American history books and textbooks. He argues that historians have used four principal methods to create or perpetuate false impressions of aboriginal Americans: obliteration, defamation, disembodiment, and disparagement. There is a selected bibliography that is limited to one aspect: the aboriginal influence on Americans. Titles include agriculture and food, art, childcare, and bibliographies.

Wakim, Yvonne B. "Get Crazy Horse Off That Beer Can and Let Pocahontas Go Home." *AIGA Journal of Graphic Design*, vol. 14, no. 1 (The Property Issue): 18–19.

This brief article addresses the stereotyping and appropriation of Indian culture and images for commercial design purposes. Religion/spirituality, dress, and Pocahontas are touched on as well as solutions to remedy the situation.

Weaver, Jace. "Ethnic Cleansing, Homestyle." *Wicazo Sa Review*, vol. 10, no. 1 (Spring 1994): 27–39. Bibliography.

This article is a survey of the representation of indigenous people throughout the development of American musicals from 1794. The author discusses native and crude images of Indians in these productions.

Weitenkampf, Frank. "How Indians Were Pictured in Earlier Days." *New York Historical Society Quarterly*, vol. 33, no. 4 (October 1949): 213–21. Illustrated.

The author focuses on the way European and American artists portrayed Indian racial traits in the faces of their models from 1500 to 1850, in which the pictures of Indians advanced from the purely fictitious through the dubious to the realistic. There are six illustrations ranging from around 1505 to 1844.

Wenrick, Jon S. "Indians in Almanacs." *The Indian Historian*, vol. 8, no. 4 (Winter 1975): 36–42. Notes.

The author encourages the use of almanacs, small pamphlets that were very popular in the United States in its first century, as historical resources. References to Indians were numerous and often filled with fear and hostility. Almanac literature in general, the author shows, is a very useful source by which to judge White attitudes toward Indians in the early years of the republic.

White, John R. "Playboy Blacks vs. Playboy Indians: Differential Minority Stereotyping in Magazine Cartoons." *American Indian Culture and Research Journal*, vol. 3, no. 2 (1979): 39–55.

The author illustrates the nature and varieties of stereotyping of Blacks and Indians, which occurred from 1954 to 1973 in *Playboy* and identifies changes in the context and frequency of that stereotyping over time. Tables of data and footnotes are included. See entry under Houts, Kathleen C. and Bahr, Rosemary S.

Wilkinson, Gerald. "Colonialism Through the Media." *The Indian Historian*, vol. 7, no. 3 (Summer 1974): 29–32.

This article analyzes the media's creation of a false image of Native Americans. He argues that image has served the interest of the white public, either the negative image of the drunken, dumb, helpless savage or "the noble savage so detached from reality that he achieves fairy tale proportions." He explains how cable TV is a cultural threat to Indians and contends they should control some of the media to protect their own image.

Williams, Cat. "The Indian Problem: Mass Media Images Create Stereotypes and False Impressions." *Winds of Change*, vol. 10, no. 4 (Autumn 1995): 129–131.

Navajo writer Cat Williams briefly surveys movies that either disregard unique tribal differences or try to be politically correct and portray Indians in a positive way. The writer also decries how the dominant culture now exploits indigenous art and religion.

Wilson, Charles R. "Racial Reservations: Indians and Blacks in American Magazines, 1865–1900." *Journal of Popular Culture*, vol. 10, no. 1 (Summer 1976): 70–79.

Wilson examines articles relating to Indians and Blacks in the late nineteenth-century American magazines and argues that although both are treated unfavorably, Indian images were frequently worse than images of Blacks. There are lengthy notes.

Woll, Allen L. "Native Americans." In *Ethnic and Racial Images in American Film and Television: Historical Essays and Bibliography*. Ed. Allen L. Woll and Randall M. Miller. New York: Garland Publishing, Inc., 1987. Bibliography.

A brief essay analyzes Native American film and television stereotypes and the role of Indians on the American screen beginning with the first filmmakers. The writer also discusses five major works analyzing the images of Indians in American film and television. A bibliography lists eighty-one titles dealing with stereotypes, some of which are film reviews.

Zolla, Elemire. *The Writer and the Shaman: A Morphology of the American Indian*. Translated by Raymond Rosenthal. New York: Harcourt Brace Jovanovich, Inc., 1969, 1973. Notes.

Zolla chronicles the many images of Indians that appear in American literature and how Indians have become part of two opposing erudite fantasies—as an Arcadian and as a savage in the sixteenth century. She touches on literature of missionaries, romanticists, enlightenment zealots, reverence, and a variety of other styles up to contemporary times. Some of the authors included are Cooper, Melville, Irving, Cooper, Morgan, Bandelier, Leland, Cather, De Angulo, Wilson, and LaFarge.

"CORRECTIVE" MATERIALS

Banks, James A. "First Americans and African Americans." In *Teaching Strategies for Ethnic Studies*. Boston: Allyn and Bacon, 1991. pp. 129–232. Bibliography.

Part II of Teaching Strategies for Ethnic Studies covers materials and methods for teaching about Native and African Americans. Included is a chronology of important dates in American history after the Spanish incursions, a synopsis of early life in the Americas, a discussion of tribal similarities and differences, and then an overview of Native American experiences after the European settlements. An analysis of contemporary conditions and teaching methodologies, starting from primary grades to high school level, are also helpful. An extensive bibliography of materials is offered as well as many other references and teaching aids.

Billman, Jane. "The Native American Curriculum: Attempting Alternatives to Tepees and Headbands." In *Young Children*, vol. 47, no. 6 (September 1992): 22–25.

The author reviews her attempts as a non–Native American teacher to teach about Native Americans. Her predominant concern, in all her references to methodology, is the problem of authenticity. She grapples with the question of whether or not teaching about Indians is in fact reinforcing their otherness, and if it is, how to present the truth effectively.

Caduto, Michael and Bruchac, Joseph. *Keepers of the Earth: Native American Stories and Environmental Activities for Children*. Golden, CO: Fulcrum, Inc., 1988. Illustrations. Notes. Bibliography.

The book contains a collection of North American Indian stories and "hands on activities that promote understanding and appreciation of, empathy for, and responsible action toward the Earth, including its people." The stories and environmental activities in the book and its companion teacher's guide, designed for kindergarten through the primary grades, roughly five to twelve years old, provide a complete program of study in ecological topics and history. The first part of the two part book gives instructions for using the book and the second part focuses on "Native American Stories and Environmental Activities," related to a myriad of subjects including Creation, Fire and Water. Fulcrum also publishes other curriculum books by these authors: *Keepers of the Animals, Keepers of the Night,* and *Keepers of Life.*

Caldwell-Wood, Naomi and Mitten, Lisa A. "'I' is Not for Indian: The Portrayal of Native Americans in Books for Young People." *Multicultural Review,* vol. 1, no. 2 (April 1992): 26–35.

The authors, officers of the American Indian Library Association, provide a bibliography of recommended titles, titles to avoid, guides to selecting books and sources of current reviews, and sources for books on Indians.

Closs, Michael. *Native American Mathematics.* Austin: University of Texas, 1986. Illustrated. This book covers time from the prehistoric to the present in its thirteen essays that introduce American Indian mathematical development.

Conn, Richard. *Robes of White Shell and Sunrise: Personal Decorative Arts of the Native American.* Denver: Denver Art Museum, 1974. Illustrated. Bibliography. The exhibition of "Robes of White Shell and Sunrise" seeks to reveal the richness and remarkable diversity of Indian design concepts. There is a map of American Indian tribes and a bibliography.

Council on Interracial Books for Children. *Guidlines for Selecting Bias-Free Textbooks.* New York: Council on Interracial Books for Children, 1980. This book contains guidelines for choosing bias-free children's storybooks, textbooks, and U.S. history textbooks. Topics covered include racism, sexism, handicapism, ageism, materialism, competition, elitism, and classicism. There are lists of materials and much more valuable information.

———. *Winning "Justice for All": A Social Studies/Language Arts Curriculum* (Teacher and Student Editions). New York: Council on Interracial Books for Children, 1980. This curriculum was designed to increase students' understanding of institutional racism and sexism and to develop their motivation and ability to challenge institutional inequities in education and in society. Three teaching modules include filmstrips and are entitled, "Stereotypes and Their Uses," "How Sexism and Racism Operate," and "How to Fight Sexism and Racism." A variety of materials—poems, nursery rhymes, diaries, biographies, newspaper accounts, charts, and filmstrips—have been included for student use.

Denver Art Museum. *American Indian Publications.* Denver, CO. Illustrated. Bibliography. The Museum has published over 100 illustrated leaflets, which cover a wide range of Native American topics. This series supplies accurate, nontechnical information about Native Americans and the North American continent. A wide range of topics are covered from Indian arts to food to languages.

Farber, Joseph C. and Dorris, Michael. *Native Americans: 500 Years After.* New York: Thomas Y. Crowell Co., 1975. Illustrated. Bibliography. This book contains hundreds of photographs taken by Farber who traveled throughout North American photographing Native Americans as they live today. There is a list of the locations photographed and a selected list of readings.

Gearing, Frederick O. "Why Indians." *Social Education*, vol. 32, no. 2 (February 1968): 128–31, 146.

The author argues that the proper classroom study of any Indian community can provide serious educational profit. The author feels that students should learn the anthropological experience that culturally patterned "bizarre" behavior does in the end make human sense. He gives examples of behavior among Eskimos and Cherokees, seemingly bizarre, and adds additional information that transforms the bizarre into the humanly believable. He argues that the proper study of Indian communities can help students see well the social world around them, which is often too familiar to quite see, because it provides dramatic comparison in realms of economic, political, and social organization.

Gilliland, Hap. *Teaching the Native American*, 3rd ed. Dubuque, Iowa: Kendall-Hunt Publishing Co., 1995. Bibliographies.

The author introduces educators to the many facets of Native American culture and values that affect students' motivation, self-image, learning styles, discipline, and more. Throughout the book, the author provides practical information and suggestions for teaching social studies, reading, whole language, creative writing, English and Native languages, mathematics, science, computers, art, and physical education.

Greenberg, Polly. "Ideas That Work With Young Children." *Young Children*, vol. 47, no. 6 (September 1992): 27–30.

The author presents a number of means by which teachers in children's classrooms could discuss and project the issues of race in a positive and constructive way. She stresses especially the need among teachers to be constantly aware of racial issues and to regularly incorporate them into the curriculum. In addition, she stresses the need to respond immediately to children's games and comments that might be erroneous or discriminatory.

Harvey, Karen D.; Harjo, Lisa D.; and Jackson, Jane K. *Teaching About Native Americans*. Bulletin No., 84, Washington, D.C.: National Council for the Social Studies, 1990.

This curriculum bulletin is "intended to provide direct and practical support for elementary and secondary teachers." Chapters, which include background information, lesson plans, and reference lists, deal with Environment and Resources, Culture and Diversity, Change and Adaptions, Conflict and Discrimination, Current Issues for Native Americans, and Resources for Teachers and Students.

"Headdresses Used by Some Native Americans." *The Weewish Tree*, vol. 4, no. 4 (1976): 15–18. Illustrated.

The article shows a few of the many headdresses worn traditionally by Indian tribes that vary in shape, design, and style.

Hirschfelder, Arlene. "Bibliography of Sources and Materials for Teaching About American Indians." *Social Education*, vol. 36, no. 5 (May 1972): 488–93.

The author lists and describes a variety of materials for creating units or courses about Native Americans. She discusses selected published teaching units, audio and visual materials, written documentary materials, and other supplementary sources (museum and historical publications).

Keller, Robert H. Jr. "On Teaching Indian History: Legal Jurisdiction in Chippewa Treaties." *Ethnohistory*, vol. 19, no. 3 (Summer 1972): 209–18. Bibliography.

The writer discusses the reasons why he uses Indian treaties with the U.S. government in the teaching of Indian history. He feels they provide a fruitful path to learning about Indian affairs and introduces students to theories justifying the European conquest of

North America and to the "legal bramble bush of state-federal relations vis-à-vis Indian tribes" as well as other reasons.

Kerner, Kathy. *They Taught You Wrong: Raising Cultural Consciousness of Stereotypes and Misconceptions about American Indians.* Lynchburg, VA: Carole Durham, 1995.

This manual directs teachers and other educators to reliable sources of information to correct misinterpretations and eliminate stereotypes of Native cultures. At the same time, the booklet provides a collection of Native voices, "Key Concepts for Non-Indians to Understand," bibliographies of books for adults, children, and other resources, and a "Thanksgiving Holiday Packet" for K–5 teachers from the Madison, Wisconsin, Metropolitan School District. The materials provide some alternatives to the traditional Pilgrim–Indian approach to Thanksgiving as well as copies of several alternative activities. (Available from Carole Durham, 1016 Woodhaven Dr., Lynchburg, VA 24502; e-mail: ribonshirt@aol.com)

Krieger, H. W. "American Indian Costumes in the U.S. National Museum." *Annual Report of the Smithsonian Institution for 1928*, pp. 623–61. Illustrated.

The writer describes the Native American clothing collection in the Smithsonian Institution. He includes information from many different nations; there are illustrations from the collection.

Lanoutte, JoAnne. "Teachers Corner: Erasing Native American Stereotypes." *Anthro News*, vol. 12, no. 3 (Fall 1990): 7–9.

This issue presents a list of items for teachers to consider when teaching about Native Americans. The author draws from a list created by the D'Arcy McNickle Center for the History of the American Indian at the Newberry Library in Chicago.

Little Soldier, Lee. "Working with Native American Children." *Young Children*, vol. 47, no. 6 (September 1992): 15–21.

The author discusses the virtues of cooperative learning in children's education over highly competitive classrooms. He feels that cooperative learning is especially preferable in teaching Native Americans to whom group learning is generally more comfortable than competition with other children. The author stresses that there is no one way to treat all Native American children because their backgrounds vary greatly, but a teacher should be nurturing and sensitive to the Native student's feelings.

Maine Indian Program, American Friends Service Committee. *The Wabanakis of Maine and the Maritimes. A Resource Book about Penobscot, Passamaquoddy, Maliseet, Micmac and Abenaki Indians.* (With lesson plans for grades 4 through 8.) Bath, Maine: Maine Indian Program, 1989. Bibliography.

This book provides sociohistorical information and materials on the history and culture of Indians in Maine and the Maritimes. Readings, lesson plans, resources, some illustrations, and interviews can all be used for a variety of classroom projects from games to prejudice to contemporary life to history.

See Mihesuah, Devon. *American Indians: Stereotypes and Realities* in Bibliography—Stereotyping of Native Americans.

Moore, Robert B. *Racism in the English Language.* New York: Racism and Sexism Resource Center for Educators, 1976.

The author discusses how language not only expresses ideas and concepts but also actually shapes thought. Aspects of racism in the English language that are discussed in this essay include terminology, symbolism, politics, ethnocentrism, and context. There are footnotes and lesson plans.

Newberry Library. *Teaching American Indian History: A Selection of Course Outlines.*
Occasional papers in Curriculum Series No. 10. Chicago: Newberry Library, D'Arcy
McNickle Center for the History of the American Indian, 1988.
In response to a special invitation for sample syllabi, the Newberry Library published
course descriptions and syllabi that cover a wide range of teaching environments.
Frederick E. Hoxie, Director of the Newberry suggests that readers draw on the syllabi
as guides as they "chart their educational course with their students."

Patton, William E., ed. *Improving the Use of Social Studies Textbooks.* Bulletin 63.
Washington, D.C.: National Council for the Social Studies, 1980.
The Bulletin is designed to show how it is possible to update the dated, strengthen reading comprehension, study pictures, correct ethnic and sex stereotypes, and evaluate the
strengths and weaknesses of today's textbooks. A bibliography is provided to encourage additional study and research.

Pewewardy, Cornel. "Fluff and Feathers: Treatment of American Indians in the Library and
the Classroom." *Equity and Excellence,* vol. 31, no. 1 (April 1998): 69–76. Bibliography.
Based on twenty years of practitioner experience, action research, and hundreds of
workshops on effective teaching practices for American Indian learners, the author, an
assistant professor in the Department of Teaching and Learning in the School of
Education at the University of Kansas, makes suggestions that have been effective in
teaching Indian youngsters. He writes: "To be a culturally responsive teacher of
American Indian children, teachers must be prepared to understand, and accept as
equally valid, values and ways of life very different from their own. Many teachers
speak of American Indian students as being disadvantaged. In reality, many Indian
students have the double advantage of knowing and living in several cultures. The
teacher, on the one hand, may know only one culture, and may have accepted that culture as being superior without any real thought or study. It is the teacher, then, who is
disadvantaged."

Reyhner, Jon. *Teaching American Indian Students.* Norman: University of Oklahoma Press,
1993. Bibliography.
This multidisplinary volume summarizes the latest research on Indian education, provides practical suggestions for teachers, and offers a vast selection of resources available to teachers of Indian students. Included are chapters on bilingual and multicultural
education; the history of U.S. Indian education; teacher-parent relationships; language
and literacy development; with particular discussion of English as a second language
and American Indian literature; and teaching in the content areas—social science, science, mathematics, and physical education.

Robinson, Barbara. *Native American Sourcebook: A Teacher's Perspective on New England
People.* Concord, MA: Concord Museum, 1988.
This unit contains activities to help counter stereotyping, especially at Thanksgiving.
Native American museums and organizations listed by states and essays by Native Peo-
ple are included.

Slapin, Beverly and Seale, Doris. *Books Without Bias: Through Indian Eyes.* Berkeley,
CA: Oyate, 1988. Revised edition. Bibliography.
This book contains a collection of essays about stereotyping, dozens of book reviews,
and a checklist of criteria to select reliable books about Native Americans. There is a
bibliography and information on ordering from Native American publishers and curriculum developers.

Stensland, Anna Lee. *Literature By and About the American Indian: An Annotated Bibliography.* 2nd ed. Urbana, Ill: National Council of Teachers of English, 1979.

This annotated bibliography, often accompanied by comments from Indian critics, now describes more than 775 books, among them newer works on the Native American experience, historical studies, and the surviving literature from the oral traditional. The books are arranged by age range and subject matter.

"Stop Stereotyping Indian Studies." *Instructor*, vol. 82, no. 3 (November 1972): 100–3.

This article contains three reports on how to teach Indian studies as practiced in three different classrooms.

Vernall, Catherine and Keeshig-Tobias, Lenore, eds. *All My Relations: Sharing Native Values Through the Arts.* Toronto: Canadian Alliance in Solidarity With Native Peoples, 1988.

This unit, which was designed to help non-Natives learn from Native people, is aimed at grades K through 6, but can be used for all age groups. Included are materials on storytelling, poetry, drama, games, songs, drawings, photographs, and other graphics.

Welch, Deborah. "American Indian Women: Reaching Beyond the Myth." In *New Directions in American Indian History.* Ed. Colin G. Calloway, pp. 31–48. Norman: University of Oklahoma Press, 1988. Bibliography.

The author provides a review of current scholarship with consideration given to the context (and stereotypes of Indian women in the past). She looks at six areas: biography and autobiography, role in American westward expansion, cultural roles, works by Indian women, leadership on tribal and national levels, and new directions in Indian women's history. The writer also gives an overview of bibliographic works available to scholars.

COLUMBUS DAY AND THANKSGIVING

Many Native Americans consider these two holidays a time for mourning. The materials listed here will provide classroom discussion by presenting more accurate accounts and an alternative to the "bountiful" stereotypes so common at these times.

Barriero, Jose, ed. "View From the Shore: American Indian Perspectives on the Quincentenary." *Columbus Quincentenary Edition, Northeast Indian Quarterly*, vol. 7, no. 3 (Fall 1990).

This issue is a collection of essays, reflections, photoessays, and bibliographies on Columbus and the impact he made on American Indian history/cultures. Included are articles by both Indians and non-Indians about the Quincentenary as well as general issues and contemporary information.

Brady, Phyllis. "Columbus and the Quincentennial Myths: Another Side of the Story." *Young Children*, vol. 47, no. 6 (September 1992): 4–14.

The writer considers the value of presenting a true image of Columbus rather than the heroic one. She outlines a Columbus Day quincentennial curriculum that focuses on aspects of both heroism and invasion and their consequences.

"Fireside: On Columbus and Conquest." *Turtle Quarterly*, vol. 4, no. 2 (Fall, Winter 1991): 36–45.

This is a transcript of a dialogue among four academics on the problem of the Western view and its choke hold on education today. They use the example of Columbus as a basis for a broad discussion touching on the origins and implications of Eurocentricism.

"500 Years of Survival." Special Supplement to *The Eagle*, vol. 10, no. 4 (July/August 1992).
This supplement to a Native-owned newspaper contains editorials, poems, photographs, stories, anecdotes, and a selective chronology about the Americans from a Native perspective. It includes testimonies of all sorts, from Susan Shown Harjo to George Bush.

Gentry, Carole M. and Grinde, Donald A. Jr., eds. *The Unheard Voices: American Indian Responses to the Columbian Quincentenary 1492–1992*. Los Angeles: American Indian Studies Center, 1993.
Essays from a fall 1992 conference in which a gathering of American Indian and non-Indian scholars examine and elucidate the Columbian experience from a variety of disciplinary and attitudinal perspectives.

Goldberg, Martin. "Searching for Columbus." *Multi-Cultural Review*, vol. 1, no. 3 (July 1992): 10–16.
This extensive annotated bibliography of children's literature on Columbus contains books dating as far back as the early 1900s. However, not all references are critiqued for the Native perspective.

Gonzalez, Ray, ed. *Without Discovery: A Native Response to Columbus*. Seattle: Broken Moon Press, 1992.
An anthology of literature by 23 Native American, Puerto Rican, and Chicano writers. The authors present their points of view on Columbus and his effect on the lives of Native North Americans.

Hirschfelder, Arlene and Califf, Jane. "A Thanksgiving Lesson Plan: Celebration or Mourning? It's All In the Point of View." *Interracial Books for Children Bulletin*, vol. 10, no. 6 (1979): 6–13. Illustrated. Resources.
Traditional Thanksgiving observances often make use of stereotypes that perpetuate false images of Native Americans and U.S. history. This lesson plan has been designed to give students a more accurate view of Thanksgiving and to raise their awareness. There are objectives, activities, and background readings provided for various age levels.

Koning, Hans. *Columbus: His Enterprise*. New York: Monthly Review Press, 1992. Bibliography.
The author addresses the myth that has grown around Columbus, largely as a result of the images depicted in textbooks. He begins with an outline of fifteenth-century European history in which he discusses the real politics behind the age of exploration—as a means to compensate for a foundering economy in a time of massive upheavals. He continues with a biography of the young Columbus, attempting to chart the growth of his mostly erroneous notions that led Columbus to his westward voyages. Also included is a realistic view of the atrocities inflicted on the Native populations by the Spanish for economic gain.

Loewen, James W. "Columbus in History and High School." *Akwe:kon Journal*, vol. 9, no. 1 (Spring 1992): 28–35.
The writer criticizes the shallow history about Columbus that appears in most modern textbooks.

Mohawk, John. "Looking for Columbus: Thoughts on the Past, Present and Future of Humanity." In The *State of Native America*. Annette Jaimes, ed. Boston: South End Press, 1992. pp. 439–44.

The author summarizes the roots and course of Eurocentrism, starting with an explanation of theological racism and the transition to scientific racism and then to "ecological" racism. He exhorts readers to learn from the past and develop a more worldly social consciousness.

National Geographic. *1491: America Before Columbus.* Washington, D.C. National Geographic Society, vol. 180. no. 4 (October 1991).

In this issue of *National Geographic,* six articles (three by Native writers) recreate Native American life in 1491. There are close-up looks at Ozette (Makah village in Washington State), Etowah (southeast Indian village), Otstungo (Mohawk village), and Pueblo (southwest) on the eve of cataclysmic change. A double map supplement "Native American Heritage: A Visitor's Guide" illustrates the heritage of Native Americans.

Ramsey, Patricia. "Beyond 'Ten Little Indians' and Turkeys: Alternative Approaches to Thanksgiving." *Young Children,* vol. 34, no. 6 (September 1979): 28–51. Bibliography.

This article describes several approaches to observing Thanksgiving that are potential vehicles for expanding children's awareness and appreciation of shared human experiences and cultural differences.

"Reflections on 500 Years." *Indian Country Today,* 8 October 1992. Section C, C1–C8.

Several editorials on Columbus, racism, and Native American History are presented. Throughout the section are tribal endorsements or the movement to change the name of Columbus Day to Native American Day.

Rethinking Columbus: Teaching About the 500th Anniversary of Columbus' Arrival in America. A Special Issue of Rethinking Schools. Milwaukee: Rethinking Schools and Washington, D.C.: Network of Educators on Central America, 1991.

The goal of the editors of *Rethinking Columbus* is "not to present 'two sides,' but to tell the part of the story that has been neglected." Native people tell some of their side of the encounter through interviews, poetry, analysis, and stories that underscore contemporary resistance to the spirit of Columbus. Designed for teachers and students from kindergarten through college, there are sections entitled "Elementary School Issues," "Secondary School Issues," "Contemporary Struggles," a selection of historical documents, and a section of resources, references, and a teaching guide for this special issue.

Viola, Herman and Margolis, Carolyn, eds. *Seeds of Change: A Quincentennial Commemoration.* Washington, D.C.: Smithsonian Institution Press,1991. Illustrated.

This well-illustrated book reexamines the massive changes since the contact of the Old and New Worlds, not a story of discovery, but rather one of "stark tragedy, the decimation of the hardy people of the New World by new diseases and by war, and the forcible removal of at least ten million people from their African homes to serve as plantation slaves in the Americas." The contributors to the volume attempt to interpret the meaning of Columbus 500 years after his landing. The essays examine many different aspects of the biological transformations begun in 1492, especially the transfer of many new plants and animals including the horse, potato, and corn.

Zinn, Howard. *Columbus, the Indians, and Human Progress, 1492–1992.* Pamphlet no. 19. Westfield, NJ: Open Magazine Pamphlet Series: May 1992.

In this essay, Professor Zinn seeks to winnow away the myth and illusion surrounding Columbus and present a truthful image of the constant racism in Western society. He refers to many other histories, both modern and primary, and attempts to refute many of the writings that perpetuate the Columbus myth and Eurocentrism.

ANTHOLOGIES OF POETRY AND PROSE

These writings are all by contemporary American Indians. We recommend that they be included in literature classes as well as in American Indian units to ensure that any curriculum will be one of inclusion.

Allen, Paula Gunn, ed. *Spider Woman's Granddaughters: Traditional Tales and Contemporary Writing.* Boston: Beacon Press, 1989.

———. *Voice of the Turtle: American Indian Literature 1900–1970.* New York: Ballantine, 1994.

Astrov, Margot, ed. *American Indian Prose and Poetry: An Anthology (Winged Serpent).* New York: Capricorn, 1946.

Brandon, William, ed. *The Magic World: American Indian Songs and Poems.* New York: William Morrow, 1971.

Brant, Beth, ed. *A Gathering of Spirit: Writings and Art by North American Indian Women.* Rockport, Maine: Sinister Wisdom Press, 1984.

Bruchac, Joseph, ed. *American Indian Writings.* Greenfield Review, vol. 9, nos. 3–4 (1981). Prose and Poetry.

———. *New Voices from the Longhouse: An Anthology of Contemporary Iroquois Writing.* Greenfield Center, NY: Greenfield Review Press, 1989.

———. *Returning the Gift: Poetry and Prose from the First North American Native Writers' Festival.* Tucson: University of Arizona Press, 1994.

———. *Songs from this Earth on Turtle's Back: Contemporary American Indian Poetry.* Greenfield Center, NY: Greenfield Review Press, 1983.

Bruchac, Joseph and Landau, Diana, eds. *Singing of Earth: A Native American Anthology.* Berkeley: Nature Company, 1993.

Cronyn, George W., ed. *American Indian Poetry: An Anthology of Songs and Chants.* New York: Liveright, 1934.

Evers, Larry and Zepeda, Ofelia, eds. *Home Places: Contemporary Native American Writing from Sun Tracks.* Tucson: University of Arizona Press, 1995.

Francis, Lee, ed. *Callaloo: Native American Literatures/A Special Issue.* vol. 17, no.1 (Winter 1994). Published by the Johns Hopkins University Press.

Green, Rayna, ed. *That's What She Said: Contemporary Poetry and Fiction by Native American Women.* Bloomington: Indiana University Press, 1984.

Hobson, Geary, ed. *The Remembered Earth.* Albuquerque: University of New Mexico Press, 1981. Prose and poetry.

Institute of American Indian Arts. *Both Sides: New Work from the Institute of American Indian Arts, 1993–1994.* Santa Fe, NM: IAIA, 1994.

———. *Voices of Thunder: New Work from the Institute of American Indian Arts.* Santa Fe, NM: IAIA, 1990.

King, Thomas, ed. *All My Relations: An Anthology of Contemporary Canadian Native Fiction.* Norman: University of Oklahoma Press, 1992.

Lerner, Andrea, ed. *Dancing on the Rim of the World: An Anthology of Contemporary Northwest Native American Writing.* Tucson: University of Arizona Press, 1990.

Lesley, Craig, ed. *Talking Leaves: Contemporary Native American Short Stories: An Anthology.* New York: Dell, 1991.

Levitas, Gloria; Vivelo, Frank; and Vivelo, Jacqueline, eds. *American Indian Prose and Poetry: We Wait in Darkness*. New York: G. P. Putnam's, 1974.

Margolin, Malcolm, ed. *The Way We Lived: California Indian Stories, Songs, and Reminiscences*. Berkeley: Heyday Books/California Historical Society, 1993. 2nd edition.

Niatum, Duane, ed. *Harper's Anthology of 20th Century Native American Poetry*. New York: Harper, 1988.

Ortiz, Simon, ed. *Earth Power Coming: Short Fiction in Native American Literature*. Tsaile, Arizona: Navajo Community College Press, 1983.

Perrault, Jeanne and Vance, Sylvia, eds. *Writing the Circle: Native Women of Western Canada*. Norman: University of Oklahoma Press, 1993.

Roman, Trish Fox, ed. *Voices Under One Sky: Contemporary Native Literature*. Freedom, CA: The Crossing Press, 1994.

Rosen, Kenneth, ed. *The Man to Send Rain Clouds: Contemporary Stories by American Indians*. New York: Viking Press, 1974.

Sarris, Greg, ed. *The Sound of Rattles and Clappers: A Collection of New California Indian Writing*. Tucson: University of Arizona Press, 1994.

Smelcer, John E. and Birchfield, D. L. *Durable Breath: Contemporary Native American Poetry*. Anchorage, Alaska: Salmon Run Press, 1994.

Trafzer, Clifford E., ed. *Earth Song, Sky Spirit: Short Stories of the Contemporary Native American Experience*. New York: Doubleday/Anchor, 1993.

Walters, Anna Lee, ed. *Neon Powwow: New Native American Voices of the Southwest*. Flagstaff, AZ: Northland Publishing Co., 1993.

Witalec, Janet, ed. *Smoke Rising: The Native North American Literary Companion*. Detroit: Visible Ink, 1995.

COLLECTIONS OF INTERVIEWS AND PERSONAL ACCOUNTS BY CONTEMPORARY NATIVE AMERICANS

Abbott, Lawrence, ed. *I Stand in the Center of the Good: Interviews with Contemporary Native American Artists*. Lincoln: University of Nebraska, 1995.

Bruchac, Joseph, ed. *Survival This Way: Interviews with American Indian Poets*. Tucson: University of Arizona Press, 1987.

Coltelli, Laura, ed. *Winged Words: American Indian Writers Speak*. Lincoln: University of Nebraska Press, 1990.

Crozier-Hogle, Lois and Wilson, Darryl Babe, eds. *Surviving in Two Worlds: Contemporary Native American Voices*. Austin: University of Texas, 1997.

Garrod, Andrew and Larimore, Colleen. *First Person, First Peoples: Native American College Graduates Tell Their Life Stories*. Ithaca: Cornell University Press, 1997.

Hirschfelder, Arlene, ed. *Native Heritage: Personal Accounts by American Indians—1790 to the Present*. New York: Macmillan Books, 1995.

Katz, Jane, ed. *Messengers of the Wind: Native American Women Tell Their Life Stories*. New York: Ballantine, 1995.

Lutz, Harmut, ed. *Contemporary Challenges: Conversations with Canadian Native Authors*. Saskatoon: Fifth House Publishers, 1991.

Swann, Brian and Krupat, Arnold, eds. *I Tell You Now: Autobiographical Essays by Native American Writers*. Lincoln: University of Nebraska Press, 1987.

CATALOGS AND CURRICULUM

There are some excellent curricular materials available for teachers who do not always have time to develop lessons that ensure quality teaching about American Indians. These resources offer a wide variety of subjects.

Akwe:kon (300 Caldwell Hall, Cornell University, Ithaca, NY 14853)
  Catalog of journals, books, special publications and curriculum—*The Six Nations Series: Student and Teacher Guide.* Publishes *Native Americas: Akwe:kon's Journal of Indigenous Issues,* a quarterly journal.

American Indian Science and Engineering Society (5661 Airport Blvd., Boulder, CO 80301-2339)
  Nonprofit organization (with college chapters) has catalog of books, curricula, posters, videos; publishes *Winds of Change,* a quarterly journal with articles focusing on the environment, science, and mathematics.

Anoka-Hennepin Independent School (District 11, 11299 Hanson Blvd. NW, Coon Rapids, MN 55433)
  Selection of teacher guides: *American Indian Astronomy, American Indian Time Keeping Devices, American Indian Communications Systems, American Indian Toys and Games, Modern Indian Issues,* cassettes, and more.

Bread and Roses Cultural Project (Bread and Roses Distribution Center, P.O. Box 1154, Eatontown, NJ 07724)
  The not-for-profit cultural arm of 1199 National Health and Human Service Employees Union published four poster sets entitled Women of Hope including Native American/Hawaiian Women of Hope—posters of twelve courageous contemporary women and Study Guide. (Also African American, Asian American, and Latina Women of Hope.)

ERIC/CRESS (P.O. Box 1348, Charleston, WV 25325; 1-800-624-9120)
  They will do a free computer search by subject. Example: curriculum materials about North Carolina Indians.

Highsmith Multicultural Bookstore (W5527 Highway 106, P.O. Box 800, Fort Atkinson, WI 53538-0800)
  Catalog of books by and about people of color for schools.

National Women's History Project (7738 Bell Road, Windsor, CA 95492-8518)
  Catalog of books, posters, videos, calendars, and curricula on women for elementary and secondary schools.

North American Native Authors Catalog (The Greenfield Review Press, P.O. Box 308, 2 Middle Grove Road, Greenfield Center, NY 12833)
  Catalog of works by American Indian poets, writers, historians, storytellers, and performers; cassette tapes.

Oyate (2702 Mathews Street, Berkeley, CA 94702)
  Catalog of books, videos, posters, and cassette tapes about Native Americans.

Teaching for Change (c/o Network of Educators on the Americas (NECA), P.O. Box 73038, Washington, DC 20056)
  Catalog of multicultural, antiracist curricula for K–12.

AUDIOVISUAL RESOURCES

Many of these listings have been directed and produced by Native Americans. Sources include cassettes and compact discs of music ranging from traditional to contemporary, photographs, videos, and slides.

Canyon Records (4143 N. 16th Street, Phoenix, AZ 85016)
Catalog of music tapes; curriculum—*American Indian Music for the Classroom* by Louis Ballard.

Library of Congress (Music Division, Recorded Sound Section, Washington, DC 20540)
Catalog of music tapes.

National Anthropological Archives (Smithsonian Institution, Washington, DC 20560)
Descriptive leaflets of historic photographs of men and women (50,000 images in collection).

National Museum of the American Indian (George Gustav Heye Center, Public Information Department, One Bowling Green, New York, NY 10004)
Native Americans on Film and Video. (2 volumes list film and videos by Native and non-Native film/video makers.)

Native American Public Telecommunications (P.O. Box 83111, Lincoln, NE 68501-3111)
Catalog of hundreds of videos for sale/rent, many produced by Native Americans.

SOAR (Sound of America Records) (P.O. Box 8606, Albuquerque, NM 87198)
Catalog of music tapes, compact discs with music by contemporary singers, rock groups, traditional, new age, powwow, and flute music.

NEWSPAPERS AND MAGAZINES

Current events are helpful in any subject, but Indian issues rarely appear in the mainstream press. These sources will help the classroom become aware of the contemporary lives of Indian people and events in Indian communities.

Aboriginal Voices (Suite 201, 116 Spadina Avenue, Toronto, Ontario M5V 2K6 Canada)
Covers arts and entertainment.

American Indian Art Magazine (7314 East Osburn Drive, Scottsdale, AZ 85251)
Covers historic and contemporary arts; full-color photographs.

American Indian Culture and Research Journal (American Indian Studies Center, University of California at Los Angeles, 3220 Campbell Hall, Los Angeles, CA 90024)
Scholarly articles about historical and contemporary American Indian lives and cultures; book reviews.

American Indian Quarterly (University of Oklahoma, Department of Anthropology, Dale Hall Tower/Room 521, 455 W. Lindsey, Norman, Oklahoma 73019-0535)
Covers historical and contemporary American Indian life and culture.

The Circle (Minneapolis American Indian Center, 1530 E. Franklin Avenue, Minneapolis, MN 55404)
Monthly newspaper covers national Indian news.

Honor Digest (Route 1, Box 79-A, Bayfield, WI 54814)
  Bimonthly journal covers important issues in Indian Country: treaty rights, sovereignty and religious freedom issues, discrimination, and stereotyping in popular culture.
Indian Artist (P.O. Box 5465, Santa Fe, NM 87502-5465)
  Covers contemporary arts in diverse media.
Indian Country Today (1920 Lombardy Drive, Rapid City, SD 57703)
  Weekly newspaper covers national Indian news.
Indigenous Women (Indigenous Women's Network, P.O. Box 174, Lake Elmo, MN 55042)
  Covers grassroots Western Hemisphere Native women involved in political, social, and environmental issues.
NARF Legal Review (1506 Broadway, Boulder, CO 80302)
  Biannual journal of legal organization protecting Native sovereignty of tribes, treaties, natural resources, legal issues, and legislation; court decisions.
Native Americas: Akwe:kon's Journal of Indigenous Issues (American Indian Program, 300 Caldwell Hall, Ithaca, New York 14853)
  Covers economic development, agriculture, community health, arts, land rights, education, environmental issues, oral history, poetry, book reviews.
Native Monthly Reader (P.O. Box 122, Crestone, CO 81131)
  Monthly newspaper for young adults (October-May).
Native Peoples (Media Concepts Group, 5333 North Seventh Street, Suite C-224, Phoenix, AZ 85014)
  Quarterly journal with feature stories about Native American culture and history; full-color photographs.
News from Indian Country (Rt. 2, Box 2900-A, Hayward, WI 54843)
  Bimonthly newspaper covers national Indian news.
News from Native California (P.O. Box 9145, Berkeley, California 94709)
  Covers California Native arts, culture, language, history, language.
Rethinking Schools (Rethinking Schools, 1001 E. Keefe Ave., Milwaukee, WI 53212)
  Journal concerned with tracking, testing, class size, antiracist education, school budgets, teachers' unions, and more. Published curriculum *Rethinking Columbus: Teaching About the 500th Anniversary of Columbus' Arrival in America* (1991).
Studies in American Indian Literatures (Robert M. Nelson, Box 112/28 Westhampton Way, University of Richmond, Richmond, VA 23173)
  Quarterly journal focuses on American Indian literature (including traditional oral); reviews.
Teaching Tolerance (400 Washington Ave., Montgomery, AL 36104)
  Biannual journal with teaching strategies; book reviews.
Tribal College: Journal of American Indian Higher Education (P.O. Box 720, Mancos, CO 80328)
  Quarterly journal covers American Indian higher education and curriculum and activities of thirty-one tribal colleges and universities in North America.
Winds of Change (American Indian Science and Engineering Society, 5661 Airport Blvd., Boulder, CO 80301-2339)
  Quarterly journal with articles covering the environment, science, and mathematics.

Web Sites about Native Americans

Native American nations, tribes, communities, and individuals have created numerous sites, more than can be listed here. A number of these important Internet sites about Indian cultures and issues are listed with the following information: name of each site, the address, and a brief description of the site's contents. **Reminder:** The Web is an ever-changing universe, and unfortunately many sites disappear.

Census data for American Indians: http://www.census.gov/
, Under A, find American Indian (choose "Businesses" or "Population") or Alaska Native (Businesses or Population).
Cradleboard Teaching Project: http://www.cradleboard.org/
The project, developed by teacher/songwriter Buffy Sainte-Marie (Cree), connects native and non-Native students to one another and provides curricula to help teach children "Indians exist." The site provides numerous links to other Native resources, including tribal sites and Native organizations.
Home Pages of Native Artists and Authors: http://www.hanksville.org/
An index provides links to the home pages of Native artists and authors as well as Native American resources on the Internet, including culture, language, history, health, education, and indigenous knowledge. See also http://www.hanksville.org/sand/stereotypes/.
Indian Country Today (newspaper): http://Indiancountry.com/
The weekly national newspaper *Indian Country Today*, covering national news and events and distributed in all 50 states and in all 12 foreign countries, can be accessed online.
National Congress of American Indians: http://www.ncai.org/
The NCAI, founded in 1944, is the oldest and largest national Indian organization. In addition to information on current issues, the site supplies the addresses of all the U.S. Indian tribal governments and links to tribal sites. Look for "Indian Nations and Alaska Native Villages."
National Museum of the American Indian Resource Center: http://www.conexus.si.edu/
Conexus is a Web site with a "window" through which people can view programs and exhibits at the George Gustav Heye Center / NMAI, New York City.
Native American Home Pages: http://info.pitt.edu/~/mitten/Indians.html/
This megasite, maintained by Lisa Mitten, a Mohawk urban Indian who is a librarian at the University of Pittsburgh, provides access to the home pages of individual Native Americans and Nations and to other sites that provide information about Native people.

Topics include Native organizations and urban Indian centers, tribal colleges, Native studies programs, the mascot issue, powwows and festivals, sources for Indian music, businesses, and general Indian-oriented home pages.

Native American Public Telecommunications: http://www.Nativetelecom.org/
This site is the national distribution system for AIROS (American Indian Radio on Satellite), Native programming to tribal communities and to general audiences through Native American and other public radio stations as well as the Internet. "Native American Calling," the nation's first live talk radio show geared toward a Native American audience, is also available at this site. The one-hour electronic talking circle can be heard Monday through Friday, 1–2 P.M. EST on local public radio stations and on the World Wide Web. Some stations opt to air the program on tape delay. Call a particular station for broadcast time. Before listening on the computer, it is necessary to click onto the RealTime Audio Web site and download its program at no charge. The site is www.realaudio.com/. This site also has music programs such as "Native Sounds–Native Voices," which features traditional and contemporary Native American music.

Native American Resource Center: http://www.wco.com/~berryhp/broadcast.html/
Produced by radio producer Peggy Berryhill, this site is a "gateway" to Native American public broadcasting and media organizations, along with community radio information.

Native American Rights Fund: http://www.narf.org/
NARF provides legal representation to Native American tribes, villages, organizations, and individuals to help untangle the maze of laws affecting their lives. The site supplies the addresses of all U.S. tribal governments and links to tribal sites. Look for "Tribal Directory" under "Resources."

Native Americas: http://nativeamericas.aip.cornell.edu/ or http://www.news.Cornell.edu/general/July97/NatAm.Online
Native Americas is the quarterly publication of Akwe:kon Press of the American Indian Program at Cornell University. The journal features articles that cover important issues of concern to indigenous peoples throughout the Western Hemisphere. Visit the site and find subscription information, Native happenings, and information on Akwe:kon Press.

NativeNet: http://www.fdl.cc.mn.us/natnet/
The NativeNet page provides an excellent connection to a group of NativeNet mailing lists as well as list archives. Also lists references to selected Web resources relating to indigenous peoples. Good for ongoing and past topics.

Native Tech: http://www.nativeweb.org/Native Tech/
A wealth of information on the technology of Native American crafts, including beadwork, clay and pottery, games and toys, metal framework, food and recipes, poetry, and much more. There is a section with articles dealing with contemporary issues about Native American art.

NativeWeb: http://www.nativeweb.org/
NativeWeb exists to use the Internet to educate the public about indigenous cultures and issue, and to promote communications between indigenous peoples and organizations supporting their goals and efforts. The content of NativeWeb is predominantly about the Americas, from the Arctic to Tierra del Fuego. Lists Native-owned enterprises and deals with issues of cultural property, genealogy, and lots more.

Repatriation Issues: http://www.uiowa.edu/~anthro/reburial/repat.html/
Deals with the Native American Grave Protection and Repatriation Act of 1990, case studies, state laws, articles, organizations, and bibliographies.

Smithsonian Institution: http://www.si.edu/newstart.htm/

The Smithsonian Institution's searchable site contains a vast amount of information from all of the Smithsonian museums, including a section with resources for teachers. The site's Native American information includes a number of bibliographies and articles, plus information on relevant Smithsonian exhibitions.

Index to Part 1: A Reader

Index to Part 2: Bibliography

335

About the Contributors

Bill Bigelow, a high school social studies teacher in Portland, Oregon, and coauthor of several book-length curricula, wrote the Afterword for Teachers in the new edition of *Columbus: His Enterprise* by Hans Koning (Monthly Review Press, 1991).

Sanda Cohen has taught fourth and fifth grades at the Elizabeth Morrow School, a renowned private school in northern New Jersey, for a total of twelve years. She specializes in curriculum development and Native American history and cultures, as well as the American Revolution and Lewis and Clark.

Gerben Earth, a member of the Winnebago Tribe of Nebraska, is married to Winona and has three children: Georgine, 18; Ari-el, 13; and Thomas, 13. A former Winnebago Tribal Chairman, Earth is now Personnel Officer for the Winnebago Tribe of Nebraska and Iowa. A 1990 graduate with a B.S. degree from Morningside College in Sioux City, Iowa, he served in the military for six years: three years in the army, 1966–1969; the 82nd Airborne Division, with eighteen months in Vietnam; and three years in the Nebraska National Guard 167th Armored Cavalry, 67th Mechanized Infantry Division.

Dorothy Grandbois is an enrolled member of the Turtle Mountain Band of Chippewa of Belcourt, North Dakota, where she was born and raised. She has many relatives and friends there. Grandbois currently resides in Corrales, New Mexico, where she operates a photography and fine art studio from her home. Grandbois is an award-winning photographer. She works in alternative processes and mixed media when creating fine-art photographic digital images. Dorothy's work is shown both nationally and internationally. An honors graduate from the University of New Mexico, Dorothy also graduated from the Institute of American Indian Arts in Santa Fe, New Mexico, where she is currently teaching photography.

Kathy Kerner was a licensed social worker for York County schools in Virginia. The author of *They Taught You Wrong: Raising Cultural Consciousness of Stereotypes and Misconceptions about American Indians* (1995), she conducted numerous workshops for teachers and human services professionals on that subject. She also co-led an annual ecological conference called "Returning Home: Healing the Earth; Healing Ourselves." Kathy died in August 1998 from complications following an automobile accident while on her way to a powwow.

At similar events, she had worked to counteract racism and stereotyping by distributing antibias materials.

Jim Northrup writes of himself, "Born on the Rez, lives on the Rez, will probably die on the Rez . . . was a lot that happened in between but it was just details. I am or have been a husband, father, grandfather, cousin, nephew, logger, Marine grunt, factory hand, ironworker, mason, editor, freelance writer (more free than lance), poet, actor, columnist, playwright, author, and Anishinaabe." Northrup writes the syndicated column "Fond du Lac Follies," which is distributed in *The Circle*, *The Native American Press*, and *News from Indian Country*. The author of *Walking the Rez Road* (Voyager Press, 1993), which won a Minnesota Book Award, and *Rez Road Follies, Canoes, Casinos, Computers, and Birch Bark Baskets* (Kodansha America, 1997), Northrup's prose and poetry have been included in many anthologies. The film *Jim Northrup: With Reservations* (1995) received an award at the Dreamspeakers Native Film Festival in 1997 and at Red Earth 1997.

Dr. Cornel Pewewardy, a Comanche-Kiowa, has spent most of his professional career as an elementary teacher and principal on the Navajo Reservation in New Mexico and was founding principal of the award-winning American Indian Magnet School in the Saint Paul, Minnesota, public school district. He is currently an assistant professor in the Department of Teaching and Leadership, School of Education, at the University of Kansas, Lawrence.

Beverly Singer is Tewa and Navajo, and grew up at Santa Clara Pueblo, New Mexico. Among her current interests are making videos about health and well-being in Native communities; writing about Native self-representation; spending time with her grandmother; baking bread; fishing; reading women's literature; and riding horses. She graduated from high school at age 16 and, fulfilling her parents' wish, continued her education. She received a B.A. from the College of Santa Fe, New Mexico; an M.A. in 1977 from the University of Chicago; and a Ph.D. in 1996 from the University of New Mexico.

Charlene Teters, a member of the Spokane Tribe in Washington, is an activist, artist, and mother. Since 1989 she has actively campaigned to eliminate racist symbols that degrade and dehumanize American Indians and Alaska natives. A board member of the National Coalition on Racism in Sports and the Media, she has used her art to protest the use and abuse of Indians as mascots. *In Whose Honor*, a 1997 documentary, features her campaign against Chief Illiniwek, the University of Illinois mascot. Teters also served as senior editor of *Indian Artist Magazine*.

About the Authors

Arlene Hirschfelder is the author of award-winning nonfiction books, as well as curricula, magazine articles, and bibliographies concerning Native Americans. Hirschfelder, who also teaches Native histories, cultures, and literature, worked for the Association on American Indian Affairs for over twenty years. She received her M.A.T. in teaching from the University of Chicago.

Paulette Fairbanks Molin is a member of the Minnesota Chippewa Tribe from the White Earth Reservation. She has worked in educational administration for many years and is the author of curriculum, articles, and other publications. A faculty member at Hampton University in Virginia, Molin serves on the board of the Wordcraft Circle of Native Writers and Storytellers.

Yvonne Wakim, Cherokee/Arab, has worked in Indian education and community services for twenty-five years. She is a writer, teacher, trainer, curriculum developer, multicultural consultant to publishers, and coauthored *Native Americans Today: A Resource Book for Teachers, Grades 4–8*. A board member of Nitchen, Inc. (*Our Children* in the Lenni Lenape language), she helped create the Family Awareness Network, a holistic preventive mental health program for American Indian youth and their families.